MW01157062

Life in Groups

Life in Groups

How We Think, Feel, and Act Together

MARGARET GILBERT

Great Clarendon Street, Oxford, OX2 6DP,
United Kingdom

Oxford University Press is a department of the University of Oxford.
It furthers the University's objective of excellence in research, scholarship,
and education by publishing worldwide. Oxford is a registered trade mark of
Oxford University Press in the UK and in certain other countries

© Margaret Gilbert 2023

The moral rights of the author have been asserted

First Edition published in 2023

Impression: 1

All rights reserved. No part of this publication may be reproduced, stored in
a retrieval system, or transmitted, in any form or by any means, without the
prior permission in writing of Oxford University Press, or as expressly permitted
by law, by licence or under terms agreed with the appropriate reprographics
rights organization. Enquiries concerning reproduction outside the scope of the
above should be sent to the Rights Department, Oxford University Press, at the
address above

You must not circulate this work in any other form
and you must impose this same condition on any acquirer

Published in the United States of America by Oxford University Press
198 Madison Avenue, New York, NY 10016, United States of America

British Library Cataloguing in Publication Data
Data available

Library of Congress Control Number: 2022947307

ISBN 978-0-19-284715-7

DOI: 10.1093/oso/9780192847157.001.0001

Printed and bound by
CPI Group (UK) Ltd, Croydon, CR0 4YY

Links to third party websites are provided by Oxford in good faith and
for information only. Oxford disclaims any responsibility for the materials
contained in any third party website referenced in this work.

For Nat, Dave, and Josh

Contents

V. RIGHTS AND OBLIGATIONS IN GROUP LIFE

Preface

This book comprises thirteen essays relating to central aspects of our life in groups, along with a general introduction and a concluding discussion. A particular focus is on what we refer to as *our* beliefs, emotions, and plans, in such everyday statements as "We think a crime was committed," "The team is delighted to have won," and "We plan to go to New York in June." It is not easy to say precisely what states of affairs "on the ground" such statements refer to.

Central to my proposals is what I refer to as *joint commitment*. Our having a certain plan, for instance, is our having a joint commitment with the appropriate content. Some of the essays defend specific proposals of this sort, others consider their implications in particular contexts, others explore closely related matters, including the nature and basis of the rights and obligations that are part and parcel of group life.

The individual essays are all relatively self-contained, so the reader can start anywhere in the book without reading what comes before. That said, there are clear links between many of their topics, as is reflected in the division of the book into different parts. Each essay retains its original citation style and is bibliographically complete.

The introduction includes an extended discussion of joint commitment for those who wish to approach that first, or to read more about it later. Among other things it clarifies certain points in response to questions others have posed. It concludes with a preview of the sections and chapters of the book.

The book's conclusion introduces some further topics relating to life in groups, responds to some comments on my approach to that life, and indicates some avenues for further research.

At the end of the book there is a bibliography of my writings relating to life in groups, with the articles divided by topic, for those who wish to go further.

While most of the essays have been previously published, many of these found their original home in a collection with a particular, limited emphasis, or in a specialist journal. This is true of the discussions that constitute chapters 1 and chapter 13, among others. I hope that bringing the essays together in one volume will increase their accessibility for those with an interest in the topics they address.

Given the opportunity, I have corrected some typological errors in the originals and made some minor changes to bring out my meaning more clearly. Thus the previously published essays are best read in this new presentation.

Acknowledgments

I am indebted to all of those who have contributed to my thinking on the topics in this book over many years. Those whose input on a particular chapter has been helpful are thanked in the chapter itself.

In connection with this book my first thanks go to Peter Momtchiloff, who commissioned it for Oxford University Press, Oxford, with further thanks to all of those involved in the production process.

I am also grateful to Matthew Dean and Giulia Napolitano for helping in preparation of the manuscript, and to Tiffany Zhu for her help with the proofs and preparation of the indices.

Thanks to my students at UCI, both graduate and undergraduate, for probing discussions of many of the topics addressed, and to Jane Goldman for discussion of the project in its early stages and beyond. Thanks also to the staff of the Department of Philosophy at the University of California, Irvine for their support, including the administration of the research funds provided through my position as Melden Chair of Moral Philosophy, which have been helpful in many ways.

Special thanks to Daniel Pilchman and James Weatherall, each of whom coauthored one of the articles that now constitute a chapter of this book. I would like also to thank Maura Priest for our collaborations on several articles on themes related to our life in groups.

More generally, I am grateful to many scholars for their interest in my work over the years. In some cases they have generously encouraged me to publish criticisms of their own views—I am thinking in particular of the late David Lewis, and Thomas Scanlon.

Others have seriously engaged with my ideas, hosted or contributed to conferences for the discussion of them, and been supportive in other ways. There are far too many to list here in these connections but I should like to mention at least Donald Baxter, Paul Bloomfield, Alban Bouvier, Michael Bratman, Antonella Carassa, Marco Colombetti, Rowan Cruft, Stephen Darwall, Roberta De Monticelli, Francesca Di Lorenzo Ajello, Miranda Fricker, Itzel Garcia, John Greenwood, Gilbert Harman, Jeffrey Helmreich, Aaron James, Peter Jones, Christine Korsgaard, Saul Kripke, Noa Latham, David Lewis, Stephen Lukes, Ruth Millikan, Herlinde Pauer-Studer, Costanza

Penna, Gerhard Preyer, Joseph Raz, Mark Sainsbury, Frederick Schmitt, Gopal Sreenivasan, Gabriele Taylor, Deborah Tollefsen, Michael Tomasello, Raimo Tuomela, Gary Watson, Leif Wenar, and Morton White.

I should also like to thank the American Philosophical Association for hosting several author-meets-critics sessions on my work along with other pertinent sessions at their meetings.

My work on this book took place during a worldwide pandemic. Much of my socializing has been on the phone or over the internet. I am deeply grateful to those colleagues, friends, and family members who have regularly provided conversation, consolation, and community during this time.

As always, my parents must bear the ultimate responsibility for this book as for everything I have ever done. I continue to be more than grateful to them not only for having me, but for their loving support and guidance throughout their lives.

Sources

The following articles are reprinted with permission:

'The Nature of Agreements: A Solution to some Puzzles about Claim-Rights and Joint Intention' (2014), in *Rational and Social Agency*, eds. M. Vargas and G. Yaffe, New York: Oxford University Press, pp. 215–54.

'Culture as Collective Construction' (2010), and 'Joint Commitment and Collective Belief' (2010), in *Kolner Zeitschrift for Sociologie*, pp. 384–410.

'Belief, Acceptance, and What Happens in Groups: Some Methodological Considerations' (2014) (with Daniel Pilchman), in *Essays in Collective Epistemology*, ed. Jennifer Lackey, Oxford: Oxford University Press, pp. 190–212.

'Collective Belief, Kuhn, and the String Theory Community' (2016) (with James Weatherall), in *The Epistemic Life of Groups*, eds. M. Brady and M. Fricker, Oxford: Oxford University Press, pp. 191–217.

'Collective Remorse' (2001), in *War Crimes and Collective Wrongdoing: A Reader*, ed. A. Jokic, Oxford: Basil Blackwell, pp. 216–35.

'How We Feel: Understanding Everyday Collective Emotion Ascription' (2014), in *Collective Emotions*, eds. Mikko Salmela and Christian van Sheve, Oxford: Oxford University Press, pp. 18–30.

'Collective Preferences, Obligations, and Rational Choice' (2001), in *Economics and Philosophy*, vol. 17, pp. 109–19.

'Corporate Misbehavior and Collective Values' (2005), in *Brooklyn Law Review*, vol. 70, no. 4, pp. 1369–80.

'Can a Wise Society Be a Free One?' (2006), in *Southern Journal of Philosophy*, vol. 44, pp. 1–17.

'Giving Claim-Rights Their Due' (2012), in *Rights: Concepts and Contexts*, eds. Brian Bix and Horacio Spector, Farnham, Surrey: Ashgate, pp. 301–23.

Introduction

Someone might say, of her family, "We intend to go to Greenland this year." Someone might say, of her book group, "We thought that novel was far too long" or "We preferred her first book to the later ones." And someone may say of her sports team, "We are thrilled by this result." Such statements are completely commonplace.

Call them *collective psychological statements*. Precisely how they are to be understood is a matter of debate. As will become clear in the course of this book, however, there is good reason to suppose that they are not simply summaries of the intentions, beliefs, and so on, of the individual group members. Nor, indeed, do they imply that the individuals in question have corresponding intentions, and so on, of their own.

If this is so, what do these statements amount to? And how, and in what way, do the states of affairs they refer to—call these *collective psychological states*—impact our individual and collective lives?

The chapters of this book represent the continuation of a sustained investigation into these and related questions beginning with my book *On Social Facts*.[1]

0.1 The Perspective of This Book

As I attempted to formulate accounts of everyday ideas of our acting, intending, and thinking, going on to our preferring, valuing, and feeling, among others—considering them one by one—a pattern began to emerge.[2]

An important clue was this: a particular set of rights against each other are understood to accrue to the parties to a given collective goal, intention, and so on. These are rights to actions and utterances that promote the collective goal, are expressive of the collective intention, and so on. Corresponding to

---

[1] Gilbert (1989). Due to publishing delays this was completed prior to Gilbert (1987), which focuses on collective belief.
[2] Starting with Gilbert (1989), which contains extensive discussions of collective goals, actions, and beliefs along with group languages and social conventions, among other topics.

Life in Groups: How We Think, Feel, and Act Together. Margaret Gilbert, Oxford University Press. © Margaret Gilbert 2023. DOI: 10.1093/oso/9780192847157.003.0001

and, indeed, equivalent to these rights are obligations to the right-holders to perform the relevant actions.

Thus suppose that we intend to eat together at six o'clock this evening. I then have a right against you that you don't do something to make it impossible that we eat together at six. You, meanwhile, have a corresponding obligation to me not to make it impossible for us to eat together at six.

The understanding that there are such rights and obligations is indicated by the rebukes and demands that may be issued when other parties to a collective action, say, speak or act in ways that are likely to undermine the success of the action. So, for example, one member of a hiking group that is intent on climbing a particular hill before turning back might call to another in a demanding tone, "Hey, if you don't speed up we won't get back before dark!" implying a right to the slower hiker's moving more quickly.

What grounds these rights and obligations? This question, among others, led me to the idea that lies at the heart of this book.

To put things generally: as they are—implicitly—conceived of in everyday life, the different components of our *collective psychology—our* intending, thinking, and so on—have a particular structure.[3] I describe this structure as a *joint commitment* of the two or more people involved, the content of the joint commitment being appropriate to the case in hand. Take our collective intention to go to Europe this year. I suggest that—in technical terms that will be explained below—for us to have this intention is for us to be jointly committed to intend as a body to go to Europe this year.

Joint commitment features in every chapter of this book, along with such explanation of its nature and functioning as is sufficient for the chapter's purposes. The next section of this introduction offers an overview of some key points, followed by some elaborations that may be useful before, or after, reading an individual chapter.[4]

0.2 Joint Commitment

To be jointly committed in the sense at issue here two or more people must be in a particular condition that is the product of a particular process. In spelling this out further I start with the product.

---

[3] Hence the title of Gilbert (2003): "The Structure of the Social Atom."
[4] Pertinent discussions outside this book include Gilbert (2002a) (ch. 2 of Gilbert (2014)) and Gilbert (2006: chs. 7 and 8).

0.2.1 The Product

When two or more people are jointly committed in some way, they are committed *as one*. In emphasizing "as one," I mean to draw attention to the fact that the subject of the commitment—the "one" whose commitment it is—comprises those two or more people.

The parties' being jointly *committed* is a normative matter: it concerns what they *ought* to do, all else being equal. The "ought" in question is not a specifically moral one, but it implies that any actions contrary to it will be at fault, all else being equal. It is an *exclusionary* "ought," in the sense that some kinds of consideration that point against it are not properly judged to license contrary action. In this case a person's contrary inclinations and desires, as such, do not count against the "ought" in question. Moral considerations, however, may do so.

Thus even though, *all else being equal*, I ought to conform to a joint commitment, it may be that, *all things considered*, I ought not to conform to it. This may be so if, for instance, the joint commitment enjoins actions that are morally impermissible, or if conformity to an otherwise innocuous joint commitment is expected to lead to consequences dire enough morally to require nonconformity.

Given that they are *jointly* committed with certain others in some way, each of the individual parties is committed to act in ways that will promote fulfillment of the joint commitment. These *individual* commitments depend on the joint commitment for their existence: they last as long as it does. By this I mean that each party continues to be (individually) committed to act in ways that will facilitate fulfillment of the joint commitment. Depending on the circumstances, my own more specific commitments or sub-commitments may change, as may yours.[5]

0.2.2 The Process

The process of joint commitment is broadly speaking psychological. It has two variants: the basic and the non-basic or authority-involving cases.

---

[5] My use of the phrase "sub-commitments" here echoes Michael Bratman's references to the parties' personal "sub-plans" in his discussion of what we intend, see e.g. Bratman (1993). A comment from Jeffrey Helmreich prompted this note.

0.2.2.1 The Basic Case

In the basic case, in terms to be explained, each of the would-be parties have openly expressed their readiness to be jointly committed in a particular way with the relevant others, as is common knowledge between the parties. As the parties understand, once this condition is fulfilled, they will be jointly committed in the way in question.[6]

A state of affairs is *common knowledge* between two or more people if and only if, roughly, it is entirely out in the open between them.[7] People express their readiness *openly* if they intend, or are at least prepared for it to be common knowledge among the relevant others.

Note that, in the above account of the basic case, what is at issue is not only behavioral *expressions* but also something that is *expressed*: actual readiness on the part of each for the relevant joint commitment to be established. One may wonder how the "inner states" of the parties can be open to all. One might allude to the philosophical problem of other minds—can one ever know what is in them? Suffice it to say, here, that I take there to be many contexts in which one person knows of another's actual readiness for a given joint commitment, or, indeed, where that readiness is common knowledge among all concerned.[8]

As I understand it, the *readiness* in question can exist in circumstances of strong external pressure. For instance, one may be ready to commit oneself in

---

[6] In some expositions I may have muddied the waters when writing that the would-be parties to a joint commitment must openly express their readiness "jointly to commit" them all in some way. (See e.g. Gilbert (2018a: 131).) This phrasing may suggest that the parties must openly express their readiness *to engage in a particular joint action*, namely, the joint action of *committing them all*. I did not mean to suggest this. I see a joint action as involving a joint or *collective goal*, something that is *constituted by* a joint commitment of a particular kind. The would-be parties to a joint commitment need not have a collective goal. Rather, each has the same individual goal: a particular joint commitment of them all, arrived at by means of open expressions of each one's readiness for the joint commitment in question. In some of the previously published essays in this volume I have altered the original text in order to avoid the suggestion just noted.

[7] Philosophical discussion of common knowledge in the relevant sense began with Lewis (1969); see also Schiffer (1972). See Vandershraaf and Sillari (2007) for a selection of proposals including my own in Gilbert (1989: 186–97). Many of these proposals are quite technical. Suffice it to say, here, that it is assumed by Lewis and myself, among others, that common knowledge in roughly his sense *is completely commonplace*. It does not require any particular sophistication in those who are parties to it. This can be so even if an exposition of what it amounts can usefully be couched in technical language. See Lederman (2018) for a distinction between "formal" and "informal" notions of common knowledge where, roughly, formal notions have been developed with no concern for the psychological realism of common knowledge, in contexts such as the mathematical theory of games, whereas informal notions, such as my own, have been developed with such a concern.

[8] For related discussion of the importance of both the "expression" and "expressed" condition on joint commitment see Gilbert (1989: 182–4). There I write of "willingness" rather than "readiness" and say that the various expressions issue in a "pool of wills"—having not yet settled on the phrase "joint commitment." This only comes into that work at and after p. 198. My understanding of joint commitment and its implications has continued to evolve since then.

a certain way as a result of threats to one's person. As long as one prefers to make the commitment to experiencing the expected penalty for not doing so, one can be ready to do so in the sense at issue. It follows that the fact that two or more people are jointly committed in some way does not mean that the circumstances in which their joint commitment was formed are morally impeccable.

The conjunction of expressions of readiness for joint commitment may amount to an agreement, but need not.[9] Nor need the individual expressions of readiness amount to promises, which people often—if wrongly—see as the constituents of an agreement.[10] Nor need words be involved. Consider, for instance, the case in which Isaac sees Maria struggling to lift a heavy suitcase into her car, and rushes to help her. In a situation like this the protagonists may establish a joint commitment to, in my technical language, *endorse as a body* a particular goal without any preliminary verbal exchange.[11]

Note that I am not supposing that each party is indicating that their personal readiness for joint commitment is *conditional* on the readiness of whichever others.[12] Rather, as is understood by the parties, if and only if they all openly express their unconditional personal readiness to be jointly committed with the others, in conditions of common knowledge, the joint commitment of them all will be established. There is, then, no "deconditionalization problem," as there would be if what each party expressed was, for instance, "I am ready for us to be jointly committed, if you are similarly ready," leaving us with two conditional expressions of readiness, requiring of at least one party a further move.[13]

An important kind of basic joint commitment is involved in what I have referred to as a moment of *mutual recognition*.[14] Here, in effect, the parties have expressed their personal readiness to be jointly committed *to acknowledge as a body the co-presence of the parties*—as when one person "catches the

---

[9] For an account of agreements as constituted by joint commitments see chapter 1, this volume.

[10] In Gilbert (1993) and elsewhere I argue that an agreement is *not* an exchange of promises.

[11] For further discussion of this point see e.g. Gilbert (2000a: 5–7); Gilbert (2006: 138–40).

[12] I may have been misunderstood on this score, in part because in Gilbert (1989: 198) I referred to an expression of a "conditional commitment," which suggests the expression of something conditional in form. As is clear by the end of that discussion (199), that was not my intent. Nor does it represent my current understanding of the matter. For further discussion on this point see Gilbert (2002a).

[13] The importance of not being left with two conditional expressions was emphasized by Velleman (1997). For further references and discussion see Gilbert (2014: ch. 2).

[14] This phrase has been used differently by others, but I have found it apt for the phenomenon I describe.

other's eye."[15] Mutual recognition in this sense may be established before, or at the same time as, the establishment of further joint commitments.[16]

The parties to a given joint commitment do not have to be present to one another when making the relevant expressions. They must, however, be directing these expressions toward one another at the level of their intended target or targets.[17] Further, the parties need not know one another personally, or even *know of* one another as particular individuals as opposed to, say, "one of those living on this island."

In relation to the last point it is important to note that in situations in which the parties do not, in general, know of one another as particular individuals, there can be common knowledge in the population in question that the relevant expressions have been made by the members of that population characterized as such. I have elsewhere referred to such common knowledge as *population common knowledge*, as opposed to *individual common knowledge*.[18]

Evidently, it may take some time for a given basic joint commitment to be established, even when the parties are face to face, and even when an agreement seems to have been made. The meaning of a word or gesture may need to be clarified; it may take a while to discern how many have made the relevant expressions, and so on.

In sum, a basic case of joint commitment can be established without words, in the absence of any promise or agreement, among people who do not know of one another, let alone knowing one another, and over an extended period of time. The fact that a case of joint commitment is a basic case, then, does not mean that its establishment has been a quick or simple matter. It is in part for this reason that *non*-basic cases are an important part of the landscape of joint commitment.

0.2.2.2 The Non-Basic Case

In the *non-basic* or *authority-involving* case, a joint commitment is established by some person or body of persons that has been authorized, through a basic joint commitment of the parties, to establish further joint commitments of them all. Such authorization may restrict the scope of the non-basic joint commitments that the authorized person or group can establish, as it may restrict the contexts and methods of their establishment.

---

[15] For discussion see e.g. Gilbert (2014: ch. 14); Gilbert (2018b).   [16] Cf. Gilbert (2003: 55).
[17] For discussion see Gilbert (2006: 175–7).
[18] See Gilbert (1989: 212–13, 261–2). Lewis (1969) recognizes these different possibilities.

An important aspect of the distinction between basic and non-basic cases is as follows. In a basic case those who are jointly committed will know that they are committed in the relevant way. In a non-basic case they may not know this—though of course they may. So—in what I take to be a reference to a non-basic joint commitment—a man may say to his wife, "Whose parents are we visiting this Christmas?" understanding that she is the one who makes their decisions on such matters, and that she will have made that decision by now, though she has not communicated it to him.[19]

0.2.3 Regarding a Possible Query

One may wonder how two or more people could impose a normative constraint upon those two or more people in the way proposed. In particular, one may wonder how the fact that the relevant individuals *will* the desired normative result—all expressing their personal readiness for joint commitment—can impose a normative constraint on them as one. It has been argued, indeed, that individuals lack the analogous normative power over themselves, at least when they also have the power to reverse themselves.[20]

Such arguments come up against what I take to be our everyday understandings.[21] That said, what is most important for an understanding of our collective psychology is the collective case, which has not been the target of the arguments just referred to, and appropriately so. The collective case is importantly different from the individual case, with respect to both its genesis—in the matching expressions of two or more wills—and its conclusion, to which I now turn.

0.2.4 The Conclusion of a Joint Commitment

Once a joint commitment has been fulfilled, it is over and done with. But how might it otherwise properly be concluded?[22] There are several ways in which this can happen. Before saying more about this, let me make a related point.

---

[19] For sustained discussion of the idea of a joint or collective intention as involving a constitutive joint commitment, along with some further references, see chapter 1, this volume.
[20] See e.g. Broome (2001).
[21] For discussion in this volume see e.g. chapter 1, chapter 12; see also Gilbert (2013a) and Gilbert (2018b: 43–5).
[22] I have often referred in a general way to the "rescission" of a joint commitment, but such language is best reserved for a relatively explicit, intentional way of concluding such a commitment.

Those who are jointly committed immediately prior to the conclusion of the commitment need not be identical to those who created that joint commitment in the first place. Consider, for instance, that people can co-create a joint commitment in their capacity as *possessors of a certain general property*, e.g., "person living on this street," and some may cease to hold that property—by moving house or, for that matter, by dying. Further, people who were not among the co-creators can "sign on" to a given joint commitment, as when a new arrival is welcomed by the original parties, or by their representative, acting in the name of them all.[23]

That said, all of those who are jointly committed *at the time the commitment is concluded* must have been involved in its conclusion in one way or another in order for it to have been properly concluded.

As with the creation of a joint commitment, we can distinguish basic from non-basic or authority-involving cases with respect to its conclusion.

In a basic case, all parties must express their personal readiness to conclude the commitment, in order that it be properly concluded. Such expressions can take a variety of forms.

Among these is participation in deliberate, explicit rescission, as by an agreement to conclude the joint commitment. There is also what I've referred to as "fade-out," in which the readiness of each party is established tacitly over what could be an extended period of time.[24] Another possibility is a more precipitous kind of "voting with one's feet," as when, without prior discussion, each of the crew members jump out of a sinking ship.

Though in principle all parties must make the relevant expressions, fewer than that may be taken to have concluded the commitment in practice—particularly if there is no hope now of fulfilling the commitment. Suppose, for instance, that fulfilling the commitment requires that appropriate actions of all five parties be performed. If one party leaves the scene, the other parties may reasonably take it that their joint commitment is at an end.

In a non-basic case, the joint commitment is concluded by a person or body authorized by the parties to do so. I take it that, though authorized to instigate a particular joint commitment, a given person or body of persons may *not* be authorized unilaterally to rescind or change it, but some other person, or body of persons, may need to concur as to any rescission or change.

Similarly, certain people might together create a given joint commitment, but authorize one of them unilaterally to decide on its rescission prior to fulfillment. This could happen when one person is known to be reluctant to

---

[23] See e.g. Gilbert (1989: 220–1, 232–4).
[24] See Gilbert (2006: 142 (example); 143 ("fade-out")).

be beholden to the others for rescission. So the members of a group aiming to scale a particular mountain may say to the least experienced climber, "We'll stop as soon as you want: just say the word."

It is important to note that the implicit *content* of a joint commitment may be such that what may look like unilateral rescission—involving, perhaps, a simple announcement that one is moving on—is no such thing. So consider the case in which the parties understand the goal they are jointly committed to espousing as "walking alongside each other for as long as it suits us both," or "playing around with a football as long as each of us feels like it," as opposed to "going for a walk together" or "playing a game of football." If one of the parties stops and says, "I'm off now!" without any "by your leave," this will, predictably, ruffle no feathers.

0.2.5 The Content of a Joint Commitment

As indicated earlier, the content of any joint commitment can be represented by a particular schema, which I shall refer to here as SJC. To make this concrete I start with one instance:

Jack and Jill (or: members of G, as such) are jointly committed to espouse as a body the goal of painting the house.

Generalizing now, one can represent any joint commitment as follows, where "phi" stands for a psychological state such as espousal of a particular goal, belief in a particular proposition, acceptance of a proposition, and so on:

[SJC] Persons X, Y, and so on (or: those with feature F) are jointly committed to phi as a body.

The joint commitment is, as said, a commitment of persons X, Y, Z, and so on (or those with feature F) as one. They are committed, as one, to phi as a body.

Some commentators have seen the phrase "as a body" in Schema SJC as qualifying "joint commitment," but that is not how I understand it. Any joint commitment does, of course, combine the individuals in question into what might be thought of as a body of sorts. They are, after all, committed *as one*. And in one of my earliest writings on the subject I spoke of people being "committed as a body" rather than as jointly committed.[25] That said,

---

[25] Gilbert (1987).

in Schema SJC, and its particular instances, I understand "as a body" as qualifying "phi."

Further, though many commentators seem to have left the matter there in their minds, I have regularly made it clear that I understand the phrases "to espouse goal G as a body," and so on, as shorthand for something else.

In one formulation, those who are jointly committed to phi as a body are—more fully—jointly committed to emulate, by virtue of their several actions and utterances, a single phi-er, for instance, a single espouser of goal G. In other, more nuanced, words, they are jointly committed to speak and act, in relevant circumstances, as if they were the representatives of a single espouser of goal G. Thus if Jack and Jill are jointly committed to espouse as a body the goal of painting the spare room this weekend, they are to speak and act, in relevant circumstances, as would the representatives of a single possessor of that goal.

Note the qualifier "in relevant circumstances." Suppose that Jack and Jill are jointly committed to espouse as a body the goal of painting the spare room this weekend. This means that they need to speak and act as would the representatives of a single espouser of that goal when conversing and otherwise interacting with each other, without preamble, or when representing the two of them to a third party. If, however, Jill's friend Babs asks her what she is doing that weekend, Jill can appropriately speak for herself, as in "I'm helping Jack paint the spare room." She may, of course, say, "We are painting the spare room," thereby speaking as a representative of herself and Jack.[26]

0.2.6 Joint Commitment, Rights, and Obligations

It can be argued that once a joint commitment is established, the parties have rights against each other to conformity with it. One's right against another, in the sense in question, is *equivalent* to that other's *obligation to* oneself.[27]

It is important to note that to say that those who are jointly committed in some way *ought* to conform to the joint commitment is *not* to say that they are *obligated to one another* to do it. Nor does it *follow from* the fact that they ought to act accordingly that they are obligated to one another so to act. In sum, to say something of the form: "John ought to perform action A" is neither to say nor to imply that John is *obligated to* anyone to do A.

That said, it can be argued that, by virtue of the *process* of joint commitment, not only *ought* the parties conform to the commitment, all else being

---

[26] See, in this volume, chapter 6.   [27] See, in particular, chapters 1 and 13, this volume.

equal, but they are *obligated to each other* so to conform. The argument for the latter point appeals to the normativity of joint commitment—to the fact that each member ought to conform—but does not stop there.[28]

It can be argued, then, that if the elements of our collective psychology—our intentions, beliefs, attitudes, emotions, and so on, as understood in everyday life—are founded in joint commitment, the origin of the associated rights and obligations has been found. I believe that they are, and it is.

The rights and obligations of joint commitment might possibly be referred to as "social" rights and obligations, though that may be too broad a characterization to be helpful. I propose that they are not, in any case, best thought of as *moral* rights and obligations. This fits the observation that, apparently, the rights and obligations associated with our collective intentions, and so on, can be rights to actions it is morally impermissible to perform, all else being equal.[29] This observation is suggested by the classic phrase "honor among thieves."

It is also consistent with the idea that joint commitment thinking is prior to at least some aspects of moral thinking in human evolution and has, to some extent at least, prompted such thinking.[30]

If it is best not to characterize the rights and obligations of joint commitment as moral, one can conclude that there is a third realm of rights distinct from the two that have been the focus of traditional rights theory: the moral and the legal realms.[31]

Evidently pursuit of an understanding of our everyday psychological statements can bear unexpected fruit, relating as it does to the theory of rights and directed obligations, and the scope and evolution of moral thinking, among other significant topics.[32]

0.3 A Note on Groups

The term "group" and even the more qualified "social group" has been used in a variety of more or less restrictive ways, both in everyday speech and in theorists' discussions.[33] This can be seen from the variety of items that may be listed as "groups" or "social groups" by a given theorist, who then goes on to

---

[28] See e.g. chapters 1 and 13, this volume; also Gilbert (2018b: ch. 8).
[29] See e.g. Gilbert (2018b: ch. 7), with special reference to promissory obligation.
[30] See Concluding Remarks, this volume, for further discussion.
[31] For an extended characterization of moral versus legal rights, emphasizing their differences, and their separateness, see Gilbert (2018b: ch. 2).
[32] See the Conclusion, this volume, for further discussion.
[33] "Theorists," here, include both philosophers and social scientists. The examples following in the text are from philosophical sources.

make various generalizations about groups, or distinctions among groups, in light of the list in question.

Thus, one list of "groups of people" includes "classes, populaces, mobs, legislatures, courts, faculties, student bodies, and so on," adding shortly after "kindergartners" and "legislators."[34] And another list of "social groups" of one sort or another includes "racial, ethnic and gender groups" along with families, teams, clubs, among other examples.[35]

There is no need to argue, here, for the correctness or otherwise of the inclusion of a given item in one of these lists, or, for that matter, to argue that one or more further items or kinds of items should have been included from some particular point of view. The main thing, for present purposes, is to establish the rough contours of "groups" in the sense of this book.

Early on, in thinking about groups, or social groups—I tended to use the latter phrase—I appealed to some lists which appeared to be at least roughly right for my particular purposes. These include the following from the great sociologist Georg Simmel, in which he gives as examples of "sociation" "getting together for a walk... founding a family... the temporary aggregation of hotel guests," and "the intimate bonds of a medieval guild."[36]

I also invoked some suggestive yet puzzling general statements from Simmel and another of the founders of sociology, Émile Durkheim, regarding the nature of groups. These included Simmel's tantalizing claim that a society is an "objective unit" of a special kind, such that "the consciousness of constituting with the others a unity is actually all that there is to that unity."[37] And Durkheim's equally tantalizing reference to a society as a "*sui generis* synthesis of individuals."[38]

Both of these references connect the idea of a society or social group with the idea of a special kind of unity of persons—a unity going beyond the possession of common features. They connect in particular with something that might be expected to be an appropriate reference for a full-blooded use of the collective "we."

Here I mean to contrast the use of "we" in question with uses one might call "initiatory," "tendentious," or (more positively) "aspirational."[39] Clearly,

---

[34] Epstein (2015: 9). Epstein notes that his is a "broad" conception of groups (133).

[35] Ritchie (2020: 1), Having first placed them together, Ritchie later notes that racial, ethnic, and gender groups lack central characteristics of another set of examples she considers, leading her plausibly to offer distinct though related accounts of each.

[36] Simmel (1971 [1908]: 24).   [37] Simmel (1971 [1908]: 75).

[38] Durkheim (1968: xvi–xvii), my translation. I discuss Simmel's statement in Gilbert (1989: ch. 4, esp. sec.1), and Durkheim's discussion in Gilbert (1989: ch. 5, sec. 2).

[39] See Gilbert (1989: ch. 4), also chapter 12, this volume, connecting social groups with use of the collective "we."

this is not true of all of the examples of groups or social groups from which one or another contemporary theorist has started.

In any case, in the present volume, what is key is groups, social groups, or, if you like, populations, of the kind with a collective psychology—those to whose members psychological predicates are standardly ascribed in a straightforward manner, using a full-blooded collective "they" or "we."

0.4 Plural Subjects

I should say something here about my technical phrase "plural subject."[40] As I understand it, a *plural subject* is, by definition, a set of people who are jointly committed with one another in some way. As I understand it, then, a joint commitment account of some element of our collective psychology—as understood in everyday life—does not bring with it any suspect appeal to a "group mind." In particular it does not bring with it any reference to any "subject of consciousness" other than the individual persons involved.

I tend not to write of "plural subjects" now because of misunderstandings along these lines. However, once the phrase is properly understood it presents a useful, compact way to refer to a set of people who are jointly committed with one another in one or more ways. Thus, interpreting "plural subject" as indicated, I have suggested that social groups—of the type at issue here—are plural subjects.[41]

Given that a plural subject is comprised of the parties to one or more joint commitments, and that the parties to a particular joint commitment may change, by addition or subtraction, the members of a plural subject can change. A plural subject account of social groups, then, can accommodate the intuitive point that it is possible for a social group to persist through a change in its members.

0.5 Regarding an Appeal to Joint Commitment

Different accounts of particular collective psychological states may have different targets. Some, for instance, may want to explain what it would be appropriate to call a "collective belief," given certain antecedently established

---

[40] First introduced in Gilbert (1989).
[41] Gilbert (1989: ch. 4); Gilbert (1990), and elsewhere.

standards for what constitutes a belief of any kind.[42] In contrast, my aim has been to elucidate everyday ascriptions of such states.

Some may think an appeal to joint commitment cannot be right in this context, since "joint commitment" is a technical term, and one cannot expect those who use the language I am trying to understand to have a grasp of that. One can, however, possess a concept or grasp a point without being able to articulate it.

Some may object to an appeal to joint commitment on the grounds of theoretical parsimony: why invoke this concept when other, more familiar concepts, such as that of a personal intention, or goal, can do the job?[43] Let us grant that sticking with existing concepts in our theories is a virtue—the virtue of theoretical parsimony—when the job in question can be done with those concepts. But what if it can't—as appears to be the case here? What if an appeal to joint commitment is the best way to understand our collective psychological states—as understood in everyday life?

Further, if we need to appeal to joint commitment in connection with other everyday concepts, it is not clear how much is gained by eschewing the idea of joint commitment in relation to collective psychological states as conceived of in everyday life. If, as I have argued, we need to appeal to joint commitment in order to give an account of everyday agreements as these are ordinarily conceived, there seems to be little benefit in avoiding it in accounting for other everyday concepts.[44]

Subsequent to my introduction of joint commitment into the discussion of collective psychological states and other social phenomena, empirical studies in developmental psychology have indicated that human children evince an understanding of, and capacity for, joint commitment from an early age.[45] These studies clearly support my contention that the concept of a joint commitment is a fundamental part of the conceptual equipment of human beings. Indeed, some primatologists have recently argued for an understanding of joint commitment in some non-human primates.[46]

Clearly, collective psychological states, understood in terms of the relevant joint commitments, are extremely consequential phenomena. One need only

[42] Such an aim may underlie much of the discussion in Lackey (2020), for instance. For a response to Lackey's concerns about my account of collective belief see chapter 6, this volume.
[43] Bratman (2014) argues along these lines.
[44] For an account of agreements as a type of joint commitment see e.g. chapter 1, this volume. On the relevance of this point to the parsimony concern, see Smith (2015).
[45] See e.g. Tomasello (2014). Tomasello and his colleagues have frequently referred to my work and, in particular, to my invocation of joint commitment.
[46] Heesen et al. (2022).

point to their unifying power—unifying disparate individuals into one "we"—
and their inherent stability—which comes from several quarters, including
the associated standings to issue demands and rebukes to other parties, and
the conditions on rescission.

Joint commitments do not necessarily promote the good. Irrespective of
the contexts in which they are formed—which may involve the intimidation
of one person by another, for example—their content may be suspect. Further,
just as they bind us together, they divide "us" from "them" in ways that are
relatively hard for any one of us to change.[47] As the essays gathered together
in this book make clear, we need to make our joint commitments wisely, support them appropriately, and change them when change is called for.

0.6 Preview

The individual chapters of this book are presented in five parts. This preview
includes an introduction to each part and a summary of each chapter in that
part. This should enable readers to focus on the chapters that most interest
them, while retaining a sense of each chapter's place in the overall scheme of
the book. After the Conclusion at the end of the book there is a list of my
publications on our collective psychology and other central aspects of life in
groups, divided by topic for ease of reference.

0.6.1 Part I: Our Intentions, Agreements, and Rights

Part I comprises an extensive essay that links together three important aspects
of life in groups, aspects which are generally either ignored or treated separately in the philosophical literature. These are: everyday agreements, rights of
the kind associated with such agreements, referred to here as "claim-rights,"
and joint or collective intentions—intentions that are ours, collectively.[48]

The nature of agreements, as opposed to promises, has largely been ignored
in the philosophical literature, central though they are to everyday life in

---

[47] For focused discussion of joint commitment as constitutive of an important form of social unity
see my "A Real Unity of Them All," reprinted in Gilbert (2014).

[48] As to claim-rights: I have elsewhere referred to them as "claim-rights*" and, most recently,
"demand-rights" in order to clarify that I have a particular understanding of them in mind, in face of
various interpretations in the literature. See chapter 13, this volume, for claim-rights* and Gilbert
(2018b) for "demand-rights."

groups.[49] The literature on promises, meanwhile, tends to focus on obligations of a type that—as I have argued—are not correlative to rights of the
appropriate kind.[50] Nor do contemporary rights theorists tend to focus on
rights of the kind most closely associated with promises and agreements,
though there are important exceptions.[51] As to joint intentions, leading con-
tributors to the discussion of this topic have rarely explored the relationship
of such intentions to rights or agreements.[52]

Chapter 1, "The Nature of Agreements: A Solution to Some Puzzles about
Claim-Rights and Joint Intention," argues that an understanding of the nature
of everyday agreements can throw light on both the constitution of a joint
intention and the ground of the rights most closely associated with both
agreements and joint intentions. After developing an account of agreements,
it proposes a concordant account of joint intentions, and a ground for rights
of the kind in question.

It starts by describing five puzzles for which an adequate account of agreements can be expected to offer a solution. Four of the puzzles relate to claim-
rights. A fifth relates to joint intentions. When people agree to meet for dinner
the following day, for instance, that seems to suffice to create a joint intention
to meet for dinner then, irrespective of the personal intentions of the parties.
That it does this, however, runs contrary to a natural assumption, one that lies
at the foundation of Michael Bratman's prominent account of joint intention
in terms of a complex of personal intentions with a particular type of
content—the assumption that a joint intention comprises, at least in part, a
pertinent set of personal intentions.

Against this background, I argue for an account of agreements as joint
decisions understood as constituted by a joint commitment with a particular
content, arrived at in a particular manner. I then show that understanding
agreements in this way suffices to solve all five puzzles. In concluding, I point
out the practical utility of agreements understood as proposed.

---

[49] An exception is Black (2012).

[50] See e.g. the prominent discussion in Scanlon (1998) discussed in Gilbert (1993), repr. in Gilbert
(2013). See also chapter 1, this volume.

[51] Hart (1955) takes rights of the kind most closely associated with promises as paradigmatic. Raz
(1984) attempts to fit promissory rights into his general interest theory framework. For further discussion of the general approach of contemporary rights theories see chapter 13, this volume, and Gilbert
(2018b: ch. 5).

[52] I have in mind, in particular, Michael Bratman, whose take on the relation of agreements to collective intentions (in e.g. Bratman 1993) is discussed in chapter 1, and John Searle, though there is an
undeveloped reference to a "social pact" in Searle (1990). I discuss this paper of Searle's in some detail
in Gilbert (2007). I focus on Bratman's account of collective intentions in several places, including
Gilbert (2009) and (2022).

0.6.2 Part II: Our Beliefs

Part II focuses on topics related in one way or another to what we—collectively—believe. Among other things it clarifies my account of collective belief and its target, defends the account against recent objections, argues for a field of general epistemology that subsumes as independent branches individual and collective epistemology, and brings my account of collective belief to bear on observations from the history and philosophy of science.

Chapter 2, "Culture as Collective Construction," takes a group's culture to include its beliefs, attitudes, rules, and conventions. What do these features of groups amount to? The discussion focuses on the case of a group's belief. It first argues that, according to a central everyday conception, a group's belief is not a matter of the personal beliefs of the group members. Rather, it is a matter of the joint commitment of the members by virtue of their several actions and utterances to emulate a single possessor of the belief in question. This means that each member has the standing to demand appropriate utterances and actions of the others and to rebuke those others for failure to produce them. Clearly when group beliefs on this conception arise they are highly consequential phenomena. The same goes for all similarly constructed features of groups, including social conventions, which are also discussed.

Chapter 3, "Joint Commitment and Group Belief," responds to some important queries from sociologist Annette Schnabel regarding the central ideas in the previous chapter. Issues addressed include the relation of joint commitments to the commitments of the involved individuals, the expression condition on joint commitment formation, and contexts in which those involved will benefit from forming a related joint commitment. These contexts include situations in which the relation of the personal inclinations of the parties is representable as constituting a Prisoner's Dilemma. The chapter concludes with discussion of motives for conforming to a given joint commitment, and the relation of joint or collective beliefs and preferences to those of the individuals involved.

Chapter 4, "Belief, Acceptance, and What Happens in Groups: Some Methodological Considerations," notes that the primary focus of epistemology—the theory of knowledge—has been the knowledge, beliefs, and related cognitive states of individual human beings. The broadest concern of this chapter is the relation between the accounts and distinctions developed within *individual* epistemology and *collective epistemology*—the theory of collective cognitive states.

The chapter approaches this relation in part by considering a relatively long-standing debate in collective epistemology that invokes a distinction between "belief" and "acceptance," in which one side argues that groups can accept but not believe propositions. With respect to this and other such contexts it argues for an important methodological caveat: one should not assume that accounts and distinctions arrived at within individual epistemology will apply straightforwardly within collective epistemology, however central they are to individual epistemology. An envisaged field of *general* epistemology will develop an account of belief and related cognitive states that takes its data from both the individual and the collective cases into account.

Chapter 5, "Collective Belief, Kuhn, and the String Theory Community," builds on ideas in my article "Collective Belief and Scientific Change."[53] There I propose that a scientific community like any other will form and be influenced by a range of collective beliefs (on my account of these), and argue that obligations accrued by the parties through these collective beliefs can be expected to act as barriers both to the generation and to the fair evaluation of new proposals and hence to positive changes in the community's beliefs. Relatedly, the established beliefs of the community, accurate or not, will be relatively stable, giving practitioners the opportunity fully to explore their implications. This chapter argues that such points help to explain philosopher of science Thomas Kuhn's famous observations on the role of paradigms in "normal science," as well as certain features ascribed to the group of physicists working on string theory by physicist Lee Smolin in his book *The Trouble with Physics*.[54]

Chapter 6, "Group Lies—and Some Related Matters," defends my joint commitment account of collective belief from a recent challenge from Jennifer Lackey, who presses the charge that the account cannot allow for either group lies or group bullshit—BS for short—and must therefore be rejected. After clarifying several aspects of the account which Lackey's discussion overlooks, I rebut the charge about lies and BS. I then distinguish my aims in presenting an account of collective belief from Lackey's.

0.6.3 Part III: Our Emotions

In everyday life people often refer to collective emotions. For instance, they talk about a team's excitement over its win, or, as a team member might

[53] Gilbert (2000a: 37–49).   [54] Kuhn (1962); Smolin (2006).

express it, "We are so excited!" Yet even theorists who are comfortable with the thought that there are collective intentions and beliefs—intentions and beliefs ascribable to us as opposed to all or most of us—may resist the very idea of a genuinely collective emotion.

One reason for this is that emotion theorists—who generally focus entirely on the emotions of individuals—have long assumed that emotions, as such, involve a particular type of experience, or feeling—a *thrill* of excitement, a *twinge* of remorse, a *gust* of anger, and so on. They may then worry that to ascribe an emotion to a *group* is illegitimately to ascribe a form of subjectivity to the group as such—as opposed to its individual members *seriatim*.

Without making the mentioned assumption about emotions as such, the discussions in this part of the book focus on one or more *collective emotion ascriptions*—in which emotions are ascribed to "us," as one—and ask after their intended referents.

Chapter 7, "Collective Remorse," focuses on a particular collective emotion: a group's remorse. This is a topic of considerable practical interest. It seems that, in general, remorse can be an important stimulus to forgiveness, and hence an important basis for reconciliation between perpetrators and victims. What, then, is remorse at the group level?

The chapter carefully considers three possible accounts of a group's remorse. Two are aggregative. The first of these takes group remorse to involve an aggregation of cases of personal remorse over acts contributing to the relevant act of the group. Three versions of this account are considered. A crucial problem for all of them is that no member of the group, on any version of the account, has to feel remorse *over an act of the group*.

The second aggregative account invokes what I call "membership remorse": a member's remorse over his or her group's act. I argue for the intelligibility of such remorse in light of doubts from philosopher Karl Jaspers and others— Jaspers both expresses and wrestles with such doubts.[55] I propose that, in spite of the intelligibility of membership remorse, generalized membership remorse does not suffice for the remorse *of a group*.

Finally, I propose a plural subject—joint commitment—account of group remorse. I propose that group remorse according to this account is of great practical importance. Its existence and expression can only move forward the emergence of peace between previously victimized groups and their oppressors.

Chapter 8, "How We Feel: Understanding Everyday Collective Emotion Ascription," starts by arguing for the importance of investigating the intended

---

[55] See Jaspers (1947).

referents of everyday collective emotion ascriptions before adopting a general thesis about emotions as such. It then discusses some important aspects of situations in which collective emotions are understood to have been established, along with important features of behavior in the context of an established collective emotion. A joint commitment account of collective emotions that respects the observations just made is then proposed. Finally, some potential relationships between collective emotions on this account and the personal emotions of the parties are considered.

0.6.4 Part IV: Our Preferences, Values, and Virtues

Chapter 9, "Collective Preferences, Obligations, and Rational Choice," focuses on collective preferences as those are expressed in such commonplace statements as "We prefer to eat dinner at 6 o'clock." It defends a joint commitment account of collective preferences in the context of related doubts expressed by economist Robert Sugden.[56]

Sugden doubts that collective preferences entail obligations of the parties. In response I begin by focusing on the kinds of reactions those with a collective preference are likely to evince when one of them acts in ways liable to prevent the satisfaction of that preference. These responses express an understanding that the person in question was obligated to the others to act in the relevant ways, an understanding that person is likely to share. As I discuss, this may well be true even when that person had little choice about whether or not to be part of the group in question. In this connection I discuss two cases referred to by Sugden: conscripts and teenagers.

I turn next to discuss the normativity of collective preferences and argue, *contra* Sugden, that one can validly argue from a premise about what we collectively prefer to a conclusion about what I ought to do, all else being equal, *without reference to what I personally prefer*. In other terms, our collective preference gives me sufficient reason to act accordingly, irrespective of any personal preferences I may have. I emphasize that neither the "oughts" nor the obligations to others associated with collective preferences need be the last word, normatively speaking, as to what a given person ought to do.

---

[56] Sugden (2000); in this paper Sugden responds to the reference to collective preferences in Gilbert (1987).

I then articulate and defend a joint commitment account of collective preferences, and conclude with some remarks connecting the foregoing discussion with aspects of the theory of rational choice.

Chapter 10, "Corporate Misbehavior and Collective Values," speaks to the question: how are we to understand corporate misbehavior? Is it a matter of a few "bad apples" or, if not, what other factors are in play? The chapter argues that when collective values are understood in terms of joint commitment, it can be clearly seen how such values, when misplaced, will be a significant source of corporate misbehavior. Emphasis is placed on the coercive power of collective values on a joint commitment account. Not only do they motivate the parties to act accordingly, they give them the standing to rebuke one another for expressing, or acting in terms of, contrary values. Even when one makes it clear that one is only expressing one's personal opinions, one may be regarded with suspicion. So one may stifle these opinions and even, eventually, cease to hold them.

Chapter 11, "Can a Wise Society Be a Free One?" invokes the idea of a wise society, an idea that has received little attention from contemporary political philosophers, though it has long been a philosophical concern. The chapter argues that, given plausible interpretations of the relevant terms, the wiser a society is, the less free it is. Even if one prefers a different account of a wise society, the argument in question is significant, for on this account a wise society possesses features that would seem to be desirable whatever their relationship to wisdom in particular: it makes many true value judgments. As the chapter explains, this comes with a cost to freedom in the sense in question. One may prefer a different account of a society's freedom, but it is natural to prefer a society that is free in the sense in question, all else being equal.

0.6.5 Part V: Rights and Obligations in Group Life

For political philosophers, "political obligations" are, roughly, obligations to uphold the political institutions of one's country. The "problem of political obligation" is the problem of showing that there are such obligations—if such there be. In my book *A Theory of Political Obligation* (2006) I offer an account of political obligations as joint commitment obligations.

Chapter 12, "Regarding *A Theory of Political Obligation*," addresses several questions and concerns that have been raised about this theory. Some are general questions about personal and joint commitments, and about acting together, on which I focus when introducing the theory. These include questions about the normativity of personal decisions, and concerns about my proposal that those acting together need to have concurred on the exit of a given party if that exit is to occur without fault.

Other questions focus on issues closer to the theory of political obligation itself. These include: the possibility of joint commitments on a very large scale, the content of a joint commitment that would constitute a political society, the temporal dimension of political societies and the possibility of "signing on" to an existing joint commitment, the nature of the relationship of obligations of joint commitment to moral requirements, concerns about the fact that my theory relates to the obligations of joint commitment as opposed to moral requirements, and the relationship of my theory to what I refer to as "actual contract" theories.

Chapter 13, "Giving Claim-Rights Their Due," focuses on rights, and, in particular, the species of rights known as "claim-rights" or, simply, "claims," which were said by the jurist Wesley Hohfeld to be "rights in the strictest sense."

In spite of general agreement on their centrality, there has been a long-standing debate as to the nature of claims. Following Hohfeld, those participating in this debate take it for granted that correlative with any claim is a duty with some feature that relates it to the claim-holder specifically. They disagree on the nature of this feature, some saying that it is the duty's relation to an interest of the claim-holder, some saying that it is the claim-holder's control over the duty. Starting from some remarks of Hohfeld's that are not generally cited, this chapter takes a different approach.

Unlike the traditional views, I do not assume that correlative with any claim is a duty plus some feature that relates it to the claim-holder. Like the traditional views, I do assume that correlative with any claim is a *duty to* the claim-holder. Where we differ is that, unlike the traditional views, I do not assume that a duty to the claim-holder is a duty plus some further feature.

One can, indeed, dispense with any use of the term "duty" in this context, and speak rather of *owing* the claim-holder the object of the claim. The claim-holder, in turn, has the *standing to demand* that object from the right's addressee.

This raises the question of how someone can obtain the standing to demand an action of someone. In other words, how are claim-rights, so understood, accrued? Going forward, for clarity's sake I refer to them as claim-rights*.[57]

I argue that standard references to the claim*-holder's interests or control over the duty does not help here. I then argue that joint commitment is a

---

[57] In Gilbert (2018b) I refer, rather, to "demand-rights," with the same intent.

source of claim-rights*. In other words, the parties to the commitment have the standing to demand conformity to the commitment of each other.

In concluding, I briefly consider the conjecture that joint commitment is the only source of claim-rights* outside what the law may accord to those within its jurisdiction. In this connection I consider, in separate sections, the claim-rights* of the parties to agreements and promises, other informal contexts for claim-rights*, claim-rights* and the law, claim-rights* and the set of canonical claim-right (without the asterisk) ascriptions, and the idea that there is a "moral community" which sustains those requirements we think of as "moral."

* * *

In sum, through the different chapters of this book, I develop a particular approach to life in groups. It offers accounts of multiple situations in which the parties understand themselves to have particular obligations towards each other and rights against each other, it allows us to make sense of the ascription of intentions, goals, beliefs, preferences, values, and emotions to groups, and it subsumes all of these under a single umbrella theory: that group psychological states, broadly construed, are grounded in a joint commitment of the parties. That, the theory goes, is how we think, feel, and act together.

Bibliography

Black, Oliver (2012) *Agreements: A Philosophical and Legal Study*. Cambridge University Press: Cambridge.

Brady, Michael (2016) "Group Emotion and Group Understanding" in Michael S. Brady and Miranda Fricker (eds.), *The Epistemology of Groups*, Oxford University Press: Oxford.

Bratman, Michael (1993) "Shared Intention," *Philosophical Review* 104.1: 97–113.

Bratman, Michael (2014) *Shared Agency: A Planning Theory of Acting Together*. Oxford University Press: Oxford.

Broome, John (2001) "Are Intentions Reasons? And How Should We Cope with Incommensurable Values?" in Christopher Morris and Arthur Ripstein (eds.), *Practical Rationality and Preference: Essays in Honor of David Gauthier*, Cambridge University Press: Cambridge.

Durkheim, Émile (1968 [1895]) *Les Règles de la Methode Sociologique*. Presses Universitaires de France: Paris.

Epstein, Brian (2015) *The Ant Trap: Rebuilding the Foundations of the Social Sciences*. Oxford University Press: Oxford.

Gilbert, Margaret (1987) "Modeling Collective Belief," *Synthese* vol.73.1:185–204.

Gilbert, Margaret (1989) *On Social Facts*. Routledge and Kegan Paul: London; (1992) Princeton University Press: Princeton.

Gilbert, Margaret (1990) "Walking Together: A Paradigmatic Social Phenomenon" in P. A. French et. al. (eds.), *The Philosophy of the Human Sciences*, vol. 15 of *Midwest Studies in Philosophy*, University of Notre Dame Press: Notre Dame.

Gilbert, Margaret (1993) "Is An Agreement an Exchange of Promises?" *Journal of Philosophy* vol. 90.12:627–647.

Gilbert, Margaret (2000a) *Sociality and Responsibility: New Essays in Plural Subject Theory*. Rowman and Littlefield: Lanham, MD.

Gilbert, Margaret (2000b) "Collective Belief and Scientific Change" in Gilbertt (2000a).

Gilbert, Margaret (2002) "Considerations on Joint Commitment: Responses to Various Comments" in Georg Meggle (ed.), *Social Facts and Collective Intentionality*, German Library of Sciences, Hansel-Hohenhausen: Frankfurt. Reprinted in Gilbert (2014).

Gilbert, Margaret (2003) "The Structure of the Social Atom: Joint Commitment as the Foundation of Human Social Behavior" in F. Schmitt (ed.), *Social Metaphysics*, Rowman and Littlefield: Lanham, MD.

Gilbert, Margaret (2006) A Theory of Political Obligation. Oxford University Press: Oxford.

Gilbert, Margaret (2007) "Searle on Collective Intentions" In: Tsohatzidis S.L. (ed) Intentional Acts and Institutional Facts. Theory and Decision Library, vol 41. Springer, Dordrecht. Available at SSRN: https://ssrn.com/abstract=3523055

Gilbert, Margaret (2009) "Shared Intention and Personal Intentions" Philosophical Studies 144 167–187.

Gilbert, Margaret (2013) "Commitment" in Hugh LaFollette (ed.), *The International Encyclopedia of Ethics*, Wiley-Blackwell: Hoboken, NJ.

Gilbert, Margaret (2014) *Joint Commitment: How We Make the Social World*. Oxford University Press: New York.

Gilbert, Margaret (2018a) "Joint Commitment" in Marija Jankovic and Kirk Ludwig (eds.), *Routledge Handbook of Collective Intentionality*, Routledge: London.

Gilbert, Margaret (2018b) *Rights and Demands: A Foundational Inquiry*. Oxford University Press: Oxford.

Gilbert, Margaret (2019) "Further Reflections on the Social World," *Protosociology* vol. 35. 257–284.

Gilbert, Margaret (2022) "Creature Construction and the Morality of Shared Agency. Response to Bratman," *Journal of the American Philosophical Association* vol. 8: 1–4.

Gilbert, Margaret (forthcoming) "Response to Four Critics on *Rights and Demands*," *Philosophy and Phenomenological Research*.

Hart, H. L. A. (1955) "Are There Any Natural Rights?" *Philosophical Review* vol. 64: 175–191.

Heesen, R., Zuberbühler, K., Bangerter, A., Iglesias, K., Rossano, F., Pajot, A., Guéry, J.-P., and Genty, E. (2022) "Evidence of Joint Commitment in Great Apes' Natural Joint Actions" *Royal Society Open Science*, https://doi.org/10.1098/rsos.211121.

Jaspers, Karl (1947) *The Question of German Guilt*, tr. H. B. Acton. Capricorn: New York.

Kuhn, Thomas (1962) *The Structure of Scientific Revolutions*. University of Chicago Press: Chicago.

Lackey, Jennifer (2020) *The Epistemology of Groups*. Oxford University Press: Oxford.

Lederman, Harvey (2018) "Common Knowledge" in M. Jankovic and K Ludwig (eds.), *Routledge Handbook of Collective Intentionality*. Routledge: London.

Lewis, David (1969) *Convention: A Philosophical Study*. Harvard University Press: Cambridge, MA.

Raz, Joseph (1984) "On The Nature of Rights" *Mind* 93.

Ritchie, Katherine (2020) "Social Structures and the Ontology of Social Groups," *Philosophy and Phenomenological Research* 100.2: 402–424.

Scanlon, Thomas (1998) *What We Owe to Each Other*. Harvard University Press: Cambridge, MA.

Schiffer, Steven (1972) *Meaning*. Oxford University Press: Oxford.

Searle, John (1990) "Collective Intentions and Actions" in P. Cohen, J. Morgan, and M. Pollack (eds.), *Intentions in Communication*, Harvard University Press: Cambridge, MA.

Simmel, Georg (1971[1908]) "How Is Society Possible?" in D. N. Levine (ed.), *Georg Simmel: On Individuality and Social Forms*, University of Chicago Press: Chicago.

Smith, Thomas (2015) "*Shared Agency* on Gilbert and Deep Continuity," *Journal of Social Ontology* vol. 1(1): 49–57.

Smolin, Lee (2006) *The Trouble with Physics*. Mariner Books: Boston, MA.

Sugden, Robert (2000) "Team Preferences," *Economics and Philosophy* vol. 20: 175–204.

Tomasello, Michael (2014) *A Natural History of Human Thinking*. Harvard University Press: Cambridge, MA.

Vandershraaf, Peter, and Sillari, Giacomo (2007) "Common Knowledge," *The Stanford Encyclopedia of Philosophy*, http://plato.stanford.edu/entries/common-knowledge.

Velleman, David (1997) "How to Share an Intention," *Philosophy and Phenomenological Research* vol. 57(1): 29–50.

PART I

OUR INTENTIONS, AGREEMENTS, AND RIGHTS

1

The Nature of Agreements

A Solution to Some Puzzles about
Claim-Rights and Joint Intention

Informal agreements pervade our everyday lives.[1] They are made by means of brief interchanges such as "Let's have supper at 5 pm," "Fine," and "Suppose you do the laundry and I walk the dog?" "Okay!" Clearly, if we want to understand the different processes that contribute to our living together, we need to understand precisely what happens in such interactions: what is an agreement?

Insofar as it needs underscoring, the interest of an understanding of agreements is made clear by the history of political philosophy, in which it has been perennially tempting to see a political society as set up by means of an agreement to which successive generations regularly sign on. There are also frequent references to "tacit" and "implicit" agreements in political philosophy and other fields. Presumably an understanding of explicit agreements—which I take to be agreements proper—will help us to understand why these references are popular.

In this chapter I argue that a satisfactory theory of agreements is also likely to make a significant contribution to the discussion of two important issues that are often discussed without reference to agreements. These issues tend to be investigated separately by theorists with different backgrounds and interests.

The first issue concerns rights, in particular those that are known by rights theorists as "claim-rights." Influential legal theorist Wesley Hohfeld regarded

---

[1] The first version of this paper was an invited presentation at a conference on agreements and shared or joint intention held at London University, June 5, 2009. The other speakers were Oliver Black, Michael Bratman, Thomas Pink, and Thomas Smith. Another version was presented at Harvard University, October 2009. I am grateful to the discussants on these occasions and to Daniel Pilchman, Maura Priest, and Frank Stewart for comments on a written draft. Renewed thanks are due to Michael Bratman for our continuing dialogue, in print, in public, and in private conversation on the topic of joint intention—a dialogue that goes back to 1992, when I was the invited commentator on his paper on shared intention at a meeting of the central division of the APA, and continues here. Discussion over the years with such a clear-headed, thoughtful, and probing interlocutor has helpfully pushed me further to clarify my own ideas and the justification for them.

Life in Groups: How We Think, Feel, and Act Together. Margaret Gilbert, Oxford University Press. © Margaret Gilbert 2023.
DOI: 10.1093/oso/9780192847157.003.0002

these as "rights in the strictest sense."[2] The second issue concerns what we are talking about when, in everyday speech, we talk of what *we* intend, where this is not simply elliptical for what I, on the one hand, and you, on the other, intend. This phenomenon has been variously referred to as "shared," "collective," or (as I will say here) "joint" intention."[3]

In both cases the issue is, roughly: *what are these things?* In each case there is a puzzle or puzzles that provoke it with particular intensity. Having introduced the puzzles that I have in mind, I sketch an account of agreements that enables us to solve each one.

This discussion builds on earlier work, referenced where appropriate in what follows. Because of the scope of the chapter, some important points for which I have argued elsewhere will be taken for granted or only briefly defended. The overarching aim of the chapter is to show that the account of agreements sketched here can in part be justified by its ability to solve the puzzles noted.

1. Some Puzzles about Claim-Rights

Claim-Rights in Rights Theory

What exactly is a claim-right? That is a central issue in the theory of rights.[4] Perhaps the least contentious point in the theory of claim-rights in particular is this: claim-right ascriptions generally are fully spelled out in sentences of the form:

X has a claim-right against Y to Y's phi-ing.

For present purposes I will take ascriptions of this form as the canonical *claim-right ascriptions.*[5] In doing so I will assume that the person referred to

[2] Hohfeld (1913). Others have concurred with this assessment, for example, Hart (1955), Thomson (1990). Hohfeld used the label "claims" rather than "claim-rights." He also refers to claim-rights simply as "rights."

[3] "Shared intention" is Michael Bratman's phrase; see, for example, Bratman (1993). It is often used by philosophers interested in the topic. I avoid it here so as not to give the impression that the phenomenon captured by Bratman's account of what he calls "shared intention" is the phenomenon at issue here. As will become clear in the text below, I doubt that is the case.

[4] Less than half of an article is not sufficient space for a full treatment of the topic. My book *Rights and Demands* (2018) offers an extended discussion, expanding on many of the points made here. See also ch. 13, this volume. I was led to this topic as a result of earlier work on issues in the philosophy of social phenomena, including joint intention.

[5] Here, then, I set aside ascriptions of other forms such as "X has a right against Y *to thing T.*" It is standard to focus on sentences of the form given in the text above, although sentences of apparently different forms would need to be considered in a full discussion.

THE NATURE OF AGREEMENTS 31

by "X" and the person referred to by "Y" are distinct persons.[6] The person "against" whom a claim-right is held is generally known as the right's *addressee*.

There is controversy among rights theorists as to how to go further with this spare and essentially formal account of a claim-right. Despite this controversy, rights theorists concur at least in this: informal *agreements* are a canonical source of claim-rights. All else being equal, at least, those who have made an agreement with one another have thereby accrued rights against each other to conformity to the agreement.[7]

The kind of claim-right that accrues to the parties to an agreement is commonly referred to by rights theorists as a "special" right. These are understood to depend on particular transactions or relationships between people. In contrast, "general" rights are not so dependent.[8]

A piece of relatively common ground on the matter of what a claim-right is, which follows Hohfeld, is this:

(1)   For X to have a claim-right against Y to Y's phi-ing is for Y to have an obligation to X to phi.[9]

Some notes on (1) follow.

This statement as a whole is intended to represent the thought that X's having a right against Y is *equivalent* to Y's having an obligation to X. I take this to mean roughly this: X's having a right against Y to Y's phi-ing, and Y's having an obligation to X to phi, are one and the same fact. I will follow custom and refer to statement (1) and to each of the similarly formulated statements that follow as an "equivalence."

Often the term "duty" is used instead of "obligation" in formulations of Hohfeld's equivalence. As far as I can tell there is generally no difference in intent when this happens. I will continue to use the term "obligation" here, without intending to make any particular point by preferring it.[10]

---

[6] There is controversy over whether one can have a claim-right against oneself, the prevailing view seeming to be that one cannot. See Hart (1955). That seems wrong to me, but I will here focus on cases involving one person's right against another. See Gilbert (2018: 17n10, and 177–81) for some related points.

[7] Here and throughout this paper the idea of "conforming" to an agreement and related phenomena will be construed broadly so as to include acting as explicitly agreed but not to be limited to such action.

[8] See Hart (1955, pp. 183–4). For Hart, general rights derive from a single "natural" right possessed, he argues, by all human beings capable of choice, independently of their actual choices (pp. 175–6). I say something about natural rights in the text below.

[9] I say this is "relatively" common ground because not everyone sees the relationship of rights and duties in this way. See, for example, Ross (1930, pp. 48–9). He sees it as unquestionably true that "A right of A against B implies a duty of B to A," but he does not think the converse is true.

[10] Hart (1955) argues that "obligation" is the more appropriate term. His recommendation, although it has merit, has not been generally accepted by philosophers.

Equivalence (1) refers to an obligation that Y has "to" X to phi. What is it for one person to have an obligation *to* another to perform some action? What, in standard terms, is a "directed" obligation?[11] Much of the just mentioned controversy in rights theory focuses on this particular question. That is not surprising, given the prominence of this equivalence. Further, it may look at first blush as if the question is relatively easy to answer. Thus theorists tend to assume that all we have to do to understand *directed* obligation is find out what further factor is involved in the pertinent cases of *nondirected* obligation.[12] Although obviously tempting, this course has brought no consensus to rights theory.[13]

Some Further Equivalences

I now offer a fuller characterization of claim-rights by setting some further equivalences alongside equivalence (1). These new equivalences pick up on important statements by rights theorists H. L. A. Hart and Joel Feinberg, among others.[14]

I take the development on which I focus to be appropriate at least with respect to the claim-rights most closely associated with everyday agreements. What follows, then, can be understood as a characterization of *the type of claim-right that is associated with agreements—at least*. This allows that other types of claim-right are possible. These are not my concern here. That understood, I will continue to write simply of "claim-rights" for brevity's sake.

The first additional equivalence that I offer links directed obligation with *owing* as follows:

(2)   For Y to have an obligation to X to phi is for Y to owe X his, that is, Y's, phi-ing.

To say something like this is quite common. Even without further explanation, it is of interest insofar as it allows us to dispense with the term "obligation"

---

[11] Other terms that have been used are "relational" and "bipolar."

[12] See, for example, Sreenivasan (2005) on the longstanding debate between the "will" and "interest" theories, and an alternative proposal, all in terms of nondirected duties with certain special features.

[13] See Chapter 13, this volume, originally Gilbert (2012), for more discussion of the standard way of proceeding.

[14] Especially Hart (1955) and Feinberg (1970).

altogether even if we want an equivalence that emphasizes the situation of the right's addressee. Thus we can derive from (1) and (2):

(3)   For X to have a right against Y to Y's phi-ing is for Y to owe X his (Y's) phi-ing.

One cannot stop there, however, in part because the verb "to owe" is currently used in a variety of senses.[15]

We need, then, to say something about what it is to owe someone an action—in the sense in question. I will pin that sense down by reference to a central notion of demanding that I take to relate to owing in the way captured by the following equivalence:

(4)   For Y to owe X his (Y's) phi-ing is for X to have the standing to demand of Y that Y phi.

From this and equivalence (3), it follows, of course, that

(5)   For person X to have a right against person Y to Y's phi-ing is for X to have the standing to demand of Y that Y phi.

Much of what follows in this paper will involve discussion of demanding in the sense that I have in mind.

A related equivalence, which I will not pursue directly, invokes an analogous notion of *rebuking*, such that

(6)   For person X to have a right against person Y to Y's phi-ing is for X to have the standing to rebuke Y for not phi-ing, should Y have failed to phi at the appropriate time.

What is it for one person to *demand* something of another? Given one standard sense of the term "demand"—which I will refer to as the *thin* sense—a demand is no more than a seriously intended utterance in the imperative mood. One can demand in this sense without possessing a right to the action one demands. More generally, one needs no special *standing* or

---

[15] A use of "owe" well known to philosophers is that of Scanlon (1998). As Kamm (2002) pointed out, it is at best not clear that Scanlon has in mind a relation that correlates with someone's having a right.

authority to make such a demand. Anyone is in a position to address such an imperative to anyone else, and people probably do this often—sometimes as a plea, sometimes in a menacing tone, and so on.[16]

There is another sense of the term "demand," however, such that one needs a special standing to demand of someone that he do something. Thus, although demanding in this sense typically *involves* a seriously intended utterance in the imperative mood, it is never simply such an utterance. It is this *thick* sense that I take to be at issue in equivalences (4) and (5) above. In writing of "demands," "demanding," and so on in what follows, I have the thick sense in mind.[17]

The special standing that one needs to make a demand is a type of power. One might think of it as a normative—as opposed to physical or mental—power. One *cannot* demand that someone act in a certain way without having the relevant standing. One can do various closely related things but not *demand* the action.[18]

One may have the *standing* to demand some action of someone without being *justified, all things considered,* in demanding it. Thus, even if I have the standing to demand of you that you meet me this afternoon, since we agreed that you would, it may be that I should not do so, all things considered, given that your ailing spouse will need your help then.

Further, I may be justified, all things considered, in uttering a *seriously intended imperative,* yet *lack* the standing to demand the action in question. Thus if I see that you are inadvertently about to walk over a cliff, I may be justified in yelling "Stop!" although I would not be thought of having the standing to *demand* that you stop.

---

[16] Compare Fuller (1978, p. 369), quoted in Barnett: "If I say to someone, 'Give me that!' I do not necessarily assert a right. I may be begging for an act of charity, or I may be threatening to take by force something to which I admittedly have no right" (1995, p. 122).

[17] Ross says, "There hangs about the notion of a 'right' the notion of its being not only something which one person should in decency respect but also something which the other person can in decency claim" (1930, p. 53). Ross may be sensitive to the point in the text; however, his "claim" could be interpretable as "demand" in the thin sense, while "in decency" suggests a moral justification for so demanding. To be justified in so demanding, however, is not necessarily to have the standing or authority to demand in the thick sense. See the text below. The phrase "hangs about" suggests a certain puzzlement as to how to accommodate the point that Ross is making.

[18] In what sense is demanding a *normative* matter—that is, roughly, a matter of what someone has or lacks reason to do? Suffice it to say here that, at a minimum, if I have the standing to *demand* that someone phi, then I have a particular means to the end of keeping him on track with respect to *something he otherwise has reason to do.* Here I make a sharp distinction between demanding and commanding. If I have the standing to *command* you to phi, *my command may be the only thing that gives you reason to phi.* If I *demand* that you phi, where saying this is not just another way of saying I commanded it, I am making it clear that I am not ready to let you get away with not doing something you otherwise have reason to do. For more on commanding see Gilbert (2006).

If I have the standing to demand a given action, must I be justified in demanding it, *all else being equal*? Given the equivalences above, for you to have the standing to demand an action is for you have a claim-right to the action. In that case it seems plausible to say that you will indeed be justified—all else being equal—in demanding an action when you have the standing to do so. After all, you then have a claim-right to it.[19]

A Puzzle about the Standing to Demand

How does one come by the standing to demand a given action of another person? We already know that, given equivalence (5), for X to have the standing to demand of Y that Y phi is for X to have a right against Y to Y's phi-ing. So one can come by the standing in question by accruing a claim-right. Similar things can be said on the basis of other equivalences listed above.

What would be helpful at this point, however, would be to find a basis for the standing to demand an action that can be specified without explicit reference to the accrual of a claim-right, getting someone to owe you an action or getting someone to be obligated to you to do something. If our aim is further to understand claim-rights, pursuit of such a basis is in order. It may lead us in fruitful new directions, allowing perhaps for further equivalences that extend our understanding of claim-rights. But can such a basis be specified and if so how? Call this *the standing-to-demand puzzle*.

Feinberg's Suggestion and Another Puzzle

A suggestion from Joel Feinberg offers a clue as to how one might say more about the standing to demand. At several points Feinberg writes, without special comment, of a right-holder demanding *as his* what he has a right to.[20] Whatever Feinberg's intention, this suggests the following: for me to have the standing to demand that someone else act in a certain way is for that action to be in an as yet unspecified sense *mine*.

Suppose one finds this idea intuitive. One may yet wonder: How *can* an action that is another person's to perform be in any sense mine?[21] Perhaps

---

[19] Paragraph added in response to a comment from Maura Priest.
[20] Feinberg (1970) and elsewhere.
[21] What is it for a given person to perform a given action? That is a good question. For present purposes I rely on an intuitive, unanalyzed understanding of this idea.

someone will say that it is mine in the sense that I have a claim-right to it. That, however, will not help us to go beyond the equivalences already presented. Nor, given these equivalences, will it help to refer to the other person's directed obligations toward me or to what he owes me.

Setting those options aside, then, the question is this: Is there another sense of "mine" that could plausibly be argued to be at issue in this case? I refer to the latter question as the *demanding-as-mine puzzle*.

Two Puzzles about the Claim-Rights of Agreements

If we can find a context in which people indisputably have the standing to demand actions of one another, we may be able to work from that to a solution to the puzzles so far noted and hence to a better understanding of what claim-rights amount to.

It seems sometimes to be assumed that in certain cases human beings have the pertinent standing "naturally." That is, roughly, they have it independently of any particular transactions or relationships. That this is so is by no means obvious. Indeed, the issue is one version of the important and long-debated question whether there are any natural rights.[22] In attempting to understand how one comes by the standing to demand an action, it seems best initially at least to look elsewhere.

An obvious place is everyday agreements. Indeed, my characterization of claim-rights in terms of the equivalences so far noted was in part derived from what it is that agreements give the parties by way of rights. How is it, then, that by making an agreement one comes by one or more claim-rights?

This is not a question on which philosophers have tended to focus. They tend to assume that an agreement is a pair of promises and have thus focused on promises. As I have argued elsewhere, however, there are serious problems with that assumption. Indeed, there is reason to think it best first to consider agreements.[23]

That said, promises and agreements are close cousins, intuitively, and an understanding of the way in which promises give claim-rights—at least to promisees—should go some way toward an understanding of how agreements

---

[22] I say "one version" because the claim-rights in question here are of a particular type. I discuss this version in Gilbert (2018). There is related discussion in the text below. The most famous opponent of natural rights is probably Jeremy Bentham, who argued that talk of such rights is "nonsense." That is not to say that he is focusing on claim-rights in the sense at issue here—as Hart (1955), for instance, is.

[23] Gilbert (1993a).

give such rights to the parties. The two standard approaches to the question of how promises give rights, however, both leave something to be desired. Let me briefly indicate some of the problems associated with these approaches.[24]

First, there is the *moral* approach. Here the rights associated with promises have been understood as being of the same genus as "natural" rights, although in the case of promises the existence of the associated rights depends on particular transactions—up to a point. The genus in question is *moral* rights.

The idea is something like this. Some moral rights exist independently of the particular transactions of human beings—these moral rights are natural rights. Some, however, come into existence only in the context of particular transactions between human beings.[25] According to the moral approach, the rights of promisees are of the latter type: they are "special" moral rights.[26]

For present purposes there is no need to try to say precisely what is meant by the qualifier "moral." Suffice it to say that there seems to be a particular interpretation at issue in the case of the moral approach, which has consequences to be detailed shortly. It is not necessary, either, to attempt to understand whether and if so how there can be "special" moral *claim-rights*, as the moral approach supposes. For it is possible to set out a significant problem for the moral approach without concerning oneself with these issues.

This problem relates to the way that those who hold the moral approach tend to react to a particular type of case. That is the case of promises to do very bad things—evil things, for short.[27]

Most likely one who takes this approach will not want to say that in such cases the promisee has a moral claim-right against the promisor to his performing the evil action promised. More likely a proponent of the approach will say that the promisee would have had such a right—were it not for the content of the promise.[28] It is not clear, however, that the promisee in such a

---

[24] In fact, most theorists of promising focus on the obligation of a promisor, not on a promisee's right to performance. Gilbert (2004) raises doubts about *moral principle* theories of promissory obligation, doubts that relate to these theories' abilities to account for the claim-rights of promisees and in particular the standing to demand performance that is associated with them. I say something along these lines in section 3 below.

[25] This would be the case if, given a certain fundamental source of moral rights generally, that source gives rise to some moral rights independently of particular human transactions and so on, while at other times the delivery of rights depends on such transactions.

[26] See Hart (1955).

[27] Here and in what follows I assume that such agreements are possible. See Gilbert (2006, ch. 10; 2011b) for further discussion.

[28] Sometimes "prima facie rights" are referred to in discussions of this point, where these are understood along the lines of Ross's "prima facie duties." As Ross (1930) emphasized, in his terms, "prima facie" duties were not "duties proper." Nor, I suppose, are "prima facie" rights "rights proper."

case lacks the usual standing to demand of the promisor the promised act. Indeed, that seems not to be the case intuitively.

Recall in this connection that for X to have the *standing* to demand of Y that Y do A is not equivalent to X's being *justified*, all things considered, in making such a demand. The present point is that if, for instance, Jack has promised Jill that he will shoot Rose, should Jill then say to Jack, "Come on, take your gun and get going!" it makes little sense for Jack to respond, "*What put you in a position to tell me to do that?*" The answer is clear, as Jill would undoubtedly aver: "Your promise to shoot her!"

Of course, Jack could now go on to explain why at this point this is not something that he feels able to do, that he now realizes that it is wrong, indeed unconscionable, that his promise is not enough to change that. To say any of these things, however, is not to deny Jill's standing to make the demand in question.

There are other problems with the moral approach that need not be detailed at this juncture.[29] Suffice it to say that this approach to the rights of promisees is problematic. The same goes, *mutatis mutandis*, for the analogous approach to agreements.

Before leaving the moral approach, I note that those who take it rarely focus on the question of precisely what it is to make a promise. Assumptions along these lines are of course explicitly or implicitly made, but these assumptions are not generally defended in any detail. That is unfortunate since, intuitively, *it is something about the very nature of promises that ensures the right of the promisee.* In other words, if a promise has been made, the promisee has a right to performance.[30] The analogous point is true of agreements.

There are two related intuitive points worth distinguishing—both worthy of more comment than I can give them here. First, as just indicated, a promise gives a right to the promisee irrespective of *the moral character of the promised act.* More generally, a promisee's right is *content-independent.* Second, a promisee's right exists irrespective of such contingent consequences as

---

[29] For further pertinent discussion of the problem discussed in the text and other problems for the moral approach see Gilbert (2006, ch. 10; 2011b); also see the text below (section 3).

[30] Compare Prichard's statement about promissory *obligation* in Prichard (1968, p. 198): "Once call some act a promise, and all question as to whether there is an obligation to do it disappears." If there are any qualifications to be made here—something I doubt—I do not think they will affect the general thrust of this paper. I therefore proceed here and in what follows on the assumption expressed in the text. See Gilbert (2011b) for further discussion.

expectations or potentially detrimental reliance in relation to which various moral requirements may come to apply to the promisor. Thus it is also, for short, *consequence-independent*.[31] The same goes, once again, for agreements.

The second of the standard approaches to the rights of promisees is the conventionalist or institutional approach. Hume took such an approach to the obligations of promisors.[32] Although he does not talk of "rights," his discussion is of great interest for present purposes.

Hume notes that, intuitively, the obligation of a promisor is willed into being when the promise is made.[33] He argues, however, that this judgment is not sustainable on reflection. As he sees it, the judgment in question is, more precisely, that the obligation of a promisor is a *moral* obligation that is willed into being. His central worry is that one cannot will a moral obligation into being. Although this point is made in terms of his own particular sentimentalist moral theory, he argues that it is more generally applicable.[34]

Seeking for an account of promissory obligation, Hume argues that it is, in the first instance, a stipulated, institutional obligation.[35] *According to the institution in question*, one who says "I promise" must do what he promised. This approach can be extended to promissory *rights* by saying that the rights of promisees are stipulated, institutional rights: very roughly, according to the institution in question, one to whom "I promise" is said has a claim-right against the promisor to the promised action.[36] The same approach can be taken to agreements and the rights of agreement, insofar as these receive separate treatment.

One problem with an institutionalist approach to the rights of agreement is that it does not represent the intuitive situation. In particular, to echo Hume on promissory obligation, the claim-rights of the parties to an agreement are

---

[31] This assumes that actual expectations, reliance, and so on are contingent consequences of a given promise as such, something that I take to be correct. The point made in the text is not always acknowledged in the literature on promising, in which there is much reference to such contingent consequences.

[32] Hume (1960, book 3, section 5).

[33] Hume does not use the term "intuitively." It seems apposite here, however. What he says is: "It is entirely conformable to our common ways of thinking, and of expressing ourselves, when we say that we are bound by our own consent, and that the obligation arises from our mere will and pleasure" (1960, pp. 516–17). For a comment on what I take the class of philosophically noteworthy "intuitive" judgments, see section 2 below.

[34] Hume (1960, p. 517, n. 1).

[35] Hume's discussion of promissory obligation is complex and involves "obligations" of different kinds. He sums up his position at one point by saying that the obligation of a promise is "merely a human invention for the convenience of society" (1960, p. 524).

[36] See Shockley (2008) for related points.

willed into being by those parties—in a way that does not involve institutional rules of the kind conventionalism envisages.[37]

Can we, after all, make sense of this intuitive judgment? I will call this *Hume's puzzle*. Note that as I have couched it, Hume's puzzle does not explicitly concern *moral* rights, nor is it intended implicitly to do so. If one wishes to save the intuitive judgment in question, while avoiding the problem noted for the moral approach, it had better not concern moral rights—or, at least, moral rights in the sense of the moral approach.

Not surprisingly, given the nature of the standard approaches to the rights of promises and agreements, Hume's puzzle has been largely ignored in contemporary theorizing about promises and agreements themselves. A different approach is called for. Yet many will doubt that anything other than a moral or institutional approach is possible. They will think that these options simply exhaust those available. Given that neither of these options is satisfactory, then, it is reasonable to think of the nature of the claim-rights of agreement as a puzzle.

Is there an alternative to the moral and institutional approaches? If so, what is it? I will call this the *third way puzzle*.

Towards a Solution to the Puzzles about Claim-Rights

I have noted several puzzles about claim-rights. First, there is the standing-to-demand puzzle: What can be said to amplify our understanding of the standing to demand? In particular, how does one come by this standing? Then there is the demanding-as-mine puzzle, stemming from Feinberg's suggestion that, in effect, one who demands an action demands it *as his*: In what sense of "his"—if any—is this true? A helpful approach to each of these puzzles will go beyond the previously listed equivalences and their various permutations.

Next there are two puzzles relating specifically to the association of agreements with claim-rights. One is Hume's puzzle: Can one make sense of the intuitive idea that the claim-rights of agreement are *willed into being*—and if so how? The other is the third way puzzle: What *kind* of claim-right is at issue in the case of agreements—if it is not as envisaged by the moral and institutional approaches?

---

[37] There is further discussion of institutional rights in Gilbert (2018) and in "Rights without Laws" (Gilbert 2011a). See also Gilbert (2006, ch. 2) on "imputed" obligations.

Evidently a good way to pursue a solution to all four of these puzzles is to attempt to understand precisely what an agreement amounts to.[38] As noted, the connection between agreements and claim-rights is particularly tight, intuitively. An agreement was made: *that's it*—now the claim-rights are there, as is the standing to demand the actions in question.

I now turn from the topic of claim-rights to another important topic to which an understanding of agreements may be expected to contribute. As I later explain, these topics are quite closely related.[39] That relationship, however, is not the concern of the next section.

2. A Puzzle about Joint Intention

The issue to be discussed in this section is: What is referred to when, in everyday life, people speak informally of what "we intend," and this is not simply elliptical for what "I, on the one hand, and you, on the other, intend." In the technical terms I am adopting here: what is a *joint intention*?[40]

In addition to joint intentions there are *personal* intentions. A "personal intention" as I use the term here is an intention that is naturally referred to by the individual who has it as "my intention."

Theorists of personal intention have distinguished intentions with regard to the future and intentions in acting. I focus here on *joint* intentions with regard to the future. I take it that these may sometimes naturally be referred to not only as "our intention" but also as "our plan," as in "our plan is to paint the house tomorrow."[41]

In the case of both personal and joint intentions one can speak of intentions *to do such-and-such* and of intentions *that such-and-such be the case.*[42]

---

[38]   One might also attempt to understand promises for this purpose. It should in any case be agreed that a focus on agreements is one way to go. See Gilbert (2011b) for further discussion of the relation of agreements and promises; also Gilbert (2006, ch. 10) and (2018, ch. 9).

[39]   See section 3 below.

[40]   For a longer initial characterization of my topic see Gilbert (2000b). There and in the present paper I assume—prior to some reason to think otherwise—that such phrases refer to a single phenomenon, which may of course occur in usefully distinguishable versions.

[41]   From the point of view of the way in which people talk in everyday speech, it may at least sometimes be a bit of a stretch to speak of an *intention in acting* as a plan. Thus suppose Jack is drinking some coffee. His wife, Phyllis, who is in the other room, calls out to him, "What are you doing?" If he says, "My plan is to drink some coffee," this is likely to be interpreted as implying that he has not yet started his coffee drinking, or as a sarcastic reference to his having been interrupted in his coffee drinking by her question. Otherwise he is likely simply to say, "I am having a coffee" or some such thing. In acting, one may of course be according one's behavior with a prior plan, one's intention in acting taking its character from that plan. I take it that this need not be the case.

[42]   Here is an example of the latter in the joint case: "Our intention is that our son go to college."

To not overly complicate matters, and following standard practice, I focus here on joint intentions to do such-and-such, such as the intention someone might express by saying, "We intend to get married in June." I do not mean thereby to disavow the possibility of joint intentions of the other sort. Indeed, they are worth more attention than I can give them here.

As I now explain, there is a puzzle about joint intention that can be brought out by reference to agreements.

Suppose that Alan and Barbara agree to have dinner together this evening. Alan says, "Shall we have dinner tonight?" and Barbara says "Yes, indeed." As soon as their agreement is made, it seems that either one is in a position confidently to say of the two of them, "We plan to have dinner together tonight." Indeed, *there seems to be no question, given their agreement, that they have this plan.* This I take to be the intuitive position.

Does this story logically entail any particular facts about the personal intentions of the participants with respect to their having dinner tonight? In particular, must each personally intend to act in ways conducive to their having dinner together?

It seems not. For we can consistently describe the following expansion of the example just given. Before entering their agreement—an agreement he fully intended to enter—Alan privately decided *not* to dine with Barbara. He would call her at the last moment to say that he was unwell and could not dine with her. By coincidence Barbara decided likewise. Nonetheless, each went ahead and agreed with the other that they would meet for dinner. Each intended to enter such an agreement, and it was made. They now had the joint intention to meet for dinner. At no point before or after their agreement was made, or during its making, did either one change his or her own personal plan or form any new intention to conform with their joint one.

This example illustrates three significant points. First, the fact that *we agreed* to do something does not entail that either of us personally intends, or ever intended, to act in ways that conform to the agreement.[43] Second, the fact that *we intend* to do something entails no more about the *personal intentions* of each than does the fact that we agreed to do it. Third—following from the first two points—the fact that *we intend* to do something does not entail that either of us personally intends to act in ways that conform to our intention or

---

[43] Compare Bratman (1999b, p. 134, n. 12; p. 127, n. 31). In both cases Bratman refers to the fact that agreements do not entail personal intentions to conform to them. I discuss the inference that he draws from this in the next section. I also say more about the case of Alan and Barbara there.

ever intended to do so. This last is *the puzzle about joint intention* to which I mean to draw attention.

I call it a puzzle because it runs contrary to a natural—if misguided—thought; namely, that a joint intention is made up of personal intentions of the participants.[44] This is, indeed, a thought that is endorsed by most theorists of joint intention, albeit without much, if anything, by way of preamble.[45] I will call it the *personal intentions thesis*.

Bratman's Discussion

It is worth seeing how the personal intentions thesis figures in the opening sections of a classic article by Michael Bratman, entitled "Shared Intention." Before doing so, I refer to a footnote fairly late in his article that is particularly pertinent to the present discussion. Here and in what follows I will assume that a *shared* intention in Bratman's sense is a *joint* intention in the sense of this paper, an assumption I justify in due course.

In the footnote in question Bratman argues that *no agreement suffices in and of itself to produce a joint intention*.[46] After all, he reasons, there are agreements such that *neither party intends to act as agreed*. This premise represents an important fact about agreements and conforms with the preceding discussion here. The conclusion Bratman draws from it, however, does not so conform.

To reach this conclusion it seems that Bratman is relying on the personal intentions thesis. I now consider whether there is anything in the discussion preceding this note that adequately justifies that thesis. To anticipate my conclusion: that discussion comes close to a justification but not close enough.

Bratman opens his discussion as follows:

---

[44] Compare Alonzo: "*It is reasonable to think that* the socio-psychological structure of our shared intention...involves, among other things, intentions on the part of each of us" (2009, p. 447; emphasis added). By "shared intention" it seems that Alonzo has in mind joint intention in my sense. I note that he sees Searle's theory as conforming to the thought he describes. Searle does not centrally invoke what I am referring to as *personal* intentions. See the next note.

[45] There may be doubt as to whether in fact the theorists whom I have in mind are indeed theorizing about joint intention in my sense. There is reason to think that many are and that they take the position noted in the text. I explore in more detail the discussion in Bratman (1993) in the next subsection. Assuming that his target is joint intention, a well-known exception here is Searle (1990), whose position was expressed earlier by Sellars (1963). These authors conjure mental states of each individual in question expressible not in sentences of the form "I intend...." but rather of the form "We intend...." I discuss some difficulties with Searle's discussion, and with the Searle-Sellars approach, in Gilbert (2000a, ch. 12; 2007).

[46] Bratman (1999b, p. 127, n. 31; see also p. 134, n. 12).

That we do sometimes have intentions that are in an important sense shared seems clear. We commonly report or express such shared intentions by speaking of what *we* intend or of what *we* are going to do or are doing. Speaking of you and myself I might say that we intend to paint the house together, to sing a duet together. In each case I report or express a shared intention.[47]

From this, I shall take it that the target of Bratman's discussion is joint intention in the sense of this paper.[48] Moving on from the introductory material just noted, Bratman asks what jobs shared intentions fulfill in our lives—what function do they fulfill? Plausibly, he describes three such jobs—the details of which need not concern us for present purposes—and, equally plausibly, he says that an account of shared intention should explain how a given shared intention performs these jobs.

This leaves things relatively open. Bratman's next points, however, close things up considerably. He argues that an account of shared intention should be in terms of "a complex of attitudes of each of the individual agents."[49] He continues quickly to posit, in effect, that personal *intentions* of the parties will lie at the core of any pertinent complex of *attitudes*. Thus he writes: "Such an approach to shared intention will need to draw on an understanding of the intentions of individuals."

The point that an account of shared intention will need to be in terms of the *intentions* of individuals is not argued for. Indeed, the point in question is *presupposed* prior to the statement just quoted.[50]

Among the framework assumptions of Bratman's discussion of joint intention, then, is the personal intentions thesis. Given this assumption, his focus naturally becomes: What *sort* of personal intention is at issue? In particular, what kind of special content must it have? And how must the intentions of the individual parties relate to one another—if there is some constraint on how they must relate? The assumption in question, however, is quite a strong one.

---

[47] Bratman (1999b, p. 127, n. 31).

[48] Bratman continues to open his discussion in a similar way in more recent work. See, for example, Bratman (2009, p. 150). More recently still, he comes close to disavowing this particular target.

[49] Bratman (1999b). This point is supported by comparing "a complex of attitudes of the individual agents" with "an attitude in the mind of some superagent consisting literally of some fusion of the two agents." It is hard to know exactly what Bratman means to rule out here. It is also hard to be sure what he means to rule in. On the face of it, a "complex of attitudes," as such, need have no particular relation to the parties' interactions past or present, another factor that could be relevant.

[50] "Now, one way in which you and I may arrive at a shared intention is to arrive at an appropriate, explicit promise to each other. But such promises *do not ensure a shared intention, for one or both parties may be insincere and have no intention to fulfill the promise*" (Bratman 1999a, p. 111; emphasis added). This is the complete discussion of the point in this location.

A different assumption along the lines of Bratman's original proposal does indeed seem reasonable: that shared intention can be explained in terms of the *actions, attitudes, and/or relationships, past and present, of the parties*— what other materials are available, after all? That, however, is far weaker than the personal intentions thesis.

I conjecture, then, that when—fairly far into his article—Bratman rejects the idea that people can share an intention by virtue simply of an agreement that they have made, he is, in effect, stipulating a sense for the phrase "shared intention" such that this rejection is indeed in order. Meanwhile, the assumption that lies behind this stipulation—the personal intentions thesis—has not been adequately defended in prior discussion.

In this section I have not meant to offer anything like a full discussion of Bratman's position on joint intention. My intention has been to illustrate in a relatively detailed way how the personal intentions thesis enters a classic discussion of joint intention.

Agreements, Joint Intention, and Personal Intentions

In discussing Bratman's work I have not meant to imply that the personal intentions thesis has no credibility. The problem, however, is that it does not respect the intuitive position on the relationship of *agreements* and joint intentions. Intuitively, in the example given, Alan and Barbara *have* the joint intention at issue as soon as their agreement is concluded, *irrespective* of whether they personally intend to act accordingly. I take it that this kind of judgment on a case with respect to whether a certain concept applies in that case is more of a benchmark for an account of shared intention than a "first-blush" judgment concerning *what joint intention is.*[51]

It is worth noting that there is an analogy with the first-blush judgment at issue here in the case of everyday talk of what we—as opposed to you on the one hand and I on the other—believe. A "summative" account of this according to which, at a minimum, all or at least most of the people in question personally believe whatever *we* are said to believe is likely to be the first that

---

[51] The important distinction between these two types of judgment is often ignored when people write critically about the use of "intuitions" in philosophy. Compare in this connection the use of "grammaticality" judgments in linguistics with proposals as to the grammar of a given language. One should presumably take seriously the former when made by those whose language is in question; while there is no reason to think that speakers generally are particularly well equipped either to propose plausible grammars or to judge proposed grammars of their own languages.

comes to mind. Yet, as I have argued at length elsewhere, there are strong reasons for rejecting a summative account.[52]

If one is still unsure that an agreement as such may suffice, intuitively, for a joint intention, some development of the example of Alan and Barbara may be helpful. Suppose that some time after he and Barbara have agreed to have dinner that evening, Alan tells her that he intends to have dinner with Clarisse—not Barbara. Barbara retorts, as well she might, "What about our plan?" Whatever her own intentions, she has no wish to let Alan off the hook of their agreement at this time.

Suppose now that Alan replies, "I know that you didn't realize it at the time, but *there never was such a plan*! It's true that I agreed to have dinner with you, but I never intended to stick by that agreement." Does this reply make sense? I would side with Barbara should she respond: "I'm not concerned with your personal intentions, Alan! You agreed to dine with me—so *we had a plan*. We *still do*—although it seems you intend to subvert it!" Of course, the idea that Alan would say "There never was such a plan!" in the circumstances envisaged is quite far-fetched, which says something in itself.

In what follows I will assume that the fact that *we* intend to do something entails no more about our *personal* intentions than does the fact that we *agreed* to do the thing in question. I will assume, further, that we can so agree without either one personally intending to act in accordance with the agreement either at the time that we make it or after it has been made. Indeed, each may persistently intend to act otherwise.[53]

These working assumptions rule out all accounts of joint intention that are, in a word, *personal-intention based* at least insofar as they are taken to be offering conditions that are both necessary and sufficient for joint intention.[54] These include many carefully wrought accounts of joint intention in addition to Bratman's.[55]

This brings us back to the puzzle about joint intention noted at the outset of this section. It will seem to be particularly challenging if one's first-blush judgment is that personal intentions must be constitutive of joint intention. How is it possible for *us* to have an intention although neither one of

---

[52] For extensive discussion, see Gilbert (1989, ch. 5, and Part 2, this volume).

[53] There is further discussion of these points in Gilbert (2009).

[54] Bratman (1999b, p. 128) is prepared to opt for having offered a set of conditions sufficient although not necessary for shared intention, although his aim had been to find a set of conditions both sufficient and necessary. I note some points that argue against its sufficiency later in the text below.

[55] Bratman (1993a, 1999b, and elsewhere, e.g., 2009). Other such accounts that at least on the face of it concern joint intention include those of Kutz (2000), Roth (2004), and Alonso (2009). For some distinctions among different personal-intention-based theories see Gilbert (2009).

us—perhaps—intends or has ever intended to play a role in implementing it? What can it be for us to intend to do something if our personal intentions do *not* constitute this phenomenon at least in part?

Evidently, an understanding of the nature of agreements should help us to solve this puzzle—and to do so without making any metaphysically extravagant claims. Agreements being pretty humdrum things, it should be possible to understand them and what they entail without going too far metaphysically speaking.

3. What Is an Agreement?

What, then, is an agreement?[56] The account that I outline here can be introduced by reference to a phenomenon that I take to be importantly analogous—a personal decision. Such decisions are typically expressed (if only in private rumination) by such words as "I'll do A!" or "I'm going to do A!"

Personal Decisions: Their Normativity

One who has decided to perform some action A may then be said to plan to do A. We might also describe the situation using not the verb "to plan" but the noun "plan," or the phrase "scheme of action." As one puts it colloquially, one who has decided now *has a plan.*

What difference does one's personal decision make to one's situation, normatively speaking? There is by now a considerable, growing, and diverse philosophical literature on this topic, central participants in which have been Michael Bratman and John Broome. I cannot undertake to explore its details here. I simply describe my own take on the pertinent part of the issue.

A simple case will exemplify the main point I want to make. Diane decides to have lunch at the Rose café. Later she absent-mindedly walks in the other direction. Realizing this, she presses her hand to her brow and says in a tone of self-rebuke, "Oh, I meant to go to the Rose café!"

I construe this as a matter of Diane's recognition of a central aspect of the normativity of personal decision: all else being equal, at least, one acts in error if one acts contrary to a standing decision. What kind of error is this?

---

[56] The present proposal draws on earlier discussions of mine including Gilbert (2006, ch. 10). See also Gilbert (2018).

I start with what it isn't. It isn't a matter of bad consequences. It isn't a matter of choosing an action that is bad in itself or worse than a given alternative. It isn't a matter of ignoring whatever reasons led one to make the decision in question.

On the positive side, it is perhaps natural to think of the error involved in acting contrary to one's decision in terms of a kind of "practical inconsistency": if my plan is to do A, my not doing A is not consistent with that decision. I am not sure that this account goes to the heart of the matter.

Rather than attempting further to characterize the error involved in "contra-decisional" action, I will work with the spare idea that there is such an error, and that the way I have so far characterized it is correct, if not exhaustive. To indicate in a phrase the idea of a generic *error in action*, such as is involved here, I will say that one's decision in and of itself gives one *sufficient reason* to act in conformity to it, where this means that if one is appropriately responsive to applicable considerations of whatever kind one will so act, all else being equal.[57] Then one ought so to act—in a generic sense of "ought"—rather than a more restrictive moral sense. A personal decision, then, creates for the decision-maker a specific type of *normative constraint* with respect to his future actions.

Commitments of the Will as a Genus

In imposing this constraint, the decision-maker may be said to have *committed* himself to act according to the plan in question. The type of *commitment* in question may be referred to as a commitment *of the will*. In this case it is a commitment both *by* and *of* the will of the person who makes the decision.[58]

A personal decision effects what I call a *personal* commitment of the will. Such commitments are created solely by virtue of an act or state of the will of the individual in question. They may be destroyed in the same manner. Thus one unilaterally *makes* and can unilaterally *rescind* one's personal decision and thus rid oneself of the commitment that it imposes.

Once I have rescinded my decision or, in the vernacular, *changed my mind*, that decision no longer imposes any rational constraint upon me. Without

---

[57] I distinguish between having reason and having a reason. See Gilbert (2006, ch. 2).
[58] For more on commitment generally and commitments of the will in particular see Gilbert (2013a).

rescission, however, my decision stands until the time for carrying it out is past, and throughout this time I am personally committed to act accordingly.[59]

Note that the notion of *commitment* at issue here is not a specifically *moral* notion—unless one operates with a particularly broad notion of morality.

One might talk of someone being *morally committed* in the following kind of context. I have regularly been offering food to a homeless person who sits on the street corner near my house. Although I have made no promise and, for that matter, no decision to continue to do this on a regular basis, I have set up expectations; the homeless person now relies on my help. Perhaps by virtue of what I have done, I now have sufficient reason to continue and may then be said to be committed to do so. My *commitment* here, if there is one, is not a commitment of my will, in the sense introduced above, but rather a commitment deriving from moral considerations, given what I have done in the past. It is true that my will was involved in these past doings, but I did not will *the continuation of my help*, as I might have done.

Agreements Compared with Personal Decisions

That informal *agreements* have some affinity with personal decisions is clear enough. A personal decision is expressed monologically by, for instance, "I'll go swimming!" An agreement may be expressed by the parties in related, dialogical ways, as in "Shall we go swimming?" "Let's!" Again, a personal decision can be rescinded by the decision-maker and by him alone. An agreement is rescinded when those who made it concur as to its rescission. It cannot be rescinded by anyone else or by either one unilaterally.[60] Most important for present purposes, in the case of both a decision and an agreement *a particular plan or scheme of action* is at issue. This plan is explicitly specified at the time the decision or agreement is made.

---

[59] Here I take there to be a difference between personal *decisions* and personal *intentions*, both of which I take to effect personal commitments of the will. In particular, a personal intention can simply *disappear* in a way that a decision cannot. See, for example, Gilbert (2006, ch. 7). If decisions are acts of will, intentions may be better described as states of will. Although also describable as states of *mind*, or mental states, the latter description omits a crucial dimension of intention. To use one relatively familiar technical term: they are *conative* states. In the present terms, they are states of a person's will.

[60] In certain cases it may look as if this is not so. I have in mind examples of the kind suggested by such interchanges as "Okay, we'll go on until you say you've had enough" and "Fine." Such examples will not be a matter of unilateral rescission of the agreement but rather of an agreement involving a certain kind of proviso. In some contexts background understandings may be such that there is no need to make such a proviso explicit. I take it, however, that the existence of such a proviso cannot be simply assumed. For related discussion see Gilbert (2006, ch. 7).

What relation to the pertinent plan do the people in question take up when, as we say, they make the decision or agreement in question?

In the case of a personal decision we might say that the decision-maker *endorses* the plan. As he understands, he thereby commits himself to act accordingly. In the agreement case, in turn, we might say that the parties *jointly* endorse the plan. What, however, does *joint endorsement* amount to? And in what way, if any, does such endorsement commit each of the parties to act accordingly?

To answer these questions in a particular way is, in effect, to offer the major part of an account of agreements. I proceed now roughly to sketch an answer. I later argue for it in the context of the puzzles about both claim-rights and joint intention noted earlier.

Joint Endorsement of a Plan

It is useful first to recall those dialogues or nonverbal exchanges through which agreements, in particular, are made. How are these to be construed?

A natural proposal in light of the idea that the parties will eventually *jointly endorse* the plan in question—call it plan P—is as follows: Each of the parties expresses to the others his personal *readiness* jointly to endorse P with the others. Once these expressions have been made, in conditions of common knowledge, P will have been jointly endorsed.[61]

This proposal may be fine as far as it goes, but it does not answer the question of what it is for the parties *jointly to endorse* plan P. It also leaves open the question of how, if at all, each party is committed to act as a result of the joint endorsement of P.

I suggest that we amplify the proposal as follows. In the precursor dialogue, each party expresses to the others his readiness to be committed with them all, *as one*, to endorse plan P as a body—where it is understood that once these expressions are common knowledge between the parties, they *are* committed, as one, to endorse plan P as a body. It is at this point that the parties jointly endorse plan P, and each party is committed, through the commitment of them all, to act accordingly.

---

[61] "Common knowledge" been variously defined since Lewis (1969). Many such definitions can be questioned for various reasons. For my own proposal in the context of a discussion of acting together, see Gilbert (1989, ch. 4). For present purposes it may suffice to say that the making of these expressions has been "out in the open" as far as the parties are concerned.

I shall refer henceforth to the commitment of them all in such cases as a *joint commitment*. In discussing this going forward, I focus on the *basic* case.[62]

Evidently, there is both a *process* of joint commitment—as I understand it—and a *state* or *condition* of joint commitment, the latter engendered by the former. The process of joint commitment is the expression of each of the would-be parties' readiness to be committed as one with the rest.[63] The state of joint commitment is a normative condition with a particular history.

The conditions under which the parties to a joint commitment cease to be jointly committed correspond to the conditions under which they come to be so committed: they must concur, in a broad sense, in rescinding their joint commitment.

To say that the parties are *jointly committed* is not to say that each now has a particular *personal* commitment, as these were characterized earlier. Given a joint commitment, each of the relevant persons *is* committed, but not by virtue of having unilaterally committed himself. Nor can any one of the committed persons unilaterally rid himself of his commitment.[64] The *individual* commitments in question, then, come into and go out of existence simultaneously and interdependently: one cannot come into existence or go out of existence without the rest doing so.

What is it to be jointly committed to endorse *as a body* a certain plan? This means, roughly, that the parties are jointly committed to emulate, by virtue of the actions and utterances of each, a single endorser of that plan. In other terms, each is to talk and act as would the representatives of single endorser of that plan.[65]

I take it that the *personal* plans of the parties, as such, are not the concern of such a commitment. It relates to how the parties are personally to *act*, rather than to how they are personally to plan. Of course, should one or another party form contrary personal plans *and carry them out*, they will then fail to act as appropriate from the point of view of the joint commitment.

Further, to act in accordance with a joint commitment of the kind in question, the parties will most likely need to form various related personal plans and carry them out. Thus, if two people are jointly committed to playing

---

[62] *Nonbasic* joint commitments involve a person or body authorized by the parties to impose new joint commitments upon them all. Basic cases involve no such authorization. For more on this distinction see Gilbert (2006, ch. 7).

[63] One might say that the parties express their readiness to "pool" or "unify" their wills in the relevant respect. See Gilbert (1989, p. 18).

[64] I say more on this point shortly.

[65] This accords with what I take to be the "general form" of all joint commitments. See Gilbert (2000b).

tennis together next weekend and one has no racquet, he would be well advised to make a personal plan to acquire one in time for the projected game. In addition, any related personal plans of the parties had better mesh well together. In short, those who are party to such a joint commitment are thereby committed to forming appropriate, meshing personal subplans with respect to the jointly endorsed plan.[66]

The Importance of Joint Commitment

There is reason to believe that to give adequate accounts of many central social phenomena including agreements we need to invoke the concept of joint commitment.[67] This raises the questions: What special jobs are joint commitments tailored to take on, or what jobs otherwise achievable do they do better than the alternatives? Why might human beings need to go beyond personal commitments to joint ones?

One reason is the *relative stability* of the commitment of each party to a joint commitment. One who makes a personal decision can unilaterally rescind that decision and so rid himself of the personal commitment involved. Similarly, those with a joint commitment can *together* rid themselves of that commitment. In a basic case, however, *no single party* to a given joint commitment can unilaterally rescind that commitment and so cease to be committed himself.

This increased stability is of great practical importance. In the case of both types of commitment of the will—personal and joint—the committed person has sufficient reason to act in certain ways, sufficient reason that may not have been present before the commitment was made. At a minimum, then, in an otherwise normatively neutral context a joint commitment is an effective way of *pinning someone else down*.

Of course, one is at the same time more effectively pinned down oneself. That is one reason for people to be somewhat shy of joint commitment. If, however, I am sure that I want something that can only be achieved by your phi-ing and my psi-ing, I shouldn't mind about being myself committed to

---

[66] I take the terms "meshing" and "subplans" from Michael Bratman's discussions in, for example, Bratman (1993). For him, these are personal subplans of the *personal* plans he puts at the center of his account of "shared intention."

[67] See Gilbert (1989) and, for more emphasis on joint commitment as such, the pertinent articles in Gilbert (1996, 2000a, 2013b) and in this volume.

psi-ing without the option of unilateral rescission, as long as you are so committed to phi-ing.

In the next section I argue that any joint commitment gives the parties claim-rights against one another, claim-rights to actions that conform to the joint commitment. If this is so, then each party to a joint commitment is in a position authoritatively to intervene if one of them threatens not so to conform. This is a further reason to prefer a joint commitment to a corresponding pair of personal commitments in cases where one wants something that can only be achieved by virtue of the actions of each of the parties. For a personal commitment seems not to carry with it anyone else's standing to demand performance of the committed person.[68]

Agreements: The Joint Decision Account

Having developed an account of the joint endorsement of a plan, I now make two proposals about *agreements*. First, for two or more people to *enter* an agreement is for them openly to express, in conditions of common knowledge, their readiness to be jointly committed to endorse as a body a certain plan *by means of a verbal or nonverbal exchange more or less akin to the simple two-part verbal exchanges showcased earlier*. In other words, they make the relevant expressions *in a particular, explicit manner*. Second, *to have made* an agreement with another person is to be jointly committed with them to endorse as a body the plan in question and to be jointly so committed by virtue of an exchange of the appropriate sort.

I will label the account of agreements just sketched the *joint decision* account. I should emphasize that a joint decision as conceived of here is *not* a matter of two or more personal decisions that fit together in relevant ways. The label is intended to indicate the analogies pointed out between the agreement of two or more parties and a single personal decision. In particular, both involve the endorsement—joint, in the case of agreement—of a given plan of action.

I take it to be possible for people to express their readiness jointly to endorse a particular plan without having a verbal or nonverbal exchange of

---

[68] Suppose that something like this is true: if there is common knowledge between two people of the personal commitment of one of them, particularly where this has deliberately been communicated to the other, the person with the commitment is morally required to perform, all else being equal. Would others then have corresponding claim-rights against the committed person to demand that he conform to his commitment, and so on? I think not. At the least, the opposite assumption is highly debatable. See Gilbert (2004). For some further related discussion, see the text below.

the kind called for by an agreement. Then, given common knowledge of these expressions, they will jointly have endorsed a plan without having made an agreement. I return to this point later.

The joint decision account of agreements respects salient analogies between the creation and rescission of personal decisions and interpersonal agreements and the nature of such decisions and agreements. It also has other virtues.

One of these virtues is its potential for avoiding the problems noted for the standard approaches to the rights of agreement discussed earlier.[69] As was then observed, agreements have a close relationship to rights from an intuitive standpoint. Indeed, it follows from what was said earlier that *an adequate account of agreements will be an account of a phenomenon such that from its existence and that alone one can infer that the parties have claim-rights against each other, rights to the conformity of the party in question to the agreement.* These rights are present irrespective of the *content* or contingent *consequences* of the agreement.

The moral approach to the rights of agreement came up against this criterion of adequacy. My discussion of that approach focused on the intuitive judgment that even the parties to an agreement to do something evil have claim-rights of some kind to one another's conformity. Those who take the moral approach are not likely to allow that even when conformity to an agreement re quires one to do something evil, the other person has a *moral* claim-right to one's doing it. Since this is the only kind of claim-right that they contemplate in relation to this issue, they are not in a position to account for the intuitive judgment noted.

In contrast, those who accept the joint decision account of agreements may be in a position to allow that in the case of an agreement to do something evil the parties have claim-rights to conformity—although these will not be moral claim-rights of the sort contemplated by the moral approach. It will then represent an advance on the moral approach from the point of view of our intuitive judgments on the relationship of agreements to claim-rights.

Whether the joint decision account is in this position depends, of course, on whether those who have agreed, on that account, thereby have ensuing claim-rights against each other to conformity, claim-rights that exist irrespective of the moral character of the conforming actions. This seems to come down to the question whether those who are party to a *joint commitment* thereby have claim-rights against each other, and so on. This is discussed in the next section—with a positive conclusion. For now, suffice it to say that

---

[69] Neither of these approaches, it may be recalled, rested on a carefully articulated, plausible account of what an agreement is.

there is no obvious barrier in principle to the *formation* of a joint commitment conformity to which would require an evil action.

With respect to the institutional approach, the problem was that, intuitively, the obligations most closely associated with an agreement are somehow "willed into being"—in a way that is not dependent on the rules of an established institution. Assuming, once again, that there is an appropriate connection between the making of a joint commitment and claim-rights and their correlative obligations, the joint decision account of agreements appears well placed to make sense of the intuitive judgment in question. In this case, of course, two or more wills are involved.

I do not mean to imply that according to the joint decision account anyone needs to have had an intention precisely to *obligate* himself or the other. Rather, the obligations of agreement and their correlative rights will come into being given only that each of the parties has expressed to the other his readiness *that they be jointly committed* in a particular way, in conditions of common knowledge.

In sum, the discussion in this paper so far suggests that the joint decision account of agreements has much to be said in its favor. It respects salient analogies between personal decisions and interpersonal agreements, and it is in a position to avoid pressing problems that confront the moral and institutional approaches to the rights of agreement.

4. Returning to the Puzzles

I now return to the puzzles introduced earlier: four relating to claim-rights and one to joint intention. It appeared that a relatively fine-grained account of the nature of agreements should help to solve all of these puzzles. As I now argue, the joint decision account of agreements does offer such help.

Claim-Rights Revisited

The Standing-to-Demand Puzzle
Can one specify a basis for the standing to demand an action of another, without explicit reference to one's accrual of a claim-right or the other's directed obligation or owing?[70]

---

[70] There is a longer discussion of the points made in this section in Gilbert (2018).

Evidently, a positive answer will be forthcoming if one's being party to a *joint commitment* suffices to give one the standing to demand of the other party or parties that they conform to the commitment. For one can make this point without any explicit reference to claim-rights and so on. Indeed, the relevant notion of a joint commitment was introduced without any such references.

That being party to a joint commitment is sufficient to give one the standing to demand an action is already suggested by the plausibility of the joint decision account of agreements. Intuitively, people accrue claim-rights by making agreements. The joint decision account of agreements is plausible on several grounds that do not refer to its accounting for the claim-rights of agreement. Given its plausibility on these grounds, there is reason to think that we come by claim-rights by establishing joint commitments. Although an agreement only comes into existence when a joint commitment is entered into in a particular way, the joint commitment that is formed lies at the core of the agreement. It is therefore the obvious candidate ground of the standing to demand compliance.

Intuitively, a joint commitment does indeed suffice to give the parties the standing to demand of one another conformity to the commitment, however it is formed. Consider a related example. David and Phyllis are—as they understand—jointly committed to endorse as a body the plan that they go hiking together at four this afternoon. Perhaps this was by virtue of an explicit process sufficient to make it the case that they made an agreement to that effect, perhaps not. Now suppose that David sees Phyllis getting ready to play tennis at a time that would not allow her to go hiking with him as planned. He goes up to her and says in a demanding tone, "Phyllis, you can't start playing tennis now!"

It seems that if she remembers their joint commitment, she is unlikely to question his standing to demand that she not start playing tennis now by saying something like, "Who are you to tell me that?" or "What puts you in a position to tell me what to do?" If she does say something like that, David can allude to their joint commitment in various ways. For instance, he could say: "You are violating *our* commitment!"

If pressed, he could in principle expand on this somewhat as follows: "*I'm the one you joined with in normatively constraining the two of us as I've just indicated!* I am not in a position to tell you to do anything I happen to want you to do, but I *am* in a position to demand that you act according to our commitment!" Intuitively, that is a sufficient answer to the question.

Although more could be said along these lines, for present purposes I leave things there, taking it that a joint commitment gives the parties the standing to demand of each other conformity to it. Thus the standing-to-demand puzzle receives an appropriate answer: to accrue the standing to demand an action it suffices to make a joint commitment with one or more other parties. One then has the standing to demand, of the other parties, action that conforms to the commitment.

This explanation of the standing to demand does not explicitly refer to the possession of a claim-right, to directed obligation, or to owing. That granted, given the equivalences listed earlier the following points must also be granted: the parties to a joint commitment are obligated to each other to conform, owe each other conforming action, and have claim-rights against each other to such action—in their capacity as parties to the joint commitment.

A Follow-Up Question

Is participation in a joint commitment the only thing that gives one the standing to demand an action of another? If it were, that would be of the greatest interest. There is no space to go into this question in any depth here.[71] One aspect of it may usefully be noted, however: its relation to some of the existing accounts of what it is to have a moral "claim-right."[72]

Suppose you are morally required to phi *because your phi-ing respects significant interests of mine* or *because it appropriately responds to my value as a human being* or some similar aspect of myself. There are philosophers who would say that in that case I have a moral claim-right to your phi-ing.[73] Indeed, to say something like this is quite standard. It seems not to be the case, however, that *in this situation and simply on account of its obtaining* I have the standing to demand of you that you phi. I may well be both morally and prudentially justified in trying to get you to phi if you are threatening not to. That, however, is another matter.

To illustrate the point, suppose you are about to hit me because you do not like something I said. Suppose I say, "Stop that!" in a demanding tone, and you ask, "What gives you the standing to demand that I stop?" The answer "You are morally required to stop because doing so respects significant interests of mine!" seems not to be an adequate answer. Nor does "You are morally required to stop because that will appropriately respond to my value as a human being!" You could quite intelligibly reply in either case: "That is true

---

[71] Gilbert (2018) pursues it in some detail. See also Gilbert (2004).
[72] I use scare quotes here not for any reason of disparagement but to signal at the outset that claim-rights of the type with which I have been concerned in this paper are not necessarily at issue.
[73] Compare, for example, Raz (1984), who emphasizes interests, and Kamm (2006), who does not.

but I don't see how it gives you the standing to demand that I don't hit you. Perhaps *something* gives you that standing—but not *those* things."

Consider now another idea about moral claim-rights that has been mooted: X has a moral claim-right against Y if Y is subject to a moral requirement of the form: you must phi unless X says you need not.[74] Intuitively, the fact that Y is subject to a requirement of this form does not mean that X has the standing to demand of Y that Y phi.[75]

Regarding some of the situations to which rights theorists have drawn attention, then, the idea that joint commitment is not just *a* but *the* source of the standing to demand has not been disconfirmed.

Isn't it the case, someone might object, that *if I see you doing something morally wrong*, then, whoever I am, I have the standing to demand that you stop? In other words, don't we all have the standing to demand of each of us that we conform to all *moral requirements*, notwithstanding such relations to our interests, our value, or our wills, as were considered above?[76] Perhaps so, but the philosophical problem is showing a *ground* of this standing—what precisely is it that links the situation described and the standing to demand that the wrongdoer cease his wrongdoing? Insofar as this remains obscure, doubt is cast on the alleged standing.

Possibly it can be argued that there is one or more *joint commitment* in the background such that the judgments about standing that are in question are warranted. If no such argument is available, then these cases may remain problematic from a philosophical point of view, however deeply one is convinced that there is a standing to demand here. If such an argument *is* available, then, of course, the hypothesis that joint commitment is the sole source of the standing to demand has not been refuted.

The Demanding-as-Mine Puzzle

The second puzzle about claim-rights relates to a suggested development of the idea of demanding: One who demands some action demands it *as his*. The puzzle is: How can an action that is one person's to *perform* be in any sense another's? In particular, what sense of "mine"—if any—could plausibly be argued to be at issue in the case of *demanding as mine*? As in the case of the standing-to-demand puzzle, a helpful answer, if there is one, will not

---

[74] This idea approximates the position on the nature of claim-rights of Hart (1955) and is relevant to the discussion in Scanlon (1998), on which see Gilbert (2004).

[75] For more on this case see Gilbert (2004).

[76] Compare Darwall (2006). Darwall alludes to many others who are inclined to endorse this position, including J. S. Mill.

allude to my possession of a claim-right, the other person's directed obligation, or owing.

We now have the basis for such an answer. If the idea that my *demanding* an
action is, more fully, the idea of my demanding an action as in some sense
mine, then that sense is *exemplified* by the relation of one party to a joint commitment to the conforming actions of the other parties, at least in his capacity
as party to the joint commitment. That is because, intuitively, he has the standing, in that capacity at least, to demand conformity of the other parties.

I will not attempt here to try to say in other terms what sense of "my action"
is here at issue. That said, it is plausible to suppose that any such sense will
relate to the following specific aspect of joint commitment: In co-creating
their joint commitment by virtue of their several expressions of readiness the
parties have *co-created a constraint on each such that a given party will not act
as he ought to, all else being equal, should he fail to respect it*. In other terms: all
equal, each party *will* so act if he acts appropriately in the circumstances.[77]

On this conception of the matter, each party to a joint commitment can
think of conforming actions as *mine, insofar as I am one of us*. In other terms,
they are *his qua co-creator of the joint commitment*. He can, then, also think
of the commitment as *ours*.

If joint commitment is the only basis for the standing to demand, and
demanding an action with standing is in some sense demanding that action as
mine, then the sense of "mine" in question will always be the one associated
with joint commitment. In the alternative situation, the sense of "mine" in
question will somehow subsume the sense associated with joint commitment.

The Third Way Puzzle

I come now to the third puzzle about claim-rights. How are the claim-rights
associated with agreements to be accounted for? In particular: Is there a
plausible alternative to the standard moral and institutional approaches that
are both problematic? A positive solution to this puzzle can now be given.

I argued earlier that the joint decision account of agreements—whose core
is a joint commitment—is plausible independently of considerations relating
to the claim-rights of agreement, respecting as it does significant analogies
between personal decisions and interpersonal agreements. I also argued that
it had the potential to avoid the problems noted for the moral and institutional approaches. I have now argued that it does avoid those problems.
The joint decision account of agreements thus appears to offer a plausible

---

[77] I develop this point further in Gilbert (2018).

alternative to the moral and institutional approaches to the claim-rights of agreement.

With respect to the case of agreements to do evil, the following should perhaps be emphasized. As long as the parties have indeed jointly committed themselves in the relevant way—to endorse a decision to perform some evil act together, say—they have claim-rights against each other to conforming action in the way of the parties to any joint commitment. They have these rights irrespective of the content of the joint commitment or the likely consequences of its fulfillment. This of course is *not* to say that *all things considered* each ought to give the other what is owed him. It is completely appropriate to consider the content of an agreement to judge what ought to be done all things considered. Once it is considered in this case the proper judgment is presumably that one should *not* do what one agreed to do. If one acts accordingly, of course, one will continue to be answerable to the other parties to the joint commitment for doing so.[78]

Hume's Puzzle

Hume's discussion of promissory obligation provoked the question: How can the claim-rights of agreement be willed into being, as is intuitively the case? We have already seen that this is solved by the joint decision account provided that a joint commitment is indeed a source of claim-rights. It remained only to argue that they are such a source. This has now been done.

A General Note on Claim-Rights

It is generally assumed that all claim-rights fall into one of two distinct classes: they are either moral rights or legal or other institutional rights. This now seems to be incorrect. The following, at least, should be noted.

The claim-rights associated with a given joint commitment are not stipulations within an institution, whether legal or otherwise. They are a function of the joint commitment itself. Whether some background institutions may need to be in place before a joint commitment can be made is not to the present point.

Are the claim-rights of joint commitment moral rights? That depends on the breadth of the notion of morality with which one is operating. At this point, suffice it to say that—as far as I can see—the argument that I have given for the claim-rights of joint commitment is a matter only of the authorship of

---

[78] The case of coerced agreements is similar. Here not the content or the consequences but the circumstances in which the agreement was made is at issue. Precisely what the all things considered judgment is when coercive circumstances are at issue may depend on the case. For more extended discussion of both immoral and coerced promises and agreements, see Gilbert (2006, ch. 10). See also Gilbert (1993b).

the commitment and its provision of those subject to it with sufficient reason to act accordingly. That would make them moral according to a broad residual notion of the moral such that a moral right is any right that is not a legal or other institutional right. Moral philosophers, however, tend to operate with a substantive, non-residual notion. Thinking along the lines in question—which vary to some extent from person to person—this does not look like a specifically moral argument to me.[79] The fact that—as it seems—the claim-rights most closely associated with joint commitment can in principle be rights to the doing of evil things further suggests that there is nothing inherently moral about them—in a non-residual sense of "moral."

Thus it makes sense to say that the claim-rights most closely associated with joint commitments are neither moral nor institutional claim-rights. More generally, *along with any legal and moral claim-rights there are claim-rights of at least one other sort—claim-rights of joint commitment*. As indicated in my discussion above of the standing to demand, it may be possible to go further and argue that the claim-rights of joint commitment are the only ones. Recall in this connection that I am talking about claim-rights on a particular understanding of what those are.[80]

Joint Intention Revisited

I now turn to the puzzle about joint intention. What can a joint intention be, if it is not constituted by a set of personal intentions of the participants? It seems that it is not so constituted, if only because an agreement to meet for dinner tonight, say, issues immediately in a joint intention to meet for dinner tonight; yet the agreement may be made by those who do not intend to carry it out—and once it is made corresponding personal intentions may not ensue. This may or may not be a common case, but it is a logically possible one. Personal intentions, then, cannot be necessary to the constitution of a joint intention.

In this connection consider first the joint decision account of agreements. It seems that I can indeed be *ready for a joint commitment* with you to endorse as a body the plan that we dine together tomorrow, although I have personally

[79] The "residual" account that I have in mind is this: a moral right is any right that is not a legal or other institutional right. Joint commitment rights are moral rights on this account. I have no concerns about that. I think, however, that philosophers tend to think of moral rights in a more substantive way—and more than one such way, one might add.
[80] Gilbert (2018) pursues the issue. See also "Giving Claim-Rights Their Due" (Gilbert 2012) [chapter 13, this volume] and, for a number of related points, Gilbert (2004).

decided not to dine with you tomorrow or have no personal intentions either way. You may be in the same position. Once we have mutually expressed our readiness to be jointly committed in the relevant way, in conditions of common knowledge we will, nonetheless, be so jointly committed. Although personal intentions that accord with the joint commitment may arise when or after it does, they need not do so. The joint decision account of agreements, then, accords with the idea that agreements need not carry with them personal intentions to act in conformity with the agreement.

That is not to deny that agreements on this account offer a stout resistance to the formation and maintenance of contrary intentions. Our joint commitment imposes a normative constraint upon my actions. If my personal decision is at odds with it, I am faced with a conflict of directions, so to speak. If I am wondering what to do, the deck is surely stacked in favor of my rescinding my decision, all else being equal.

For one thing, I cannot unilaterally rescind the joint commitment, whereas I am in a position to rescind my own decision—to change my mind. There is therefore at least one reason for doing so—to resolve the conflict.

For another, I owe you my conformity to the joint commitment. Perhaps I also owe myself conformity to my decision. Even if so, I am in a position to waive my right in that respect. I cannot waive *your* right to my conformity to our commitment!

Given your right, you are in a position to demand that I conform to our agreement should I threaten not to. Similarly, should I not rescind my decision but rather go ahead and act accordingly you will have the standing to rebuke me and make related demands, such as a demand for some kind of substitute action or compensation. Generally speaking, you will be in a position to intervene in my life in an authoritative manner. In short, there will be interpersonal consequences that I may well prefer to avoid.

What, however, is a *joint intention*? Although very commonly a joint intention results from the making of an agreement, this is not true of all such intentions. Thus consider the following case. Thelma and Bob are sitting idly in a rowing boat at the side of a lake, when they realize that their friend Frank is in danger of drowning in the middle of the lake. Each starts rowing in Frank's direction, making sure that his or her movements are well-coordinated with that of the other. Soon after, Bob calls out, "Shouldn't we go a bit faster?" Thelma does not reply but increases her rowing speed, as does Bob.

One would not very naturally say that any agreement was made in the course of this story, yet at some point it may well be true that Bob and Thelma have formed a joint intention to rescue Frank. Indeed, in normal circumstances I take it that they will at some point have formed such an intention, and might truly say to a third party, later, "We intended to rescue Frank."

I propose that a joint intention, as such, is *a joint commitment to endorse as a body a certain plan*. A joint commitment of this type results from the making of an agreement *when and only when there are the pertinent explicit preliminaries* to the formation of the joint commitment in question. Without such preliminaries, a joint intention arises when people otherwise indicate to one another, possibly through a long process, that they are personally ready to be jointly committed to endorse as a body some plan, in conditions of common knowledge.

In neither case is the joint intention as such constituted by personal intentions of any sort. Of course, given a joint intention in the sense indicated, the parties are likely to develop all manner of corresponding personal intentions and to reject any personal intention whose fulfillment would work against fulfillment of the joint commitment. For instance, they will develop personal intentions to act in ways that will most likely lead to fulfillment of the joint commitment given the expected actions of the other party or parties. Again, each may form a personal intention to help, encourage, or appropriately direct the other party or parties if they are struggling to act in such a way that the joint intention will result in appropriate action.[81]

My point has been that—puzzling and, indeed, surprising as this may initially seem—it is logically possible for there to be a joint intention in the absence of any corresponding personal intentions—any personal intentions, to use a phrase of Michael Bratman's, *in favor of* the joint intention. This puzzle must be solved in a satisfactory manner by an adequate account of joint intention. This speaks in favor of the proposed joint commitment account of joint intention. This account may need some fine-tuning. As long as a joint commitment remains at its core, the spirit of the proposal will have been maintained.

Joint Intention and Claim-Rights

I now briefly discuss one further consideration I take to speak in favor of a joint commitment account of joint intention, not meaning to say that these two are the only such considerations.[82] This, however, links closely to the foregoing discussion.

---

[81] Compare the discussion of acting together in Gilbert (1989, ch. 4).

[82] For further argumentation in favor of a joint commitment account of shared intention, see, for example, Gilbert (2000b; 2009). These include reference to a concurrence condition (on rescinding

Suppose that, by hypothesis, Bob and Thelma jointly intend to rescue Frank and that they have recently increased their rowing pace at Bob's suggestion. Now suppose that without saying why, Thelma suddenly begins to row very slowly. Bob may be surprised—Thelma is a very strong rower capable of rowing for miles without slacking off. Bob may also be upset, worried, and so on. In addition, and most important for present purposes, he may sense that he has been offended against, and that he has both the standing to rebuke Thelma for going so slowly and the standing to demand that she hurry up, if she can, insofar as hurrying up is more appropriate to their shared intention. Thus he understands that he has a claim-right to her acting in the spirit of that intention. This seems to be something that is so *just by virtue of the fact that the two have the joint intention in question.* Thus Bob may call out in a demanding way something like this: "Get a move on! *We won't get to Frank in time at this pace!*"

Claim-rights are, of their nature, "waivable" in at least the following sense: One with such a right may decide not to enforce it by means of demands, rebukes, and the like and may make it clear to the right's addressee that he has made this decision. It is therefore no objection to the contention that joint intentions ground claim-rights of the parties to observe that these rights may sometimes be waived, in this sense, either explicitly or implicitly.

The envisaged joint commitment account of joint intention easily accommodates these observations. So would any account with joint commitment at its core.

An aspect of the foregoing discussion that may seem surprising at first is this. Assuming that claim-rights are inherent in joint intention—that there cannot be a joint intention without the parties having associated claim-rights—then one who inquires into the nature of joint intention must be prepared carefully to consider the nature and sources of such rights. That is quite a heavy load for a theorist of joint intention. On the more positive side, it can be noted that *one who investigates joint intention puts himself in a position to throw light on the nature and sources of claim-rights in addition to joint intention.*

Summary and Concluding Remarks

In this paper I introduced several puzzles: four concerning claim-rights and one about joint intention. Intuitive judgments about claim-rights and joint

---

the shared intention) and the several roles that joint intention on a joint commitment account can play, roles of a type Michael Bratman has stressed in Bratman (1993) and other writings.

aTHE NATURE OF AGREEMENTS   65

intention led to these puzzles. I offered solutions to the puzzles by reference to an account of agreements. One would expect that solutions based on an account of agreements should be available, since those who make agreements are generally acknowledged thereby to accrue claim-rights against each other, and one can bring a joint intention into being simply by making an agreement.[83]

The joint decision account of agreements offers solutions to the puzzles. It does this by virtue of its incorporation of a joint commitment.

As to claim-rights: intuitively, the parties to a joint commitment are in a position to demand conforming actions of the other parties, and they relate to those actions in such a way that speaking of those actions as in a sense theirs, qua parties to the joint commitment, rings true. Finally, the account shows that there is an alternative to the standard moral and institutional approaches to the claim-rights most closely associated with agreements.

As to joint intention, the joint decision account of agreements suggests the following general account: A joint intention is, in effect, a joint commitment to endorse as a body a certain plan. Given the joint decision account of agreements, joint intentions on this account immediately result from the making of an agreement and do not entail the existence of appropriate personal intentions. They do not *require* prior agreements. Further, the parties have the pertinent—waivable—claim-rights.

Three further aspects of the discussion in this essay may be mentioned before leaving these topics here.

First, I have argued that to understand joint intention we need to understand claim-rights and their source or sources. This is not to deny that the existence of a joint intention is to a significant extent a matter of the *psychological states* of the parties. On my account each must be *ready* to contribute to the creation of a particular joint commitment and that is a matter of his psychological state, as is (in part) his intentional expression of this readiness and the existence of common knowledge between the parties that each has expressed this readiness.[84]

Nonetheless, as the parties understand, the kind of interaction with mutual expressions of psychological states envisaged here inevitably results in a *normative situation* of great importance for the practical reasoning of the

[83] Do *all* agreements bring joint intentions into being? I think this is plausible. My focal example was an agreement to do something together (in particular to dine together) and a corresponding joint intention to do something together. Here is another type of example: Nina and Ted agree that he will do the dishes and she will take Fido for a walk. I think it natural for either of the two now to report, "Our plan is for Nina to take Fido for a walk and for Ted to do the dishes," or for one of them to say, "We have a plan!"

[84] This situation can exist in a specific form among those who do not know each other personally; see Gilbert (2006, ch. 7).

parties—their *being jointly committed*, with the associated claim-rights and directed obligations.

Second, in much previous work I have used the technical phrase "plural subject" to refer to the parties to a given joint commitment. It is useful to have such a general label. This, however, has attracted some concern, with people wondering if I mean to claim that when people make a joint commitment there comes into being, in addition to the conscious states of each of the individual human beings concerned, another set of conscious states situated somewhere "over and above" those of these individuals.

This is one reason I have not used the phrase in discussion here. That has not, I think, prevented me from making any pertinent points. However, the label was intended to indicate something for which I have argued, although not the point about a "superindividual" consciousness noted above.

The point I intended to make was roughly this: When people use what one might refer to as the collective "we"—when they use *the first person plural pronoun* as the subject term in such sentences as "We intend to go shopping" and do not mean this to be elliptical for "Each of us intends to go shopping," they mean to refer to a plural subject *in my sense*. This can be argued in contexts other than that of joint intention.[85]

Third, whether or not either an *agreement* or a *joint intention* as initially characterized here is a matter of joint commitment, people who wish effectively to use their respective forces in the service of an aim that can be best reached by those forces in conjunction would do to make a joint commitment *to endorse as a body the plan of achieving that aim*—whatever we call such a joint commitment.

References

Alonso, Facundo. (2009). "Shared Intention, Reliance, and Interpersonal Obligations." *Ethics* 119: 444–75.

Barnett, Randy E. (1998). *The Structure of Liberty*. Oxford: Clarendon.

Bratman, Michael. (1993). "Shared Intention." *Ethics* 104: 97–113.

Bratman, Michael. (1999a). *Faces of Intention*. Cambridge, UK: Cambridge University Press.

Bratman, Michael. (1999b). "Shared Intention and Mutual Obligation," in *Faces of Intention*, by Michael Bratman. Cambridge, UK: Cambridge University Press.

[85] See Gilbert (1989, chs. 4, 7, in particular).

Bratman, Michael. (2009). "Modest Sociality and the Distinctiveness of Intention." *Philosophical Studies* 144: 149–65.

Darwall, Stephen. (2006). *The Second-Person Standpoint*. Cambridge, MA: Harvard University Press.

Feinberg, Joel. (1970). "The Nature and Value of Rights." *Journal of Value Inquiry* 4: 243–60.

Fuller, Lon. (1978). "Forms and Limits of Adjudication." *Harvard Law Review* 92: 353–409.

Gilbert, Margaret. (1989). *On Social Facts*. London: Routledge and Kegan Paul; (1992) Princeton, NJ: Princeton University Press.

Gilbert, Margaret. (1993a). "Is an Agreement an Exchange of Promises?" *Journal of Philosophy* 90: 627–49.

Gilbert, Margaret. (1993b). "Agreement, Coercion, and Obligation." *Ethics* 103: 679–706.

Gilbert, Margaret. (1996). *Living Together: Rationality, Sociality, and Obligation*. Lanham, MD: Rowman and Littlefield.

Gilbert, Margaret. (2000a). *Sociality and Responsibility: New Essays in Plural Subject Theory*. Lanham, MD: Rowman and Littlefield.

Gilbert, Margaret. (2000b). "What Is It for Us to Intend?," in *Sociality and Responsibility*, by Margaret Gilbert. Lanham, MD: Rowman and Littlefield.

Gilbert, Margaret. (2004). "Scanlon on Promissory Obligation: The Problem of Promisees' Rights." *Journal of Philosophy* 101: 83–109.

Gilbert, Margaret. (2006). *A Theory of Political Obligation: Membership, Commitment, and the Bonds of Society*. Oxford: Clarendon.

Gilbert, Margaret. (2007). "Searle and Collective Intentions," in *Intentional Acts and Institutional Facts: Essays on John Searle's Social Ontology*, edited by Savas L. Tsohatzidis. Dordrecht: Springer.

Gilbert, Margaret. (2009). "Shared Intention and Personal Intentions." *Philosophical Studies* 44: 167–87.

Gilbert, Margaret. (2011a). "Rights without Laws." Working paper, University of California, Irvine.

Gilbert, Margaret. (2011b). "Three Dogmas about Promising," in *Promises and Agreements: Philosophical Essays*, edited by H. Scheinman. New York: Oxford University Press.

Gilbert, Margaret. (2012). "Giving Claim-Rights Their Due," in *Rights: Concepts and Contexts*, edited by Brian Bix and Horacio Spector. Farnham, UK: Ashgate. [Chapter 13, this volume.]

Gilbert, Margaret. (2013a). "Commitment," in *International Encyclopedia of Ethics*, edited by Hugh Lafollette. Malden, MA: Wiley-Blackwell.

Gilbert, Margaret. (2013b). *Joint Commitment: How We Make the Social World*. New York: Oxford University Press.

Gilbert, Margaret. (2018). *Rights and Demands*. Oxford: Oxford University Press.

Hart, H. L. A. (1955). "Are There Any Natural Rights?" *Philosophical Review* 64: 175–91.

Hohfeld, Wesley N. (1913). "Some Fundamental Legal Conceptions as Applied in Judicial Reasoning." *Yale Law Journal* 23: 16–59.

Hume, David. (1960). *A Treatise of Human Nature*, edited by L. A. Selby-Bigge. Oxford: Clarendon Press.

Kamm, Frances. (2002). "Owing, Justifying, and Rejecting." *Mind* 111: 323–54.

Kamm, Frances. (2006). *Intricate Ethics: Rights, Responsibilities, and Permissible Harm*. New York: Oxford University Press.

Kutz, Christopher. (2000). *Complicity: Ethics and Law for a Collective Age*. Cambridge, UK: Cambridge University Press.

Lewis, David K (1969). *Convention: A Philosophical Study*. Cambridge, MA: Harvard University Press.

Prichard, H. A. (1968). *Moral Obligation and Duty and Interest*. Oxford: Oxford University Press.

Raz, Joseph. (1984). "On the Nature of Rights." *Mind* 93: 194–214.

Robins, Michael. (1984). *Promising, Intending, and Moral Autonomy*. Cambridge, UK: Cambridge University Press.

Ross, W. D. (1930). *The Right and the Good*. Oxford: Clarendon.

Roth, Abraham. (2004). "Shared Agency and Contralateral Commitments." *Philosophical Review* 113: 359–410.

Scanlon, T. M. (1998). *What We Owe to Each Other*. Cambridge, MA: Belnap.

Searle, John. (1990). "Collective Intentions and Actions," in *Intentions in Communication*, edited by Philip R. Cohen, Jerry L. Morgan, and Martha E. Pollack. Cambridge, MA: MIT Press.

Sellars, Wilfrid. (1963). *Science, Perception, and Reality*. New York: Humanities.

Shockley, Kenneth. (2008). "On That Peculiar Practice of *Promising*," *Philosophical Studies* 140: 385–99.

Sreenivasan, Gopal. (2005). "A Hybrid Theory of Claim-Rights." *Oxford Journal of Legal Studies* 25: 257–74.

Thomson, Judith. (1990). *The Realm of Rights*. Cambridge, MA: Harvard University Press.

Vandershaaf, Peter, and Giacomo Sillari (2013). "Common Knowledge," in *The Stanford Encyclopedia of Philosophy*, edited by Edward N. Zalta, https://plato.stanford.edu/entries/common-knowledge.

PART II

OUR BELIEFS

2

Culture as Collective Construction

Introduction

The term "culture" in the title of this paper is intended to refer to a constellation of relatively permanent features of social groups, including organizations. Such features tend to provide numerically distinct groups with some degree of qualitative distinctness one from the other. Though that may be generally agreed among social theorists, there is controversy as to what the features in question amount to. Assuming that a group's culture includes its beliefs and values, its rules and conventions, what does it take for a group to have a particular belief, and so on?

There is more than one way of approaching these questions. In discussing two possibilities I focus on the case of group belief.

One possibility is to offer an explicitly stipulative account of what it is for a group to believe something. To say that the account is stipulative is not to say that it is arbitrary. It is to say, rather, that it does not purport to be the articulation of an existing idea. In particular, it does not purport to articulate the idea expressed by the relevant terms in vernacular speech.

How a given stipulative account is criticizable will depend in part on the type of justification offered for it. Perhaps the claim is simply that group beliefs, on the proposed account of them, are important phenomena, as indeed they may be.

A stipulative account of a group's belief may also be criticizable from the point of view of the intuitive aptness of the label adopted for the phenomenon in question, or for its tendency to deflect attention from a phenomenon more intuitively apt to be referred to as a group's belief.

Another approach is to attempt to articulate the idea expressed by the relevant terms in vernacular speech. Naturally, this approach allows that there may be ambiguities in everyday discourse, in which case the different *ideas* in question will need to be revealed.

One might wonder how helpful the second approach can be for scientific purposes. After all, as both Max Weber and Émile Durkheim emphasized, "everyday concepts" as one might call them, were not framed for such purposes

Life in Groups: How We Think, Feel, and Act Together. Margaret Gilbert, Oxford University Press. © Margaret Gilbert 2023. DOI: 10.1093/oso/9780192847157.003.0003

but rather for broadly speaking practical ones. The possibility remains that these concepts—in particular the central concepts at issue here—are themselves geared to pick out important phenomena, phenomena that might, indeed, escape one's attention were one to limit oneself to the first approach mentioned.

I have myself in a series of papers and books adopted the second approach to group beliefs and other elements of culture.[1] This paper focuses on the question of a group's belief and reviews some of my main conclusions about it.[2] It also briefly touches on the question of social convention.

Group Belief Statements

What I shall refer to here as "group belief statements" are exemplified by such sentences as: "The union believes that the strike should be continued," "In the opinion of the search committee, Jones is the best candidate," and "Our discussion group thought it was a great poem."

In what contexts are everyday group belief statements considered to be true, or false, by those who make them? One should not assume that the answer is obvious, or easily retrievable after a moment's thought.

In approaching it my method has been somewhat analogous to that of many linguists. Rather than operating in terms of interviews and questionnaires, I have largely drawn on my own "participant observations" of the contexts in which group belief statements are made, and of a variety of reactions that occur in such contexts.

Problems with the Summative Condition

The first hypothesis that occurs to many people is what I call the "simple summative account" of group belief. This maintains that—according to everyday understandings—a group believes something when and only when all or most of its members believe that thing. For instance, to say that the union believes the strike should be continued is to say that all or most members of the union believe this.[3]

---

[1] See, initially, Gilbert (1989).
[2] Previous sometimes quite extended discussions include the following articles and book chapters: Gilbert (1989: ch. 5, 2000, 2002, 2004a, 2004b, 2006a).
[3] See, e.g., Quinton (1975).

More complex variants of the simple summative account may also be proposed. All have at their core what I shall call the "summative condition," which comprises the whole of the simple summative account.[4]

It can be argued that all or most of a group's members believing that such-and-such is neither necessary nor sufficient for the group's believing that such-and-such. More complex accounts that are not exhausted by the summative condition could in principle avoid the sufficiency problem. Insofar as they purport to offer a set of conditions that are individually necessary as well as jointly sufficient, however, they will be criticizable, as is the simple summative account, for the non-necessity of the summative condition.

i. It Is Not Necessary

I turn first, then, to the question of necessity. Must all or most members of a group believe that such-and-such in order that the group believes that such-and-such?

Consider first two of the examples of group belief statements offered earlier: "The union believes that the strike should be continued" and "In the opinion of the search committee, Jones is the best candidate." Such statements are commonly made in light of the results of a voting procedure that has been previously agreed upon by the parties. The application of any such procedure is liable to result in an opinion of the group that runs contrary to the opinions of most of its individual members. For what ultimately determines the group belief is the votes of the members as opposed to their personal beliefs.

Thus suppose that in the union case it is understood that a two-thirds majority of votes in favor of continuing the strike is both necessary and sufficient to determine that the union is in favor of such continuance. It is possible that when there is a two-thirds majority of votes in favor of continuance those members who voted in its favor do not themselves believe that the union should continue the strike.

For one thing, many of these individuals may lack a personal opinion on the matter. They may then vote as they imagine others will vote; or they may make arbitrary choices of how to vote, mentally "tossing a coin." And so on.

---

[4] Several such complex accounts are discussed in Gilbert (1989: ch. 5). See also the following proposal from social psychology (which I assume is seen as stipulative): group beliefs are "convictions that group members (a) are aware that they share and (b) consider as defining their 'groupness'" (Bar-Tal 1990: 16). I take the implied condition that group members "share a given conviction" to be, in effect, the summative condition.

In addition, there are many reasons why someone might vote in a way contrary to his personal opinion, should he have one. For instance, he may believe that the rest will vote in favor of continuance. Not wishing to defend himself after the vote, or be the target of various negative emotions, he may vote as he believes others will vote, contrary to his own opinion.

The scenario just envisaged may or may not be a common one. The point is that it is possible—indeed, familiar motivations could lead to it. It follows that a group may believe something that is not believed by all or most of its members.

This case involves people who vote for a position that is not their own. Given a different—but common—voting procedure, however, one can easily describe a case in which everyone votes in accordance with his personal beliefs and the group then believes something that is not believed by all or most of its members.

Thus suppose that in the search committee case there are six committee members and it is agreed that the committee's opinion is to be determined by the majority of positive votes. The members are to vote on whether Jones is the best candidate. Three members find themselves sitting on the fence on the matter and vote "Abstain." A fourth thinks Jones is the worst candidate and votes "No." The two remaining members think Jones is the best candidate and vote "Yes." All vote according to their personal beliefs, then, but the resulting opinion of the group is not the view of the majority of the members: only two out of six believe that the job should be offered to Jones.

Evidently, voting procedures vary, and are to some extent arbitrary. What, then, of cases that do not involve a previously agreed upon voting procedure? It is plausible to suppose that the most basic cases of group belief are of this kind, and should be one's initial focus in coming to understand what a group's belief amounts to. It is also plausible to suppose that these most basic cases will not involve an authoritative person or body that has been charged with formulating opinions for the group. In what follows I focus on such basic cases.

Suppose that at a meeting of a "leaderless" poetry discussion group one member speaks admiringly of certain poem, and each of the others responds in a similar way. "Truly, it's great!" says one. "It's very accomplished," says another. Several others nod their heads in concurrence. And so on through each of those present. I take it that on some such basis someone might with confidence say, "The poetry discussion group thinks this is a good poem."

Why might one then be confident that the poetry discussion group thinks the poem is a good one? It may be proposed that it is because one can reasonably assume, in this context, that all of the members personally think the poem is a good one. There is reason to reject this suggestion, however.

First, it cannot be the whole story. As I argue in the next section, even if each member explicitly and sincerely avows his personal belief that the poem is a good one, this does not suffice to establish that the group believes this. So something more is needed to ground the latter claim. Further, there is a plausible alternative story that does not even entail that the members personally think well of the poem, though of course they may.

The alternative story is roughly this. It suffices for the group to think the poem a good one if, roughly, the individual members of the group have publicly expressed their personal readiness to see the belief that the poem is a good one established as that of the group. More must be said in clarification of the proposed sufficient condition, which, as stated, assumes an understanding of what it is for a belief to be the belief of a group. I say more in clarification of it shortly. For now, the main points to be made about it are these.

Those expressing their readiness to see a favorable view of the poem established as the view of the group do not thereby express their personal views regarding the quality of the poem. Nor, indeed, need they personally believe that the poem is a good one.

There are many reasons why, in practice, a given group member might be ready to see a particular opinion established as the view of the group, and to express this readiness, even though the opinion in question is not his own. He may have no opinion of his own, but guess that most people will be of the opinion in question, and not want to stand out from the crowd. He may wish to curry favor with a group member who has already expressed a particular opinion, and be willing therefore to suppress the contrary personal opinion he himself has formed. And so on.

ii. It Is Not Sufficient

Is the fact that all or most members of a certain group believe that such-and-such *sufficient* for the group's belief that such-and-such? There are several ways of arguing for a negative answer.

Here is one. In the discussion imagined earlier among the members of the poetry discussion group no one said anything about his or her personal views. Suppose, however, that we imagine a different discussion. One of the members, Jane, mentions a certain poem and says, "It's a wonderful poem—as I see it, anyway." Her "as I see it, anyway" suggests that she is not yet ready to have the wonderfulness of the poem established as the view of the group. She is ready only to have it established that she personally sees the poem as wonderful. Even if everyone does likewise, and the truth of their statements is not in doubt, it seems that the judgment that *the group* thinks the poem is wonderful has not yet been made true.[5]

Another line of argument is as follows. Each of the members of the poetry group may be familiar with a certain poem, and each may think it is excellent. Yet it has not yet been a topic of discussion among the members of the poetry group. No one has said anything to anyone else about it. It would then seem right to say that, as of now, the group has no opinion of this poem.

It seems, then, that it is not sufficient for a group to have a certain opinion that each of its members has that opinion. This conclusion accords with that of the classic sociological discussion of Durkheim in the *Rules of Sociological Method* where he discusses "the beliefs of a group taken collectively." He says there that the *generality* of a given belief—that the group members generally have the belief—is not what makes it *collective*. Rather, its being collective may account for its generality. One may be helped to see how collectivity could lead to generality by considering the following observation.

An Observation Concerning the Standing to Rebuke

If one is attempting to formulate an alternative to the simple summative account, the following observation should be born in mind. Once a group belief is established, the parties understand that any members who bluntly express the opposite belief in conversation with other members may appropriately be taken to task by other members. The same goes for the blunt expression of beliefs that logically imply the opposite of the group belief.

That the other members have the standing to rebuke the member in question appears to be a function of the group belief itself. An adequate account of group beliefs as these are ordinarily conceived of, then, should explain how a group belief is such as to give the members this standing.

Returning to Durkheim, one can see that if someone knows he is likely to be rebuked for bluntly expressing the belief that a certain poem is not a good one, for instance, he is less likely to be willing so to express that belief even if

---

[5] For further discussion of this kind of case see Gilbert (1989: 268–70).

he has it. His suppression of his tendency bluntly to express what he believes may lead his belief itself to be diminished or simply to disappear.

Rather than bluntly saying something that runs contrary to an established view of one's group, one may make use of such prefatory phrases as "In my personal opinion." I take it that the use of such a phrase would be enough to forestall the kind of rebuke just envisaged, which is a rebuke precisely for bluntly saying something contrary to the group's view, in circumstances where this is not appropriate.

Though such locutions are available, however, there is likely to be some cost attached to using them. One makes it clear that one's personal view is different from that of the group. Others may regard one with suspicion, thinking one more likely to go on bluntly to say things that run contrary to the group's view, and hence to be worthy of rebuke. One may therefore be almost as reluctant to say, "In my personal opinion it is not the case that such-and-such" as to say the sentence that results from omitting "In my personal opinion."

The Plural Subject Account of Group Belief

The foregoing discussion suggests certain criteria of adequacy for an account of group belief: (1) It should clarify the point that a group belief can be established, roughly, by virtue of public expressions of readiness on the part of the individual group members to let a particular belief be established as that of the group. In particular, it should not presuppose that one understands what it is for a belief to be the belief of a group. (2) It should explain how the very existence of a particular group belief gives group members the standing to rebuke each other for bluntly expressing a contrary view. (3) It should not entail that all or most group members believe what the group believes. (4) It should not entail that if all or most of them believe something then the group believes it too. At the same time, of course, (5) it should allow that the members may believe what the group believes: that is not ruled out.

I now give a rough statement of the account of group belief that I have developed and then briefly explain its key terms. As will emerge, this account fares well in light of the criteria of adequacy just stated:[6]

---

[6] I have formulated this account differently on different occasions. This is in part because essentially the same idea is expressible in different ways. Naturally the most acceptable version will be as clear and free of ambiguity as possible. I explain the way the main formulations I had used to date relate to one another in Gilbert (1996: 7–10; see also 1989: ch. 7). This account subsumes both (what I

A group G believes that p if and only if the members of G, as such, are jointly committed to believe as a body that p.

One can give a parallel account of a collective belief that does not presuppose a pre-existing group, to cover cases of a type I refer to later in the text.

The *phrase* "joint commitment" as I use it is a technical one. There is reason to believe, however, that the concept it expresses, as I understand it, is fundamental to our everyday conceptual scheme concerning social relations. In other words, it is not a technical *concept*.

The kind of commitment involved is what I have called "a commitment of the will." One species of such commitment is engendered by my decision to go to the beach tomorrow. In making this decision I commit myself to go to the beach tomorrow. A *personal commitment* of this kind is one that the person in question unilaterally creates—for himself—and that he is in a position unilaterally to rescind.

He is committed to do what he decided to do in the following sense: he now has *sufficient reason* to do it—unless and until he rescinds his decision. This does not mean that it is, in and of itself, a good thing to do, or that doing it will have good consequences. It means that as long as his decision stands, rationality in an intuitive sense of the term requires him to do it.[7] He is thus in a clear sense, and to a certain extent, "tied down" with respect to what it is appropriate for him to do in the future.

A joint commitment, as I understand it, is the commitment of two or more people. It is not a conjunction of a personal commitment of one party with personal commitments of the others. Rather, all, together, commit all. And they remain thus committed absent the concurrence of all on the alternative.

Any given party is of course physically capable of acting against a standing joint commitment, if he so desires. But then the commitment will be violated, as all of the parties will understand.[8]

In order together to commit them all, each of the two or more people involved must express his personal readiness to participate in the creation of this commitment, in conditions of common knowledge. I use "common

call) basic and non-basic or authority-involving cases. On that distinction see the Introduction, this volume.

[7] This is not rationality in the game-theorist's sense of "maximization of utility" but rather the rationality of reacting appropriately given those considerations that bear on the case.

[8] For discussion of the consequences of such violation see Gilbert (1996: 14–15). I there incline to the view that generally speaking violation by one or more parties renders a joint commitment voidable by the remaining parties, as opposed to immediately voiding it.

knowledge" in roughly the sense introduced by David Lewis.[9] To put it informally, these things are out in the open as far as the relevant people are concerned. Once each of the necessary expressions has been made in conditions of common knowledge, the parties are jointly committed in the relevant way.

Of course, there is sometimes some unclarity as to what a given person is expressing. There will be various ways of clarifying the situation in a given case. One obvious method is to ask that person to make his intentions explicit.

Having explained—to some extent—the nature of joint commitment in general, I now focus on the particular joint commitment invoked in my account of a group's belief.[10]

On that account, a group's belief that p involves a joint commitment of the members, as such, *to believe that p as a body*. What does this particular joint commitment require of the individual parties to it?

On the negative side, and importantly, it does not entail that each of them is personally to believe that p.

On the positive side, it requires them, in appropriate circumstances, *to speak and act as would the representatives of a single believer of the proposition that p*. This requirement will be fulfilled, to some extent at least, if in appropriate circumstances those concerned say that p with an appropriate degree of confidence, and generally behave in a way consistent with the belief that p.

I have elsewhere introduced the technical phrase "plural subject" as a label for those who are jointly committed to do something as a body, where believing that p counts as an instance of "doing something." I therefore call the account of a group's belief that I have sketched here "the plural subject account." If for some reason that label is found to be uncongenial, "the joint commitment account" would do just as well.

Social Groups as Plural Subjects

My discussion in this paper has focused on the beliefs of established groups such as unions, search committees, and discussion groups. All of these may be thought to have as their primary feature a certain aim or mission.

---

[9] See Lewis (1969). For further discussion along these lines see Gilbert (1989: 188–95) and elsewhere.
[10] I have discussed joint commitment more extensively in a variety of places including Gilbert (1996: 7–15, 2003, 2006b: ch. 7).

I have elsewhere argued that it is necessary and sufficient for the existence of a social group in a certain central sense of the term that there be a plural subject in the sense just indicated.[11] This central sense includes unions, search committees, and discussion groups, among others, within its extension.

If all plural subjects are social groups in the sense in question, it follows that any persons A, B, and so on, who are jointly committed to believe something as a body, thereby constitute a social group, irrespective of any other relationship they have. This seems to me to be correct intuitively. Indeed, there are established groups that appear to have not so much a certain mission as a certain belief or credo as their primary feature. The Flat Earth Society is but one example.

Joint Commitment and the Standing to Rebuke

I return now to the criteria of adequacy for an account of group belief proposed earlier and discuss how the plural subject account fares in relation to them.

According to criterion (1) an adequate account should clarify the point that a group belief can be established, roughly, by virtue of public expressions of readiness on the part of the individual group members to let a particular belief be established as that of the group. The plural subject account offers, in effect, a particular interpretation of that point, an interpretation that does not presuppose that one understands what it is for a group to believe something.

According to criterion (2) the account should explain how the very existence of a particular group belief could give group members the standing to rebuke each other for bluntly expressing a contrary view. I leave discussion of this criterion till last, since it requires the longest treatment.

According to criteria (3), (4), and (5) the account should not entail that all or most group members believe what the group believes; it should not entail that if all or most of them believe something then the group believes it too, and it should allow that the members may believe what the group believes: that is not ruled out. All of these criteria are satisfied by the plural subject account.

I return now to criterion (2): the need to explain how the members of a group with a given belief have the standing to rebuke each other for bluntly expressing a contrary view. It is clear enough that by virtue of their having

---

[11] See Gilbert (1989: ch. 4).

jointly committed one another in some way, the parties to any joint commit-ment gain a special standing in relation to one another's actions. Precisely how to characterize that standing is a good and important question, and gets us into some fairly deep waters. Here I summarize some aspects of the matter as I see it.

First, the parties to a joint commitment are *answerable* to one another, qua parties to the commitment, should they fail to conform to it. Each will under-stand that if one party asks another why he failed to conform, it will not be appropriate to respond, "That is none of your business!" Second, one who fails to conform to a given joint commitment has *offended against* all of the parties to the commitment as such.

I propose that the offense in question can plausibly be characterized as a violation of each party's *right* to the offender's conformity. Correlative to this right is an *obligation* or duty of conformity on the part of each, an obligation or duty *towards* the other parties. In other terms, each *owes* each his conformity.

I take it that one owes someone an action in the sense in question here if that action is already in an important sense *his*. Its occurrence is not, of course, a matter of his behaving in a certain way. It is not his action in *that* sense. In what pertinent sense is an action that is owed to me *mine*? Apparently—if my proposal is correct—in a sense exemplified by a situation of joint commitment.

If all this is right, then we can see how the parties to a joint commitment have the standing to rebuke one another for nonconformity to the commit-ment. To spell this out, it will be useful first to introduce the notion of a *demand*. In the pertinent relatively narrow sense of "demand" one needs a special standing in order to be capable of demanding that someone act in a certain way. I take it that one has this standing if the action in question is one's own in the sense in which an action that is owed is one's own.

A rebuke is an after-the-fact demand. One can sensibly demand the action *before* it has been performed—if, perhaps, the person who must carry it out seems to be planning not to do it. When the time for carrying it out has past, one can no longer sensibly demand it, but one can rebuke the person in ques-tion for not carrying it out. In the case of the demand one says, in effect, "Give me what is mine!" In the case of the rebuke, one says, rather, "You did not give me what was mine!" implying, perhaps, that some kind of recompense or at least apology is called for.

There is, then, a way of linking group belief on the plural subject account to the standing to rebuke, a way that makes this standing part and parcel of the fact that the group belief exists. It is unclear that any other way of characterizing group belief will fare so well in terms of the criterion of adequacy in question.

Group Belief as Belief

I propose that the concept of group belief as articulated in the plural subject account is an everyday concept that permeates everyday life. In this section, in writing of "group belief" I mean group belief according to the plural subject account.

To say that there are group beliefs is not to say anything metaphysically disreputable, or so I suppose. It is clear enough what group beliefs involve.

If it is said that group beliefs are not really beliefs, this will need to be supported. For when people speak of what their group believes, they are apparently speaking seriously and non-metaphorically.

One can of course make important distinctions among the statements about belief that are made in everyday life. In a story for children a train might be said to believe something. A computer user might find himself saying in response to an error message that his computer thinks he is stupid. Or someone might attribute an overly sophisticated belief to his cat: "She thinks she is the President of the United States." Many such statements can presumably be excluded from consideration as in some sense playful, or not intended to be taken seriously or literally. Group belief statements, in contrast, are commonly made with serious intent.

It would be reasonable to assume that there are both analogies and disanalogies between the beliefs of groups—or, if you will, the phenomenon to which group belief statements refer—and the beliefs of individuals. Precisely what these analogies and disanalogies are is a good question.[12]

Elements of Culture beyond Group Beliefs

I have focused in this paper on the nature of group beliefs as these are conceived of in everyday life, and offered an account of such beliefs in terms of joint commitment. I should like to close by noting the plausibility of joint

---

[12] For some discussion of analogies between group or collective belief and the beliefs of individuals in light of various philosophical doctrines about belief, based on the individual case, see Gilbert (2002).

commitment accounts of many other potential cultural elements, one of these being social conventions.

A popular account of social convention comes from the philosopher David Lewis via the philosopher Hume and the economist Thomas Schelling. According to this account, roughly, there is a convention in a given population—which may or may not be a social group—if there is a regularity in the behavior of its members combined with expectations on the part of the members that such behavior will continue and preferences for such continuation on the part of all, if most so continue.

Lewis may have described an important phenomenon with this description of a convention. However, he set out not only to do this, but to give an account of our everyday concept of a social convention. That he has achieved this particular aim is debatable. That depends, of course, on what one thinks an account of this concept must explain—what one thinks the firm contours of the everyday concept of a social convention are.

In my view, in parallel with the everyday concept of a group's belief, the—or at least a central—everyday concept of a social convention is such that the parties to such a convention understand themselves to have the standing to rebuke one another for non-conformity to the convention, and to have this standing by virtue of the fact that this is their convention. It is hard to see how this can be explained given only the elements of Lewis's account of social convention.

I have elsewhere proposed an account that can explain it, an account that retains none of the elements of Lewis's account. According to this plural subject account of social convention, there is convention in a given population if and only if the members are jointly committed to accept as a body a certain fiat with respect to their behavior. Given this account, which is to be understood along similar lines to the plural subject account of collective belief, the parties do have the standing to rebuke one another for non-conformity with the "fiat" that characterizes the particular convention at issue, insofar as non-conformity contravenes the joint commitment that lies at the heart of the convention.[13]

Though I shall not attempt to discuss other elements of culture here, I believe that, as I have argued elsewhere, plural subject accounts of central elements of

---

[13] For further discussion of both Lewis's and my account of social convention see Gilbert (1989: ch. 6, and 2008).

culture other than beliefs and conventions are very plausible. These include a group's language and its moral code.[14]

References

Bar-Tal, Daniel. 1990. *Group Beliefs: A Conception for Analyzing Group Structure, Processes and Behavior.* New York: Springer-Verlag.

De Munck, Victor, and Giovanni Bennardo. 2019. Disciplining Culture: A Sociocognitive Approach. *Cultural Anthropology* 60: 174–93.

Gilbert, Margaret. 1989. *On Social Facts.* Princeton: Princeton University Press.

Gilbert, Margaret. 1996. *Living Together: Rationality, Sociality, and Obligation.* Rowman and Littlefield. Lanham: MD.

Gilbert, Margaret. 2002. Belief and Acceptance as Features of Groups. *Protosociology* 16: 35–69.

Gilbert, Margaret. 2003. The Structure of the Social Atom: Joint Commitment as the Foundation of Human Social Behavior, in *Social Metaphysics: The Nature of Social Reality*, ed. F. Schmitt, Rowman and Littlefield: Lanham, MD, pp. 39–64.

Gilbert, Margaret. 2004a. Durkheim on Social Facts, in H. Martins and W. Pickering (eds.) *Debating Durkheim.* London: Routledge: 86–109.

Gilbert, Margaret. 2004b. Collective Epistemology. *Episteme. A Journal of Social Epistemology* 1: 95–107.

Gilbert, Margaret. 2005. Shared Values, Social Unity, and Liberty. *Public Affairs Quarterly* 19: 25–49.

Gilbert, Margaret, 2006a. Can a Wise Society Be a Free One? *Southern Journal of Philosophy* 44: 1–17 [Ch. 11, this volume].

Gilbert, Margaret, 2006b. *A Theory of Political Obligation: Membership, Commitment, and the Bonds of Society.* Oxford: Oxford University Press.

Gilbert, Margaret. 2008. Social Convention Revisited. *Topoi* 27: 5–16.

Lewis, David. 1969. *Convention.* Cambridge, MA: Harvard University Press.

Quinton, Anthony. 1975. Social Objects. *Proceedings of the Aristotelian Society* 76: 1–27.

[14] See Gilbert (1989: ch. 3), on group languages, and, on a group's moral code, Gilbert (2005). For an anthropologist's adoption of a joint commitment account of culture (subsequent to the original publication of this essay) see De Munck and Bennardo (2019).

3

Joint Commitment and Group Belief

In chapter 2, "Culture as Collective Construction," I focused on group belief as a central aspect of culture, proposing that *a group G believes that p* if and only if the members of G are jointly committed to believe that p as a body. In this chapter I respond to some questions raised by sociologist Annette Schnabel in connection with that discussion, questions which may have occurred to others as well. They relate both to joint commitment in general and to group belief in particular. I turn to some questions about joint commitment first.

1. Joint Commitment and the Commitments of the Parties

Professor Schnabel asks, "What are the particular properties of the joint commitment that are not reducible to individual commitment and under what conditions do they develop?"[1] In response I shall amplify somewhat the discussion of joint commitment in chapter 2.

When, in conditions of common knowledge, two or more people have openly expressed their readiness for them all to be *jointly committed* in some way, I say that these people *are jointly committed*, that *a joint commitment* has been created, and so on. When this is the case *each of the participating individuals* is indeed committed. That is, each is now subject to the kind of constraint in question—a commitment of the will. It is important to note, however, that to say this is not to say that each of these individuals now has what I have referred to as a *personal commitment* such as is created by a personal decision. By definition, a *personal* commitment is created unilaterally by the party in question, and can be rescinded unilaterally by that party. If you like, he is the sole *author* of his commitment and, as such, he can do away with it when he pleases.

In contrast, a joint commitment has a *joint author* in the sense that the input of each party is required in order that it be established. That is how the parties to it understand what is happening. It is created, and must be

---

[1] Schnabel (2009: 402).

Life in Groups: How We Think, Feel, and Act Together. Margaret Gilbert, Oxford University Press. © Margaret Gilbert 2023.
DOI: 10.1093/oso/9780192847157.003.0004

rescinded, by all. Thus, for its creation, it must at a minimum be common knowledge between the parties that each is ready for the commitment of them all, *as one*, in the relevant way.

Here I would like briefly to insert a point that is not strictly relevant to the reducibility issue. I have long supposed that in basic cases it is necessary that each party's readiness to join with the pertinent others in creating a given joint commitment be *expressed*, in conditions of common knowledge, in order that the joint commitment be formed.[2] This indeed is how I represented the situation in "Culture as Collective Construction."

It may be, however, that there are some special contexts in which no "expression condition" need be met. These will presumably be cases—if such there be—in which something like the following is true: As is common knowledge between them, each of several people is ready to join with the others in creating a particular joint commitment, *and desires to have that readiness taken for granted in the absence of his expression of it.* There is no space to pursue this possibility here, so for present purposes I set it aside.

One thing for which I take the jointness of a commitment to be crucial —is the existence of rights of the parties to each other's conformity to the commitment, along with the standing to demand conformity and to rebuke for nonconformity. A set of mutually expressed *personal* commitments, as in the dialogue "I've decided to…" "…and so have I," would not in and of themselves create a situation in which each party was in a position to demand the other's conformity or, more fully, to demand such conformity *as his*. In the case of a joint commitment formed in the way on which I focus, a fuller elaboration of *as his*, here, would be *as his, in his capacity as one of us, where the joint commitment was the result of our combined expressions of readiness for it.*

2. Contexts Conducive to the Formation of Joint Commitments

When and why are joint commitments likely to develop? My discussion of this question here will focus on an important type of situation in which one can argue that the development of a joint commitment is predictable.[3] Though this situation as described involves a degree of idealization in terms of the

---

[2] I argue in favor of an "expression" condition as well as an "expressed" condition in Gilbert (1989: ch. 4).
[3] There is related discussion in Gilbert (2007).

way human beings operate, I take it to be relevant to our understanding of less than ideal circumstances.

Thus consider a situation in which two people, Anne and Bea, are *rational* in the sense that each one always acts appropriately given the considerations that bear on her situation. It is also common knowledge between Anne and Bea that each one is in this sense rational. Each has to choose between two actions, which I shall label "defect" and "not defect." The personal *inclinations* of each with respect to the possible combinations of their actions have the profile associated with the payoffs to each agent in a classical Prisoner's Dilemma payoff matrix. Crucially, each is inclined to defect both on the assumption that the other defects and on the assumption that the other does not defect, though she is more strongly inclined to defect on the assumption that the other does not defect. And so on.[4]

In this situation it seems reasonable to assume that if there is no joint commitment to the contrary both Anne and Bea will defect. Certainly such defection accords with each one's "strictly dominant strategy" given the profile of her inclinations, a fact which would appear to recommend defection if it does not rationally require it.

If the parties can achieve a joint commitment to adopt as a body the plan of non-defection by each, however, then each will choose the option of non-defection. Here I assume that conforming to the joint commitment and hence not defecting is the rational response in this context, all else being equal. In other words, the joint commitment "trumps" the inclinations of each from the point of view of what rationality requires.

Granting this assumption, as I shall in what follows, it is clear that people who are rational and wish to do as well as possible *according to the profile of their inclinations* in the situation envisaged will be well advised to make an appropriate joint commitment with the other party or parties prior to the time they must act, if it is feasible to do so.

I assume that, more generally, *when the pattern of personal inclinations in a population is not enough to guarantee a satisfactory outcome for rational agents*, an appropriate joint commitment can ensure such an outcome for such agents by providing a consideration for all parties that "trumps" whatever course is recommended or required by virtue of their inclinations

---

[4] In the classic Prisoner's Dilemma, each player has to choose between confessing and not confessing to a particular crime. Given the structure of the payoffs to each player, if each makes the dominant or payoff-maximizing choice (confessing), then each does less well than would both making the alternative choice (not confessing). In my example, the satisfaction of a stronger inclination stands in for a higher payoff.

considered on their own. It will do this as long as there are no further considerations that trump the joint commitment itself.

How might one argue for this trumping quality of joint commitment in
this context? Apart from the fact that it seems right on the face of it, the following way of arguing for it seems plausible.

Commitments of the will generally are such that they mandate the action
in question, all else being equal. Inclinations only recommend actions rather
than require that they be performed. Hence, when a commitment of the will
is added to the situation, it wins out over a contrary inclination in terms of
what one is rationally required to do.

That said, a *joint* commitment in contrast to a pair of personal commitments is an especially powerful tool in face of contrary inclinations. In the
case of the personal commitment that a personal decision engenders, it is easy
enough for the committed person to do away with it by rescinding the decision. When one is party to a joint commitment, however, he is not in a position unilaterally to do away with his commitment. Once established, then, a
joint commitment provides a stable point of reference for the parties.

A joint commitment also introduces certain important *relational facts* into
the situation: it endows all of the parties with rights to the conforming actions
of the others. That I am inclined to act otherwise appears to be a weak counter
to the claim that another has a right against me to my acting in a particular way.

Trumping inclinations is, I propose, one of the central purposes served by
everyday agreements, which are plausibly interpreted as involving a joint
commitment of a particular type arrived at by a particular explicit process.[5] It
is also a central role played by social rules and conventions understood in
joint commitment terms.[6]

3. Why Conform?

The foregoing remarks are part of the reply to another of Professor Schnabel's
questions. This concerns the precise mechanisms that force people to keep
their commitments, to which I now turn.

---

[5] See Gilbert (2006: ch. 10) for a discussion of agreements and promises as joint commitment phenomena. See also, on agreements, chapter 1, this volume.

[6] I discuss social convention in "Culture as Collective Construction" (chapter 2, this volume). For
discussion of social rules, with particular reference to the theory of the British philosopher of law
H. L. A. Hart, see Gilbert (1999). See also Gilbert (2006: ch. 9).

First, there are mechanisms internal to the person, in that they concern how each person understands his situation. Insofar as he is rational, his understanding that the joint commitment trumps his inclinations as such will lead him to conform to the commitment, all else being equal.

Second, there are mechanisms external to the person, in that they concern how the other parties understand their situation and are likely to react given this understanding. For example, the other parties will understand that if a given person fails to conform to the commitment, each of them has the standing to rebuke him. Insofar as it is unpleasant to be rebuked, the parties to a joint commitment have here an additional reason to conform: their desire to avoid a rebuke.

Of course, even given a tendency of human beings to act rationally in the sense in question, one can expect them to act *irrationally* at times. And factors other than those to which I have alluded will doubtless play a role in bringing people to act in conformity with their commitments—or to fail to do so.

One significant factor that may argue *against* conformity with a joint commitment from a rational point of view is one's sense that it would be *morally wrong*, all things considered, to conform. Indeed, it is worth emphasizing that though every joint commitment brings with it rights and obligations of a kind, that does not mean that one is always rationally required to act in accordance with these rights and obligations, all things considered.

Thus we can expect that in certain circumstances rational agents will act contrary to their joint commitments, though they know this will lay them open to the authoritative rebukes of the other parties. These are the circumstances in which all things considered it would be morally wrong—perhaps it would be a great evil—to conform to the joint commitments in question.[7]

4. Group Beliefs and Preferences

I turn finally to some of Professor Schnabel's questions specifically about group beliefs and preferences: "How do joint beliefs and preferences relate to individual beliefs and preferences? Do they overwrite them? Are they able to be overwritten by them?"[8]

---

[7] For discussion of a conflict between one's personal decision and a joint commitment to which one is a party, see Gilbert (2006: 158–9). One notable aspect of that situation is that the former but not the latter is unilaterally rescindable by the deliberating agent. Rescinding the decision is therefore the only way to avoid leaving a standing commitment unfulfilled.

[8] Schnabel (2009: 402–3).

Perhaps the following development of a particular example involving a group beliefs on my account of these will go some way to answer these questions.[9] Among other things it will bring out in relation to a concrete case how well the account corresponds to the observations on everyday group belief statements offered in the first part of "Culture as Collective Construction."

Suppose that scientists in a particular research team collectively believe that a particular hypothesis H is probably true. Suppose now that Clara Jones is a member of this team. She participates in the collective belief, *being jointly committed with the others* to believe as a body that H is probably true. Personally, however, she has her doubts. Perhaps she did not have them when the collective belief was formed, but on subsequent reflection, in private, she has come to think that H is probably false.

The development of a contrary personal belief is certainly possible in the circumstances of an existing collective belief and does not in and of itself destroy the collective belief. These two—the collective belief and the contrary personal belief—can coexist, whether or not this is comfortable for the person in question.

If Clara's doubts about H are strong enough, and she wishes to bring the team to a better position on the matter, she may decide to speak out. However, in deciding whether or not to do so, she will need to take into account *the fact of her joint commitment.* This requires that she not baldly—without a special preamble—deny that H is probably true. Indeed, she owes it to her fellow team members not so to deny it.

What she can do, it seems, without defaulting on her obligations to the other members, is say something with an appropriate preamble such as "Personally, I have my doubts." This makes it clear that she is speaking in her own name and not that of the research team.

Though this option is available, taking advantage of it will not necessarily be without cost for Clara. For her doing so may well seem to her colleagues to throw doubt on her reliability with respect to her obligations according to their joint commitment. Thus she risks a negative reaction whether she acts contrary to the joint commitment or takes advantage of the possibility of speaking "in her own name."

One can see, then, that as a causal matter, an existing group belief may tend to suppress the expression of contrary beliefs, whether in a qualified or unqualified manner. This tendency may carry with it another: the tendency to prevent contrary personal beliefs from being formed. Rather than saying one

---

[9] The example is derived from discussion in Gilbert (2000a).

thing and thinking another, people may prefer to stop thinking differently altogether, suppressing or turning away from ideas that appear to threaten the plausibility of some proposition that their group believes.

Group beliefs, then, have an inherently repressive tendency. When what a group believes is true, that may be all to the good. When what a group believes is false, that may be little short of tragic. Though repressive, however, group beliefs do not logically exclude the contrary personal beliefs of the participants. And if one or more people have the courage to speak out, either in their own names or in a more challenging fashion, they may succeed in changing things at the collective level. Indeed, the end result of one person's speaking out could be the demise of the group itself, as together the members agree on the error of their previous beliefs.[10]

5. Concluding Remark

I use the phrase "plural subject" as a label for any collection of persons linked by a joint commitment of one kind or another. If the concept of a joint commitment roughly as I have characterized it is as fundamental a part of the conceptual scheme with which human beings approach their lives together as I have suggested, it behooves not only philosophers but also social scientists to do their best to understand the nature and functioning of plural subjects. I thank Professor Schnabel for engaging with me in this exchange of ideas on this important topic. I hope that our exchange will encourage others both to explore more of the literature on the topic and to continue the discussion.

References

Gilbert, Margaret (1989): *On Social Facts*. London: Routledge and Kegan Paul.

Gilbert, Margaret (1999): "Social Rules: Some Problems for Hart's Account and an Alternative Proposal." *Law and Philosophy* 18, 141–71.

Gilbert, Margaret (2000a): "Collective Belief and Scientific Change." In Gilbert (2000b).

---

[10] This is all that I shall say here about the way groups come to an end, a topic which Schnabel raises in several places. Here I refer her and the reader to Gilbert (2006: ch. 7), where the topic of how joint commitments end is discussed in more detail.

Gilbert, Margaret (2000b): *Sociality and Responsibility: New Essays in Plural Subject Theory*. Lanham, MD: Rowman and Littlefield.

Gilbert, Margaret (2003): "The Structure of the Social Atom: Joint Commitment as the Foundation of Human Social Behavior." In Frederick Schmitt (ed.), *Socializing Metaphysics*. Lanham, MD: Rowman and Littlefield.

Gilbert, Margaret (2006): *A Theory of Political Obligation*. Oxford: Oxford University Press.

Gilbert, Margaret (2007): "Collective Intentions, Commitment, and Collective Action Problems". In Fabienne Peter and Hans-Bernard Schmid (eds.), *Rationality and Commitment*. Oxford: Oxford University Press.

Schnabel, Annette (2009): "Group Beliefs, Group Speakers, Power and Negotiation." *Kolner Zeitschrift fur Soziologie und Socialpsychology* 393–404.

4

Belief, Acceptance, and What Happens in Groups

Some Methodological Considerations

Introduction

The vast majority of the discussions in epistemology have focused on the epistemic states of human individuals.[1] Thus those discussions consider, for example, what it is for individual human beings to believe that such and such or to know that such and such. For present purposes we will call the inquiry such theorists engage in *individual epistemology*.

Individual epistemology leaves outside its purview a whole range of everyday ascriptions of epistemic states. For in everyday thought and talk ascriptions of belief and other epistemic states commonly include ascriptions to both human individuals and collectives made up of individuals, including unstructured informal groups.

Thus we might speak of Jones's belief that the team will win, or of the team's belief that it will win. We might speak of Smith's belief that there is an afterlife, or of her bible study group's belief in an afterlife. Robinson might say that she believes her country is the best in the world, or she might say, in reference to the relevant citizen body, "We believe this is the best country in the world."

Such ascriptions of epistemic states to collectives raise the question of what these ascriptions refer to. In other words, what is it for a group to have beliefs, knowledge, and so on? We shall call the inquiry that focuses on these

---

[1] This chapter was co-authored with Daniel Pilchman, who is the other half of the authorial "we" in the text. In writing of "epistemic states" in this paragraph and below we use "states" in a broad non-technical sense to include e.g. episodes and dispositions.

Life in Groups: How We Think, Feel, and Act Together. Margaret Gilbert, Oxford University Press. © Margaret Gilbert 2023.
DOI: 10.1093/oso/9780192847157.003.0005

questions *collective epistemology*.[2] This inquiry is by now well under way, with a rapidly growing literature.[3]

The broadest concern of this paper is the relation between individual and collective epistemology.[4] It approaches this relation by considering some prominent contributions to collective epistemology. These include a relatively long-standing debate that invokes a distinction between "belief" and "acceptance" in specified senses of these terms.

We shall argue that these contributions to collective epistemology throw into high relief an important methodological caveat: one should not assume that accounts and distinctions arrived at within individual epistemology will apply straightforwardly within collective epistemology, however central they are to individual epistemology.

Cohen on Belief and Believers

Twenty years after its publication, L. Jonathan Cohen's *An Essay on Belief and Acceptance* is still one of the most cited sources for authors engaged in collective epistemology. Cohen has made his own contributions to the subject. In addition, his accounts of the nature of belief and acceptance have heavily influenced the continuing debate in collective epistemology that we shall discuss. We start, therefore with some discussion of Cohen's work. We focus, first, on his ideas about belief.

On Cohen's view, "belief that p is a disposition, when one is attending to issues raised, or items referred to, by the proposition *p*, normally to feel it true that *p* and false that *not-p*."[5] This account of belief, as Pascal Engel points out, has much in common with Hume's conception of belief as belonging to the passive side of the human mind.[6] At some length, Cohen situates "credal feelings" within the realm of sentiments when, on his use of the phrase, he writes:

---

[2] Cf. (Gilbert 2004). We allow that either collective epistemology or individual epistemology could in principle have one or more skeptical outcome. Some have argued that individuals are not knowers; some have argued that they are not believers. Some, as we shall see, have argued that groups are not believers.

[3] See e.g. (Gilbert 1987; Gilbert 1989; Tuomela 1992; Clark 1994; Schmitt 1994; Cohen 1995; Tuomela 2000; Wray 2001; Tollefsen 2002; Bouvier 2004; Mathiesen 2006; Pettit 2010).

[4] We take *social epistemology* to be something of a mongrel category depending on how it is interpreted. In any case, it is not our specific focus here. For a classic source see (Goldman 1999).

[5] (Cohen 1995, 4).   [6] (Engel 2000, 11); echoing (Cohen 1989, 20).

What is important here is not to provide a phrase that is a synonymous equivalent for the word 'belief', but to place belief in its right conceptual category. Specifically, it is classifiable as a disposition to have a certain kind of mental feeling, not as a disposition to perform a certain kind of action.[7]

While the ability to believe, on this view, is inextricably linked to feelings, what Cohen refers to as "acceptance" is not. In his words,

> To accept that *p*, is to have or adopt a policy of deeming, positing, or postulating that *p*—i.e. of including that proposition or rule among one's premises for deciding what to do or think in a particular context, whether or not one feels it to be true that *p*.[8]

Cohen holds that the distinction between belief and acceptance is significant because it makes an important difference to human life that we are able both to believe and to accept propositions and that we understand that this is so.[9]

Cohen on Groups and Belief

Given his understanding of belief it is no surprise that Cohen was skeptical about group or collective belief.[10] Thus he says:

> When we look closely enough, and get behind the metaphor or the accidents of vocabulary, we find that organizations are typically engaged in accepting premises or pursuing goals, not in experiencing beliefs or desires. No doubt this is for two main reasons. First, organizations share with human adults the ability to formulate what they accept or decide in language…Secondly, an organization is not exposed at all to the chemical or physiological stimulation of feelings.[11]

This suggests the following argument. Groups are incapable of having or being disposed to have feelings; believing involves having or being disposed

---

[7] (Cohen 1995, 11).   [8] (Cohen 1995, 4).
[9] (Cohen 1995, 61). Cohen maintains that the distinction between belief and acceptance also gives us important insights into questions about the epistemology of animals, infants, and artificial intelligences as well as into persistent philosophical problems including Moore's paradox and self-deception. Compare (Engel 2000, 11).
[10] We use the phrases "group belief" and "collective belief" interchangeably in what follows.
[11] (Cohen 1989, 383; Cohen 1995, 55).

to have feelings, in particular credal feelings; so groups are incapable of belief. Though Cohen does not explicitly draw this conclusion in the quotation just given, we shall take it to express the position he holds on the basis of something like the argument just sketched.

In assessing that argument, let us assume, first, that groups cannot be *disposed* to have feelings if they cannot *have* feelings, and, second, that groups are indeed incapable of having feelings in the sense at issue here. The second assumption would seem to be true, if feelings are understood essentially to involve *subjective experiences*. We shall so understand feelings here.[12] It follows from these assumptions that groups cannot be disposed to have feelings. Given these assumptions, then, we must allow that *if* any believer must be disposed to experience credal feelings, then groups are not believers. This argument, however, does not clinch the case against group belief.

For one thing, Cohen's account of belief has not generally been accepted, and a variety of criticisms have been made of it. Raimo Tuomela, for instance, argues that, when distilled, Cohen's credal feelings are little more than "the thought that the content of the belief is true."[13] In other words, so-called credal feelings are not really *feelings* at all. Leslie Stevenson criticizes Cohen's appeal to credal feelings in another way. Stephenson identifies examples that one might very naturally call credal feelings—like the feeling that one's spouse is in the house despite knowing that he or she is dead—but that do not intuitively seem like beliefs. So credal feelings may not, after all, be the mark of *belief*.[14]

Irrespective of the correctness of Cohen's account of belief, there is another reason for thinking that the above argument does not clinch the case against group belief. The argument relies on Cohen's account of belief. That account, however, was based on the individual human case.[15] A plausible way of seeing Cohen's account, then, is as an account of belief *as it occurs in individual human beings*. If Cohen's account of belief is seen in this way, then, even if it is correct, it leaves open the nature of belief *in the collective case*.

---

[12] Cf. Cohen's phrase "mental feeling" in one of the above quotations. It is of course common in everyday speech to refer to the emotions of groups as in "The team was furious with their manager" and "We just loved the opera." One can take these seriously without allowing that groups have subjective experiences of their own. For detailed discussion of a particular ascription of collective emotion see (Gilbert 2001). On collective emotions generally see (Gilbert 2014): ch. 8, this volume.

[13] (Tuomela 2000, 128).   [14] (Stevenson 2002, 111).

[15] That this is so is clear enough from his discussion in, say, (Cohen 1989), where all of the initial expository examples concern individual human beings. He is, of course, operating in the context of a long epistemological tradition in philosophy and cognitive science that betrays no interest in the collective case. Cohen is an exception here, but his discussion of the collective case is relatively cursory and comes after the main expository work has been accomplished.

Methodological Remarks: With Reference
to Plato's Approach to Justice

The point just made suggests some important methodological points. We preface our discussion of them by recalling Plato's methodology in the *Republic*. Though he is primarily concerned with justice, as opposed to belief, his procedure is instructive.

Plato's overarching aim is to understand what it is for an individual human being to be just. Early in his discussion, however, he notes that justice is commonly ascribed both to individual human beings and to political societies (*poleis*). Accordingly, he suggests that an inquiry into the nature of justice in the human case may benefit from an inquiry into the nature of justice in the collective case. Presumably justice in the one case and justice in the other will have something in common. Both, after all, are cases of *justice*.[16]

Plato investigates the collective case first. Taking account of some of the salient features of this case he goes on carefully to probe the human case, an inquiry that proceeds to a large extent in its own terms.

For present purposes the main point about Plato's procedure is not his starting with the collective case. His stated reason for doing so is not, indeed, particularly convincing. The main point is that Plato clearly sees it as both possible and appropriate to engage in *two distinct inquiries* in relation to justice: an inquiry into the nature of justice in the collective case, and an inquiry into the nature of justice in the human case. Though he believes the results of the former may be expected to help with the investigation of the latter, he also believes that, by and large, each should be investigated on its own terms.

There are several lessons for epistemology here. In contemporary epistemology inquiries into the nature of belief and so on have started with the individual case. The results of these inquiries may well help to throw light on the nature of the collective case. Nonetheless caution is required with respect to the use of results deriving from the individual case in approaching the collective case. There may be significant disanalogies between these cases, despite their having some features in common. Careful, independent investigation of the collective case—as of the individual case—is required in order properly to understand it. Quite possibly, such careful investigation of the collective case will help to throw light on the individual case as well.[17]

---

[16] (Plato 1992 Bk II, 368 b–e).   [17] See e.g. (Priest ms).

Let us return for a moment to the argument, drawn from Cohen's work, to the effect that groups are not believers. A proponent of this argument may be ignoring the methodological points just made. For he (or she) may be adopting uncritically a concept of belief developed within individual epistemology—the concept articulated in Cohen's credal feelings account—when approaching the collective case.

Whether or not application of Cohen's concept is *warranted* in relation to the collective case can only be decided given a careful examination of that case. We take it that this will involve an inquiry into the intended referents of those everyday statements that, on the face of it, ascribe beliefs to groups—an inquiry central to collective epistemology.

Later we shall argue that the methodological points made in this section are apt to help us to understand the stalemate that has arisen in a current debate in collective epistemology. This debate owes much to Cohen, though its proponents generally do not accept all of the particulars of his account of belief. The debate focuses on a particular account of the referent of those everyday statements that appear to ascribe beliefs to groups, an account whose accuracy it does not dispute.

Before turning to that account, and the debate it has prompted, we briefly note some of the problems associated with a different type of account. This is the account that may first come to mind, and that Cohen, for one, appears to espouse. It is the failure of this type of account, among other things, that has led theorists to focus on something different.[18]

Collective Belief Ascriptions: The Failure of Summativism

Although Cohen doubts that there are collective beliefs—in light of his understanding of belief—he is aware of the prevalence in everyday life of what are, on the face of it, ascriptions of beliefs to groups, utterances such as "The team believes it will win," "My bible study group believes in an afterlife," and so on. We shall refer to all such statements as *collective belief ascriptions*. We include under this label statements such as "We believe that…" where no established label for a type of group is at issue. In such cases it may be clear both to the speaker and the audience that the speaker's words are not simply

---

[18] The next section covers ground familiar to those specializing in collective epistemology, and is intended largely for non-specialists.

elliptical for "We all believe that..." or "We both believe that..." Rather, a belief is here cribed to *us* as opposed to each one of us.

This is what Cohen says about collective belief ascriptions:

> When a community or nation is said to believe or desire that *p* this is normally a figurative way of saying that most of its individual members or most of its official representatives believe or desire that *p*.[19]

He suggests, then, that when someone appears to be ascribing a belief that p to a group he (or she) is really ascribing that belief to most of the group's members or most of its official representatives.

Years earlier, Anthony Quinton had written something similar:

> Groups are said to have beliefs, emotions, and attitudes...But these ways of speaking are plainly metaphorical. To ascribe mental predicates to a group is always an indirect way of ascribing such predicates to its members. With such mental states as beliefs...the ascriptions are of what I have called a summative kind. To say the industrial working class is determined to resist anti-trade union laws is to say that all or most industrial workers are so minded.[20]

Suppose we call an account of the referent of everyday collective belief ascriptions an account of *collective belief*. Then we can think of Quinton and Cohen as offering such an account.

Irrespective of these authors' contributions, one's initial attempt at providing an account of collective belief is likely to take the following form:

A group G believes that p if and only if all or most of the members believe that p.

Borrowing Quinton's term, we shall refer to this as a "summative" account of collective belief. *A summative account of collective belief*, by definition, places at its core the condition that *all or most members of the group in question have the belief that is ascribed to the group*. We shall refer to this as the *summative condition*.[21]

---

[19] (Cohen 1989, 383).

[20] (Quinton 1975, 9), cited in (Gilbert 1987; Gilbert 1989). Since then Quinton has become the poster-philosopher for views of the kind he expresses here.

[21] Call an account of collective belief "correlative" if, according to that account, a group cannot believe that p unless at least one member of the group believes that p. All summative accounts are correlative, but not vice versa.

More complex summative accounts than the one just formulated are possible. For instance, one might add to the above the condition that everyone in group G knows that all or most of members of G have the pertinent belief.[22] We shall therefore refer to the account consisting of the summative condition alone as the *simple summative account* of collective belief.[23]

The simple summative account clearly has its attractions. For one, it appeals only to the beliefs of individual human beings, an appeal with which we can assume most theorists are comfortable. Further, it makes no allusions, implicit or explicit, to a "group consciousness" or the subjective experiences of groups. It is, one might say, completely realistic. As Margaret Gilbert has argued for some time, however, there are good reasons to reject the simple summative account and, indeed, to reject all summative accounts of group belief.[24]

The following simple example may help to make the point. Joe meets Karen and, wanting to say something pleasant, comes out with "Lovely day!" Karen, wanting to be agreeable, says "Yes, indeed!" Joe and Karen then come across Fred, who grumbles about the day's weather. Karen confidently responds, on behalf of Joe and herself, "We think it's a lovely day!" Karen's statement seems to be on target, as a statement of collective belief, irrespective of the personal beliefs of the parties regarding the weather, whatever those happen to be.[25]

This is not the place further to discuss this example or to pursue the issue of summativism more generally. For present purposes the important point is that this and related examples strongly suggest that what is properly acknowledged to be "our" belief may not be the opinion of all or most—or, indeed, any—individual group members. If, indeed, a group G can believe that p without any of its members believing that p, no form of summativism, however complex, can be right.

Collective Belief Ascriptions, Belief, and Acceptance

Suppose that no summative account of collective belief is correct. The question remains: to what exactly do everyday collective belief statements

---

[22] An account discussed in (Gilbert 1989, ch. 5) and elsewhere adds a more complex, "common knowledge" condition to the summative condition. The initial philosophical discussion of "common knowledge" is in (Lewis 1969).

[23] For presentation of several different summative views see (Gilbert 1989). For a smaller range see (Gilbert 1987).

[24] See e.g. (Gilbert 1987; Gilbert 1989; Gilbert 1996). See also ch. 2, this volume.

[25] Cf. (Gilbert 1989).

refer? In what follows we shall not pursue this question for its own sake. Rather, we focus on a debate that has arisen in connection with a particular non-summative account of collective belief, the joint commitment account of Margaret Gilbert.[26]

As a way into this debate we return briefly to Cohen's discussion. Cohen denies that groups have or, indeed, can have beliefs, and offers a summative account of the referents of collective belief ascriptions. He does not deny that groups can *accept* propositions in his sense. Indeed, he asserts that they can and sometimes do accept propositions in that sense.[27] Cohen's openness to the idea of a group's being able to accept propositions may prompt the following question. Is the phenomenon to which collective belief ascriptions refer a matter of acceptance in Cohen's sense?

In the years following Cohen's publications on belief and acceptance several authors have considered an analogue of this question with respect to collective belief according to Gilbert's joint commitment account of it.[28] More specifically, they have considered Gilbert's account in light of distinctions between belief and acceptance that to some extent echo Cohen's distinction, though the pertinent accounts of belief generally either ignore or fail to give a central role to credal feelings.[29]

Before focusing on these discussions, we need to explain Gilbert's joint commitment account. This was developed in order to account for a range of contexts in which everyday collective belief ascriptions are made, with further reference to important aspects of the situation once a collective belief was formed. With respect to the latter, Gilbert focused in particular on the fact that parties to an established collective belief take themselves to be in a position to rebuke one another for denying the truth of the proposition in question in certain contexts—though they may choose not to issue such rebukes, which may be the right decision all things considered.

---

[26] We explain "joint commitment" and what we are calling the joint commitment account later in the text.

[27] As far as ordinary language use is concerned, to say that someone "accepts" a certain proposition is at least sometimes to say that he believes it. For instance, were X to say "Jack will not be elected" and Y to reply "I accept that," a reasonable gloss on what Y says may well be "I believe that." Evidently Cohen would not agree that groups accept propositions in this vernacular sense.

[28] These authors include (Meijers 1999; Tuomela 2000; Wray 2001; Gilbert 2002; Tollefsen 2003); (Hakli 2006) continues the discussion with reflections on the foregoing material. We say more about the belief-acceptance distinction as it tends to figure in the debate shortly.

[29] (Wray 2001) is one who does include credal feelings in his account of belief.

Gilbert's Joint Commitment Account of Collective Belief

As the label we are using for it suggests, joint commitment in Gilbert's sense is central to her account of collective belief.[30] The account runs roughly as follows:

The members of a population, P, *collectively believe that p* if and only if they are jointly committed to believe that p as a body.

This formulation involves several technical terms that will now briefly be explained.

First, what is it for two or more individuals to be *jointly committed* in some way?[31] We can answer this question by starting with the more familiar idea of the personal commitment of a given individual.

If Jake decides to go to the store, then there is a sense in which he has *committed himself* to going to the store. He now has, if you like, a commitment of the will. A commitment in this sense is a normative constraint on behavior. Roughly, all else being equal, the committed person ought to conform to his commitment, in a sense of "ought" that is not specifically moral.[32]

Through Jake's decision he accrues a personal commitment. By definition, when there is a *personal* commitment the committed person has unilaterally brought his commitment into being and can rescind it unilaterally by changing his mind.[33]

In order that two or more people are jointly committed in some way, it is neither necessary nor sufficient for each of those involved to make an appropriate personal commitment. That would indeed involve all of their wills. For joint commitment, however, their wills must be involved in another way.

In the basic case of joint commitment, on which we shall focus, all of those involved must openly express their readiness for a particular commitment of them all, *as one*, in conditions of common knowledge.[34] This suffices to commit them all: they are now jointly committed in the way specified.

---

[30] In prior work Gilbert has referred to this and related accounts of other collective phenomena as "plural subject" accounts. This is because, in her technical terminology, those who are jointly committed with one another in some way constitute, *by definition*, a plural subject. Since some have tended to read more than was intended into the phrase "plural subject," we have avoided that phrase here.

[31] For a longer treatment see e.g. (Gilbert 2006, ch. 7). See also the introduction and ch. 2, in particular, of (Gilbert 2013a), and the introduction, this volume.

[32] (Gilbert 2013b).

[33] There are richer notions of commitment, but we are operating with a simpler, yet important, notion. See (Gilbert 2013b).

[34] "Openly" will suffice for present purposes. See (Gilbert 1989, ch. 4) for a more detailed discussion of the requirements of joint commitment formation that appeals to a particular account of "common knowledge."

Once they are jointly committed the concurrence of each is required for the joint commitment to be rescinded, absent special background understandings. Thus one cannot unilaterally free oneself from its constraints. Things would be different if, rather than jointly committing them all, each had made a personal commitment of some kind. In that case each would be in a position to free himself from his personal commitment, without any input from the others.

In non-basic cases there are special "authorizing" joint commitments such that, for example, one person can bring it about that a given plurality of persons are jointly committed in some way. For instance, the members of a given group may be jointly committed to believe as a body whatever proposition their leader expresses belief in, in a particular context. So, if the leader, in the right context, says "Eating meat is wrong," the members are now jointly committed to believe as a body that eating meat is wrong. In this kind of case the jointly committed persons may in principle be unaware of the content of their joint commitment. Cases involving special background commitments of the kind in question are, evidently, special cases, though they may be common. We set them aside here.

What is it to be jointly committed to believe *as a body* that p, for some proposition p? Roughly, the parties are jointly committed to emulate, in relevant contexts and in relevant respects, a single party who believes that p, by virtue of the actions, including the verbal utterances, of each. In order to conform to the commitment so understood, an individual member of P must act, or refrain from acting in certain ways, in relevant contexts. For instance, she must not express beliefs contrary to or inconsistent with p in those contexts—not in an unqualified manner. It may be unproblematic for her to express such contrary beliefs when she is not speaking as a party to the joint commitment. But when she is, she must keep to "the company line." Alternatively, she must qualify her statement as in "*Personally*, I doubt whether p."

On this account, certain collective beliefs, such as those about the repugnance of an activity, will be more demanding than others, strongly impacting as they do our actions other than our verbal utterances. If we collectively believe that it is bad to smoke cigarettes, then I am not only constrained with respect to my speech, I am also constrained with respect to my cigarette smoking. If we collectively believe that everyone should do what they can in favor of energy conservation, I am constrained in my decision as to what car to buy, and so on. In contrast, if we collectively believe that the universe came into being with a big bang, while this may restrict my liberty to publicly doubt the theory, our joint commitment is unlikely to affect the way any of us goes about the daily round.

Gilbert has argued elsewhere for an important aspect of joint commitment that goes beyond anything that is involved in a concatenation of personal commitments. If Jake and Sue have jointly committed one another in some way, then, by virtue of that joint commitment and that alone, Jake is *obligated to* Sue to act in a way that conforms to the joint commitment, and the same goes for Sue.[35] Each has the correlative right against the other. In other terms, each owes the other conforming action.

This feature of Gilbert's account counts in its favor, she argues, since it provides an explanation for central aspects of the way people behave in the context of what they take to be a collective belief. These include something mentioned earlier: the parties to an established collective belief take one another to be in a position to rebuke one another for denying the truth of the proposition in question in certain contexts. One whose right to an action has been violated has the standing to rebuke the person who has offended against them.

The simple summative account favored by both Cohen and Quinton lacks this advantage. More generally, the prevalence of a particular belief among the members of a given population does not suffice to endow them with obligations towards each other to express, or at least not outwardly deny, the belief in question.[36]

Note that there is nothing in the joint commitment account of collective belief that entails that all, most, or, indeed, any of the members of the relevant population personally believe what they believe *collectively*, either before or after the collective belief is formed. Prior to its formation, people can be ready, and express their readiness, together to commit one another to believe that p as a body without believing that p themselves. Of course all or most of them may believe that p, and this may be a common situation. It may also be the most desirable situation from a variety of points of view. In principle, however, one or more or even all of the parties may fail to have any personal views on the matter, or themselves think that p is false. Nonetheless each one may be ready to join with the others to commit them all to believing that p as a body, as explicated here. Their motives may vary: one may wish to be done

---

[35] See e.g. (Gilbert 2006, ch. 7).   [36] See (Gilbert 1987; Gilbert 1989, ch. 5).

with discussion, one may be deferring to a more powerful person or wish to curry favor with him, and so on.[37]

Once the collective belief is formed, there may be a tendency on the part of the people involved to form the corresponding personal belief. After all, they are committed to expressing that belief when acting as members of the group, and owe such expression to the other parties. It is plausible to suppose that one with no prior personal view on the relevant matter is likely to form the corresponding personal belief. Here too, however, it is not logically necessary that the personal views of any of the members will come to align themselves with the collective view.

Clearly, then, the joint commitment account is not a summative account. It neither states nor logically implies that all or most members of the population in question themselves believe what the population believes in a given case.

Plausibly, conversations, whether brief or extended, are a primary context for the formation of collective beliefs. Gilbert has argued elsewhere that this idea fits well with her account of collective belief: one can interpret what happens in a typical conversation, short or long, as at least in part a matter of collective belief formation according to her account.[38] In a conversation, propositions are proposed for collective belief by one participant and accepted or rejected by the other or others. If the proposal is accepted, the interlocutors are jointly committed to believe the pertinent proposition as a body.

One other aspect of Gilbert's account should be mentioned here. She has argued that a central type of collective or social group is constituted by one or more joint commitments. Thus, for example, two or more people who previously did not together constitute such a group constitute one by virtue of the emergence among them of one or more collective beliefs.[39] Examples of groups of the kind in question include typical families, teams, clubs, and associations of various kinds. Granting, for the sake of argument, that the parties to any joint commitment, as such, constitute a social group, we return to this point later.

---

[37] See (Gilbert 1989, ch. 5) for further discussion. In arguing for her account of collective belief including the radical conceptual disjunction between a collective belief and the beliefs of the people involved, Gilbert has tended to focus on cases in which a group belief emerges in informal discussion or on the basis of a simple majority voting procedure. More recently, drawing on work of Laurence Sager and Lewis Kornhauser, and often in collaboration with Christian List, Philip Pettit has noted various formal procedures for "aggregating" the personal beliefs of group members such that the resultant belief is distinct from that of any of the members. See e.g. (Pettit 2010).

[38] See (Gilbert 1989, ch. 5); for an extended discussion see (Gilbert and Priest 2013).

[39] For detailed discussion of social groups see (Gilbert 1989: ch. 4; Gilbert 2006).

Generally speaking, the authors we primarily engage with here—the "rejectionists"—do not question the accuracy of Gilbert's account of the referent of at least some collective belief ascriptions. That is not their central concern. Rather, assuming that Gilbert's account more or less accurately describes a real phenomenon, they argue that—whatever people may call it in everyday speech—the phenomenon in question is not belief but acceptance.

To keep things clear and avoid prejudging the issue, we shall refer to the phenomenon Gilbert's account describes as collective belief*. Here the asterisk after "belief" is intended to imply agnosticism on the question whether the phenomenon in question is belief or not. The previously mentioned authors have become known as *rejectionists*, then, on account of their rejection of the idea that collective belief* is belief.[40]

Although our primary interest in the debate between rejectionists and their opponents is methodological rather than substantive, our methodological points will usefully be made in light of a relatively detailed focus on the substance of the debate.

Belief and Acceptance after Cohen

The following accounts of belief and acceptance are representative of those appealed to by rejectionists.[41] Notably, these accounts are quite complex: both acceptance and belief are characterized in terms of as many as six features.

Acceptance is: (1a) voluntary, (2a) aimed at utility, (3a) shaped by pragmatic goals, (4a) not subject to the ideal of integration, (5a) context-dependent, and (6a) does not come in degrees. Belief, in contrast, is (1b) involuntary, (2b) aimed at truth, (3b) shaped by evidence, (4b) subject to the ideal of integration, (5b) context-independent, and (6b) comes in degrees.[42]

These accounts and others much like them may be found appealing for several reasons. One is descriptive efficacy. These conceptual distinctions between belief and acceptance seem to track a real distinction among propositional attitudes that is represented in everyday speech. Thus we might say that a philosopher accepted that moral statements are truth-evaluable for

---

[40] (Gilbert 2002) introduced the label "rejectionist"; (Tollefsen 2003) labeled those who argue that collective belief is belief as "believers." We shall refer to those who oppose rejectionists simply as their opponents for reasons that will emerge.

[41] There are some exceptions, including (Hakli 2006) and (Wray 2001), who, as noted earlier, associate belief with credal feelings. In order to keep our discussion to manageable proportions we shall work with these representative accounts.

[42] See (Mathiesen 2007, 209–16).

the sake of a particular argument, though he did not believe that moral statements are truth evaluable. Or we might say that a scientist provisionally accepted a hypothesis he knew to be unproven, while working out how to test it experimentally. We might also say that in constructing his closing argument a trial lawyer refused to accept his client's guilt, though he believed his client was guilty. Finally, we might say that a philosopher accepted God's existence for the purposes of a proof of some kind, while acknowledging that, at the same time, the philosopher believes that God exists. Thus, depending on the context one may be said to accept a proposition one does not believe, not to accept a proposition one does believe, or to accept a proposition that one does believe.

The Rejectionist Credo (1): Collective Belief* Is Acceptance

We now turn to the debate between rejectionists and their opponents. Rejectionists agree with Wray when he asserts that "the phenomenon that concerns Gilbert is a species of acceptance" and not a species of belief.[43] They have put forward a number of arguments for rejectionism which, evidently, has two distinct parts. First, in brief, collective belief* is not belief. Second, collective belief* is acceptance.

Gilbert countered the rejectionists' conclusions in her paper "Belief and Acceptance as Features of Groups."[44] She argues, for one, that collective belief* is not acceptance, as the rejectionists claim.[45]

In so arguing she focuses on what rejectionists say about the relationship of the will to acceptance, as opposed to belief. According to rejectionists a belief cannot be voluntary. That is, I cannot bring a belief of mine into being by an act of will, or not directly. Acceptances, in contrast, are directly willed into being: in order for me to accept some proposition I must directly will this acceptance into being.[46]

The identity of the agent who wills the acceptance and the agent who thenceforth bears the acceptance is important in this connection. It seems that, without special authorization, no person or group can accept a proposition on behalf of another person or group. Rather, acceptances must be willed *by the relevant agent*. That is, they must be willed into being by the one who thereafter accepts the proposition in question.

---

[43] (Wray 2001, 319). See also (Wray 2003).   [44] (Gilbert 2002).
[45] (Gilbert 2002, 59–63).   [46] In this discussion, Gilbert focuses on (Meijers 1999).

In the case of my acceptances, then, I am the relevant agent. In the case of your acceptances, you are the relevant agent. In the case of collective belief*, if it really is acceptance, as the rejectionists claim, the collective or social group whose acceptance is in question is the relevant agent—the social group itself, and not its members taken one by one.

If there can be a collective belief* that is not willed into being by the relevant agent, however, then it is not a case of acceptance, since acceptances, by their nature, are willed into being by the relevant agent. It follows that collective beliefs* as such are not, of their nature, acceptances.

In support of this general conclusion Gilbert argues that there are cases of collective belief* such that those who jointly commit one another to believe as a body that such and such have not previously together constituted a collective. Rather, it is this very joint commitment, the commitment to believe as a body, that constitutes them as a collective.

Consider the following case: six unrelated people are sitting in the same compartment of a train.[47] Each is minding his or her business, reading, staring out of the window, talking on a cell phone, and so on. None of them has yet made eye contact with any of the others. We take it that they do not together form a collective at this time. After a while one of them says, "Phew! It's far too stuffy in here." There is a general murmuring of assent, as each person says something like "Yes indeed" or "Agreed!" Let us assume that the collective belief* that it is far too stuffy in the carriage has now been established among the six people in question, as is plausible given no special background circumstances.[48] Given that the parties to any joint commitment constitute a collective, then, at the moment their collective belief*—with its constitutive joint commitment—is formed, and not before, these six people constitute a collective, if only a collective whose central feature is its believing* that it is too stuffy in the carriage.[49]

This example shows that, at least in some cases, collective beliefs* are not willed into being by the social group to whom the belief* is subsequently attributed. The relevant group simply did not exist, qua social group, at the time. Since any acceptance is only appropriately attributed to the agent that willed it, such collective beliefs* cannot be acceptances.

---

[47] This example draws on one in (Gilbert 1989, 310).

[48] This assumption in no way disputes the possibility that, at the same time, all of the six personally believe that the compartment is too stuffy. The point relates only to generation in this context of the applicable collective belief*.

[49] On the possibility of groups whose central feature is a particular belief, consider, for instance the Flat Earth Society. Cf. (Gilbert 1989, ch. 5).

Examples like the one above suffice to reject the central tenet of rejectionism: that collective belief* is a species of acceptance. Moving to a different example allows us to consider the question of collective belief* and acceptance in a different, more familiar, context, that of an already existing collective.

Suppose the faculty members of a philosophy department gather for the department's weekly meeting. After the meeting has gone on for many hours, one professor interrupts the conversation and says, "This meeting has gone on long enough." There is a general murmur of assent. Absent any special background considerations, this has the character of a non-controversial case of collective belief* formation. Unlike the previous case, however, the relevant group predates the collective belief* in question, so it could in principle have willed the belief* into being.

Did the group will its collective belief* into being in this situation? We would say not. The wills of the members, qua members, even when publicly expressed, do not suffice to constitute the will of the group itself. They do, of course, establish a new feature of the group: the group has a new collective belief*. A group will, however, must be established as such by the group, how-ever informally.

We take the following to be an example of the formation of a group will. Before they tired, the same faculty members were discussing the dwindling morale in the department. Students are disaffected, faculty do not talk to each other outside department meetings, and so on. A professor who has studied the way in which morale is kept high in athletic teams says, "We have [collect-ively] to believe[*] that this department is one of the best in the world."[50] The others concur.

We take the resolution established by this interchange to represent the will of the group of department faculty. Indeed, we take it that the group has now willed that it believe* something, namely, that it is one of the best depart-ments in the world. In more familiar terms, it has *decided* to believe* that this is so.[51]

We do not deny, then, that there is a sense in which a group can will that it believe* something. We take it, however, that in many cases, even though the individual wills of the group members, qua group members, are involved,

---

[50] The square parentheses are intended to indicate what he means; were he to have written out his statement, he would not have included any such parentheses, but rather understood it (we are assum-ing) in the terms indicated by the parentheses.
[51] Note that we do not say that the group has in fact *willed a belief* into being*. Rather it is the group's will that it have a particular belief*. We consider the former possibility in due course.

a group believes* something without itself first willing that it believe* it, let alone willing the collective belief* in question into being.

With respect to the rejectionist claim that collective belief* is acceptance, then, this seems to be false. There are humdrum cases of collective belief* that do not bear the relationship to the will of the collective that would be required for these to be cases of acceptance. More precisely, the collective with the belief* did not *itself* will the belief* into being, though that belief* came into being as a result of the exercise of its members' wills. Contrary to the rejectionists, then, collective belief* as such is not acceptance. If it were, it would always be a creature of the group's will.

The Rejectionist Credo (2): Collective Belief* Is Not Belief

Rejectionists argue that collective belief* is not belief.[52] This may seem to be a doubtful conclusion, if one allows that collective beliefs* are what everyday collective belief ascriptions refer to. Everyday collective belief ascriptions are, after all, ascriptions of so-called "beliefs" to collectives. Setting that consideration aside, we shall consider a particular segment of the debate over this part of the rejectionist credo.

Gilbert argued at length in "Belief and Acceptance as Features of Groups" that rejectionist arguments to the effect that collective belief* is not belief are not as strong as might be thought. In this vein she has addressed both the rejectionists' claim that beliefs "aim at truth," and their claim that a belief cannot be willed into being, or, in the terms we used above, the claim that belief is involuntary.[53] Here we continue the discussion with a focus on the latter claim, with special reference to an article by Raul Hakli that responds to that part of Gilbert's material.[54] For the purposes of our discussion here we shall accept that there is a sense in which belief cannot be willed into being.[55]

A central premise in the rejectionists' argument is that whereas belief is such that one *cannot* will one's belief into being, or not directly, collective

---

[52] If rejectionists constitute a collective, then they would seem to be a collective whose credo is that they have no credo—given that a credo is a matter of what is believed.

[53] (Gilbert 2002) discusses the issue of "aiming at truth" at pp. 51–9, and the issue about the will at pp. 59–64.

[54] (Hakli 2006).

[55] The extent to which this is true in the individual case has itself been a matter of some debate, a debate we shall not enter here.

belief* *can* be directly willed into being.[56] Following Gilbert, we have so far argued that collective beliefs* are not *always* willed into being—not by the group itself. The examples of the people on the train and the faculty members, which were offered in order to argue that collective belief* is not acceptance, both speak to this point. We now address the question: is it *possible* for a group to will its collective belief* into being, even if collective beliefs* are not always generated this way?

In discussion of this question Gilbert focused on an example akin to the second one in the last section, an example we develop a little further for present purposes. Fran and her partner Trudy explicitly adopt as their collective goal their collectively believing* that their future is bright.[57] Perhaps Fran says to Trudy "We need to believe[*] that our future is bright" and Trudy agrees. The setting of such a collective goal can, we have allowed, be seen as a case of a group's willing that it believe* something.

Gilbert observes that the setting of this collective goal—this instance of group willing—does not *immediately* produce the desired collective belief* of Fran and Trudy. A new joint commitment must be made, a joint commitment constitutive of the collective belief* in question. Thus, after a pause, Trudy might say, in a cheerful tone, "Our future is indeed bright!" and Fran concur, thus establishing their collective belief* that their future is bright. It seems, then, that the pertinent collective belief* may yet count as a belief, granted the rejectionists' assumption that beliefs cannot be willed into being.

Reflecting on Gilbert's discussion, Hakli disputes her judgment that the relevant collective belief* in this case is not the direct effect of the will of the group. He writes, "Granted that a new joint commitment must be made, nothing special is required for that."[58] He concludes that "there is no necessary or conceptual obstacle for the group to form a view according to its will."[59]

One might agree with the point about the lack of necessary or conceptual obstacles while wondering if that is sufficient for the requisite directness of willing. After all, there are many humdrum ways in which some kind of slippage might have occurred between the formation of the group's will to believe* and the formation of the collective belief* itself. For instance, the

---

[56] A typical case of willing a belief *indirectly* would be such as this: a husband wishing to believe his wife does not flirt with other men on social occasions deliberately turns away when a man approaches his wife on such an occasion. He thus deliberately precludes himself from confronting evidence contrary to his desired belief. No one disputes that people can will their beliefs into being indirectly in this way.

[57] (Gilbert 2002) notes that there may be something off-color about the adoption of precisely such a goal in both the collective and the individual case.

[58] (Hakli 2006, 296).   [59] (Hakli 2006).

conversation might have been interrupted, the parties thereby losing the opportunity to make the crucial joint commitment. Or one party might have rethought the matter and told the other that she is not sure, after all, if a belief that their future is bright is what is needed, thus stalling or possibly aborting the process of collective belief* formation. Or the parties might simply have lost interest in the whole business and failed to make the necessary final move.

One sympathetic to Hakli's position might respond that, in spite of this, it is relatively easy for a group to bring a collective belief* into being after resolving to do so. He might, indeed, aver that when Judy and Fran move from setting their collective goal to forming the desired collective belief* without a hitch, this is *direct enough* a connection between the group's will and the collective belief* to deny to it the name of belief—assuming, of course, that belief is such that it cannot be willed into being directly.

At this point we want to step back from the discussion of collective belief* and belief and note the following. Suppose that, when a collective belief* arises through a series of steps such as those involving Judy and Fran when they do proceed to form their desired collective belief*, it *has* been willed into being in such a way that it cannot be belief. Then the result of this and the last section taken together would be this: collective belief* is neither acceptance nor belief.

Further Methodological Observations

We shall not pursue further the debate between rejectionists and their opponents. Nor shall we attempt a final conclusion on that debate. Suffice it to say, here, that though the rejectionists' claim that collective belief* is not belief as they understand it may be sustainable, there is reason to reject their claim that collective belief* is acceptance as they understand that.

We shall focus on the following two observations. First, the disagreements within the debate over rejectionism are about categorization, rather than facts of the matter. They concern, more specifically, whether or not certain concepts of acceptance and belief apply in a particular context. Second, in the work of both Cohen, discussed earlier, and those who, by and large, follow him, the relevant articulations of the concepts of belief and acceptance derive from the individual case. The debate over rejectionism concerns the application of these concepts, so articulated, to the case of collective belief*, the details of which are agreed upon by all parties.

This brings us back to the methodological points we brought up in relation to Cohen's rejection of group beliefs, citing Plato's procedure in the *Republic*. These points are clearly pertinent to the debate over rejectionism, in relation both to the account of belief and to the account of acceptance at issue.

We now briefly develop this observation. In order to mark the fact that the basis for the relevant articulations of the concepts of acceptance and belief lies in the individual case, we shall in what follows refer not simply to belief and acceptance but rather to belief-i and acceptance-i.[60]

With some development, the points made in our earlier discussion suggest that though there is some interest in asking whether collective belief* is belief-i, or, rather, acceptance-i, this is not the most important question to be asked. Indeed, these points recommend an alternative approach to collective epistemology.

For the purposes of the following discussion we shall assume that collective belief* is the referent of everyday collective belief ascriptions. Our points apply to any relevantly similar phenomena that may be invoked as the referents of everyday collective belief ascriptions. We shall also assume for present purposes that belief-i and acceptance-i—belief and acceptance roughly as characterized by the rejectionists and others writing after Cohen—are the referents of everyday ascriptions of belief and acceptance to individual human beings.

As illustrated earlier, when we try to apply either the concept of belief-i or the concept of acceptance-i to the case of collective belief*, we run into difficulties. It is perfectly possible, indeed, that though collective belief* is rampant in groups, groups neither believe-i nor accept-i.

This might tempt us to reconsider the articulated concepts of belief-i and acceptance-i themselves, thinking that collective belief* needs to be accommodated by one or the other—in particular the former, given the way it is labeled in everyday life. So long as we are interested in individuals, however, these concepts and the distinction they mark, or something close to them, may be indispensable.

Conversely, we might be tempted to use the fact that it is hard to fit collective belief* under the concept of belief-i as evidence that it is not the referent of everyday collective belief ascriptions. Collective belief ascriptions could just be a *façon de parler* whose real target is some fact about the beliefs-i of

---

[60] In using the terms "belief-i" and " acceptance-i," we mean to indicate that they refer to belief and acceptance as understood on the basis of observations of individuals. Cf. the use of the phrase "individual belief" in Gilbert (2002).

individuals, in this way bringing the concept of belief-i into play. The problem here is that, as discussed earlier, there are arguments against both summative and, indeed, correlative accounts of the target of such ascriptions.[61]

We advocate a third perspective on the significance of the fact that collective belief* fails clearly to fit on either side of the distinction between belief-i and acceptance-i. As we have emphasized, the concepts of belief-i and acceptance-i, roughly following Cohen's work, were developed from considerations about individuals. But groups are not individuals, and it is unclear why we would expect concepts and distinctions designed to characterize the cognitive states of the latter to apply cleanly to the former, as the rejectionists, for instance, seem to do.[62]

The approach we advocate is to see the concepts of belief-i and acceptance-i, on the one hand, and collective belief*, on the other as belonging to two distinct inquiries. The concepts of belief-i, and acceptance-i, roughly following Cohen, are primarily concepts for individual epistemology. The concept of collective belief* is primarily a concept for collective epistemology. This being so one should not be surprised if collective belief* fails clearly to be belief-i, let alone acceptance-i. Indeed, though the relations between collective belief* and belief-i and acceptance-i are of some interest, the question "Is collective belief* belief-i or acceptance-i?" insofar as it assumes that collective belief* must be one of these, appears to be misplaced.

Generic Epistemology

Supposing that collective belief* is neither belief-i, nor acceptance-i, what is it? If we want a parallel label, we could reasonably call it belief-c. Here we are assuming, as before, that it is collective belief* to which everyday collective belief ascriptions refer.

The naturalness of this labeling suggests that our discussion should not end with the distinction between collective and individual epistemology. Even if we understand that these are separate inquiries, there will be important questions that straddle the two. For instance: What are the analogies and disanalogies between belief-i and belief-c? What, for that matter, are the analogies and

---

[61] For concordant remarks see (Tollefsen 2003, 401–4). For the term "correlative" see footnote 21 above.
[62] Cf. Gilbert (2002, 49) with special reference to the rejectionist use of an account of belief derived from the individual case.

disanalogies between acceptance-i and its opposite number, acceptance-c?[63] How can these analogies and disanalogies be explained?

Answers to such questions are likely to throw into better relief the cognitive characteristics of both individuals and groups.[64] From this perspective, then, there is considerable value in the debate over rejectionism, which has occasioned much consideration of analogies and disanalogies between belief-i and acceptance-i and belief-c.

The pursuit of such questions can be part of either collective or individual epistemology. It can also be part of a third inquiry, which may be labeled *generic epistemology*. The questions of generic epistemology will include such questions as: What—if anything—is common to belief-i and belief-c? What, for that matter, is common to belief *whatever it characterizes*, whether human individuals, groups of human individuals, animals perhaps, or other beings?

With reference to our discussion of Plato's methodology earlier in this essay, it may be noted that the author of the *Republic* does not attempt to formulate a general characterization of justice. His main target, as noted, is what we may now call justice-i. He works towards an account of that by a careful examination of justice-c. He does not, however, go further than these two accounts, or advance to a further inquiry, beyond both the theory of individual justice and the theory of political justice, an inquiry that might be referred to as generic justice theory. To use his own terms, he does not attempt to come to grips with the very *form* of justice, the *idea* of justice itself, justice as it pertains both to polities and to human beings.

Plato does not explain why he does not pursue a theory of justice in general. Whatever his reasons, and they may be good ones, it is not clear that epistemologists should follow his lead. There may well be merit in pursuing generic epistemology.[65] At least part of the basis for this would presumably be the combined results of individual epistemology on the one hand and collective epistemology on the other.

In that case there are surely some good pointers already in the literature, features of both belief-i and belief-c. For instance, the idea of belief "aiming at truth," when suitably articulated, could be a central characteristic of belief in general, something possessed by both individual and collective believers.[66] We must leave any extended forays into generic epistemology for other occasions.

---

[63] See (Gilbert 2002; Tollefsen 2003) on acceptance when "said of" groups.
[64] See (Tollefsen 2003; Hakli 2006).   [65] (Gilbert 2002, esp. 47–9).
[66] See (Gilbert 2002) on how various ideas, from individual epistemology, of belief as having the aim of truth fit collective belief*.

Concluding Summary

We first distinguished between the projects of individual and collective epistemology. The former is concerned with the cognitive states of individual human beings, and the latter with the cognitive states of collectives. We then argued that those engaged in one of these projects should not rely on accounts and distinctions developed specifically for the other, though they may find much of interest in the results obtained by those engaged in the other project.

As we explained, this methodological point has not generally been respected by researchers in collective epistemology. The opposite methodology is exemplified in influential work by L. Jonathan Cohen, in which he denies that groups have beliefs, as opposed to acceptances, as he understands these states. It is exemplified further by a recent debate in which revised versions of Cohen's distinction have been brought into play. This is the debate between "rejectionists" and their opponents with respect to whether or not the phenomenon Margaret Gilbert has argued to be the referent of standard everyday ascriptions of collective belief is belief—or acceptance.

The debate over rejectionism has reached something of a stalemate. After reviewing some of its central features, we argued that though important points have been made on both sides, there is reason to think that the debate itself is misguided. For, although the collective case is at issue, the debate operates with accounts and distinctions tailored specifically to the case of the individual. This is surely the wrong procedure. Though individual and collective epistemology will doubtless have related results, neither one should rely on accounts and distinctions tailored specifically for the other. Rather, those working on either one of these projects should develop concepts of belief and acceptance appropriate to the particular project at hand, without being constrained by the results of the other, however helpful these results may be from a heuristic point of view.

With respect to collective epistemology, then, supposing for the sake of argument that Gilbert's account of collective belief is correct, the collective epistemologist needs primarily to be concerned with the particular features of collective belief*—its relation to truth, the will, and so on. The same goes, *mutatis mutandis*, for whatever account of collective belief the collective epistemologist prefers.

In concluding, we briefly argued for the interest of generic epistemology. This is an inquiry that, while paying attention to the results of both individual and collective epistemology, can be seen as a subject in its own right.[67]

---

[67] Margaret Gilbert would like to thank all of those who have taken account of her work on collective belief and contributed to the discussion of it both formally and informally, including the

Bibliography

Bouvier, Alban. 2004. "Individual Beliefs and Collective Beliefs in Sciences and Philosophy: The Plural Subject and the Polyphonic Subject Accounts Case Studies." *Philosophy of the Social Sciences* 34 (3) (September 1): 382–407.

Clark, Austen. 1994. "Beliefs and Desires Incorporated." *The Journal of Philosophy* 91 (8) (August 1): 404–25.

Cohen, L. Jonathan. 1989. "Belief and Acceptance." *Mind* 98 (391) (July 1): 367–89.

Cohen, L. Jonathan. 1995. *An Essay on Belief and Acceptance.* Oxford: Clarendon Press.

Engel, Pascal. 2000. *Believing and Accepting.* Dordrecht; Boston: Kluwer Academic.

Gilbert, Margaret. 1987. "Modelling Collective Belief." *Synthese* 73 (1) (October 1): 185–204.

Gilbert, Margaret. 1989. *On Social Facts.* Princeton: Princeton University Press.

Gilbert, Margaret. 1996. *Living Together.* Lanham; Boulder; New York [etc.]: Rowman & Littlefield Publishers.

Gilbert, Margaret. 2001. "Collective Remorse." In *War Crimes and Collective Wrongdoing: A Reader,* edited by A. Jokic Maiden. Rochester, NY: Blackwell Publishing.

Gilbert, Margaret. 2002. "Belief and Acceptance as Features of Groups." *Protosociology: An International Journal of Interdisciplinary Research* 16: 35–69.

Gilbert, Margaret. 2004. "Collective Epistemology." *Episteme* 1 (02): 95–107.

Gilbert, Margaret. 2006. *A Theory of Political Obligation: Membership, Commitment, and the Bonds of Society.* New York: Oxford University Press.

Gilbert, Margaret. 2013a. *Joint Commitment: How We Make the Social World.* New York: Oxford University Press.

Gilbert, Margaret. 2013b. "Commitment." In *International Encyclopedia of Ethics.* Wiley-Blackwell Publishing Ltd.

Gilbert, Margaret. 2014. "How We Feel: Understanding Everyday Collective Emotion Ascriptions." In *Collective Emotions,* edited by Mikko Salmela and Christian van Sheve. Oxford: Oxford University Press.

Gilbert, Margaret, and Maura Priest. 2013. "Conversation and Collective Belief." In *Perspectives on Pragmatics and Philosophy,* edited by Alessandro Capone,

rejectionists. Thanks also to Aaron James for discussion of aspects of the present paper. Daniel Pilchman would like to thank Amanda Trefethen for helpful conversation, and to personally thank Alban Bouvier for introducing him to the rejectionist debate in a graduate seminar on social epistemology during the 2008–9 academic year at UC Santa Cruz. Both of us would like to thank Alban Bouvier, Raul Hakli, Jennifer Lackey, Daniel Siakel, K. Brad Wray, and an anonymous referee, for comments on a late draft, and Boaz Miller for related discussion. We have done our best to respond to all of the comments while keeping within the time and space available.

Lo Piparo, and Marco Carapezza. Perspectives on Pragmatics and Philosophy 1. Cham: Springer.

Goldman, Alvin I. 1999. *Knowledge in a Social World*. Oxford; New York: Clarendon Press; Oxford University Press.

Hakli, Raul. 2006. "Group Beliefs and the Distinction Between Belief and Acceptance." *Cognitive Systems Research* 7 (2–3) (June): 286–97.

Lewis, David K. 1969. *Convention: A Philosophical Study*. Oxford: Blackwell.

Mathiesen, Kay. 2006. "The Epistemic Features of Group Belief." *Episteme* 2 (03): 161–75.

Mathiesen, Kay. 2007. "Introduction to Special Issue of Social Epistemology on'Collective Knowledge and Collective Knowers'." *Social Epistemology* 21 (3): 209–16.

Meijers, A. W. M. 1999. "Believing and Accepting as a Group." In *Belief, Cognition and the Will* Tilburg: Tilburg University Press.

Pettit, Philip. 2010. "Groups with Minds of Their Own." In *Social Epistemology: Essential Readings*. Alvin Goldman and Dennis Whitcomb, eds. New York: Oxford University Press.

Plato, trans. G. M. A Grube, and C. D. C Reeve. 1992. *Republic*. Indianapolis: Hackett Pub. Co.

Priest, Maura. (ms). "Doxastic Voluntarism: From the Collective to the Individual."

Quinton, Anthony. 1975. "Social Objects." *Proceedings of the Aristotelian Society* 76 (January 1): 1–27.

Schmitt, Frederick F. 1994. "The Justification of Group Beliefs." In *Socializing Epistemology*, edited by F. F. Schmitt. Lanham, MD: Rowman & Littlefield Publ. Inc.

Stevenson, Leslie. 2002. "Six Levels of Mentality." *Philosophical Explorations* 5 (2): 105–24.

Tollefsen, Deborah. 2002. "Organizations as True Believers." *Journal of Social Philosophy* 33 (3): 395–410.

Tollefsen, Deborah. 2003. "Rejecting Rejectionism." *Protosociology* 18–19: 389–405.

Tuomela, Raimo. 1992. "Group Beliefs." *Synthese* 91 (3) (June 1): 285–318.

Tuomela, Raimo. 2000. "Belief versus Acceptance." *Philosophical Explorations* 3 (2): 122–37.

Wray, K. Brad. 2001. "Collective Belief and Acceptance." *Synthese* 129 (3) (December 1): 319–33.

Wray, K. Brad. 2003. "What Really Divides Gilbert and the Rejectionists." *Protosociology* 18–19: 363–76.

5

Collective Belief, Kuhn, and the String Theory Community

1. Introduction

Authoritative scientific assertions often take the form of an ascription of belief to a particular population of scientists.[1] For instance, one regularly hears or reads statements such as, "Physicists believe that elementary particles obey the laws of quantum mechanics," or "Biologists think the chimpanzee and bonobo share a recent common ancestor." A chemist might say, speaking of his colleagues, "We believe that there may be additional undiscovered elements." Let us refer to these statements as assertions of *scientific consensus*.

Many philosophers take understanding the development of and (especially) changes in scientific consensus to be essential to understanding science. Despite their ubiquity, however, statements of the above form may appear puzzling. For it is natural to construe them as ascribing beliefs not to individual scientists, *seriatim*, but rather to collections or communities of scientists—to physicists, for instance, as a group. One may wonder what a *group*'s belief can amount to.

Evidently, if one wants to understand the nature of scientific consensus, and by extension, change in scientific consensus, one would do well initially to explore what is intended when one ascribes a belief to a group. Several proposals have been made on this score in the literature.

According to one immediate and widely accepted suggestion a group of scientists, for instance, is rightly said to hold a given belief about a relevant scientific topic just in case all or nearly all members of the group hold the belief (cf. Quinton [1975–6, 17]). And perhaps in some cases, this or

[1] This chapter was co-authored with physicist and philosopher of science James Owen Weatherall, the other half of the authorial "we" of the text. Section 4, "The Rise of Strings," was written by Weatherall. For present purposes I have made some minor revisions to the original paper that do not affect the sense. The authors are grateful to Jeff Barrett, Michael Brady, Miranda Fricker, Cailin O'Connor, and K. Brad Wray for helpful comments on various drafts, and to audiences at UC Irvine and Objectivity 2010 to which an earlier draft was presented.

Life in Groups: How We Think, Feel, and Act Together. Margaret Gilbert, Oxford University Press. © Margaret Gilbert 2023.
DOI: 10.1093/oso/9780192847157.003.0006

something very like it *is* what is meant when one says that a group has a belief. But there is also a radically distinct possibility.

In her writings on the subject one of us (Gilbert) has pointed out that in standard cases of ordinary usage, when one ascribes a belief to a group, one seems not to be asserting that all or most of the members of the group hold the belief. Indeed, it often seems that group beliefs are not a matter of the beliefs of the members of the group at all—that is, it is neither necessary nor sufficient for a group to a hold a belief that all or most of its members hold that belief. The account of group belief that Gilbert has developed over the last several decades (see e.g. Gilbert [1987], [1989], and [2002]) accords with this observation.

It is now standard to call the first sort of account of group beliefs a "summative" account. Gilbert's, in contrast, is a "collective" account.

Gilbert's account was intended to capture a central intuitive meaning of assertions of the general form "G believes that p," where G is some group of people. On this account, members of groups that hold beliefs in this collective sense have certain obligations regarding the belief. And it is the ground of these obligations and not necessarily the beliefs of the members of the group that determine whether a group has a belief.[2]

Suppose now that assertions of scientific consensus are accurate ascriptions of group beliefs to scientific communities, in the collective sense of group belief described by Gilbert. In that case members of a scientific community holding a consensus have the obligations associated with being party to a group belief.[3] In her (2000a), Gilbert suggests that this would have consequences for the conditions under which scientific change can occur. In particular, she argues that the obligations associated with a group belief on her account can act as barriers both to the introduction of new ideas by members of the group and to the fair evaluation of ideas proposed by experts outside the group.[4] This suggests a way of explaining some of historian of science

[2] The ground of the obligations is what Gilbert refers to as "joint commitment." See the next section.
[3] Wray (2001) and others have argued that one should not think of the phenomenon Gilbert describes as group "belief," but rather as group "acceptance," because the phenomenon differs in certain ways from belief as traditionally understood. We will not address the belief/acceptance worry here (for more on this, see Gilbert [2002] and Gilbert and Pilchman [2014] [chapter 4, this volume]). The important point for the present paper will be that members of certain scientific communities act as though there is a *joint commitment* with a particular content in place. Whether this joint commitment is better referred to as constituting a case of belief or, rather, acceptance has no direct bearing; for convenience, we will continue to refer to the phenomenon in question as group belief.
[4] Much of the literature on collective epistemology has focused on group *knowledge*, rather than group *belief*. (For examples, see Longino [1990], Kitcher [1994], Knorr-Cetina [1999], Giere and Moffatt [2003], Mathiesen [2006], Wray [2007], Rolin [2008, 2010], and Fagan [2011].) See also Schmitt (1994). This debate, however, is orthogonal to the present discussion, as the question we are addressing here is

Thomas Kuhn's best-known observations on scientific change, in particular his focus on the way "normal science" proceeds, a point we develop in what follows.[5]

This paper focuses on some commentary, by contemporary physicist Lee Smolin, on certain "sociological" features of a particular high-profile branch of contemporary physics known as string theory, and the way in which his observations can be explained in Gilbertian terms, which are in turn supported by these observations. It thus presents a particular case study in relation both to Kuhn's and to Gilbert's work—with an emphasis on the latter.

The commentary we discuss arises in connection with Smolin's (2006) criticism of string theory. In particular, Smolin argues that string theory has failed to provide an adequate or compelling account of nature, and yet it continues to have a dominant role in theoretical physics (or at least, in high-energy physics, which is concerned with elementary particles). As a result, high-energy physics has failed to make significant progress in the last thirty years.

In part, Smolin claims, the continued interest in string theory despite the problems he identifies can be explained by appealing to sociological factors. He goes on to list "seven unusual aspects of the string theory community" (284) that, on his view, have contributed to the recent failure of high-energy theory.

For our purposes here, we take no stand on whether Smolin's broader critique has merit, or whether string theory is a fruitful or promising research program. Rather, we focus on the sociological considerations Smolin raises. Our purpose is to explore the relationship between the features one would expect of a group holding a belief on Gilbert's account and the features of the string theory community as described by Smolin.[6]

We argue that the features that Smolin ascribes to the string theory community are precisely what one would expect if Gilbert's suggestion that such

---

not whether a scientific community has knowledge, but rather whether certain features of one such community are well explained by the hypothesis that the community has a group belief with its attendant obligations. Such group belief may, of course, be a central component in group knowledge, at least on a collective construal; that is a topic on which we do not attempt to pronounce here.

[5] Kuhn (1962). Gilbert had privately noted this connection some while back without planning to write about it. The present discussion was prompted by Miranda Fricker, commenting on a draft of this paper. For an earlier, brief discussion of Gilbert's ideas in relation to Kuhnian normal science, see Bird (2010).

[6] As Gilbert points out in her (2000a), whether and to what extent scientific communities hold group beliefs is ultimately an empirical question. In this regard, the present paper can be understood as a study in the vein of Beatty (2006) and, especially, Bouvier (2004), which seek to evaluate whether real scientific communities are well-described as groups with group beliefs by studying these communities.

communities hold group beliefs on her account is correct.[7] In other words, *if* Smolin's picture of the sociology of string theory is accurate—something we assume for the sake of our discussion here—then the string theory community has properties that are very well explained on Gilbert's account of group belief, applied to the string theory community with the assumption that the community holds relevant group beliefs.

Gilbert's account offers, in particular, an effective explanation of why the string theory community may appear to act *irrationally* with regard to certain countervailing evidence.[8,9] It is here that the connection to Kuhn arises. We will suggest that the apparent irrationality of the string theory community, as described by Smolin, is symptomatic of the conservatism Kuhn attributes to normal science.

At the end of the paper, we will address an apparent conflict that arises between our argument here and Smolin's characterization of his seven features, related to the fact that he explicitly characterizes the features as *unusual*, whereas if Gilbert's account is correct, one should expect such features to be exhibited by *any* group holding a belief—including any scientific community holding a consensus view. We will argue that these features seem unusual to Smolin not because they are actually unusual, but because he occupies an unusual position from which to observe them.

We should note that the goal of this paper is not to evaluate or dispute Smolin's picture of the string theory community. Likewise, we will not directly

[7] Wray (2007) has argued that *research teams* can have group beliefs (or rather, group acceptances—see footnote 2), but that *communities of scientists associated with research fields* (such as the community of astrophysicists or of biologists) and *the community of scientists* as a whole cannot. (For a compelling reply, see Rolin [2008].) It is not clear where string theorists fit into Wray's categorization of groups of scientists—surely string theorists are not systematically organized as a research team, and yet they are only a sub-group of high-energy physicists. In any case, the present claim is that one does well to understand string theorists as the kind of community that not only *can* but *does* have group beliefs. One may well take this as an argument against Wray's view that only research teams can have group beliefs. We shall not, however, attempt to engage with the specifics of Wray's discussion here.

[8] Wray (2001) and Mathiesen (2006) have argued that groups holding group beliefs on Gilbert's account may not be epistemically rational, in the sense that group beliefs may not be updated appropriately in light of new evidence. This is taken to be a criticism of Gilbert's view. We will not address this criticism in any detail in the present work, though we will note that if, in fact, groups holding group belief tend not to account for evidence in an epistemically responsible way, then it is a *virtue* of Gilbert's account that it appears to predict this behavior. (For another response to Wray and Mathiesen, see Rolin [2010].)

[9] Gilbert (2000a) argues that postulating that certain scientific communities hold group beliefs is apt to explain certain features of scientific communities and theory change related to resistance to heterodoxy. This argument has been criticized by a number of authors, including Wray (2001, 2007), Rolin (2008), and Fagan (2011), on the grounds that it is not clear how generic the features Gilbert mentions are, and thus that it is not clear that such features stand in need of explanation. For present purposes, one can set this general discussion aside and focus on the *specific* explanatory question presented by Smolin's work, namely, does Gilbert's account provide a compelling explanation of the striking features of the string theory community? If so, then it seems that there is a potentially interesting question to be explored concerning the role of group belief in at least some scientific communities.

evaluate Gilbert's account of group belief. Any evaluative content with regard to Gilbert will be implicit in how effectively her theory accounts for the string theory community, at least as described by Smolin. Similarly, insofar as Smolin's perceptions of the string theory community accord with Gilbert's collective account of group belief, which was arrived at independently by reflection on everyday thought, talk, and behavior in multiple domains, the latter has some tendency to confirm the accuracy of the former.

The remainder of this chapter is organized as follows. We begin with a brief presentation of Gilbert's theory of social groups and group belief, along with its connection to scientific consensus and change, as described in her (2000a). We then link her theories to Kuhn's observations on scientific change. Next, we give a brief history and description of string theory, explaining how it has now come to have a dominant role in the broader high-energy physics community. Finally, we discuss the seven points of Smolin's sociological critique of string theory in light of Gilbert's account of group belief, arguing that the striking features of string theory Smolin describes are well explained by the hypotheses that group beliefs on Gilbert's account are at issue and that the string theory community holds relevant group beliefs.

2. Gilbert on Collective Belief and Scientific Change

Gilbert's account of group belief offers an interpretation of such statements as, "The seminar believes that the second article is less convincing than the first"; "The European Union believes that the euro will rebound in light of the economic indicators released today"; or "Ben and AJ believe Jim is coming, even though he's already a few minutes late." In each of these sentences, a belief is ascribed to the subject. These subjects are not individual human beings, but rather something that is made up of human beings. One might call them "groups of people," or just "groups," to capture that they refer to something of which several (or many) people are members. The problem, then, is to understand what such "group belief" amounts to.

Gilbert's account of group belief can be expressed as follows.

A group G believes that p if and only if the members of G are *jointly committed* to believing that p as a body.[10]

---

[10] For more on Gilbert's account see e.g. Gilbert (1987, 1989), her earliest discussions, and Gilbert (2000a, 2004).

When this condition obtains (and only then), each member of G may truly say, "We believe that p," where "we" is intended with respect to G.

The phrase "as a body" is not meant to be sacrosanct. "As a unit" or "as one" would do just as well. The idea the phrase is meant to encapsulate is that the object of the commitment, the thing being committed to, is the parties' talking and acting as would the representatives of *a single believer* of the proposition in question.

This analysis relies on the technical concept of "joint commitment." We will not define this term outright; instead, we will explain it by describing some central features of a joint commitment.[11]

When two or more people are jointly committed in some way, they are in a particular normative situation—they are committed *as one*—as the result of a specific process that involves them all. As to that process, in the basic case, on which we focus here, ach of the people in question has expressed his or her personal readiness for the commitment in question to be in place, in conditions of common knowledge.[12] Each is then committed to appropriate action through the commitment of them all. Thus, in the case of a group belief that p, each member of G has expressed his or her willingness together with the others to commit them all to emulating a single believer of p by virtue of their combined utterances and actions, and it is common knowledge among the members of G that this is the case.

It is important to emphasize that in order for the parties to be jointly committed in this way, it is neither necessary nor sufficient for each member of G to make what Gilbert refers to as a *personal* commitment to do his or her part in emulating, in conjunction with the others, a single believer of some proposition. A personal commitment in Gilbert's sense would be engaged by Jim's decision to work late tonight, for instance. A joint commitment is not composed of personal commitments, which are the unilateral product of the committed person's will and unilaterally rescindable by that person.

In order that a joint commitment be rescinded, in a basic case, the parties must concur in its rescission. If an individual fails to conform to a joint commitment, then, absent certain background understandings, she offends against all of the other parties to the joint commitment.

---

[11] For a longer but still compact general introduction to the notion see Gilbert (2013, Introduction) and for further details see Gilbert (2013, ch. 2); see also the Introduction, this volume.

[12] "Common knowledge" is usually construed as a technical term in philosophy and the technical sense we have in mind is akin to that in Lewis (1969). However, for the current purposes, the everyday concept is sufficient. We will not later make any use of a specific formulation of common knowledge. For the difference between basic and non-basic, or authority-involving cases, of joint commitment see e.g. the Introduction, this volume.

Amplification of this last point is important for a full understanding of the concepts of joint commitment and *collective belief*, that is, group belief on Gilbert's account of it.[13] The offense just referred to is a matter of violating one's obligations to the other parties, who have rights to one's conformity to the joint commitment. These obligations are a function of the joint commitment itself: a joint commitment obligates each party *to every other party* to conform to it, at the same time endowing them with rights to such conformity.[14]

Once party to a joint commitment, a person is required to act in accordance with the commitment under penalty of rebuke from the other members of the group. Should someone indicate that he is about to fail to accord with the commitment, the other parties have the standing to demand that he conform after all.[15]

The notions of "rebuke" and "demand" here are strong ones. As just indicated, in order to rebuke someone or demand some action of him, in the relevant senses, one must have a certain standing or authority. Thus it is not the case that everyone who finds one's action distasteful is in a position to rebuke one for it, or that everyone who thinks one ought to perform some action can demand that action of one.

Further, there is a sharp distinction between having the standing to demand a certain action of another and being justified in making that demand. The same thing holds for rebukes. Sometimes one will have the standing to make a demand, but will be unjustified, all things considered, in making it. Perhaps the psychological makeup of the potential addressee makes that inadvisable, for instance. Or perhaps the otherwise acceptable action one has the standing to demand is not acceptable, all things considered, in the circumstances. In that case, presumably, one will not be justified in demanding that action. Again, one might lack the standing to make a certain demand, though, if one had that standing, one would be fully justified in exercising it. Finally, one may be justified in pressuring someone to do something or in letting them know that one thinks poorly of their doing it, without having the standing to demand that they do it or the standing to rebuke them for doing it.

---

[13] Henceforth we use the phrase "collective belief" as short for "group belief on Gilbert's account of it."

[14] For discussion of the relationship of joint commitment and directed obligation see Gilbert (2012) [Chapter 13, this volume] and elsewhere.

[15] Gilbert sees the following as "equivalents" in roughly the sense of the rights theorist Wesley Hohfeld: (1) A has a right against B to B's doing φ, (2) B is obligated to A to do φ; (3) A has the standing to demand that B φ (before the time for A's appropriately φ-ing has passed); (4) A has the standing to rebuke B for not φ-ing. See e.g. Gilbert (2012) [chapter 13, this volume].

In the particular case of a collective belief, these consequences of joint commitment mean that if an individual is party to a collective belief and if she speaks in a way that contradicts the belief (without significantly qualifying her statement), then she has offended against the other members of the group.[16] In other terms, she has failed to fulfill obligations she has to them, and they have the standing to rebuke her for this failure. To see how this works in a particular case, imagine that the parents of a teenager disagree about when the teen's curfew should be. The mother believes it should be 9 p.m., whereas the father says 11 p.m. They compromise, and later tell the teen, "We think you should be home by 10." If the father then says, "Actually, 11 is fine," the mother would rightly feel affronted. In addition to any other reactions she may have when or after their son is present, she may well rebuke the father for speaking as he did, and he will understand that she has the standing to do so.

According to Gilbert, if a certain group of people holds a given collective belief, that suffices for them to be a social group. A group of people is a *social group* for Gilbert just in case the members are jointly committed in some way. In that case, she argues, each member appropriately thinks of the group as "we" or "us" where this is not short for "we all," "each of us," and so on. She refers to social groups of this sort as "plural subjects". Two or more people constitute a plural subject of φ-ing, where φ-ing is the activity/belief/etc. about which they have a joint commitment.

Even though "social group" is a technical term here, it is intended to capture the same content as would the words interpreted informally, at least in a certain central sense.[17] Intuitively, the idea is that a collection of people becomes a social group when they openly decide to "join forces" in a coordinated action, say. Thus suppose Wolfgang comes across Alice struggling up a hill with her groceries. Wolfgang stops and offers to help; Alice accepts. Wolfgang takes a few of Alice's bags, and then the pair walk up the hill together. Now Alice and Wolfgang are jointly committed to espousing as a body the goal of carrying Alice's groceries up the hill. Suppose a few minutes pass and Alice sees her friend Jacques. Jacques stops and asks what is going on, to which Alice can justly reply, "*We* are carrying my groceries home." They are sharing the action in a way that they would not be if they both happened to be carrying groceries up the same hill at the same time. It is for this reason

---

[16] The kind of qualification at issue includes in particular one's using such a preliminary as "Personally, I think…" that makes it clear that one is about to express one's personal belief as opposed to the collective's belief. See e.g. Gilbert (2000a).

[17] See e.g. Gilbert (1989, ch. 4); also the Introduction, this volume, "A Note on Groups."

they count as a social group. Collective belief, or rather, the joint commitment to believe that p as a body, then, is just one example of the kind of joint commitment necessary and sufficient for social group formation.

As noted above, it is helpful to distinguish Gilbert's position from another possible view that is common in the philosophical literature. Gilbert's account of group belief is not "summative," in that Gilbert does not take statements of the form "G believes that X," where G is a group, to mean "all or most of the members of G believe that X," or any of the possible variations on that theme. Indeed, it is neither necessary nor sufficient on Gilbert's view for most (or even any—recall the curfew example) of the people in G to *personally* believe that X. A group can believe a proposition even if few or none of its members believe it, so long as the members are jointly committed in the right way.

It is of particular importance for what will follow that this joint commitment to believe that p as a body does not entail a commitment on behalf of each member personally to believe that p, or even personally to act as though he believes that p. Rather, the members of the group are to act as separate *mouthpieces* of the group, expressing the belief in that role in any setting in which they are acting in their capacity as group members. Conversely, if every member of a group happens to believe something, it does not follow that they believe it as a group, as it is possible that they have not yet jointly committed to believe it as a body.

As observed above, if Gilbert's analysis of sentences of the general type in question is correct, it should apply equally well to assertions of scientific consensus understood as ascriptions of belief to the relevant group. One can thus construe scientific consensus as a matter of collective belief. Scientific change, then, which amounts to moving from one consensus to another (at least according to a prominent vein in the history and philosophy of science), can be thought of as collective belief revision.

Before asking whether the features Smolin attributes to the string theory community are well explained by the suggestion that the community has one or more collective belief, it is worth pointing out some consequences that a consensus qua collective belief would have for a scientific community, on Gilbert's account. The most important of these all follow from the fact that the existence of a scientific consensus would imply that a scientific community is a social group with a joint commitment, which in turn implies that members of the community have obligations to behave in certain ways. In particular, the members of the community are obligated to one another to act as mouthpieces of the group with respect to the consensus, or risk rebuke from other members of the community.

Expressing a contrary view—bucking the consensus—is an offense against the other members of the community and threatens to put the contrarian outside the bounds of the social group.[18] So irrespective of their personal beliefs, there are pressures on individual scientists to speak in certain ways. Moreover, insofar as individuals are psychologically disposed to avoid cognitive dissonance, the obligation to speak in certain ways can affect one's personal beliefs so as to bring them into line with the consensus, further suppressing dissent from within the group.

Finally, if scientific consensus is a set of collective beliefs, then effecting scientific change is not necessarily a matter of convincing a majority of individual scientists that a new view is correct. Instead, it is necessary to get the members of the community to jointly commit to believing, as a body, a new proposition. That is a particularly arduous undertaking in that it requires one or more individual scientists at least temporarily to risk rebuke from their colleagues as they attempt to build public support for the new view, expressing support for that view in the face of a contrary consensus.

Considerations of cognitive dissonance and potentially conflicting commitments may have another consequence as well, regarding how scientists, both individually and collectively, deal with evidence for propositions that conflict with their consensus. Bringing up such evidence will itself have costs, in the form of possible professional rebuke, akin to those associated with outright denial of the consensus.

In some cases, these costs may prevent new results from being submitted by individual scientists or research teams to scientific peers for consideration, or from being selected by relevant individuals or committees for presentation to scientific peers.[19] In others, individual scientists or research teams may avoid pursuing potentially transformative research in the first place.

Even when evidence against a consensus is found by an individual scientist, one might expect it to be ignored, suppressed, or explained away by its discoverer, since such evidence would force a psychologically unsustainable conflict between the scientist's commitment to act in a certain way and his (or her) beliefs concerning the epistemic warrant for those actions. In the case of evidence contrary to a consensus that is made public, the scientific community

---

[18] A qualified expression such as "Personally, I have my doubts about the theory" may avoid outright default on an obligation, but it is likely to make one stand out as a potentially unreliable group member. See Gilbert (1987, 2000).

[19] As may have happened in the case of the initial proposal of a bacterial theory of ulcers—now well entrenched. This was one of very few papers rejected for a gastroenterology conference when the received view was that ulcers were caused by other, including dietary, factors. See Gilbert (2000a) citing Thagard (1999), then in ms. form, which to some extent inspired it.

may also ignore, suppress, or explain it away. For instance, it may be collectively affirmed that a crucial experiment cannot have been properly done, or it may be assumed that facts that are not at odds with the consensus can explain it, however implausible such an assumption really is. For these reasons, scientific communities may be expected to hold certain beliefs in the face of considerable conflicting evidence, to the point of being, or at least appearing, irrationally dogmatic or epistemically irresponsible.

3. Kuhnian Paradigms and Gilbertian Collective Beliefs

Gilbert's account of scientific consensus and change can be brought to bear on what are sometimes called "two-process" views of scientific change, including the view developed and defended by Kuhn (1962).[20] On Kuhn's picture, scientific change (at least in "mature" sciences) occurs in two distinct modes.

One mode, which Kuhn calls "normal science," is characterized by the broad acceptance of a "paradigm." A paradigm, meanwhile, consists in (at least) a collection of theoretical commitments, acceptable research methods, and recognized problems of pressing interest. When working within a paradigm, scientists may apply their accepted methods to make incremental progress on the problems recognized by the community. This is change *within* a paradigm.

The other mode, meanwhile, which Kuhn calls "revolutionary science," consists in change *between* paradigms. That is, during revolutionary science, scientists reject a previously accepted paradigm and adopt a new collection of theoretical commitments, research methods, and important problems.

The connection to Gilbert's proposal can be seen by observing that the theoretical and methodological commitments associated with a paradigm may best be understood as a set of foundational collective beliefs of the community of scientists working within the paradigm.[21] In other terms, the collective beliefs in question create the overarching framework within which the work

---

[20] The terminology of "one-process" and "two-process" views is due to Godfrey-Smith (2003). Aside from Kuhn, one might recognize Carnap (1956), Lakatos (1970), Laudan (1977), and Friedman (2001) as defending two-process views. Much of what is said here relating to Kuhn and Gilbert could be extended to relate Gilbert's proposal with these other views.

[21] In a more nuanced treatment one would most likely bring in phenomena other than group beliefs as Gilbert construes these, phenomena such as the joint acceptance of certain methodological rules or conventions, each of which can be construed in terms of joint commitment. (On the latter see Gilbert [1989, ch. 6; 2013, ch. 9].) Doubtless, however, beliefs of one kind or another play a central role in any Kuhnian paradigm and, for present purposes, we write as if all of its elements are matters of belief.

of this community is conducted. Revolutionary change, then, may best be conceived as a variety of collective belief revision, consisting in the rejection of a prior joint commitment with respect to one or more core propositions associated with a paradigm, and the institution of at least one new joint commitment that conflicts with these core propositions.

This way of thinking about Kuhn's views offers an explanation of one of the most striking and controversial features of normal science as he characterizes it. Specifically, Kuhn argues that during periods of normal science, "anomalies," which are theoretical or experimental discoveries that are apparently incompatible with the central tenets of a paradigm, are either not recognized or ignored. In other words, during normal science, researchers seem to focus on evidence that appears to confirm the beliefs associated with the paradigm, and to disregard contrary evidence. Given that on many views of evidence, high-quality contrary evidence should be taken to be of especially high value, this tendency to ignore contrary evidence may seem (at least) strange, and perhaps irrational.

Note, however, that if a paradigm is a collection of foundational collective beliefs of a scientific community, this attitude towards conflicting evidence should be expected. As discussed earlier, some degree of resistance to contrary evidence is predictable given the nature of the joint commitment constitutive of any collective belief whatsoever. That is so both for individual members or sub-communities of a given scientific community and for the community as a whole.

Given the foundational nature of the beliefs constitutive of a paradigm, one would expect an even greater tendency to resist contrary evidence than is present in every case of collective belief. Such resistance would be evident in, for example, the particular harshness of the rebukes meted out should one challenge these core collective beliefs. At the extreme, a given member of the community may be judged to have removed himself from the community—to have excommunicated himself. After all, acceptance of a challenge to a given foundational belief is apt to bring down the whole edifice of beliefs within which this community has been working—perhaps for a very long time.

In sum, the apparent conservatism that Kuhn attributes to scientific communities may be explained by the general nature of scientific consensus understood as collective belief. This conservatism would be amplified given the centrality of the beliefs in question.

One might push this idea still further. Kuhn seems to suggest that despite the apparent failures of rationality associated with ignoring or suppressing contrary evidence, the epistemological features of normal science provide a partial explanation of the *success* of science.[22] The idea, here, is that science is successful in part because of a distinctive kind of focused, collaborative research. And this sort of collaborative research is enabled by the existence of a paradigm insofar as a paradigm provides a stable shared agenda and collection of methods for realizing that agenda. The resistance of a scientific community to accepting changes in the paradigm thus provides a mechanism for preserving this collaboration.

Gilbert's account of group belief suggests a way to understand this mechanism. Indeed, it suggests a way of understanding any relatively long-term collaborative process.

Suppose one accepts that science, at least as understood in the modern period, is an essentially collaborative activity of relatively long duration, and that any such collaboration requires a framework of beliefs, concerning, at least, the nature and viability of its goals and the best way to achieve them. If these beliefs are conceived as group beliefs in Gilbert's sense, then they will be constituted by an appropriate set of joint commitments. As we have discussed, such joint commitments, once established, are apt to provoke resistance against anyone who is inclined to push against them. Thus, the resistance to change on which Kuhn focused need not be conceived as a special feature of scientific communities. Instead, these may be seen as characteristic features of *any* long-term collaborative activity. The participants can be expected to resist change with respect to the framework of collective beliefs that help to define its goals and the means to be adopted to achieve them—its methods, if you will.

In the case of a long-standing scientific discipline, of course, there will be a special corpus of collective beliefs that represent not only the approved aims and methods of the enterprise, but an increasingly sophisticated body of theory, supported where possible with accredited empirical results, involving a host of linkages between foundational propositions and others. The collaborative enterprise that is science in its various branches is, then, of particular interest to the collective epistemologist. The collective beliefs of a mature science go far beyond those that concern a set of goals and methods, or that arise incidentally in the course of pursuit of a collective goal. They involve a

---

[22] Here we are largely setting aside the question of what it means to say that science is successful—that is, whether the success of science should be measured by the empirical adequacy of scientific theories, the truth of those theories, their explanatory power, etc. Kuhn's own notion of the success of science was deeply entwined with his notion of normal science as "puzzle solving." Roughly, Kuhn argued that science is very successful at solving the puzzles deemed to be important within a paradigm, and that the features of normal science described explained this sort of success. Our point here is merely that Kuhn gave reasons to believe that the conservatism of normal science may not be the impediment to the success of science that it would appear to be.

multiplicity of highly articulated, closely interwoven, and mutually sustaining collective beliefs about the world.

Indeed, the point of the enterprise, prescinding from various epistemic cautions, is that those beliefs be true. Hence conservatism with respect to scientific paradigms, in particular, has its problematic side. Though it helps to provide a climate in which fledging theories can grow and flourish, it also helps to hide from view alternative theories that may in fact be better.[23]

4. The Rise of Strings

We now turn to string theory, and offer, first, a brief history of this theory. Today, string theory is a would-be "final theory," that is, a theory with foundational aspirations. It originated in the late 1960s, however, in a role rather different from its current one.[24]

Initially, string theory was a phenomenological attempt to understand one of the four fundamental forces, known as the strong nuclear force.[25] The strong force acts on particles known as "hadrons," among which are the relatively familiar proton and neutron that form the nuclei of atoms. By the late 1960s, it was believed that these hadrons were composed of smaller particles, called "quarks," but their properties were not well understood. All that was known was that quarks must be, in some sense, "confined" to hadrons, since no one had ever observed any free quarks. String theory was supposed to explain this confinement via very small elastic bands (the strings) that bound the quarks together. Although the theory was fairly successful, its progress halted abruptly in 1973 with the remarkable experimental success of a competing theory of the strong force, known as quantum chromodynamics (QCD). As Galison points out, however, string theory had flaws of its own: in

---

[23] Here there is a connection to recent work by Stanford (2006) on the problem of "unconceived alternatives." Stanford argues that scientists' systematic failure to identify alternative theories that can deal with available evidence as well as or better than current theory is the strongest threat to scientific realism. If the conservatism of normal science as we have described it here contributes to that failure to recognize alternative theories, then it bears severe epistemic costs. Of course, Kuhn was not a realist in the sense Stanford attacks.

[24] As mentioned in the introduction, the material here is derived from Smolin (2006) and Galison (1995); for additional perspectives, see Cappelli et al. (2012) and Dawid (2013). This section is intended as background and not argument. If anything of the history presented here is contentious—aside, of course, from Smolin's claim that string theory has not accomplished its stated goals and should now be viewed as a failure—it is unintentionally so.

[25] As a matter of vocabulary, physicists use "phenomenological" to refer to models/theories intended to describe specific phenomena. The contrast class would be "fundamental" theories, which claim to be generally valid and universally applicable (at least in principle).

its capacity as model of the strong force, string theory predicted a new particle with no counterpart in the phenomena to be explained.

As it became clear that string theory was a dead end with regard to hadronic physics, committed devotees, convinced of the power of the theory's mathematical structure, looked for new applications. In 1974, John Schwarz and Joël Scherk, and independently T. Yoneya, proposed a reinterpretation of string theory. This new theory was essentially identical to the old one, except now the strings were 10^{20} times smaller. Instead of binding the constituents of hadrons together, strings were now proposed as the fundamental building blocks of both elementary particles and spacetime itself. In this role, the unobserved particle that threatened to derail the hadronic theory could be interpreted as a carrier of the gravitational force. (The problem of finding an adequate quantum mechanical theory of gravitation had proved remarkably stubborn, and any candidate for a particle corresponding to gravitation was considered a promising one.) In this new role, however, the theory had some worrisome and undesirable properties: for one, it predicted that the universe had at least six additional, unseen spatial dimensions. Whether for this reason or some other, over the next decade string theory was largely ignored by the physics community, aside from a small group of researchers.

All this changed in 1984, with such dramatic suddenness that the period is often referred to as the first superstring revolution.[26] The tipping point was a calculation by Schwarz and a young collaborator named Michael Green that appeared in August of that year. They showed that string theory lacked an inconsistency that had plagued other so-called unified theories then under consideration. The response was surprise, celebration, and a massive movement of physicists into the field. In 1984, there were about 150 articles published on string theory in total, about three times the average annual output in the previous decade. In 1985, the number was well over four hundred, and then over a thousand in 1986.

This explosive growth can be attributed to a variety of factors. One was that the then dominant theory—called the Standard Model, which included QCD as one of its two subparts—had been around for a decade and was doing too well. None of its predictions had been falsified and a good number had been confirmed to a high degree of accuracy. Wonderful as this sounds, it was widely believed that the Standard Model could not be a fundamental theory, because it left too many of its own parameters unexplained; yet, without any

---

[26] "String theory" is now common shorthand for a theory that was known as "superstring theory" when it was first developed in its modern form, during the 1980s.

experimental disagreement, there was little to point the way towards more fundamental theories.

After the Schwarz-Green calculation, string theory was a promising possibility in a landscape where all other options seemed exhausted. It was in this period, between 1984 and 1989, that string theory first rose to be the leading candidate for a theory of everything. Smolin also describes the mid- to late-1980s as the time when the string theory community began to exhibit the sociological features he highlights. (We will state and discuss these in detail below.) He writes of string theory, "It was the hottest game in town...Very quickly there developed a cultlike atmosphere. You were either a string theorist or you were not" (Smolin [2006, 116]). One reason for this appearance of division, according to Smolin, was that string theory required new technical tools that most physicists would not have learned in graduate school. The investment of time and energy were risky, and were taken as evidence of one's commitment to the new project. Theorists who did not take the time to learn the new tools were viewed as either incapable of understanding the new developments (a stance common among younger physicists towards their elders, when the elders began to question the unconventional new research). And it was easy to tell who had devoted themselves to the new theory, because the research methods were distinct enough to distinguish "string theorists" from others based solely on the sorts of papers they published.

It was also during this period that the first outspoken dissenters appeared. Among these critics numbered many of the most prominent theorists of the previous generations. Nobel laureate Richard Feynman, for instance, wrote in 1988, "[string theory] doesn't produce anything; it has to be excused most of the time. It doesn't look right." Another Nobelist, Sheldon Glashow, who was largely responsible for a big chunk of the Standard Model, wrote in the same year that string theorists "cannot demonstrate that the standard theory is a logical outcome of string theory. They cannot even be sure that their formalism includes a description of such things as protons and electrons. And they have not yet made even one teeny-tiny experimental prediction" (both of these are quoted in Smolin [2006, 125]). Howard Georgi, who with Glashow proposed the first Grand Unified Theory (and thus started the path of which string theory was supposed to be the end), wrote in 1989, "I feel about the present state of GUTs as I imagine Richard Nixon's parents might have felt had they been around during the final days of the Nixon administration" (quoted in Galison [1995, 392]).

Interest in string theory calmed down somewhat during the early 1990s. Approximately six hundred papers were published each year between 1990 and 1993—half the peak of twelve hundred in 1987. Although many still found the theory to be promising, the wide interest of the late 1980s had revealed several new undesirable features. Most prominent was that there appeared to be a handful of *different* theories, all justly going by the name string theory and between which there was no way to adjudicate. This was in conflict with one of the principal virtues many physicists hoped and expected string theory to have, namely that its mathematical structure would lead to an essentially unique theory. Physicists felt that a highly constrained theory of this sort was desirable because, if confirmed, it would carry a sense of necessity with it. The world is the way it is, one might then say, because small changes (in the true theory) would lead to a mathematical inconsistency.

Soon physicists were able to classify five possible string theories. This number might have seemed manageable, except that to make any of these five theories physically acceptable it was necessary to "compactify" (literally, roll up and hide from view) the six extra dimensions. By the late 1980s, it had been observed that there were millions of consistent ways to do this, and picking the one that corresponded to the world appeared arbitrary and ad hoc. In other words, string theory appeared incapable of making substantive predictions at all, since the geometry of the theory was so radically underdetermined by known mathematical constraints that almost any possible experimental data was compatible with the theory. Twenty years later, these features continue to be among the ones that string theory's critics cite.

The field accelerated once again in 1995, however, when Edward Witten made a rather striking proposal. He said that although it seemed there were five different string theories, he believed it was possible that all of these were examples of a single underlying theory, with seven extra dimensions (instead of six). This new theory did not have strings in it, per se. Now, it had two dimensional surfaces. One of the dimensions of these surfaces was tightly wound in the new extra dimension, so that the objects would appear to be one-dimensional strings in a ten-dimensional space, much as in the older theory. Witten conjectured, and later proved, that the five string theories that were discovered in the late 1980s corresponded to different ways of winding the two-dimensional objects around in this eleventh dimension. He named the new theory M-theory. Once it was understood that the five theories were actually different parts of one theory, physicists' interests were reignited. (The additional problem of compactification, however, remained.)

This period, following Witten's proof and a handful of developments that followed quickly from it, is often called the second superstring revolution. Since then, string theory and its descendant, M-theory, remain hegemonic, despite the fact that some of the earliest concerns—about the prediction of unseen particles without any details of their properties; about the non-uniqueness of the scheme for hiding the theory's extra dimensions; and about the lack of connection with experiment—remain unresolved.[27] The mid-1990s saw a slew of popular books, by such authors as Michio Kaku and Brian Greene, that spread the word of the superstring revolutions to non-scientists, and helped create the sense that, despite its problems, string theory was already established science.[28] Now, however, many (perhaps most) outsiders to the theory, in both the public press and in other areas of physics, tend to be more critical. Despite the efforts of some string theorists, such as Leonard Susskind of Stanford and Lisa Randall of Harvard, to present new developments of the theory and sustain a feeling of hopefulness, an increasing number of physicists outside of the string theory community have come to believe that the grace period during which the theory's problems could be excused has ended. And yet, it continues to be dominant within its sub-field of physics. In other words, from Smolin's and others' perspectives as outside experts evaluating string theory, given the current state of the field string theorists appear to be epistemically irrational in their continued confidence that string theory is the best available proposal for approaching questions in quantum gravity.[29] This is where Smolin suggests that sociology plays a role.

5. Smolin's Sociological Critique: String Theory and Collective Belief

In his (2006), Smolin describes seven features of the contemporary string theory community that are intended to explain why it continues to be the

---

[27] This is not to say that nothing has changed in the last fifteen to twenty years. In particular, the interests of string theorists have shifted to new topics, including questions concerning the role of strings in cosmology and the early universe and the so-called AdS/CFT correspondence, which attempts to draw a connection between string theory and more traditional approaches to high-energy particle physics. Curiously, some string theorists have also had success in applying the methods characteristic of their discipline to problems in other, radically different areas of physics, including atomic and nuclear physics. (This latter work has led some string theorists to claim that string theory *has* made testable predictions. But they are not predictions concerning fundamental physics, the supposed domain of the theory. At best, predictions of this other sort provide evidence that some of the mathematical and physical reasoning used by string theorists is not inherently fallacious; it emphatically does *not* provide evidence that string theory is the correct fundamental theory of nature.) Importantly for present purposes, the *sociological* features of string theory that Smolin emphasizes were already well-established by the mid-1990s and, he claims, had not changed significantly by the time he wrote his book.

[28] Greene (1999, 213–14) in particular provides quotes from some of the same critics Smolin and Galison cite—including Georgi and Glashow—that are more conciliatory.

[29] String theory has not been without "outside" defenders—for instance, the particle-physicist-turned-philosopher Richard Dawid (2013) has recently argued that not only is string theory not a failure, but its success should force a change in how we understand science.

dominant candidate for a fundamental theory, despite the widely held view of experts outside the fold that the theory is no longer as promising as it once seemed.[30] We first state them in their entirety, and then we relate them to Gilbert's description of a scientific community holding one or more collective beliefs. Smolin writes that string theory has qualities of:

- *Tremendous self-confidence*, leading to a sense of entitlement and of belonging to an elite community of experts.
- *An unusually monolithic community*, with a strong sense of consensus, whether driven by the evidence or not, and an unusual uniformity of views on open questions. These views seem related to the existence of a hierarchical structure in which the ideas of a few leaders dictate the viewpoint, strategy, and direction of the field.
- In some cases, a *sense of identification with the group*, akin to identification with a religious faith or political platform.
- A strong sense of the *boundary between the group and other experts*.
- A *disregard for and disinterest in* the ideas, opinions, and work of experts who are not part of the group, and a preference for talking only with other members of the community.
- A tendency to *interpret evidence optimistically*, to believe exaggerated or incorrect statements of results, and to disregard the possibility that the theory might be wrong. This is coupled with a tendency to *believe results are true because they are "widely believed,"* even if one has not checked (or even seen) the proof oneself.
- A lack of appreciation for the extent to which a research program *ought to involve risk*. (Smolin [2006, 284], emphasis in original)

In what follows, we work with the hypothesis that string theorists are a group of people with collective beliefs concerning the fundamental nature of the world. (Given the connection we have noted with Kuhn's work, one might rephrase this as "a group of people working within a Kuhnian paradigm.") We will use the proposition "string theory is true" as shorthand for whatever

---

[30] We should emphasize that Smolin's claim is not that string theory has failed—insofar as it has—because of these sociological features. Instead, string theory has failed because it is not an adequate theory of nature. It continues to enjoy a privileged place in the physics community, however, for these sociological reasons; this continued dominance, meanwhile, has prevented other possible theories from receiving much attention, which, Smolin claims, explains why high-energy physics has stalled. Thanks to Gerald Cantu for pointing out this possible ambiguity.

those beliefs are supposed to be, setting aside the worry that "string theory" may not refer to a single, well-defined set of propositions. The actual views of string theorists are more subtle and would involve a number of technical propositions and beliefs about the relation between these propositions and the world, plus opinions about the ontology of the world and the prospects for string theory's ultimate success. It is not important precisely what statements are part of the core set of collective beliefs of the string theory community, so long as there *is* such a core set.

We will treat the features that Smolin describes in turn, grouped according to their explanation in terms of collective belief. We will argue that each of these features have natural explanations given the assumptions made thus far concerning the string theory community and the nature and implications of collective belief. The central assumption regarding the string theory community for present purposes is its possession of a core set of collective beliefs—group beliefs in Gilbert's joint commitment sense. Then, in section 5.iv, we will turn to the question of why, if the features Smolin describes are precisely what one should expect of a scientific community, Smolin describes them as "unusual."

5.i Features 2, 3, and 4: Identification with the Group and a Boundary with Other Experts

Features 2, 3, and 4 of Smolin's description are direct consequences of collective belief. Holding a collective belief is a sufficient condition to constitute a social group, which means that string theorists can justly refer to themselves as "we," with regard to the consensus of the community. So it is unsurprising that the parties to the collective belief tend to have a sense of identification with the group holding the belief. After all, they are *members* of that group. The point will presumably pertain even more strongly to a population of scientists with many interconnected collective beliefs.[31]

Likewise, the sense of a boundary between the string theory community and individuals and other groups of a different persuasion follows from the string theory community's status as a social group. Insofar as the people

---

[31] Can a given group have inconsistent beliefs? If so it could indeed be described as a house divided. Supposing that this can happen within a given scientific community, it is clearly a special though interesting case that we shall set aside here.

who collectively believe that string theory is true can refer to themselves collectively as "we," there is an available distinction between "us" and "them." And so features 3 and 4 can be expected of any social group.

Similarly, feature 2 should be expected of any social group holding one or more collective beliefs. A monolithic community with a strong sense of consensus is precisely what would characterize a group with multiple joint commitments to speak and act in ways expressive of particular beliefs—particularly if there is a large number of interconnected beliefs with a central core.

Indeed, Smolin's description of the early history of string theory suggests the process by which an initial joint commitment, out of which the social group arose, was formed. Early string theorists needed to devote significant amounts of time to learning new theoretical methods—so different from other methods that Witten once described the theory as "a piece of 21st-century physics that fell by chance into the 20th century" (Cole 1987)—and it was clear who among the broader physics community had chosen to do so. As Smolin explains, physicists who *did* choose to learn string theory quickly came to view themselves in opposition to those physicists who did not.

Some physicists used plural subject language to refer to those committed to string theory: as Harvard string theorist Andrew Strominger put it later, reflecting on the early days, "We were once considered semi-crackpots working on some bizarre idea" (Johnson 1998). Their expenditure of time and energy, with consequences that could be easily observed by their peers, amounted to a public commitment on the part of those who made the investment. By the mid- to late-1980s, at least, it seems likely that through their interactions in the course of their work the relevant group of physicists had thus openly expressed their readiness *jointly* to commit to work as a body on string theory, in conditions of common knowledge, so that the conditions for a Gilbertian social group obtained. As described above, it was during the same period that a consensus concerning the basic propositions of string theory was first arrived at by those physicists jointly committed to working on string theory, and that Smolin's feature 4 became apparent.[32]

---

[32] As indicated in footnote 2 above, the distinction or rather distinctions between belief and some form of "acceptance" made by various philosophers is not strictly germane here. *Mutatis mutandis*, the points made here about collective belief can be made about collective acceptance, on whatever construal. The question whether it is better to characterize string theorists as collectively believing as opposed to collectively accepting the basic propositions of string theory is an interesting question that we shall not pursue. For some it will hang on whether they are collectively agnostic as to the truth of these propositions, as opposed to the desirability of supposing their truth for the purposes of scientific inquiry.

5.ii　Features 5, 6, and 7: Disinterest in Other Ideas, Tendency to Interpret Evidence Optimistically, and Poor Appreciation of Risk

Features 5, 6, and 7 follow only slightly less obviously from Gilbert's account. There are two things to say here: the first is to explain why these features might *appear* to be true of the string theory community to an outside expert like Smolin, and the second is to explain why they might in fact come to be true of the members of the community.

As parties to a joint commitment, members of the string theory community are obligated to act as mouthpieces of their collective belief. This means that if they speak in a way that contradicts the consensus, without significant qualification, they risk offending against the other parties to the collective belief. As it is difficult (and professionally unwise) to offend against other members of one's community, one expects parties to any collective belief to refrain from speaking approvingly about ideas that contradict or challenge the consensus.[33]

Moreover, no individual can rescind the commitment alone, even in the face of overwhelming evidence against it—at most, she can choose to violate the commitment and risk rebuke. Thus the collective belief entails that the members of the group have an associated obligation to dismiss evidence or viable alternative views that might instill doubts about the consensus. Likewise, any evidence that can be taken in favor of the collective belief is embraced. Someone who is obligated to speak as (for short) the mouthpiece of a group is naturally inclined to emphasize evidence in its favor—i.e., to take a rhetorical stance in evaluating and communicating the evidence. So features 5 and 6 seem to follow on Gilbert's account. Or, at least, it is to be expected that an outsider would characterize a group with a collective belief as having features 5 and 6.

As Gilbert argues in her (2000a) and as we briefly noted above, features such as these may run deeper still. When a person is obligated to speak or act in certain ways, it can affect his private thoughts, inhibiting him from pursuing spontaneous doubts about the group view or from fully accounting for available evidence. Even though being party to a joint commitment to believe that p as a body does not require one to in fact believe that p individually, it is awkward and often difficult to believe one thing and say another with

---

[33] This is most likely true even if the approval is qualified as in "Personally, I approve..." See e.g. Gilbert (2000a).

conviction. Whether consciously or not, this difficulty can impede a party to a collective belief from exploring possibilities that seem likely to lead to a contradiction between one's personal beliefs and the belief referenced in the pertinent joint commitment. An individual's personal beliefs, then, are liable to be strongly influenced by considerations directly arising from the collective belief. And so the collective belief can in fact change how an individual will react to and interpret new evidence in such a way that features 5 and 6 become true of the members of a group with a collective belief.[34]

To explain how the appreciation of risk in a research program relates to these considerations, and to the obligations arising from joint commitments in particular, it is important to say just what Smolin means by risk. Risk-taking scientists "invent their own directions" and "tend to provoke strongly polarized reactions" (342). Risk-taking within a research program amounts to exploring ideas that oppose the "entrenched approaches" on one's own initiative (294). That is, risk, according to Smolin, amounts to systematically and sustainedly bucking the consensus—precisely what one cannot do as a party to a collective belief.

On this account of riskiness in research, an obligation publicly to endorse string theory makes risk-taking even more unlikely, since if one succeeds in taking risks, one violates the applicable joint commitment and may well be excluded from the social group by one's fellows, who take one to have indicated one's own readiness to be so excluded. And so it is unsurprising that Smolin finds few risk takers within the string theory community. One cannot take risks as Smolin understands them and yet still be sure of retaining one's membership of the social group.

Smolin's biography is telling here. He worked successfully as a string theorist for many years, before deciding to explore new possibilities; now, by his own lights, he is no longer a member of the string theory community.

5.iii Feature 1: Tremendous Self-Confidence and Sense of Eliteness

Tremendous self-confidence or the sense that the group holding a belief is somehow elite are not features that Gilbert has previously discussed in relation to her account of collective belief. But there are considerations in the

---

[34] This phenomenon of avoiding cognitive dissonance is not pure speculation. For instance, see Festinger and Carlsmith (1959) and the subsequent literature on forced compliance.

spirit of Gilbert's account that lead one to expect string theorists to appear to exhibit this feature, and, indeed, to do so.

The first consideration is an explanation of the appearance to an outside expert of tremendous (or irrational) confidence in the beliefs collectively held. Take Smolin as an example. He understands string theory, its consequences, and the evidence for and against it as well as any string theorist. On the basis of this knowledge, he has determined that the status of string theory is at best uncertain. And yet members of this community speak as though string theory is true. We may suppose that, for the reasons described above, they inure themselves against evidence and ideas that might conflict with their collective belief. An outside expert, however, might not realize this, assuming that they are taking account of all of the evidence he is (especially evidence he might present in argument). In other words, the apparent irrationality of the string theory community—its unwillingness to update its beliefs in an epistemically responsible way, according to some outside experts—is naturally interpreted by those outsiders as certainty bordering on dogmatism—or even as hubris.

Once again, as with features 5 and 6, this effect may also run deeper.[35] When a member of a social group with a collective belief speaks as a mouthpiece of the group, she is acting on an authority partially independent of and likely more significant than her own. She speaks for the group, and the views that she expresses have the blessing of the group's other members with respect to their status as the group's views. If we add to this that there are distinguished intellectuals and academics for whom the speaker has great esteem among the members of the group, that would seem to make the effect only more prominent. When a string theorist says that string theory is true—or unassailable—she can do so with confidence derived from the understanding that she speaks with and for these distinguished members of the group. Moreover, members of the group see other string theorists behaving similarly. When they express the views of the group amongst themselves, they do so assuredly and with the gravitas that comes from the assumption that they will not be contradicted. Seeing this confidence can be impressive: the members of the group appear to have authority and expertise. Each member of the group, seeing the other members behave thus, can easily come to believe that the group is populated with elite experts on the subjects that the collective belief concerns.

---

[35] Thank you to Cailin O'Connor for pointing out this consequence of Gilbert's view.

5.iv Seven *Unusual* Features?

As we have just seen, all seven of Smolin's features appear consistent with Gilbert's account. But there is still one aspect of Smolin's description of these features that does not appear to mesh. Specifically, if, as Smolin says, string theory is *unusual* in having these sociological features, then Smolin's view is in tension with the idea that joint commitments of the kind that constitute collective beliefs are likely to be present in *all* scientific communities. So why does Smolin claim that the features he describes are unusual, if in fact they obtain for any group holding a collective belief?

One way to resolve the tension is simply to suggest that what makes string theory unusual in this regard is a matter of degree—that is, perhaps the manifestations of the string theory community's joint commitment are particularly emphatic, for reasons independent of their group belief. On this suggestion, scientific communities may often have just the sociological features Smolin describes, and may even be monolithic in general. But for various reasons, string theory has turned out to be an especially striking case. (Indeed, Smolin describes string theory as "unusually monolithic, with a strong sense of consensus." One might take this as an acknowledgement that *all* scientific communities are monolithic to some degree, and all such communities have some sense of consensus; string theory is merely an extreme example.)

A second possibility—compatible with the first—is that Smolin considers these features striking (or rather, they *appear* unusual to him) not because they are in fact unusual, but rather because Smolin and his collaborators stand in a different relationship to string theory than they do to other areas of physics. One might even think that Smolin's position with regard to string theory is, historically speaking, an unusual one for *any* prominent scientist to occupy.

The idea is that it is uncommon for the physics community to fracture into such clearly defined sub-groups with conflicting collective beliefs. This means that it is unusual for a scientist to be a leader in his or her field—a fully competent expert—who nonetheless stands outside of a given collective belief within the field. But if and when this does happen, experts in the disagreeing communities would have a perspective that would make the features of the other communities—features such as those Smolin describes—more transparent, since such experts are well-equipped to evaluate the evidence for and against a particular theory without being party to the consensus. If this is right, then string theory would seem quite different to Smolin than other areas of physics.

One can connect this point with the discussion of Kuhnian paradigms above. There we suggested that paradigms might be thought of as collections of fundamental collective beliefs, that is, beliefs to which the members of a given community of scientists are jointly committed. The apparently irrational features of normal science, then, are just consequences of the existence of core joint commitments obligating scientists to speak and act in certain ways on pain of severe rebuke or even excommunication. In these terms, Smolin's perspective on string theory is that of an expert in an area of science that is divided into groups with different paradigms, who stands outside of one of these paradigms, peering in.[36] From this perspective—not so different, perhaps, from Kuhn's own perspective in *The Structure of Scientific Revolutions*—certain epistemic pathologies that most scientists never notice are cast into stark relief.

Of course, on Kuhn's view, there is nothing unusual about science within a paradigm. It is *normal science*, after all. But the fact that normal science has certain features does not mean that those features are obvious to working scientists. Quite the contrary. If anything, what is unusual is the ability to recognize these features at all, since to do so, one needs to be able to step outside of one's own particular corner of normal science and its associated paradigms and examine it from this external perspective. We suggest that this, in effect, is what Smolin has done. He has stepped outside the string theory community and is able to view it from an uncommon perspective, that of an informed outsider.

6. Conclusion

We have argued here that, given (1) Gilbert's joint commitment account of group belief and (2) the hypothesis that the consensus within the string theory community can be properly construed as an example of group belief in Gilbert's sense, the seven sociological features that Smolin attributes to string theory are precisely what one should expect of a group holding relevant group beliefs. In particular, we have observed that, apparently *contra* Smolin, and

[36] Kuhn believed there could be at most one paradigm in a field at a time—a view famously challenged by Lakatos (1970) and Laudan (1977). So there is something un-Kuhnian about the suggestion that there are multiple competing paradigms in quantum gravity. Thus, one might take the fact that Smolin does seem to stand outside of string theory when he criticizes it as evidence that Kuhn was mistaken, or perhaps as evidence that quantum gravity is in a period of crisis, during which paradigms are permitted to fracture on Kuhn's account. One way or the other, however, it is fully consistent with Kuhn's views that Smolin's perspective is *unusual*, insofar as he has the expertise to evaluate string theory without being committed to the paradigm.

consistently with a Kuhnian approach to normal science, these features may not be *unusual* after all.

What *may* be unusual, however, is that such a circumscribed social group has come to exist as a sub-group within the physics community. Particularly, it may be uncommon for there to be practitioners in a given field with full accreditation and expertise who are not party to the joint commitments of the relevant scientific community. Then it would only be because Smolin occupies this "outside expert" vantage point that the features of string theory appear unusual to him. These considerations suggest that, at least in some cases, the social features of scientific communities are well explained by supposing that scientific consensus, both with respect to paradigms and otherwise, can be understood as a variety of group belief in Gilbert's sense, with its attendant obligations.

Before concluding we would like to emphasize the following. As a matter of logic, that a given scientific community believes, in Gilbert's sense, that p, implies neither that p is true nor that p is false. Again, it does not imply that the community's belief that p is well-grounded empirically, or that it is not. The most that can be said along these lines is that *if* the core beliefs of a scientific community are false, or poorly grounded, there are the noted barriers to that community's coming to reject these beliefs, *in spite of* their falsity or poor grounding. That is all that this paper means to imply with respect to the string theory community, or any other.

Works Cited

Beatty, John (2006). "Masking Disagreement among Experts." *Episteme* 3(1), 52–67.

Bird, Alexander (2010). "Social Knowing: The Social Sense of 'Scientific Knowledge'." *Philosophical Perspectives* 24, 23–56.

Bouvier, Alban (2004). "Individual Beliefs and Collective Beliefs in Sciences and Philosophy: The Plural Subject and the Polyphonic Subject Accounts." *Philosophy of the Social Sciences* 34(3), 382–407.

Capelli, Andrea, Elena Castellani, Filippo Colomo, and Paolo Di Vecchia (2012). *The Birth of String Theory*. New York: Cambridge University Press.

Carnap, R. (1956). *Meaning and Necessity: A Study in the Semantics of Modal Logic*. Chicago: University of Chicago Press.

Cole, K. C. (1987). "A Theory of Everything." *New York Times Magazine*, October 18. Archived at: http://www.nytimes.com/1987/10/18/magazine/a-theory-of-everything.html.

Dawid, Richard (2013). *String Theory and the Scientific Method.* New York: Cambridge University Press.

Fagan, Melinda Bonnie (2011). "Is There Collective Scientific Knowledge? Arguments from Explanation." *The Philosophical Quarterly* 61(243), 247–69.

Festinger, Leon, and James M. Carlsmith (1959). "Cognitive Consequences of Forced Compliance." *The Journal of Abnormal and Social Psychology* 58(2), 203–10.

Friedman, Michael (2001). *Dynamics of Reason.* Chicago: University of Chicago Press.

Galison, Peter (1995). "Theory Bound and Unbound: Superstrings and Experiments." In *Laws of Nature: Essays on the Philosophical, Scientific and Historical Dimensions*, ed. Friedel Weinert. Berlin: de Gruyter, 369–408.

Giere, Ronald N., and Barton Moffatt (2003). "Distributed Cognition: Where the Cognitive and the Social Merge." *Social Studies of Science* 33(2), 301–10.

Gilbert, Margaret (1987). "Modeling Collective Belief." *Synthese* 73(1), 185–204.

Gilbert, Margaret (1989). *On Social Facts.* Princeton, NJ: Princeton University Press.

Gilbert, Margaret (2000a). "Collective Belief and Scientific Change." In *Sociality and Responsibility: New Essays in Plural Subject Theory.* Lanham, MD: Rowman & Littlefield, 37–49.

Gilbert, Margaret (2000b). "What Is It for *Us* to Intend?" In *Sociality and Responsibility: New Essays in Plural Subject Theory.* Lanham, MD: Rowman & Littlefield, 14–36.

Gilbert, Margaret (2002). "Belief and Acceptance as Features of Groups." *Protosociology* 16, 35–69.

Gilbert, Margaret (2004). "Collective Epistemology." *Episteme* 1, 95–107.

Gilbert, Margaret (2012). "Giving Claim-Rights Their Due." In *Rights: Concepts and Contexts*, ed. B. Bix and H. Spector. Farnham, Surrey: Ashgate, 301–23. [Chapter 13, this volume]

Gilbert, Margaret (2013). *Joint Commitment: How We Make the Social World.* New York: Oxford University Press.

Gilbert, Margaret, and Daniel Pilchman (2014). "Belief, Acceptance, and What Happens in Groups: Some Methodological Considerations." In *Essays in Collective Epistemology*, ed. Jennifer Lackey. Oxford: Oxford University Press, 190–212. [Chapter 4, this volume]

Godfrey-Smith, Peter (2003). *Theory and Reality: An Introduction to the Philosophy of Science.* Chicago: University of Chicago Press.

Greene, Brian (1999). *The Elegant Universe: Superstrings, Hidden Dimensions, and the Quest for Ultimate Theory.* New York: W.W. Norton & Company.

Johnson, George (1998). "Almost in Awe, Physicists Ponder 'Ultimate' Theory." *New York Times*, September 22. Archived at: www.nytimes.com/1998/09/22/science/almost-in-awe-physicists-ponder-ultimate-theory.html.

Kitcher, Philip (1994). "Contrasting Conceptions of Social Epistemology." In *Socializing Epistemology: The Social Dimensions of Knowledge*, ed. Frederick F. Schmitt. Lanham, MD: Rowman & Littlefield, 111–34.

Knorr-Cetina, Karin (1999). *Epistemic Cultures: How the Sciences Make Knowledge*. Cambridge, MA: Harvard University Press.

Kuhn, Thomas (1962). *The Structure of Scientific Revolutions*. Chicago: University of Chicago Press.

Lakatos, Imre (1970). "Falsification and the Methodology of Scientific Research." In *Criticism and the Growth of Knoweldge*, ed. Imre Lakatos and Alan Musgrave. New York: Cambridge University Press, 91–195.

Laudan, Larry (1977). *Progress and Its Problems: Toward a Theory of Scientific Growth*. Berkeley: University of California Press.

Lewis, David (1969). *Convention: A Philosophical Study*. Oxford: Wiley-Blackwell.

Longino, Helen (1990). *Science as Social Knowledge: Values and Objectivity in Scientific Inquiry*. Princeton, NJ: Princeton University Press.

Mathiesen, Kay (2006). "The Epistemic Features of Group Belief." *Episteme* **2**(3), 161–75.

Merali, Zeeya (2011). "Collaborative Physics: String Theory Finds a Bench Mate." *Nature* **478**, 302–4.

Quinton, Anthony (1975–6). "Social Objects." *Proceedings of the Aristotelian Society* **76**, 1–27.

Rolin, Kristina (2008). "Science as Collective Knowledge." *Cognitive Systems Research* **9**, 115–24.

Rolin, Kristina (2010). "Group Justification in Science." *Episteme* **7**(3), 215–31.

Schmitt, Frederick (1994). "The Justification of Group Beliefs." In *Socializing Epistemology: The Social Dimensions of Knowledge*, ed. Frederick F. Schmitt. Lanham, MD: Rowman & Littlefield, 257–87.

Smolin, Lee (2006). *The Trouble with Physics*. New York: Mariner Books.

Stanford, Kyle (2006). *Exceeding Our Grasp: Science, History, and the Problem of Unconceived Alternatives*. New York: Oxford University Press.

Thagard, Paul (1999). *How Scientists Explain Disease*. Princeton, NJ: Princeton University Press.

Wray, K. Brad (2001). "Collective Belief and Acceptance." *Synthese* **129**(3), 319–33.

Wray, K. Brad (2007). "Who Has Scientific Knowledge?" *Social Epistemology* **21**(3), 337–47.

6

Group Lies—And Some
Related Matters

Introduction

Does the possibility of group lies cast doubt on the account of collective belief that I have developed?[1] Jennifer Lackey has argued that it does.[2] She has focused, more precisely, on what she refers to as *the joint acceptance account*, under which generic title she includes my own.[3] She alleges that group lies, along with group bullshit present a "decisive" objection to that account.[4]

In the discussion that follows I focus on Lackey's contention as it relates—or not—to my own account. I argue that group lies pose no problem for that account. Nor, I argue, does group BS. I then turn to what appears to be Lackey's real concern, and highlight a difference between Lackey's aim in providing an account of collective belief and my own.

I start with some preliminary ground-clearing, correcting two impressions that Lackey's discussion may give of my account of collective belief, emphasizing an aspect of the account that it is important not to overlook, and noting an important support for the account.

---

[1] Beginning with Gilbert (1987) and, much more fully, (1989: ch. 5). See chapters 2, 3, 4, and 5, this volume, for some later discussions. I often write of *collective* belief rather than *group* belief. One reason for this is that, in my view, a group may—though it need not—be *constituted* by a single collective belief. In that case the group in question did not pre-exist the collective belief, as might be suggested by the phrase "group belief." In the present discussion I refer both to "collective belief" and "group belief" without meaning to make a significant distinction.

[2] See, Lackey (2021), on which I focus here, and Lackey (2020). The present discussion derives from my contribution to a symposium on Lackey's book, at the social ontology conference held online in August 2021. I thank Matt Dean, Giulia Napolitano, and Deborah Tollefsen for helpful comments on a draft.

[3] She also includes under this heading the somewhat similar—though importantly different—account in Tuomela (1992) and, indeed, focuses on this in her discussion.

[4] Lackey (2021: 22). At times in that book she seems to waver on the topic of group lies, though not on the topic of group bullshit. Some, however, have found her contention that the joint acceptance account cannot account for either group lies or group bullshit "compelling and effective" (Dunn 2021). I therefore pursue this contention here.

Life in Groups: How We Think, Feel, and Act Together. Margaret Gilbert, Oxford University Press. © Margaret Gilbert 2023.
DOI: 10.1093/oso/9780192847157.003.0007

1. Correcting Some Impressions of My Account of Collective Belief

1.1 There Is No Essential Reference to a Particular Attitude of "Acceptance"—as Opposed to Belief—in My Account

As I noted in the introduction to my book *Living Together*, early references to "acceptance" in my account of collective belief were not intended to invoke a special notion of acceptance as distinct from belief.[5] I was using "accept" in what I took to be one standard way, as a synonym for belief.[6] In order to avoid any misunderstandings on that score, I long ago dropped any reference to acceptance in my account of collective belief. Here, without any immediate explanation of its technical terms, is the account:

> Persons A, B, and so on (or members of population P) *collectively believe* that p if and only if they are jointly committed to believe that p as a body.

Lackey's rough version early in her book is close to the gist of this account, though her use of the phrase "jointly agree" as opposed to "jointly commit" wrongly suggests that in my view there has to be something we would properly call an agreement in the picture.[7]

Though I believe that an agreement is a particular kind of joint commitment, joint commitments can be established without the kind of explicitness necessary for an agreement proper.[8] Relatedly, joint commitments can be established in large populations, whose members neither know nor know of one another—contrary to Lackey's drift at one point.[9]

An appropriate label for my view would be the *joint commitment* account. Perhaps the most striking thing about this account is that it does not require that any of the individuals involved personally believe that p. It is not, therefore, what I have called a *correlativist* account: not even *one* member need have a personal belief that p in order for a group to believe that p. Nor, of course, is it a *summative* account, in the sense that it entails that *all* or *most* of

---

[5] See Gilbert (1996: 7–8, section entitled "Group belief, 'joint acceptance,' and joint commitment").

[6] Here my account differs from Tuomela's. Lackey focuses on the latter, while implying the coincidence of the accounts as to their essentials.

[7] Lackey (2021: 16).

[8] Regarding a possible concern as to the role of something *agreement-like* in an account of collective belief, see section 5 below.

[9] In a discussion of groups early in the book (at p. 13). I discuss large-scale cases in e.g. Gilbert (2006). See chapter 12, section 3, this volume for related discussion.

the individuals in question believe that p. Of course, as a matter of fact, collective beliefs on my account *will often* be accompanied by many correlative individual beliefs. Though they may raise eyebrows at first blush, these features of the account reflect my understanding of the contexts in which everyday collective belief ascriptions are comfortably made.

It is worth noting in the present context that I have proposed a parallel joint commitment account of collective *acceptance* that p, in a sense in which "accepts" is not a synonym for "believes." According to this account persons A, B, and so on (or members of population P) collectively accept [in the relevant sense of "acceptance"] that p if and only if they are jointly committed to accept [in the relevant sense] that p as a body.[10]

1.2 The Joint Commitment Account Allows for the Determination of the Content of a Group's Belief by a Proper Subset of the Members

Contrary to Lackey's drift, my account of collective belief allows that, on occasion, a group's belief may be determined by a set of "operative" members who do not comprise the whole group, to use Tuomela's (and now Lackey's) terminology.[11] Thus I have in many places distinguished between *basic* and *non-basic* cases of joint commitment. These differ precisely as to the *mode of establishment* of the joint commitment in question.

Briefly to review this distinction here: a *basic* joint commitment is established, roughly, by all of the parties openly expressing their readiness for the establishment of that very joint commitment. In contrast, a *non-basic* joint commitment is established for all members of a certain population by a proper subset of the members—or, for that matter, by an external person or body—*given a prior authorization to do so through an appropriate joint commitment of all parties.*

Thus a married couple may be jointly committed to accept as a body that spouse A is to establish their collective political beliefs. It would then make sense for spouse B to ask spouse A, "Which mayoral candidate do we think

---

[10] See Gilbert (2002).

[11] This terminology is fine, except insofar as it suggests that members other than the "operative" ones need play no role in the group's accrual of a given belief. I take it that these particular members only have their "operative" status with respect to a belief of the group as a whole by courtesy of all. See the discussion that follows immediately below.

will do best for the town?" implying both that A is in a position to determine what they collectively think in this case, and that he has already done so.

The possibility of non-basic joint commitments is particularly important in relation to collective beliefs in large populations. Once the relevant authority—whether a single person or collective body—is established by a joint commitment of the whole, the way is open for new collective beliefs of the whole to be established without any kind of population-wide referendum, which can be expensive in terms of the time and energy of all.

2. An Important Aspect of the Joint Commitment Account: The Audience for Expressions of Collective Belief

In approaching Lackey's concerns, it is important to understand the primary audience, so to speak, for the parties' expressions of their collective belief on my account. As I understand it, for certain people be jointly committed *to believe that p as a body* is, at a minimum, for them to be jointly committed to speaking and otherwise acting in ways appropriate to the representatives of one who believes that p *when they are among themselves* and speaking in the relevant capacity, for instance, as members of a particular committee. It is therefore not primarily, let alone solely, for them jointly to commit to acting appropriately *in relation to outsiders*, when speaking in the relevant capacity.

Thus, for example, it is incumbent upon the members of a committee not bluntly to express a belief contrary to the committee's belief *while at one of their meetings*. In contrast, were two committee members to meet socially at a non-member's house, for instance, it would not automatically be incumbent upon either of them to express the group's belief on some matter. The default assumption among those present is likely to be that each of them is speaking "in her own name" on whatever topics come up.

In the context of the committee meeting, if members want to speak in their own name in the context of an established collective belief they can indicate this by prefacing what they say with "Speaking personally..." At a social gathering, that would generally not be necessary. In that context, one might alert people, should one wish to speak as member of the committee, with a similar locution: "Speaking as a member of the...committee..."

3. On "Calling People to Order" in the Name of the Group's Belief

It was partly on account of the kind of "calling to order" one finds in acknowledged cases of collective belief—when people say such things as "How can you say that?" in a rebuking tone to one who bluntly expresses a contrary belief—that I was drawn to an account in terms of joint commitment.[12]

As I have argued elsewhere, those who are party to a given joint commitment have the standing to issue demands and rebukes relating to non-compliance with their commitment.[13] Further, it is hard to establish another ground for such standing. That is a point worth emphasizing to those seeking an account of collective belief that respects the observation just noted.[14]

As I have proposed, once there is a collective belief on my account, the individual parties have reason to express the belief in question in the appropriate contexts, irrespective of their personal beliefs, insofar as each is committed, through the joint commitment, to do so. They also understand that the others have the standings just mentioned or, in other terms, that the others have a right against them to their expressing the belief in question.

These considerations give collective beliefs on the joint commitment account considerable resilience in face of any contrary personal beliefs of the participants, or any inclinations they may have to say something contrary to the collective belief in relevant circumstances. One can thus expect a collective belief on that account to be relatively stable, all else being equal.

4. Group Lies and BS

I now turn to what Lackey has represented as her central concerns regarding what she refers to as "standard accounts"—alternatively "joint acceptance" accounts—among which she includes my own.

---

[12] See the discussion of the "poetry group" case in Gilbert (1987). This argues against a number of possible alternative explanations of the kinds of rebukes I reference here.

[13] See e.g. this volume, chapter 13, section 3.

[14] For extended discussion, see Gilbert (2018: chs. 11, 12).

4.1 Group Lies

Lackey has argued that accounts like my own cannot make room for group lies. Indeed, early in her book she says that the "group lie" problem—along with a "group bullshit" problem—is *the central problem* for these accounts. For they "crucially lack resources to be able to explain how groups can lie and bullshit."[15] Focusing on my own account, I now consider this claim, starting with group lies.

Can the joint commitment account make room for group lies? It can.

Here is a small-scale example of a group lie that can easily be understood in terms of the joint commitment account of collective belief.

It has two stages. I call it HAIRSTYLE:

HAIRSTYLE

First stage:
Jack: I hate Pat's new hairstyle.
Jill: Agreed. It's terrible.

(Now—I take it—they collectively believe that Pat's hairstyle is terrible.)

Second stage:
Jill: We can't tell her that. We must tell her we like it!
Jack: Of course.

(Now they collectively intend to lie to Pat.)

Third stage:
Pat arrives on the scene.
Jack to Pat, speaking on behalf of himself and Jill: "Hi Pat! We think your hair looks great!"
With a smile, Jill nods in agreement.
Jack and Jill secretly exchange a wink and a smile.

The wink and the smile are not essential to the case, but they would very naturally occur in a case like this, which I take to be a clear case of a group lie.

Lackey has invoked a far more consequential situation than HAIRSTYLE, a case where the lie is particularly reprehensible. However, I think something similar can be said of the situation of the cigarette manufacturer Philip Morris, among others, as that is described here:

---

[15] See e.g. Lackey (2021: 17).

The judge ruled that the companies had coordinated their public relations, research and marketing efforts *in order to advance their scheme to defraud by denying the adverse health effects of smoking*...The companies also suppressed and destroyed information related to the dangers of smoking in order to maximize their profit and enhance the market for cigarettes.[16]

Reference to a "scheme to defraud" in this report suggests precisely the kind of two-stage process of group lie production involved in HAIRSTYLE.

First, there is a collective belief that p—smoking is harmful in various ways. Next, there is a collective decision to tell others that not-p. In short, there is a decision to lie to others. Presumably it could take some time for this situation to develop but these would be its central elements.

4.2 A Note on Lackey's Reference to an "Official Position"

Lackey describes her TOBACCO COMPANY case, which alludes to Philip Morris, as follows—I leave out some inessential words:

Philip Morris...is aware of the massive amounts of scientific evidence revealing...the addictiveness of smoking...also the links it has with lung cancer and heart disease. While the members of the board of directors... believe this conclusion, they all jointly agree that, because of what is at stake financially, the official position of Philip Morris is that smoking is neither highly addictive nor detrimental to one's health, which is then published in all of their advertising materials.[17]

Consider the phrase "official position" in this quotation. As I would use it, a group's "official position," if it has one, *need not be something that it believes*. Indeed, I would be more likely to use that phrase to refer to a case in which I was either *agnostic* as to what the group believed, or *thought it believed something other than the official position*.

Thus, going back to HAIRSTYLE, we could say that Jack and Jill's official position is that Pat's hairstyle is wonderful, whereas what they collectively believe is something different.

---

[16] Quotation at https://www.linkedin.com/pulse/lies-tobacco-companies-told-us-united-states-v-philip-jim-wigmore; my emphasis.

[17] Lackey (2021: 28).

In the above quotation Lackey says that Philip Morris "is aware of the...scientific evidence." She does not tell us how to parse this claim, so let's suppose that the operative members of Philip Morris—those who are in a position to establish its beliefs—are jointly committed to believe as a body that the scientific evidence is thus and so, having discussed the relevant scientific reports among themselves and reached that conclusion. Lackey tells us that they then proceed to agree, for financial reasons, that their official position will be a denial of what this evidence shows, setting the company up to lie to anyone outside who asks. Understanding "official position" as I do—in a way I take to be standard—this in no way undercuts the joint commitment account of collective belief.[18]

That said, I shall return to what I take to be Lackey's real concern with the joint commitment account after rebutting her claim that the account cannot deal with group BS.

4.3 Group BS

According to Harry Frankfurt, the world expert on the subject, bullshitters seek to convey a certain impression *without being concerned with its truth or falsity*. Thus bullshitting is different from lying, since the liar aims to deceive. I don't see how the possibility of this phenomenon presents any problems for the joint commitment account of group belief.

Consider this variant of HAIRSTYLE, HAIRSTYLE-2:

HAIRSTYLE-2
First stage:
Jack: Have you seen Pat's new hairstyle? I'm not sure what to think of it.
Jill (sounding bored): No, I haven't.
Jack (dropping the subject): Huh.

Second stage:
Pat appears.
Jack—wanting to ingratiate himself with her, and implicitly inviting Jill to bullshit with him: "Hi Pat. Super hairstyle!"
Jill—taking up his invitation: "Yes, indeed!"

---

[18] Interestingly enough, sometime after the previous quotation, Lackey refers to a group's "official position" in a way that implies that a group's having such a position is *not* for it to have a group belief (2021: 42).

Jack and Jill secretly exchange a wink and a smile. They didn't lie, exactly. They were bullshitting.

Once again, the wink and smile aren't necessary, but would be entirely in keeping with the situation.

5. Lackey's Real Concern?

Now, though early in *Group Epistemology* Lackey suggests—as she had in earlier articles—that accounts like mine "lack resources to be able to explain how groups can lie and bullshit" and sees this as the crucial mark against them, she seems to concede, not long afterwards, that such accounts can, after all, account for group lies—though not group bullshit, describing briefly, in general terms, what a group lie would look like on such accounts.[19] She goes on to express what seems to be a different concern. She says that if it's in Philip Morris's financial interests to believe that smoking is safe, then:

> all that needs to be done to deny culpability for deceiving smokers on most non-summative accounts is to *get the operative members of the group in a room and have them agree that smoking is safe,* and thus there is no lying when this is reported to the public.[20]

Let us consider a more detailed example of this kind, which I call INTIMIDATION:

Jack is a particularly powerful operative member of a company that manufactures cigarettes. At a meeting of the operative members he says, falsely, "It's clear that smoking is harmless!" He stares balefully at the other members, implicitly challenging them to gainsay him, and they don't, even though, as is common knowledge, each has read contrary reports. Cowed into submission, they nod in agreement with Jack, without a trace of demurral. No one winks at anyone or gives any other indication that this is all for show. Indeed, it is not all for show.

I propose that, indeed, in a situation such as this the operative members could now truly say, "We agreed that smoking was harmless"—without any implicit scare quotes around "agreed."

---

[19] Lackey (2021: 17); (2021: 32).   [20] Lackey (2021: 43), my emphasis.

This accords with the joint commitment account of collective belief insofar as an agreement *that such-and-such is the case* is constituted by a joint commitment to believe as a body that such-and-such, arrived at in a particularly explicit way. I would argue that an agreement that such-and-such is precisely so constituted.[21]

Even if one is inclined to accept this, one might wonder if INTIMIDATION is a good example of an *agreement*—given that it is entered into as a result of the intimidation of some or all of the parties. Certainly, the fact that I was intimidated into participating in an agreement is a mitigating circumstance with respect to my responsibility for the concluding of an agreement that is open to criticism. I take it, however, that joint commitments, and hence agreements, can take effect even in broadly speaking coercive circumstances. All that is needed is that the parties are indeed ready jointly to commit themselves in the relevant way. I have argued this elsewhere in relation to agreements on some course of action.[22] I take it that the same is true for agreements that such-and-such is the case.

Let me emphasize that to say that by the end of INTIMIDATION the operative members collectively believe that smoking is harmless is not to say the situation is fine. It's a bad scene, involving Jack's (successful) attempt to intimidate others and, we may suppose, a degree of cowardice on the part of his audience. Moreover, we may suppose, it is part of an attempt on the part of Jack, at least, to deceive the general public for the sake of the company's profits, at the cost of many lives. In short, there is plenty of blame to go around.

None of this, however, seems to undermine the joint commitment account of collective belief. It shows, if you like, that the formation of a collective belief can be part of a highly disreputable process. So can many things that are fine, or at worst, neutral, in themselves, from an evaluative point of view. Most to the point, there is no clear reason a priori to suppose the contrary for collective belief in particular.

Lackey may respond that her real concern in saying that "all that needs to be done … is to have them agree" in a situation like INTIMIDATION is that collective beliefs on my account can, in effect, be willed into being by the relevant parties—just as an agreement, coerced or not, can be willed into being by the parties to it.

That a belief cannot be willed into being by the believer has sometimes been regarded as axiomatic, though this claim has found its detractors. Be

---

[21] For the analogous point about executory agreements—agreements on future actions—see chapter 1, this volume.

[22] In Gilbert (1993). See also Gilbert (2006: 77ff.).

that as it may, those who regard it as axiomatic have focused on the individual case, not the collective case. Even if they are right about the individual case, that does not close the question of the collective case.[23] That depends, of course, on what specifically collective belief amounts to. The point in question cannot, therefore, be used to fault a given account of the latter.

6. Stepping Back

I have the impression that one of Lackey's aims is to construct an account of collective belief such that it necessarily lacks certain egregious flaws. Among the things she wishes to avoid, for instance, is what she refers to as the—potential—"base-fragility" of collective beliefs.[24] Given this desideratum, Lackey does not wish to embrace an account like mine such that collective beliefs can in principle be base-fragile—though they need not be.

Hers is a possible project, but not one I have myself undertaken.[25] I want to understand what people have in mind when they ascribe beliefs to us, collectively, or to a particular group as such in everyday life.

I expect, of course, that, as understood in everyday life, collective beliefs and the beliefs of individuals will have significant features in common. For instance, it seems fair to expect—indeed, it seems to be true—that both my belief and my group's belief are understood to be assessable as true or false. It seems fair to expect, again, that both my and our belief are understood to be assessable in terms of their relation to the evidence available to me—or, in the collective case, to us. In other terms, both individual and collective beliefs can be assessed as well- or ill-founded.[26]

That said, a thorough exploration of the similarities and differences between collective and individual beliefs would compare and contrast their features, giving equal time to both the individual and the collective case.

In doing so, we pursue the project of general epistemology. This project is, I take it, a compelling one.

[23] For discussion on this point, see chapter 4, this volume.   [24] See Lackey (2021: 38ff.).
[25] I cannot speak for Raimo Tuomela, the other "joint acceptance" theorist referenced by Lackey. My impression is that he is not concerned with everyday understandings, as I am.
[26] Paragraph added in response to a comment by Deborah Tollefsen.

References

Dunn, Jeff (2021) "The Epistemology of Groups," review of Lackey (2021). *Notre Dame Philosophical Reviews.* https://ndpr.nd.edu/reviews/the-epistemology-of-groups

Gilbert, Margaret (1987) "Modeling Collective Belief." *Synthese* 73: 185–204.

Gilbert, Margaret (1993) "Agreements, Coercion, and Obligation." *Ethics*, 103(4): 679–706.

Gilbert, Margaret (1996) *Living Together: Rationality, Sociality, and Obligation* (1996) Lanham, MD: Rowman and Littlefield.

Gilbert, Margaret (2002) "Belief and Acceptance as Features of Groups." *Protosociology* 16: 35–69.

Gilbert, Margaret (2006) *A Theory of Political Obligation: Membership, Commitment, and the Bonds of Society.* Oxford: Oxford University Press.

Gilbert, Margaret (2018) *Rights and Demands: A Foundational Inquiry.* Oxford: Oxford University Press.

Gilbert, Margaret, and Pilchman, Daniel (2014) "Belief, Acceptance, and What Happens in Groups: Some Methodological Considerations." In *Essays in Collective Epistemology*, ed. Jennifer Lackey, Oxford: Oxford University Press (pp. 190–212). [Chapter 4, this volume]

Lackey, Jennifer (2020) "Group Belief: Lessons from Lies and Bullshit." *Aristotelian Society Supplementary Volume*, 94(1): 185–208.

Lackey, Jennifer (2021) *The Epistemology of Groups.* Oxford: Oxford University Press.

Tuomela, Raimo (1992) "Group Beliefs." *Synthese*, 91(3): 285–318.

PART III

OUR EMOTIONS

7

Collective Remorse

Remorse is an important response to wrongdoing. Among other things, it can be a vital precursor to forgiveness and an important basis for reconciliation. Can a group feel remorse over its wrongful acts? If so, what does group remorse amount to?

In this chapter, I consider three accounts of group remorse. Two are aggregative. The first of these takes group remorse to involve an aggregation of cases of personal remorse. Three versions of this account are considered. A crucial problem is that no one, on any version of the account, has to feel remorse over an act of the group. The second aggregative account invokes what I call "membership remorse": a member's remorse over his or her group's act. I argue for the intelligibility of such remorse in light of doubts from Karl Jaspers and others. I propose that, in spite of this, generalized membership remorse does not suffice for the remorse of a group. Finally, I present the plural subject account of group remorse that I prefer. I call the phenomenon characterized in the account "collective remorse" and argue for its practical importance.

I. Introduction

As she discovered after the fact, Irene Anhalt's father had been a high-ranking member of the Gestapo in Nazi Germany. In a memoir addressed to him she writes: "I still could not give up my hope that you would feel remorse." Later she describes his deathbed scene: "With infinite effort, as if you already had to call up the words from another world, you spoke: 'It was wrong of the Spaniards to murder the Incas and steal their land.' My throat tightened with tears as I answered you: 'Yes, Daddy—thank you.'"[1]

Moral theory has a tendency to focus on the right and the good rather than on the wrong and the bad. This is not surprising. What we need, it would seem, is instruction as to how to act rightly, not on how to act wrongly.

[1] Anhalt (1993).

Life in Groups: How We Think, Feel, and Act Together. Margaret Gilbert, Oxford University Press. © Margaret Gilbert 2023.
DOI: 10.1093/oso/9780192847157.003.0008

Yet in the world we live in there is much wrongdoing. Anyone concerned with the right and the good must consider how we should respond to wrongdoing, as perpetrators, victims, and observers.

In this chapter I focus on one possible response to wrongdoing. The response in question is remorse. It is not a particularly predictable response.[2] But if and when it does occur it is liable, as Anhalt's story shows, to have significant positive consequences in terms of the feelings of those other than the perpetrator and their relationship to him or her.

Anhalt's father referred not yet to the Nazis or Nazi Germany but rather—as a first step, perhaps—to the Spaniards: "It was wrong of the Spaniards to murder the Incas and to steal their land." This raises the question of wrongdoing by groups and the appropriate responses to that. Insofar as a group can act wrongly, can *it* subsequently feel remorse over its wrongful act?

What could the remorse of a group amount to? This is the question I explore in what follows.

II. Remorse

Remorse in General

To feel remorse over one's act, one must at a minimum judge that one has done something seriously wrong. The term "remorse" suggests that the wrong is definitely more than a mere peccadillo. Regret might suffice for trivial matters. Remorse would be too strong in such a case.

I shall assume that remorse involves a judgment of serious *moral* wrongdoing. That one judges one's act to have been *morally* wrong may or may not be essential to remorse as such. Many instances, however, clearly involve such a judgment.

This does not yet distinguish feeling remorse over one's act from feeling guilt over it. One difference between these two may be that one who feels remorse could always sincerely exclaim, "Would that I had not acted so!" This may not be true of one who feels guilt.[3]

---

[2] People will often remark of someone who has done some dreadful thing, "He showed no remorse." Sometimes they say this with a degree of incredulity, as if they are thinking, "How could he not feel remorse for *that*?" Presumably, though, the more horrible an intentional act, the less one would expect the perpetrator to feel remorse. The very performance of such an act suggests that the agent lacks moral perspicacity; yet some such perspicacity is necessary for remorse.

[3] Thus Morris (1971): "A person who feels guilty may not be disposed to say, 'I'm sorry' or 'Forgive me'; he may not feel sorry about what he did... He may be neither contrite nor repentant... We need

For present purposes I shall assume that we are concerned with altogether *well-founded* remorse. That would mean at least that it is not founded on a mistake about what, if anything, one has done. Nor does it depend on a false judgment to the effect that what one did was seriously morally wrong. It may be that remorse over one's act involves a judgment of one's blameworthiness. In that case well-founded remorse would involve no mistake on that score.

Consequences of Remorse

If one truly feels remorse over what one has done, this is liable, when recognized, to find a response in others. There may be a sense that one has undergone a major transformation, a transformation deep enough for something approaching forgiveness to take place.

The reason for this sense of transformation is clear. Remorse is liable to involve a fundamental change of perspective: one did a certain thing without hearkening to any doubts one might have about it. When one feels remorse it is as if, when it is too late to avoid the action, one finally hearkens to such doubts, perhaps *having them* for the first time. Were the original situation to repeat itself now, one is apparently now so disposed that one would not perform the action.

On this account of it, one who experiences true remorse is clearly liable to act differently in the future. Thus it may reasonably provoke not just backward-looking forgiveness but a renewal of forward-looking trust.

Remorse and Relationships

Given its connections to forgiveness and the restoration of trust, remorse is clearly of great importance where what is at stake is *a relationship* between a perpetrator and a victim, a relationship that either may or must continue in some form or other.[4] Some such relationships are relationships between

only think of the young boy who disobeys his father and who, while feeling guilty, also looks upon himself with more respect. He feels guilty but prefers being damned to renouncing his act."

[4] Irene Anhalt's case and others like it may fall under this rubric in a rather special way. Anhalt would seem to have had several motives for her persisting hope for her father's remorse. She clearly wished her father finally to embrace the values she held dear; this would be a precondition of his remorse and would be liable to give rise to it. She may have felt his remorse would benefit him in that he would at last see true and judge himself accordingly. She evidently also felt it would benefit her in allowing her to experience more positive feelings toward him. Among other things, she would

groups—for instance, nations, different factions within a nation, and families. Can groups feel remorse over what they have done?

III. Is Group Remorse Possible?

Skepticism about Group Emotions in General, and an Initial Response

It may be argued that a group or collectivity cannot feel remorse because remorse is an emotion, and groups cannot have emotions of their own. Their individual human members can, of course, have emotions of *their* own, but *groups* cannot. Why might one think this?

Emotions, it may be argued, essentially involve *feelings*, which are somewhat on a par with *sensations*. An example of such feelings would be the so-called pangs of remorse. Let us call feelings with this "sensation-like" quality "feeling-sensations." It may be proposed that nothing that is not a living organism can have feeling-sensations.

One response to this type of argument might be that it is not clear that emotions essentially involve feeling-sensations. It may be questioned, more specifically, whether to feel remorse is essentially to feel anything of the nature of pangs, twinges, and so on. I have supposed that remorse centrally involves a judgment of serious wrongdoing plus a thought of the form, "Would that I had not done that!" Such a thought encapsulates, one might say, a desire not to have acted in such a way. Might this judgment and this desire not be the central core and essence of remorse?[5]

The skeptic about collective emotions might respond that even if it is correct, this last proposal requires that emotions are properties of *minds*. And there are no group minds. Hence there can be no group emotions.

Whatever we think of these skeptical arguments, what are we to make of the fact that people often quite comfortably say things like, "Our family

presumably be able both to understand and to respect him more. She seems also to have felt his actions cast a shadow on his family, including herself. In that case she may have sought a basis for her own act of forgiveness. As has often been claimed, it is not clear that anyone other than someone's victim can have the standing to *forgive* him or her. Here Anhalt would not be forgiving her father in the name of his primary victims, but she might have a basis for forgiveness nonetheless.

[5] Shaffer (1983) contemplated an analysis of emotion that takes beliefs and desires as essential to emotion in general, though not exclusively so. The possibility of an analysis purely in terms of beliefs and desires is mooted at p. 171. I thank Professor Shaffer for bringing this article to my attention. His concern there, it should be said, concerns the emotions of individuals rather than the emotions of groups.

mourns the loss of a dear friend," "The department is in a state of shock," and "The nation views with great remorse what happened in those years?" People ascribe a whole range of emotions to groups, including remorse. What do these ascriptions mean? Alternatively, what are people talking about when they speak this way?

In what follows I shall understand by "a group's remorse" whatever it is that people refer to when they speak in those terms. Let us now pursue the question: What is it for a group to feel remorse over what it has done?[6]

Skepticism about a Group's Action, and an Initial Response

The skeptic about group remorse in particular may observe that this raises the question whether a group as such can act. One of the founders of sociology, Max Weber, asserted, indeed, that "there is no such thing as a collective personality which 'acts.'"[7]

Weber may have had in mind the fact that for him action was defined in terms of what he calls "subjective meaning."[8] It may seem to follow that groups as such cannot act. If we take this line, we have a problem similar to that of denying the possibility of group emotion.

There is a problem because people talk all the time as if groups act: "The USSR invaded Afghanistan," "The department elected Jack chair," and so on. Are they referring to some actual situation, and if so, what are the components of that situation? What, in other words, do the group actions of common parlance amount to?

I shall at first proceed on the basis of two rough assumptions about group actions. I take it that many group actions conform to these assumptions. They thus help to define a *standard type* of group action.

I shall assume, first, that when a group acts, one or more members of the group *contribute directly* to the group's action. For example, someone's flying over enemy territory may be a direct contribution to his group's act of war making.

I shall assume, second, that some members of a group that acts may *not* directly contribute to the group's action. Thus a university department may elect Jack Jones chair, though one member of the department, Peg, is on leave

---

[6] As will appear from considerations to be advanced later, this is not the only kind of remorse a group might feel. But this question is fine for present purposes.

[7] Weber (1922/1978: 14).

[8] For discussion of the nature of subjective meanings in Weber's sense see Gilbert (1989: ch. 2).

abroad and does not know the election is being held. Though Peg did not contribute directly to the group's action, she can properly say of the department, "We elected Jack."

In relation to a given action of a group, I shall call the members who directly contribute to the action "active" members and the rest "passive" members. The distinction between active and passive members may be hard to characterize precisely, but the examples here fall clearly enough on one or another side.

It is now time to appraise some candidate accounts of group remorse. I shall consider three such accounts.

IV. Group Remorse I: The Aggregated Personal Remorse Account

The first account is what I call the aggregated personal remorse account. It involves a sum or aggregate of states of personal remorse. By *personal remorse* I mean an individual person's remorse over an act of his or her own.

This account runs roughly as follows:

A group G feels remorse over its act A if and only if each active member of G feels remorse over an act or acts of his or her own and taken together these acts compose all of the members' acts that contributed directly to the group's act A.

For instance, an officer may feel remorse for having ordered the killing of a group of civilians, and each of his men may feel remorse for following his orders and killing several people. According to the account, the group comprising this officer and his men satisfies the conditions for feeling remorse over the group's act of killing the civilians.

This account has some attractive features. The state of affairs it takes to be a group's remorse is clearly a possible one. No "mysterious" entities, such as a group mind that operates independently of the minds of the group members, are posited. It is clear that only individual human minds are involved. In addition, insofar as some individual members of a group did morally repugnant things, their personally feeling remorse would appear to be desirable. Among other things, it is likely to lead to better things in the future.

In spite of these advantages, several things suggest that this account must be rejected. For one thing, according to the account each of the relevant people must feel remorse over his own action or actions, and that is all. But it is supposed to be saying what it is for a *group* to feel remorse over *its* act. Here no one is even focusing on an action of the group.

In response to this concern, the original account could be amended to run something like this:

A group G feels remorse over its act A if and only if each active member of G personally feels remorse over having directly contributed to the group's act A.

In this case there is a sense in which all of the relevant people are, indeed, *focusing on* an action of the group. No one yet, though, feels *remorse over* an action of the group. Each of the relevant members' remorse is over an action of his own, namely, his contribution to the group's action, as such.

This account also shares the following problem with its predecessor. Perhaps very few people directly contributed to the group action in question. Now suppose these people feel remorse over their contributions as such. It would surely seem odd to say, just for that reason, that the *group* felt remorse over its action. Yet if these few do feel remorse, the conditions laid down in the amended account are satisfied.

We could try amending the account again to include remorseful feelings on behalf of the passive members over having acted in such a way as to be associated, *as group members*, with the act in question. Then we would have something along the following lines:

A group G feels remorse over its act A if and only if each member of G feels remorse *either* over his or her direct contribution *or*, for those not directly contributing, over his or her association with the group's act A.

A problem here is that it may not be *reasonable* for the various passive members to feel remorse of this kind. Some may have had little choice, for instance, regarding their membership in this particular group. Some may personally have fought against the performance of the group act as best they could. And so on.

When all or most of the passive members reasonably do *not* feel personal remorse over anything they have done relating to their group membership or to the group's act, can there be no group remorse over the group's act? That is at least not obvious, but the newly amended account makes it true by definition.

Suppose that, as may sometimes be the case, every group member *is* personally remorseful over his or her *contribution to* or *association with* the group act. This situation still involves no remorse over the group's act itself.

It seems, then, that both the original aggregated personal remorse account and two variants on it are problematic. The two variants both require that the personal remorse bear some relation to the group's act, but none involves remorse over the group's act itself. In addition, all seem to give the wrong result for the case in which there are few active members and they are the only group members to feel personal remorse in relation to the group's act. On the first two accounts, which both refer to the active members only, there will be group remorse solely by virtue of the personal remorse of these few, which seems wrong. On the third account, which requires all members to feel personal remorse over their participation or association with the group's action, *group remorse is ruled out by definition*. This, too, seems wrong.

V. Group Remorse II: The Aggregated Membership Remorse Account

Is there any other type of account available? In particular, is there an account that does not appeal to the remorse of particular group members over their personal contributions to or association with an act of the group? At this point what I shall call the *aggregated membership remorse account* may suggest itself. It runs roughly as follows:

A group G feels remorse over its act A if and only if the members of G—both active and passive—personally feel remorse over act A.

Does it make sense for any individual member of a group personally to feel remorse over the *group's* act? Common experience suggests that it does. Reflecting on what her group has done, Sarah may think remorsefully, "We did a terrible thing!" referring precisely to what *her group* did and not to what she personally did. She is not likely to question the intelligibility of her emotional response.

That does not mean its intelligibility cannot be questioned. In *The Question of German Guilt*, philosopher and psychiatrist Karl Jaspers movingly recounts his own similar responses to the acts of his country but worries that in so responding he has "strayed completely into the realm of feeling" without the warrant of reason.[9]

Before pursuing this question, let me give the emotional response at issue a label. I shall call it "membership remorse." It is (more fully) a group member's remorse over the act of a group of which he or she is a member.

What does the present account of group remorse seem to have in its favor? Some of its attractions are as follows.

First, there is here—finally—remorse over the group's act itself. Second, on this account a group could in principle feel remorse even if, reasonably, only a few members felt personal remorse over either personal contributory actions or association with the group. For what is required is that members feel membership remorse, not personal remorse. Precisely which and how many members feel personal remorse—if any—is not relevant to the issue of group remorse on this account.

Third, insofar as membership remorse is intelligible at all, it will apparently be appropriate for all members to feel it in relation to a relevant action of the group's. Its appropriateness, in other words, is not restricted to active members or to any other special category of member. It concerns what the group has done, not what the member has personally done. Hence the conditions postulated by the account are not themselves unfeasible for a group of reasonable people even when most members have no reason for remorse over actions of their own.

Is membership remorse intelligible? Can it indeed be appropriate for both active and passive members in relation to a candidate group action? What of someone who did not know the action was taking place at the time? Or someone who protested the action, or ...?

One can argue that there need be no exceptions among group members with respect to the intelligibility of group remorse. The argument I have in mind appeals to a relatively fine-grained model of group action. This will be useful not only in relation to the evaluation of the aggregated membership remorse account but for other purposes of this chapter as well.

---

[9] Jaspers (1947: 80–1). I discussed this passage in more detail in "How to Feel Guilt: Three Different Ways," presented at the conference Guilt, Shame, and Punishment at Columbia University School of Law, March 8, 1998, in honor of Herbert Morris. In relation to Jaspers's concern see Gilbert (2000: ch. 16, "On Feeling Guilt for What One's Group Has Done") and the more extended discussion in Gilbert (1997).

VI. Group Action Revisited

I now sketch an account of group action that goes beyond the assumptions I have been operating with so far. It allows us to grant intelligibility to the idea of membership remorse. I first introduced this account of group action in my book *On Social Facts* in 1989.[10] I have been elaborating it since and continue to do so. The core of this account is the following necessary condition on group action:

For a group to act or (initially) to have its own goal for action, group members must be *jointly committed* to accept the relevant goal as a body.

What is it to accept a goal *as a body*? I understand this somewhat as follows.

For two or more people to accept a goal as a body is for them to emulate, through their several actions (including their utterances), in relevant ways, a single body or person who accepts that goal. To put it somewhat quaintly, these two or more people must attempt by virtue of their several actions to emulate in relevant ways a two or more-bodied person who (single-mindedly) accepts that goal. *Reaching* the goal in question will, of course, require that the individuals perform a range of specific actions of their own.

The type of commitment appropriate accepting a goal as a body is a *joint* commitment.[11] One way to understand what a joint commitment amounts to is to compare and contrast it with a *personal* commitment. Consider first a personal decision, which is, I take it, a form of personal commitment.

Suppose Mike decides to vote for candidate C in the election. One way of thinking about this decision is as embodying a special kind of order or command: a *self-addressed* command. Mike, in effect, commands himself to vote for candidate C. He is the sole author of the command, he is also in a position to rescind the command unilaterally by, as we say, "changing his mind." Until he does so, however, the command stands, and if he fails to vote for candidate C he can be criticized in light of it.

This "self-addressed" command model of personal commitment can be extended to cover joint commitment also. A joint commitment—as I understand it—is not a sum of personal commitments but a truly joint commitment, the commitment of two or more people by those two or more people.

---

[10] See especially Gilbert (1989: 154–67). See also, e.g., Gilbert (2000: ch. 8).

[11] For relatively extensive discussions of joint commitment see Gilbert (1996: Introduction and ch. 1), and (2000: ch. 1) More recently see the Introduction, this volume, and references therein.

By virtue of their several actions, expressing their willingness to be committed jointly with the others, these people constitute the author of the relevant command. Thus Harry may ask Frank "Shall we meet at six?" If Frank replies, "Sure, that'd be great," they now have a joint commitment, indeed, an explicit agreement.[12]

Given this understanding of joint commitment one can argue that one who defaults on a joint commitment offends against the other parties. They have a clear ground for calling the offender to account, and to rebuke or impose other forms of punitive pressure on him or her.[13]

No one of the parties is in a position unilaterally to rescind a joint commitment. The parties must rescind it together.[14]

All joint commitments can be represented in the same way. For some psychological predicate @, the people in question jointly *commit to @ as a body*. People enter joint commitments by mutually expressing their willingness to be jointly committed in the way in question with the relevant others. This is how the relevant joint order is issued.

In a large group where people do not know one another personally, they must openly express their willingness to be jointly committed with others of the relevant type. For instance, each might openly express his or her willingness to be jointly committed in some way with others living on a certain island. The commitment in this case might be to abide "as one" by a certain rule of the road, say, or as a body to accept certain people as arbiters in their disputes. It must be apparent that all of the relevant expressions have been made.[15]

The existence of these expressions should, indeed, in all cases be "common knowledge" in roughly the sense introduced by David Lewis in his book *Convention*.[16] Informally speaking, one might say there is common knowledge in a group G that *p* if and only if the fact that *p* is "out in the open" in G.

Going back to group action, we can say:

---

[12] An explicit agreement is not required for the formation of a joint commitment; see e.g. Gilbert (2000: ch. 1). I take it, though, that everyday agreements are joint commitment phenomena. More specifically, an agreement may be characterized as a joint decision, a joint decision as constituted by a joint commitment to uphold a certain decision as a body. See e.g. Gilbert (1993) and chapter 1, this volume, for further discussion.

[13] In Gilbert (2000: ch. 4), there is a related argument that those who are party to a joint commitment have inextricably associated obligations toward and rights against the other parties. On this point see also several chapters in this volume including chapters 1 and 13.

[14] I elaborate on the "self-addressed command" interpretation of commitment and joint commitment in Gilbert (2000: ch. 4).

[15] For further discussion of the large-group case see, for instance, chapter 12, this volume.

[16] Lewis (1969). For further discussion and references on common knowledge see Gilbert (1989: ch. 4). See also, e.g., Gilbert (2000: ch. 1).

A group G performed an action A if and only if, roughly, the members of G were jointly committed to accepting as a body the relevant goal X, and *acting in light of this joint commitment*, relevant members of G acted so as to bring X about.

For instance, you and I may be jointly committed to accepting as a body the goal of having the house painted by virtue of the painting activity of each of us. Subsequently we may both act in the light of our commitment, coordinating our behavior in such a way that our goal is reached. It can then be said that we (collectively) painted the house.

Acting in the light of a joint commitment will often involve the parties in a variety of side agreements or in carefully monitoring one another's behavior or both. The initial joint commitment need not specify a procedure for its satisfaction.

For present purposes it is important to note that members of G may be jointly committed to accepting a certain goal as a body, and the like, without all knowing or even conceiving of the content of the commitment. This can happen if there is a "ground-level" joint commitment allowing some person or body to make decisions, form plans, and so on, on behalf of the jointly committed persons. Thus an established leader and his or her henchmen may formulate and carry out a plan in the group's name, and the members properly say of the group as a whole, "We did it."

VII. Group Blameworthiness

Does remorse over an act imply the blameworthiness of that act? I have not taken a position on this issue here. But if the answer is positive, it seems that feelings of membership remorse can only be fully intelligible if the idea of a blameworthy group makes sense. Many theorists have supposed it does not, or at least they have supposed the unintelligibility of what they refer to as "collective guilt." As they conceive of it, this seems to amount to much the same thing as group blameworthiness.

It is not clear that this skepticism is warranted. Some pertinent points follow.

I take it as a good axiom to respect the intelligibility of common pre-theoretical thoughts so far as is possible. Thus if remorse implies blameworthiness, the existence of membership remorse itself suggests the intelligibility of a group's blameworthiness, as it suggests its own intelligibility.

The idea that a group may indeed be blameworthy is also supported by the way people talk outside the context of membership remorse. Outsiders frequently say such things as "Switzerland must take the blame for the current crisis," suggesting that in our everyday conception of things groups can be worthy of blame.

Is there an intelligible basis for speaking of the blameworthiness of a group as such? Insofar as this requires a collective or group agent, I have suggested satisfiable conditions of group action. The framework of analysis I have used in relation to group action can also be applied to such things as group belief, including a group's moral belief. Thus I argued in *On Social Facts* that according to our everyday conception, a group as such believes something if and only if the members are jointly committed to believe that thing as a body.[17]

One can, then, make sense of the idea that a group did something it took to be wrong. It also makes sense to distinguish between the coerced and the uncoerced actions of groups. A group may cave in to external pressure—or it may act in disregard of such pressure or in its absence. Thus a group can do something it knows to be wrong without being pressured into it.

If in spite of these things a group for some reason cannot be considered blameworthy for its act, and if membership remorse implies the group's blameworthiness, then membership remorse will be that much less intelligible.[18]

VIII. Membership Remorse and the Remorse of a Group

Leaving aside the intelligibility of a group's blameworthiness (in favor of which I have argued), the joint commitment account of group action supports the intelligibility of another aspect of membership remorse. That is its suggestion that the group's members all bear some relevant relation to the act of their group.

The joint commitment underlying a group act, on this analysis, provides such a relation. The remorseful person may be linked to his (or her) group's act not by any directly contributing act of his own but rather by his participation in such a commitment. This provides an intelligible basis for, if you like,

---

[17] I have discussed collective belief in a number of places; see Gilbert (1996: 7–8) for some terminological points. See also Gilbert (2000: ch. 3). Part II, this volume, includes several more recent discussions.

[18] See Gilbert (2000: ch. 8) for a discussion of philosophical skepticism about collective guilt and the relationship of such skepticism to an account of collective guilt along the lines sketched here.

his *identification* with the group as agent in this case. It allows him to say, with point, "We did it"—as opposed to "They did it" or "Some of us did it."

Some authors appear to see a person's identification with a group's act as self-justifying. In other words, if I identify with a group's act, there is no issue as to whether this identification is justified.[19] I see such identification as, on the contrary, raising the question of justification.[20] And I see participation in an appropriate joint commitment as sufficient justification. Identification has also been brought forward as a ground of political obligations.[21] Here, too, it remains seriously obscure how identification is supposed to do the necessary work of justification.[22]

If Jane—with justification—feels remorse over an act of her group, she may feel no remorse on her own account. She may know that she has acted honorably in the matter of the group action. She may have attempted to stop it or been ignorant of it without culpability for that ignorance. She is still tied to the group and its action by virtue of her participation in the underlying joint commitment.

She can therefore intelligibly think not only that "We did it" but "We should not have done it!" and "Would that we had not done it!" and "We must never do that again!" And she may feel an accompanying pang of remorse. Given its context, this might reasonably be called "a pang of membership remorse."

Suppose now that we grant that those who express membership remorse are doing something that is fully intelligible and that may be entirely appropriate even for those with no personal culpability. Should we accept the membership model of group remorse? I suggest not.

Note first that this account, like the previous ones, is an aggregative account. What is aggregated here is the (membership) remorse of the individual members. It is not remorse over their own acts, or what I have been calling "personal remorse." Rather, it is remorse over the group's act. Still, on the ground, so to speak, we have what is clearly a number of *separate subjects of remorse* rather than one undivided subject of remorse—the group.

---

[19] See, for instance, Morris (1987: 239–40); Horton (1992: 151–4).

[20] For further remarks on the appeal to identification see Gilbert (1997).

[21] See, for instance, Tamir (1993): "Our obligation to help fellow members derives from a shared sense of membership." On the need for some grounding to a "shared sense of membership" (in a distributive sense of "shared") see the discussion in Gilbert (1989: 146–52).

[22] Cf. Simmons (1996: 247–73). Simmons says: "Identification with a political community or with the role of member within it is not sufficient for possessing political obligations" (264). Simmons goes on to envisage that one might "cast identification as a sort of consent," rightly seeing this as an additional move, wrongly (I would say) seeing it as tantamount to a reassertion of the "voluntarism that the identity thesis was originally advanced to replace" (265). For some explanation of why I say "wrongly" here, see Gilbert (1996: ch. 12) and (2000: ch. 6).

Another point, briefly, is that in principle this aggregated membership remorse could be hidden from public view. Each group member may think that he (or she) alone feels remorse. He may therefore not express his remorse openly but suffer it secretly. Once one brings this possibility out, the idea that we should say that the group feels remorse in this case is likely to seem even more suspect.

One could posit common knowledge of the generalized feeling of membership remorse. This, however, does not overcome the first problem. We will then have common knowledge that a set of individuals, the members of group G, feel membership remorse. What of the group as such? There still seems to be a gap between what we have here and something we can with clear aptness refer to as the remorse of a group as such.

It is worth pointing out that this new common knowledge condition can be fulfilled without anyone having publicly expressed remorse. In addition, there may be serious barriers to such public expression. Imagine that in this group the members are jointly committed together to uphold the view that the group can do no wrong. Unless something is done about this joint commitment, it stands as a barrier to anyone's saying that the group has indeed done something wrong.[23]

In this situation group members may constantly speak to one another as if the group's act, A, was perfectly fine, properly justified. This may be the continuing tenor of public discourse. All may realize that they risk rebukes in the name of the joint commitment should they speak otherwise without qualification. And few may wish to risk even the use of the legitimate qualifier "I personally" as in "I personally feel that we acted badly when…"[24] Though this does not amount to outright subversion of the joint commitment, it could be seen as inherently subversive; hence one risks being seen as disloyal to the group even if going only so far.[25]

In the case as it has now been described, it would surely be reasonable to say that *the group* did not yet feel remorse over its act A, though the members individually felt membership remorse over A, and this was common knowledge within the group. One might be reluctant to give up the aggregated membership remorse account, perhaps in its common knowledge version, if no alternative was available. There is an alternative, however, to which I now turn.

---

[23] See the discussion of collective belief in Gilbert (2000: ch. 3). See also e.g. chapter 2, this volume.
[24] On the permissibility of the use of such qualifiers in the context of an established group belief see Gilbert (1989: ch. 5, especially 288–92), or the similar discussion in Gilbert (1996: 200–3).
[25] Cf. Gilbert (2000: ch. 3).

IX. The Plural Subject Account of Group Remorse

The Account

I now come to the account of group remorse that I favor. It is perhaps predictable given all that has gone before. I call it the "plural subject" account. It runs thus:

A group G feels remorse over an act A if and only if the members of G are jointly committed to feeling remorse as a body over act A.

Following what was said earlier, the joint commitment of the parties is (more fully) *to emulate, in relevant ways, by virtue of their several actions, including utterances, a single subject of remorse.* In my terminology, people who are jointly committed to doing something as a body constitute the *plural subject* of the "doing" in question. Thus I call this the plural subject account of group remorse.[26]

There is no doubt that the phenomenon characterized by this account is possible. One who takes it to exist is not committed to the existence of any dubious entities. The existence of a joint commitment is a function of the understandings, expressive actions, and common knowledge of the parties.

Pangs of Remorse in the Context of Group Remorse

Here is a possible worry about this account. Are what I have been calling "feeling-sensations" part of the phenomenon in question? If not, can it really be remorse?

Let us first consider the case of remorse in general. Can one who does not feel pangs of remorse really feel remorse? Contrary to the drift of the questions, the correct answer may be affirmative.

Consider the case of an individual human being. When I say to you, "I feel great remorse," must I be saying something false unless there are pangs or the like in the background? On the face of it, I need not be saying something false. Note that some apparently equivalent expressions do not use the term "feel" at all: "I am full of remorse"; "I am truly remorseful."

---

[26] I introduced the phrase "plural subject" with the meaning I am giving it here in Gilbert (1989: ch. 4).

If this is right, a joint commitment to constitute with certain others, as far as is possible, a body that feels remorse would not require the production of associated pangs of remorse. Nor would it require that one attempt to produce such pangs.

Be that as it may, pangs of remorse are presumably common accompaniments of remorse in an individual human being. Witness the commonplace nature of the phrase "pang of remorse." Is group remorse, on this account, a type of remorse essentially devoid of these natural accompaniments of remorse in an individual human being?

Against this idea, consider the following. Suppose one is intentionally conforming to a joint commitment to feel remorse as a body over some group act. One's conformity is likely to involve one in saying such things as, "What we did was truly terrible," "Would that we hadn't done that!" and so on. In saying such things and acting accordingly in light of one's joint commitment, one may well experience certain associated "pangs."

It is worth considering how best to describe these pangs. Are they associated most directly with one's personal remorse, with one's membership remorse, or with the remorse of the group itself?

By hypothesis, the pangs in question are directly responsive to the group's remorse rather than to any remorse of one's own. Had the group not come to feel remorse, one might never have felt this way. And one's feeling this way may not correspond to any judgments one has made in one's heart with respect to the group's act or to any associated act of one's own.

The pangs in question, then, may best be described as pangs of remorse associated with the group's remorse or, more succinctly, as "pangs of group remorse." That there can be pangs of group remorse in this sense does not fly in the face of common sense, reason, or science. There is no suggestion that there are pangs of remorse experienced within some kind of collective consciousness that exists independently of individual human minds. Pangs of group remorse, in the sense envisaged, exist in and through the experiences of particular group members. Nonetheless, this way of labeling them makes sense.

This is an intriguing line of argument. Whatever one makes of it, for reasons already given the plausibility of the plural subject account of group remorse does not hang on its conclusion—namely, that on that account there is some likelihood of plausibly so-called pangs of group remorse.

I propose that if we are faced with a case of group remorse according to the plural subject account, it is more apt for the title of "group remorse" than the phenomena captured by any of the aggregative or summative accounts considered. It alone brings remorse to the collective level. I propose further that standard everyday claims to the effect that we collectively feel remorse are well interpreted in terms of this account. To make it clear that I am talking about group remorse according to the plural subject account, I shall in what follows refer to it, exclusively, as "collective remorse."

Collective remorse does not rule out personal remorse for one's personal role—and in many cases it will be entirely appropriate to feel such remorse. It does not, however, entail personal remorse for one's personal role—and in many cases it will not be appropriate to feel such remorse.

What I have called "membership remorse" is a person's remorse over the actions of his or her group. This is expressible as "I feel remorse over what my group has done," as opposed to "I feel remorse over what I have done." Evidently, I can feel membership remorse in the absence of collective remorse. Indeed, such membership remorse can be widespread without collective remorse being present, as in the case imagined earlier.

It is possible, too, that there can be collective remorse without membership remorse. In other words, I might be able correctly to avow, "We feel remorse over our act" without being able correctly to avow, "I personally feel remorse over our act." Perhaps I have not reached my own decision on the matter, though I was willing to be jointly committed with the other members of my group to feel remorse as a body.[27]

Clearly, though, there are likely to be de facto connections between membership remorse and collective remorse. If membership remorse is widespread, it is presumably apt to give rise to collective remorse, though it may not do so in special circumstances. If, by virtue of my participation in the prevailing collective remorse, I regularly allude to the wickedness of what we have done, express the wish that it had not happened, and so on, I may well come to reflect privately on the group act in question. I may myself judge it to be evil, myself wish that we had not acted so. In other words, I may come to experience membership remorse, my own remorse over what we have done.

X. Remorse as a Beginning

Remorse may seem at the end of the day too passive a basis for the reconciliation of victims and persecutors—and of two parties each may have played

---

[27] Compare the discussion in Gilbert (1996: 206–7) of reasons why one might be willing to participate in one's group belief that such-and-such though not personally believing that such-and-such.

both roles at some time in their relationship. Yet it is unlikely that without remorse such reconciliation can take place.

Given the existence of remorse, one can expect that perpetrators will go on to perform relevant acts, for instance, to provide restitution or compensation for victims or (in the case of groups) to make relevant changes in their constitution or their laws. Refusal to engage in such acts, when appropriate, will throw doubt on the claim of remorse, if it does not actually refute it.

Thus collective remorse according to the plural subject account is liable to lead to important reconciling actions. When people understand that they are jointly committed as far as is possible together to constitute a single body that feels remorse, they will understand that their remorsefulness (as a body) calls for them to carry out appropriate actions.

I hazard that without collective remorse, where appropriate, intergroup relationships are likely to remain stuck at a level of continuing defensiveness and hostility. Periods of calm are likely to erupt into war over and over again. Collective remorse and collective forgiveness may be required for any genuine reconciliation and any lasting peace.[28]

References

Anhalt, Irene (1993) "Farewell to My Father," in *The Collective Silence: German Identity and the Legacy of Shame*, Barbara Heimannsberg and Christoph J. Schmidt, eds., trans. C. O. Harris and G. Wheeler, Jossey-Bass: San Francisco.

Gilbert, Margaret (1989) *On Social Facts*, Routledge and Kegan Paul: London.

Gilbert, Margaret (1993) "Is an Agreement an Exchange of Promises?" *Journal of Philosophy* 90, 12: 627–49.

Gilbert, Margaret (1996) *Living Together: Rationality, Sociality, and Obligation*, Rowman and Littlefield: Lanham, MD.

Gilbert, Margaret (1997) "Group Wrongs and Guilt Feelings," *Journal of Ethics* 1, 1: 65–84.

---

[28] Versions of this chapter were presented in November 1997 to the Philosophy Department at the University of Connecticut, Storrs; to my undergraduate class in philosophy of social science at the same university, and to an international conference on war crimes at the University of California, Santa Barbara. I also used some of this material in a presentation at the University of Illinois, Urbana-Champaign, in December 1998. I received many useful and stimulating comments on those occasions. I am particularly grateful to Thomas Fote and Jerry Shaffer. Thanks also to Anthony Ellis for written comments and to James Robertson for lending me the book in which I found Irene Anhalt's essay. The subject is a rich one, and this chapter only begins to explore it.

Gilbert, Margaret (2000) *Sociality and Responsibility: New Essays in Plural Subject Theory*, Rowman and Littlefield: Lanham, MD.

Horton, John (1992) *Political Obligation*, Humanities Press International: Atlantic Highlands, NJ.

Jaspers, Karl (1947) *The Question of German Guilt*, trans. E. B. Ashton, Capricorn: New York.

Lewis, David K. (1969) *Convention: A Philosophical Study*, Harvard University Press: Cambridge, MA.

Morris, Herbert (1971) "Guilt and Suffering," *Philosophy East and West* 21, 4: 107–8.

Morris, Herbert (1987) "Nonmoral Guilt," in *Responsibility, Character, and the Emotions: New Essays in Moral Psychology*. Ferdinand Schoeman, ed., Cambridge University Press: Cambridge.

Shaffer, Jerome (1983) "An Assessment of Emotion," *American Philosophical Quarterly* 20, 2: 161–72.

Simmons, A. John (1996) "Associative Political Obligations," *Ethics* 106, 2: 247–273.

Tamir, Yael (1993) *Liberal Nationalism*, Princeton University Press: Princeton, NJ.

Weber, Max (1922/1978) *Economy and Society* vol. 1, G. Roth and C. Wittich, eds., University of California Press: Berkeley) (from the posthumous German original, 1922).

8

How We Feel

Understanding Everyday Collective Emotion Ascription

In everyday life people frequently ascribe emotions of various kinds to "us" or "them." Here are some examples of the kind of statement I have in mind:

We are very excited!
We feel terrible about what happened.
We feared the worst.
We kept hoping things would get better.
We are truly angry.

Those who say such things may sometimes intend them to be elliptical for "We are both so excited!" or "We are all so excited!" and so on. I take it, however, that much of the time what is intended by the speaker is what seems to be intended: the ascription of an emotion to *us*, not to "me, on the one hand, and him, on the other" or the like.[1] For the sake of a label I refer to such statements, under the latter interpretation, as *collective emotion ascriptions*.

To which presumed states of the world are collective emotion ascriptions intended to refer? The easy answer is that "We are very excited" refers to our being very excited, and so on. The question of this chapter is: Can we go further than this unexceptionable but unhelpful explanation? In other terms, can we say more about *collective emotions* as they are conceived of in everyday thought and talk?[2] After some preliminary remarks intended both to clarify and justify the question, a positive answer is offered, and some consequences of the existence of collective emotions according to that answer are considered.[3]

---

[1] I take this to be the default interpretation but there is no need to argue that point for present purposes.

[2] Thenceforth my use of the phrase "collective emotions" and the like is intended to be short for "the referents of everyday collective emotion ascriptions."

[3] I have previously discussed collective emotions in several places, including Gilbert (2000), focusing on collective remorse [chapter 7, this volume], and Gilbert (2002), focusing on collective guilt feelings. This paper offers a more general focus. Given space limitations I concentrate on the exposition of my own position. See Salmela (2012) for some other perspectives.

Life in Groups: How We Think, Feel, and Act Together. Margaret Gilbert, Oxford University Press. © Margaret Gilbert 2023. DOI: 10.1093/oso/9780192847157.003.0009

Preliminaries

Collective Emotions and Collectivities

Consider the following statements:

The football team is so excited!
Our family feels terrible about what happened.
The department feared the worst.
The couple kept hoping things would get better.
The union was very angry.

How do these relate to the previous list? One who says "We are excited" if asked who "we" are, may well say, for instance, "the football team." More generally, he (or she) may invoke a familiar *collectivity concept*. Nonetheless, it is possible to say of oneself and one or more other people "We are excited" without there being any familiar collectivity concept to invoke in answer to the question. Thus, if asked who "we" are, one's best answer may be "she and I" or "These people and I." Or one may best say something like "the people in this room," "those living in this territory," and so on. Here one specifies the people in question by reference to some quality they share. For this reason the items in the first list can be taken to exemplify the most basic type of collective emotion ascription.

The point just made does not speak to the question whether a collective emotion is always the emotion of a collectivity, whether or not that collectivity is of an already recognized kind. It may seem, indeed, that if I can properly ascribe an emotion to us, then we constitute a collectivity, a collective "we." I return to this point in due course.

Collective Emotions and Descriptive Social Science

One may wonder how useful the pursuit of the question of this paper can be for social scientific purposes. To amplify this concern I distinguish between the descriptive and the interpretive aspects of social science.[4] Roughly speaking, *descriptive* social science attempts to describe how things are in the social

---

[4] Here and in what follows I have in mind those social sciences that focus on the human as opposed to the broader animal world.

world; *interpretive* social science attempts to describe how the participants in that world think about it. To that end interpretive social science needs to understand the participants' concepts.

How things are in the social world includes the thoughts and concepts people have, so descriptive social science has a broader purview than interpretive social science. Within descriptive social science, however, one can always ask: Are these thoughts *true*? Do these concepts *apply* to anything in the world?

If the concepts with which people operate fail to apply to anything in the world, they may still be of great interest. Indeed, their existence will call for explanation. They will not, however, be acceptable for descriptive purposes that go beyond those of interpretive social science (cf. Weber, 1964).

One may wonder about the utility of understanding collective emotion ascriptions for the purposes of descriptive social science in particular. One will do so if one holds that, considering human beings and the groups they constitute, only individual human beings can have emotions. I now briefly consider what may prompt this thought.

Collective Emotions, Individualism about Consciousness, and the Emotion Thesis

Suppose one accepts the thesis I shall call *individualism about consciousness.* This thesis runs roughly thus: Considering individual human beings and the groups they constitute, only the former are conscious or have their own states of consciousness or phenomenological states, where a group's state of consciousness would be independent of the states of consciousness of its individual members. This, it may be alleged, means that only individual human beings can have emotions.

Whether or not the point about emotions follows from individualism about consciousness depends on what emotions are. Many will find appealing *the emotion thesis:* To have a specific emotion is at least in part to be in a particular state of consciousness. That is, for a particular being to have a specific emotion is for *that very being* to be in a particular state of consciousness. Given the emotion thesis, it would seem that for a group to have an emotion would be for there to be an associated state of consciousness of its own.

Given both the emotion thesis and individualism about consciousness, it appears that collective emotions are impossible. Some such line of reasoning may have led such philosophers as Christopher Kutz (2001) to dismiss the possibility of, as he puts it, "collective affective states" (p. 196).

Evaluating the Emotion Thesis

Is the emotion thesis true? One can see this as essentially a matter of definition of the word "emotion." Definitions can be *reportive*—answering, for instance, to current everyday usage—or *stipulative*, in which case the definition is likely to be geared to a specific purpose.

Suppose one seeks a reportive definition of "emotion" that is sensitive to everyday usage. Suppose, further, that one accepts individualism about consciousness. Then the emotion thesis is hard to sustain in light of the prevalence of collective emotion ascriptions-statements that ascribe emotions to *us* rather than to me, on the one hand, and you on the other.

People who make collective emotion ascriptions do not generally see themselves as speaking in a fanciful or humorous fashion. There are no implicit scare quotes as in "We *feared* the worst," or, for that matter, "*We* feared the worst." They cannot therefore be discounted on such grounds.

If individualism about consciousness is correct, and if you and I can have an emotion that is ours, rather than mine, on the one hand, and yours, on the other, then it is not the case that one must be in a particular state of consciousness oneself in order to have an emotion. That is to say, the emotion thesis is false.

This does not rule out the appropriateness for some purposes of a *stipulative* definition of "emotion" that allows for the truth of the emotion thesis. If one's focus is on the emotions of individual human beings in particular, it may be reasonable stipulatively to define an "emotion" as something tied to its possessor's possession of a particular conscious state. I speak cautiously here, since the extent to which the emotions of an individual necessarily involve his or her conscious states is a matter of debate.

People may tend to assume that the emotions of individuals are centrally a matter of sensation-like conscious experiences or, as I shall label them, *feeling-sensations*. Thus one who, as we put it, "feels remorse" may be presumed to experience "pangs" of remorse. One who says "I was jealous" may be supposed to have experienced the "sting" of jealousy. One who is afraid may be assumed to feel the "cold hand" of fear. And so on.

Even if one is not inclined to assume that something sensation-like is central, one may assume that to each emotion corresponds a specific phenomenological state, so that, for instance, to be afraid is to be in the grip of a particular kind of experience, or, as I shall put it here, in the grip of a particular *feeling*.

Among philosophers who have focused on the emotions with reference to the individual case, however, several have argued that particular feeling-sensations or, more generally, feelings, are not central to the constitution of a given emotion. They may not even be considered essential.

Focusing on the discourse of everyday life, John Dewey (1895, pp. 16–17) writes:

> When we say that John Smith is very resentful at the treatment he has received, or is hopeful of success in business, or regrets that he accepted a nomination for office, we do not simply, or even chiefly, mean that he has a certain 'feel' occupying his consciousness. We mean he is in a certain practical attitude, has assumed a readiness to act in certain ways.

Several of Dewey's various statements about what "we mean" in the discussion from which I quote refer exclusively to dispositions to act in certain ways. Theorists writing more recently have also questioned the centrality of both feeling-sensations and feelings to the emotions of individuals.[5]

There is no need to take a stand on this issue for present purposes, and I do not do so. I mention it simply to show that even in the case of individuals the role of particular conscious states in the constitution of emotions has been subject to debate.

A Pressing Question of Independent Interest

Evidently the nature of emotions in the individual case has long been discussed, sometimes in an attempt to track the referents of everyday ascriptions of emotions to individuals. The project of seeking a general reportive definition of emotion that covers *both* ascriptions of emotion to individual human beings *and* collective emotion ascriptions has not received such attention. Nor has the question: To what states of affairs "on the ground" do everyday *collective* emotion ascriptions refer?

---

[5] Shaffer (1983, p. 171), for instance, envisages—though he does not ultimately endorse—an analysis of emotion purely in terms of beliefs and desires. For Nussbaum (2001), emotions are forms of evaluative judgment.

The last question is of independent interest. One may not be concerned to develop a general reportive definition of the kind just mentioned. One may simply want better to understand everyday collective emotion ascriptions. Apart from anything else, they may direct one to a significant phenomenon whose existence may otherwise be overlooked. Going back to concerns mooted earlier, they may direct one to a phenomenon that descriptive social science, for one, will ignore at its peril.

Summative Accounts: A Caution

Before entering the question of the referent of collective emotion ascriptions or, more briefly, *the nature of collective emotions*, I should emphasize the following.

Suppose one assumes that everyday collective emotion ascriptions do not implicitly deny individualism about consciousness. *This does not imply any particular account of collective emotions.* Nor can any account of the referents of everyday collective emotion ascriptions beyond the purely trivial be taken for granted.

In particular, if someone says, "We are very excited about this news!"— when this is not elliptical for "Each of us is very excited about this news!"— one cannot assume without argument that, nonetheless, the situation he is referring to just is each one's being very excited about the news in question, or even that it includes that situation. In technical terminology I have used elsewhere, one cannot assume without argument the correctness of a *summative* account of collective emotions. (Gilbert, 1989, ch. 5, takes the term "summative" from Quinton, 1975.)

There is more than one type of summative account that might be offered. One is the simple account according to which a group has emotion E if and only if each of its members has emotion E. Another is that a group has emotion E if and only if each member has emotion E and this is common knowledge in the group. More complex summative accounts may also be offered. (Gilbert, 1989, ch. 5, considers several potential summative accounts of collective *belief*.)

That collective emotions can be given some form of summative account may be a natural assumption. (It finds expression in, e.g., Quinton, 1975.) That does not mean that the correct account is a summative one.[6] Any account

---

[6] For a lengthy rebuttal of summativism in relation to collective belief, see also chapter 2, this volume. For a briefer version, see Gilbert (1987).

of collective emotions needs to be justified. More precisely, one needs to justify one's account of the referents of everyday collective emotion ascriptions by appeal to the kinds of context in which such ascriptions are commonly made and by the implications that those who make them attribute to them.[7] This will be my procedure in what follows.

Toward an Account of Collective Emotions

Some bases for a collective emotion ascription

Consider the following imaginary discussion:

ALICE (SPEAKING EXCITEDLY TO BEN AND CHRIS): "Stella won the prize!"
BEN (ALSO IN AN EXCITED TONE): "Wow!"
CHRIS: "That's terrific!"

This might be extended as in:

BEN: "She's worked so hard for this!"
ALICE: "She really deserves it!"
CHRIS: "It's definitely matter for celebration!"

There may also be further related non-verbal behavior such as:

ALICE SMILES BROADLY.
BEN AND CHRIS EXCHANGE A "HIGH FIVE."

In any of these increasingly complex contexts Alice, Ben, or Chris may well feel comfortable making the collective emotion ascription: "We are excited by the news about Stella." Indeed, at least on the face of it, any one of them would be right to say this.

No one need actually say, "We are excited" for it to be true. Nor would the involvement of words be necessary to justify the collective emotion ascription, given the initial announcement or some other happening that serves the

---

[7] Something that is likely to have little if any evidentiary value is asking people to give off-the-cuff judgments as to what they mean by the collective emotion ascriptions they make. Though there is surely is a sense in which they "know what they mean" by what they are saying, it is unlikely that they will be able quickly to come up with an accurate account of the type sought here.

same purpose. For instance, Stella comes into the room carrying the prize. The occurrence of appropriate non-verbal behavior would be enough.

What general description should we give of contexts such as these that suffice to establish a particular collective emotion? It will be easier to say with some further data in mind. The data on which I focus here concern the ways in which two or more of the people in question might speak to each other after the establishment of their collective emotion. I call these people the *parties* to the collective emotion.

Behavior in the Context of Collective Emotions

Suppose that on the basis of verbal and non-verbal interchanges such as those just envisaged, Alice, Ben, and Chris understand themselves to be collectively excited about Stella's prize. Alice, Ben, and Chris remain together and talk about something else. Alice suddenly looks gloomy and angrily bursts out, "Why did Stella have to win *another* prize!"

Such an outburst is clearly not expressive of excitement over Stella's prize. It is therefore not in the spirit of the collective emotion in question. It may well surprise the others. They are likely to act, however, as if more than a failed prediction is at issue.

They may well feel that Alice is doing something wrong: that Alice *should* not be speaking like this. Indeed, they may well feel that she *owed* it to them not to do this. They may, in other terms, feel *offended against*. Thus Ben or Chris might well say, in a rebuking tone, "How can you say that?" or simply "*What?*" They will take it for granted that they have *the standing to rebuke* Alice for failing to act in ways expressive of excitement over Stella's prize. There is an important family of concepts involved here. To introduce some elements not yet in play in the foregoing discussion, if one has the standing to rebuke someone for doing x, there is some other action that one has *the standing to demand*, one precluded by their doing x.[8] If one has the standing to demand some action, then one has a *right* to that action, and the addressee of the demand has an obligation to perform it, a *directed obligation*, directed toward oneself. In terms previously invoked, this person *owes* one the action. (For further discussion with an emphasis on rights, see Gilbert, 2012.)

A satisfactory account of collective emotions will account for the fact that the parties have the standing to rebuke one another for behavior that is not in

---

[8] There are some exceptions to this that are irrelevant here.

the spirit of the collective emotion, and all of the accompanying standings, rights, and obligations just mentioned. To put the point more briefly: an adequate account of collective emotions generally will satisfy *the obligation criterion.*

This immediately shows that both the simple summative account of collective emotions and the summative account with common knowledge are inadequate. For the conditions they posit do not suffice to satisfy the obligation criterion.

It also suggests that the establishment of a collective emotion involves something like an agreement. (See chapter 1, this volume, which discusses the connection between collective or "shared" *intentions* (what *we* intend) and agreements.) As to the nature of agreements themselves, there is reason to think that at the core of any completed agreement or promise is a special type of commitment—a *joint* commitment. (See, e.g., Gilbert, 2006, ch. 10; Gilbert, 2013b, ch. 13, and ch. 1, this volume.)

The same goes for many central social phenomena other than agreements and promises. These include collective goals, beliefs, and values. (On collective goals see, e.g., Gilbert, 2006, chs. 6 and 7; on collective beliefs see e.g., Gilbert, 1989, ch. 5, also Gilbert, 2013b, chs. 6 and 7; on collective values see, e.g., Gilbert, 2013b, ch. 8, and chapter 10, this volume.) All involve standings, rights, and obligations of the sort at issue in the case of collective emotions. Given these points, the idea of an account of collective emotion in terms of joint commitment suggests itself.

A Joint Commitment Account of Collective Emotion

In what follows I first set out the account I have in mind, then explain the technical terms involved. The core of any joint commitment account of collective emotion is of the following general form, where "E" stands for the emotion in question:

Persons X, Y, and so on (or: members of population P) are collectively E if and only if they are jointly committed to be E as a body.

Thus a joint commitment account of collective excitement, for instance, would run:

Persons X, Y, and so on are collectively excited if and only if they are jointly committed to be excited as a bod y.

There are several technical terms to explain here. The first is what I mean by "joint commitment." I discuss this copiously in, e.g., Gilbert, 2006, ch. 7, and in Gilbert, 2013b, especially in ch. 2. What follows should suffice for present purposes.

I start by saying something about the general notion of commitment at issue. To be *committed* to doing something, A, in the broadest applicable sense is to *have sufficient reason* to A, where this means that one would be wrong not to do A, all else being equal.[9] In other terms, one would be *acting in error* if one did not do A. Thus being committed is a normative rather than a psychological matter.

It is important to emphasize that in saying one would be wrong or be acting in error if one did not do A, I do not mean that one's action would, necessarily, be *morally* wrong. On some plausible conceptions of moral wrongness it may not be.

An example of the relevant kind or error in action is that made possible by a personal decision, such as Dina's decision to call Joe this evening. I take it if that Dina makes this decision, and does not later change her mind, she is committed, in the sense just described, to calling Joe this evening. (For further discussion of the normativity of personal decisions see Gilbert, 2013a.)

Joint commitments in my sense have important affinities with personal decisions. Centrally, in making her decision Dina *committed herself* to calling Joe this evening. In doing so she created what I refer to as a commitment *of the will.* In this case the commitment is a *personal* one. In such cases—as I define them—the committed person unilaterally brings the commitment into being and can rescind it unilaterally by changing his mind.

In order *jointly* to commit them all, it is neither necessary nor sufficient for each of those involved to make an appropriate personal commitment. That would indeed involve all of their wills. For joint commitment, however, their wills must be involved in another way.

In the *basic case* of joint commitment, on which I focus here, all of those involved must express their readiness, in conditions of common knowledge, *for their all being committed, as one,* in some particular way. As all understand, *these expressions of readiness, in conditions of common knowledge, suffice to commit them all*: they are now *jointly committed.* Once they are jointly

---

[9] I use "have sufficient reason" in the technical sense indicated. Others may have used the phrase with a different meaning. For further discussion of what I have in mind and some contrasting ideas see, e.g., Gilbert (2006, ch. 2).

committed, the concurrence of each is required for the joint commitment to be rescinded. No one party is in a position unilaterally to rescind it.[10]

Things would be different if each had made a personal commitment of some kind. For example, suppose each had decided to go for a walk with the other on the weekend. Even given common knowledge of these personal decisions, each would be in a position unilaterally to free himself from his self-imposed commitment. He would not need the others' concurrence.

As noted earlier, I have argued elsewhere that the core of any completed agreement is a joint commitment. More specifically, it is a joint commitment to endorse as a body a particular plan of action. (See, e.g., Gilbert, 2006, ch. 10; chapter 1, this volume.) In this case there is a preamble, often verbal, making clear what plan of action is proposed, as in "Shall we go to the meeting?" "Yes, let's." Importantly, the expressions of readiness necessary for joint com-mitment can be made non-verbally, and their exchange may well not consti-tute an agreement strictly speaking. References in many fields to "tacit" or "implicit" agreements may be responsive to the phenomenon of joint com-mitments that do not amount to agreements.

When two or more people are jointly committed in some way, the parties are committed, as one, to a single cause. By virtue of this, each of the parties is individually committed to act in ways appropriate to the fulfillment of the joint commitment by all.

The content of every joint commitment is of the form indicated earlier: the parties are jointly committed to do something *as a body*—in a broad sense of "do" relating specifically to psychological states. This formulation is to be understood in a particular way. Focusing on the case of a collective emotion, it means roughly this: the parties are jointly committed to emulate, by virtue of their several actions and utterances, in relevant circumstances, a single subject of the emotion in question.

As to the mode of emulation, what is at issue is each party's overt actions— each party's *public performance*. Use of the term "performance" may help to emphasize the importance of aspects of behavior such as manner and tone. The qualifier "public" indicates that *what goes on in each mind and heart* is not at issue with respect to what the parties are committed to. In the case of col-lective excitement over some happening, then, the parties are to emulate a

---

[10] In *non-basic* cases there is a background basic joint commitment to the effect that a given person or body is in a position to impose further joint commitments on them all. For some discussion see, e.g., Gilbert (2006, ch. 8), and the Introduction, this volume.

single subject of excitement over that happening by virtue of the combination of their public performances.

I shall say that a joint commitment *instructs* the parties to act in a certain way if it is manifest *from the content* of the joint commitment that the parties must act in that way if they are to fulfill it. It is evident, then, that the joint commitment constitutive of a case of collective excitement does not instruct the parties to be personally excited over the happening in question. In other terms, no one of the parties need be able truly to say "I am excited over..." with regard to the happening in question.

Again—assuming this is a different point—the joint commitment constitutive of a case of collective excitement over some happening does not instruct the parties personally to experience a "thrill" of excitement or any particular feeling-sensation or feeling.

These aspects of the joint commitment in question may be just as well, insofar as human beings may not be able to conjure up personal emotions, feeling-sensations, or feelings at will. It may be pointed out that one can often bring these things about by various means. Be that as it may, the envisaged joint commitment does not instruct one to take any such steps, as long as one's public performance, including its "expressive" quality, is adequate.

I take it to be intuitive that if, say, Alice, Ben, and Chris are jointly committed to be excited, as a body, over Stella's win, then by virtue of that fact Ben and Chris have the standing to rebuke Alice for angrily bursting out, "Why did Stella have to win *another* prize?" given that her outburst does not conform to the pertinent joint commitment.

Again, each has the standing to demand conforming behavior of the other, and so on. A joint commitment account of collective emotion, then, satisfies the obligation criterion. This is an important argument in favor of such an account.[11]

A joint commitment account also predicts that given the responsiveness of the parties to their normative situation, and given a case of collective excitement, for instance, then, all else being equal, the parties are likely to behave and talk, in appropriate circumstances, as if they were of one—excited—mind. This is something we would expect once it has been established that the parties in question are collectively excited.

---

[11] Though I cannot enter the pertinent discussion here, it is possible that no other kind of account can satisfy this criterion. See Gilbert (2012) for further discussion of this point and of the relationship between joint commitment and having the standing to make pertinent demands and rebukes.

A joint commitment account of collective emotion also accords with earlier considerations on the ways in which a given collective emotion may be established, allowing for a particular interpretation of the scenarios envisaged earlier. In particular, they suggest that each party is, at a minimum, expressing his readiness to be subject to the relevant joint commitment.

In saying that the *core* of any joint commitment account of collective emotion will be a joint commitment with the content indicated, I meant to allow for complex joint commitment accounts of collective emotion that add further conditions to this core. That said, an account that has only the core condition specified has much promise. I shall focus upon it in what follows, referring to it for present purposes as, simply, *the joint commitment account* of collective emotion.

In addition to the virtues just noted, this account accords with and, indeed, helps to explain an intuitive idea mooted earlier: if one can properly ascribe an emotion to us, then we constitute a collectivity. For it can be argued that any set of jointly committed persons constitutes a collectivity or social group in a central sense of the term. (See, e.g., Gilbert, 2006, ch. 8.) Thus the joint commitment constitutive of a collective emotion makes a collectivity of the parties, whether or not they constituted a collectivity before the establishment of this joint commitment.

It is not possible to offer a full elaboration of the joint commitment account here. Enough has been said, however, to facilitate consideration of the relationship of collective emotions on the joint commitment account to the personal emotions of the parties. This will be my focus in the rest of the chapter.

Collective Emotions and the Personal Emotions of the Parties

If there is a particular collective emotion what, if anything, does that tell us about the personal emotions of those involved? For present purposes a *personal* emotion is the emotion of a particular human being: Joe's anger, Phyllis's sadness, and so on.[12]

I shall focus on a somewhat more limited question: If there is a particular collective emotion, can we infer that all or some or at least one of the parties has *the corresponding personal emotion* or at least had it when creating the

[12] I include here, therefore, such emotions as what I have referred to elsewhere as the "membership guilt" and "membership remorse" of an individual human being. See, e.g., Gilbert (1997) and chapter 7, this volume.

collective emotion? By my definition, if a collective, C, has emotion E, then a given member of C with emotion E* has *the corresponding personal emotion* provided that the correct description of E and E* is identical at the applicable level of detail.

To illustrate: suppose we collectively feel guilty over our waging a particular war of aggression. If I am one of us, what would the corresponding personal emotion be for me? As I am defining this, the corresponding emotion would be my feeling guilty *over our waging that particular war.* It would not be my feeling guilty over my participation in the war, supposing that I did participate in its waging, or my feeling guilty over my membership in this particular group, to cite two other possibilities. One way of bringing out the difference is to say that these other emotions have a different *object* from the collective emotion.

There has been discussion as to whether it would make sense for *me* to feel guilty over *our* waging a war (Jaspers, 1947, pp. 80–1, poignantly expresses doubt on this point). After all, I didn't myself wage it—not me, myself, alone. Nor need I have actively participated in its waging. Perhaps I did not even know, at the time, that it was being waged. I have argued elsewhere that it does make sense for me to feel guilty over our waging a war, by virtue of being one of us (Gilbert, 1996, ch. 16; 1997; 2013b, ch. 3). Importantly, my feeling guilty over our waging a war does *not* presuppose that I bear any *personal* guilt for the war. The same goes for remorse, or pride.

If there are collective emotions such that there *is* no intelligible corresponding personal emotion, then collective emotions are not always associated with the corresponding personal emotions—assuming that an unintelligible emotion is also an impossible one: someone who purported to have that emotion would have to be wrong.[13]

I shall consider cases where the corresponding personal emotion is possible. I start with the situation prior to the collective emotion's existence.

In practice it could often be the case that the corresponding personal emotion of at least one party plays an important role in the genesis of a collective emotion. Thus, in a scenario such as the first one considered earlier, one or more of the speakers may well be excited over Stella's win. Nonetheless, there is no logical necessity that those who together co-create a given collective emotion have the corresponding personal emotion before or while they are doing so.

Though it is logically possible that a collective emotion can arise without each of the parties first personally having the emotion in question, one might

---

[13] An example of an unintelligible emotion would be one person's purported pride over the action of another person in which he had had no involvement. "How can *he* be *proud* of that?" one might think.

wonder if this is a possibility in practice. In particular, one might wonder why anyone would be ready jointly to commit himself with others to emulating one with a certain emotion when he did not have that emotion himself. In fact there are many possible reasons, some of which I note briefly here.

An important possibility is that one's helping to create a particular collective emotion is a practically wise thing to do. For instance, it may be that bringing a given collective emotion into being will help the parties move forward in some collective endeavor in which one hopes they will succeed. Thus, if we are collectively excited about our prospects in the upcoming game then—irrespective of our personal feelings—we may be more likely to win. For it will be incumbent upon each of us to act in ways expressive of the collective emotion, such as continuing to train for the event and foregoing activities likely to impede our success. No one should let his actions express the attitude "We are not going to win, so why bother…?"

Again, there may be a social norm in one's society requiring the formation of certain collective emotions, to which one is responding, without reference to one's personal emotions with respect to the matter at hand. For instance, it may be incumbent upon a person's friends to be collectively excited on hearing about her success. Such a norm would seem to be of practical utility, being apt both to reward individuals for their successes and to help keep in check some of the more painful human emotions connected with the successes of others.

Finally—in this particular list—a threatening member or outsider to this particular group may make it clear that any collective emotion other than one this person indicates will not be tolerated by him. For instance, the others must collectively regard him with awe. I do not mean to endorse such coercive behavior, but to point out that someone may be ready to capitulate and help to form the relevant collective emotion with others, though he lacks the corresponding personal emotion. (On the relation of coercion to the possibility of joint commitment and related matters see, e.g., Gilbert, 2006, ch. 10.)

Suppose that, in a given case, the kinds of expression of readiness required for the establishment of a collective emotion are made in the absence of the correlative personal emotions. This does not mean that there is something "fake" about these expressions. No one is pretending to feel the personal emotion in question. Rather, each is indicating to the others which collective emotion he is ready to establish. Nor does it mean that the resulting collective emotion itself is "fake."[14]

---

[14] People *can* together fake a collective emotion. As when, in a new scenario, Alice says to Ben and Chris as Stella approaches, "I know what each of us is thinking, but let's pretend we're overjoyed that she's won the prize!" Here she proposes that they participate in a bit of *collective pretense*. In another

Turning now to the situation in which a given collective emotion has been formed and is functioning properly, must the corresponding personal emotions come into being alongside the collective emotion? On the face of it, they need not. It will be good, however, to look at a particular case in some detail.

Suppose that Chris was originally disappointed by Stella's prize, and only said "That's terrific!" in order to curry favor with Alice and Ben. Once the collective emotion of excitement has been formed, he has accordingly joined in all the smiling and hailing of Stella that is now incumbent on the parties. It seems that he might do this without himself being excited about Stella's win. In case this seems questionable, let us consider the situation in more detail.

As far as his public performance goes he is acting pretty much exactly as he would were he excited about Stella's win. Here we can set aside considerations relating to pertinent demands and rebukes he might deliver to or receive from the others. On the basis of his behavior, an observer might well judge that Chris is excited over Stella's win. Yet what underlies his so acting does not seem to be of the right type for us to say that this judgment would be correct.

Whatever precisely the right foundation would be, it would not seem to be a joint commitment with certain others to emulate one who is excited, by virtue of their several actions and utterances. In other terms, if that joint commitment, and that alone, is what drives Chris's excited behavior, he could yet not truly say, "I, personally, am excited about Stella's win."

That is not to say that he could not be personally so excited. It is just that the existence of the complex comprising the pertinent joint commitment and behavior on his part that is solely responsive to it does not entail that he, personally, is excited about Stella's win. It seems, then, to be an empirical question whether, in the context of a given collective emotion, however well-functioning, people tend to develop the corresponding personal emotions.

Whether or not the corresponding personal emotions are triggered when a given collective emotion is present, other personal emotions may well be triggered, as in the following example. A crowd of people has assembled to listen to a local politician, Rose Smith. Her associates cheer excitedly when she speaks, hoping to whip up some more general enthusiasm. They succeed, insofar as, in due course, the crowd members have mutually expressed their readiness jointly to commit with all present to emulate a single subject of excitement about Smith's speaking, and this is common knowledge. The crowd members are now collectively excited. Accordingly they clap and cheer,

version of this, Alice is not so explicit about what is going on: she winks at Ben and Chris before she launches into a show of excitement over Stella's prize, in which the others knowingly join.

call out Smith's name with enthusiasm, and so on. By now, some members of the crowd are personally excited about Smith's candidacy. Many are personally excited, rather, about being part of a cheering crowd.

It may happen that as he plays his part in the collective enactment of excitement over Smith's candidacy, Jake's feeling-sensations, or other conscious states, are those typical of an excited person, though it is not correct to say that he is himself excited over Smith's candidacy, or over being part of a cheering crowd, or anything else. It is his playing his part in the collective excitement, acting on the basis of the constitutive joint commitment, that has triggered his feeling-sensations of excitement. Precisely how we should categorize such feelings is a question I set aside here. Suffice it to say that, if there are feeling-sensations of this kind, it is worth understanding their etiology and exploring their consequences. (See Gilbert, 2000, 2002, for further discussion.)

Conclusion

Earlier I referred to the emotion thesis: one with a certain emotion is in a particular conscious state, one that is, if you like, criterial for that emotion. If a collective emotion is, at base, no more than a joint commitment with a particular type of content, that will be a strike against the emotion thesis—if one is looking for an account of emotion that applies both to the emotions of individuals and to collective emotions.

One need not choose to look for such a generic account. One may prefer to treat the emotions of individuals and collective emotions as separate areas of inquiry (cf. Gilbert and Pilchman, 2014, chapter 6, this volume). Whatever one's preference in this respect, and however one prefers to pursue one's goal, it is important to understand our everyday collective emotion ascriptions.

I have argued in favor of an account of the referents of such ascriptions that has an appropriate joint commitment at its core. The situation then picked out will be a consequential one for all of the parties, whatever their personal emotions. In particular, each will be committed to act in appropriate ways and obligated to the others to do so. Everyone, participant or observer, will have a new basis for predicting what each of the parties is most likely to do. Collective emotions on a joint commitment account are apt to be highly consequential social phenomena.[15]

[15] Warm thanks for their comments on a draft to Linda Levine, Maura Priest, Philip Walsh, and Christian van Sheve and Mikko Salmela, the editors of the collection in which this chapter was first published.

References

Dewey, J. (1895). The theory of emotion, 2: The significance of emotions. *Psychological Review*, 2, 13–32.

Gilbert, M. (1987). Modeling collective belief. *Synthese*, 73, 185–204.

Gilbert, M. (1989). *On Social Facts*. London: Routledge and Kegan Paul.

Gilbert, M. (1996). *Living Together*. Lanham, MD: Rowman and Littlefield.

Gilbert, M. (1997). Group wrongs and guilt feelings. *Journal of Ethics*, 1, 65–84.

Gilbert, M. (2000). *Sociality and Responsibility*. Lanham, MD: Rowman and Littlefield.

Gilbert, M. (2002). Collective guilt and collective guilt feelings. *Journal of Ethics*, 6, 115–43.

Gilbert, M. (2006). *A Theory of Political Obligation*. Oxford: Oxford University Press.

Gilbert, M. (2012). Giving claim-rights their due. In B. Bix and H. Spector (eds.), *Rights: Concepts and Contexts* (pp. 301–24). Farnham: Ashgate. [Chapter 13, this volume.]

Gilbert, M. (2013a). Commitment. In H. LaFollette (ed.), *International Encyclopedia of Ethics* (pp. 899–905). Oxford: Wiley-Blackwell.

Gilbert, M. (2013b). *Joint Commitment*. New York, NY: Oxford University Press.

Gilbert, M. (2014). The nature of agreements: a solution to some puzzles about claim-rights and joint intention. In M. Vargas and G. Yaffe (eds.), *Rational and Social Agency* (pp. 215–256). New York, NY: Oxford University Press. [Chapter 1, this volume.]

Gilbert, M., and Pilchman, D. (2014). Belief, Acceptance, and What Happens in Groups: Some Methodological Considerations. In J. Lackey (ed.), *Essays in Collective Epistemology* (pp. 189–212). New York, NY: Oxford University Press. [Chapter 4, this volume.]

Jaspers, K. (1947). *The Question of German Guilt*. New York, NY: Capricorn Books.

Kutz, C. (2001). *Complicity*. Cambridge: Cambridge University Press.

Nussbaum, M. (2001). *Upheavals of Thought*. Cambridge: Cambridge University Press.

Quinton, A. (1975). Social objects. *Proceedings of the Aristotelian Society*, 76, 1–27.

Salmela, M. (2012). Shared emotions. *Philosophical Explorations*, 15, 33–46.

Shaffer, J. (1983). An assessment of emotion. *American Philosophical Quarterly*, 20, 161–72.

Weber, M. (1964). *The Theory of Social and Economic Organization*. New York, NY: Free Press.

PART IV

OUR PREFERENCES, VALUES, AND VIRTUES

9

Collective Preferences, Obligations, and Rational Choice

1. What Is a Collective Preference?

Can teams and other collectivities have preferences of their own, preferences that are not in some way reducible to the personal preferences of their members? In short, are *collective preferences* possible?[1] In everyday life people speak easily of what *we* prefer, where what is at issue seems to be a collective preference. This is suggested by the acceptability of such remarks as "My ideal walk would be…along rougher and less well-marked paths than we prefer as a family."[2] One can imagine, indeed, that *each* member of a given family prefers something other than what the family prefers. What, then, do the collective preferences of everyday understanding amount to?

In his paper "Team Preferences" Robert Sudgen argues that an account I have proposed is unsatisfactory, because it implies that when a collectivity has a preference, its members have associated *obligations*.[3] In this chapter I defend my account against this criticism.

I should emphasize at the outset that there are distinct species of obligation. To say that obligations are associated with collective preferences is not yet to specify which type is at issue.

I should also stress that the focus of most of my discussion is the conception of collective preferences implicit in everyday discourse as opposed to any technical notion. When I refer to "collective preferences" without qualification, this should be understood.

---

[1] I prefer to write of "collective" preferences rather than "team" preferences (Robert Sugden's phrase) insofar as teams are a species of collectivity rather than the whole genus. Families, for instance, would not standardly be referred to as teams. The word "collectivity" is rather cumbersome so I shall sometimes use the term "group" for short.

[2] Sugden, 2000, p. 175. Sudgen writes here *in propria persona*. All references to Sugden in what follows are to this paper.

[3] Sugden, 2000, pp. 189–90.

Life in Groups: How We Think, Feel, and Act Together. Margaret Gilbert, Oxford University Press. © Margaret Gilbert 2023. DOI: 10.1093/oso/9780192847157.003.0010

2. Collective Preferences and Obligations: Is There a Connection?

2.1 Footballers

Do collective preferences involve obligations? In order to answer this it would be good carefully to consider some cases in which there is, by hypothesis, a collective preference.

Consider Sugden's preferred example of a collectivity, a football team. Assume that the team's objective is to maximize the probability that a goal is scored. Assume, further, that at a certain point in the game—call it t1—this probability will be maximized if and only if team members Art and Ben both move to the right. The other possible combinations of an action of Art's with an action of Ben's all fare worse in this regard. All this is common knowledge between Art and Ben and the rest of the team.[4]

I have not yet explicitly referred to a collective *preference*. Given that the team has a unique objective, however, it presumably follows that it would rather reach that objective than fail to do so. More generally, a collective objective implies a preference for reaching that objective over failing to do so, absent any countervailing considerations.[5] In addition, given its specific objective, at t1 the team presumably prefers Art's moving to the right while Ben does to any other possible combinations of actions of these players.

Now suppose that at t1 Art moves left. We would expect Ben and indeed the other team members to be surprised. We would also expect their reactions to go beyond mere surprise.

Given that Art's moving left is not obviously explicable by some mitigating circumstance, his teammates will feel *aggrieved*. That is, they will understand that Art has offended against them. Either at the time or at some later point when conversation is more feasible they may say things like "What do you think you are doing?" in a *punitive, rebuking* tone. Such rebukes are not likely to come from members of the opposing team.

---

[4] Many accounts of "common knowledge" have been offered. Philosophers may be best acquainted with the pioneering discussion in Lewis, 1969. Economists may be more familiar with the independent work in Aumann, 1976. Informally one might say that the matter that is common knowledge is "out in the open" with respect to the people in question. For some further discussion see Gilbert, 1989: ch. 4.

[5] A collectivity could of course have multiple objectives and rank them differently, where it was considered better to reach one while failing to reach another than vice versa.

Members of that team might, indeed, express surprise after the fact. They are not likely to attempt to tell Art off.[6]

Whether or not rebukes are uttered by his teammates, Art will understand that *they have the standing to rebuke him*. He will understand, further, that there is a sense in which they were *entitled* to his moving to the right rather than to the left. Correlated with this entitlement is an obligation to them, an obligation to move to the right. His default on this obligation gives them the standing to tell him off. As to members of the opposing team, he had no such obligation to *them*, hence they lack the standing to rebuke him that his teammates have.

Why do the members of Art's team have this standing? Their opponents may have the same expectations as to what Art will do, and may rely on these expectations in deciding what to do themselves. Thus, though it may be tempting to do so, it is hard to argue that the basis of Art's fellow team members' standing is disappointed expectations or reliance.

The obligations and entitlements in question are grounded, rather, in the existence of Art's team's collective preference for his going to the right, a preference deriving from the team's objective. Thus those rebukes that are uttered may be backed up with such remarks as "We're trying to win this game, not lose it!" and "How are we going to win if you do things like that?" Indeed, such remarks may themselves be made as rebukes. If these observations about likely reactions and the understandings underlying them are granted, they must be accommodated by any adequate account of collective preferences.

2.2 Conscripts and Teenagers

Sugden takes two examples to cast doubt on the idea that there are obligations associated with collective preferences. These are the examples of a conscript and his unit and a teenager and her family. He writes that "it is hard not to feel uneasy about the assertion that these individuals have obligations to participate in the plural agency of their groups."[7]

---

[6] A member of the opposing team might possibly tell Art off if what he did amounted to ruining the game, thus making impossible the objective of the complex collective constituted by the two opposing teams, which is, one may assume, to play a decent game of football. He would then be making this rebuke on the basis of his membership in the complex collective as opposed to one of the opposing teams. I am assuming that Art's action, though flawed from the point of view of his team, does not amount to ruining the game in this sense, so a rebuke on behalf of the complex collective will not be in place.

[7] Sugden, 2000, p. 190.

Sudgen does not explain why he feels uneasy about these individuals. I suspect it is because a conscript has indeed been conscripted, with little choice as to whether or not to join his unit, while a teenager has little choice as to which family she is a member of. One may find it hard to accept that those entering a group in such circumstances thereby accrue obligations to promote the group's objectives and to act in accordance with any ensuing preferences.

In order to defuse this concern one might start by comparing the conscript and the teenager with the footballers. I shall take the case of the conscript first. In reality the situation of many conscripts is complicated by background circumstances involving some kind of consent to the practice of conscription, so I shall consider a case that does not involve such a complication.

Suppose that Jake is kidnapped and flown to a remote desert, where he finds many other men who, like himself, have been kidnapped and flown to the site. A loudspeaker announces to the assembled men that they constitute a military unit called the Desert Rats whose immediate objective is to advance five miles west on foot before sunrise.

It is unclear at this point that Jake is the member of a group with an objective, as opposed to a collection of individuals all in the same unfortunate situation. That there is such a group according to the announcement does not mean that there is one in fact.

Little may be needed to create such a group. For example, suppose Jake begins to talk without irony of *our* objective when referring to the objective ascribed to the Desert Rats. The other men who were kidnapped accept these references without demur. This may be enough to create the relevant collective objective and with it a collectivity comprising Jake and the others.[8]

Suppose, then, that in some such manner Jake and the others come to possess a collective objective. I propose that obligations corresponding to those of the footballers would then arise. Let us assume that, as is common knowledge among the men, in order to fulfil their collective objective, each must walk west without a break till sunrise. Should Jake decide to stop for twenty minutes, he will surely understand that the other group members have the standing to rebuke him for stopping. He will understand that they have this standing because they were entitled to his not stopping, or, to put it another way, he was obligated to them not to stop—by virtue of the collective objective.

Though Jake is a conscript of sorts, he is obligated to help promote the objectives of his unit. The circumstances that ground his obligation—his

---

[8] See section 4 below.

references without irony to our objective, and so on—are surely those of many conscripts.

The case of the teenager is similar. Suppose that Jane, a teenager, is speaking of her family. Without irony she refers to what we collectively prefer, and has such speech accepted as appropriate by the other family members. She will understand that now, if not before, they have the standing to rebuke her for failing to support the satisfaction of those preferences.

3. Collective Preferences as Sufficient Reason for Acting

In spite of the foregoing observations one may still be uncomfortable with the idea of a tight connection between collective preferences and obligations. The following concerns are suggested at various points in Sudgen's paper.[9]

Given that collective preferences are not reducible to a set of correlative individual preferences, it may be proposed that a *collective* preference as such cannot provide any of the *individuals* who make up the collectivity with sufficient reason for acting. In my terminology, if one has *sufficient reason* to do something, then rationally speaking one *ought* to do it, absent any countervailing considerations. By "rationally speaking" here I mean something like "given that one is appropriately responsive to the applicable considerations."

Accepting the proposal that collective preferences cannot provide the parties with sufficient reason to act accordingly, one may infer that they cannot obligate the parties, insofar as one with an obligation has sufficient reason for acting accordingly. A common form of reasoning suggests, however, that the proposal is false.

According to everyday understanding the following argument is valid: "Our preference is to advance five miles west by sunrise. I, Jake, can best help to achieve our aim by resisting the urge to take a rest. Therefore I ought to resist that urge." This argument goes from a premise about (in Jake's terms) *our* preference to a conclusion about what he ought to do and hence has sufficient reason to do. There is no additional premise stating a correlative personal preference of his own.[10]

---

[9] Sudgen, 2000, pp. 189–90, 195. I may not always have understood Sudgen's drift. In any case these are possible concerns that merit consideration.

[10] To my knowledge the intuitiveness of this form of reasoning was first pointed out by Wilfrid Sellars. See, for instance, Sellars, 1963. Having observed it independently I discussed it in Gilbert, 1989, and elsewhere, most recently in 1999 ms. See also Gilbert, 1994, and the text below.

I do not see how one can consistently accept the validity of this form of argument while maintaining that a collective preference does not provide group members with sufficient reason for acting. It is true that, without more, it may be unclear precisely *how* collective preferences provide members with sufficient reason for acting. But that is only to say that an explanation could usefully be forthcoming. I provide such an explanation shortly.

To say that collective preferences provide each member with sufficient reason for acting is not to say that the *balance of reasons* must favor a given member's doing his best to satisfy the collective preference in a particular case. Rationally speaking, one may well be able to ignore the collective preference in the sense of not, at the end of the day, doing one's best to satisfy it.

One might think that were collective preferences to *obligate* one could not, rationally speaking, ignore them in this way. But this is not true of obligations of the type associated with collective preferences. According to everyday understandings, one may have a valid excuse for not fulfilling the obligation associated with a collective preference. Thus one might without logical oddity say to one's fellows: "I'm sorry, but my conscience did not permit me to do it," where "it" is what I needed to do in order that our preference be satisfied. Note that here one implicitly grants that one's audience is entitled to an explanation and indeed an apology, though—at the same time—reason allowed one to act as one did.

4. The Plural Subject Account of Collective Preferences

The following key points have emerged in the foregoing discussion. First, collective preferences are not reducible to a set of correlative individual preferences. Second, they provide members of the group with sufficient reason for acting. Third, they provide group members with obligations. More specifically, everyone is obligated *to* everyone else, an obligation violated if appropriate action is not performed. Thus each is entitled to appropriate action from the others, and entitled to rebuke those others for not acting appropriately. Fourth, these obligations are such that in certain circumstances a member can fail to fulfill them without irrationality.

My own account of collective preferences respects these points. I have been developing the details of this account since the mid-1980s.[11] I sketch it briefly here.

---

[11] I first discussed collective preferences in Gilbert, 1987. That article focuses on collective belief, of which it presents and defends an account, and argues for an analogous account of collective

The core of the account is a concept of joint commitment. I take this to be fundamental for the understanding of everyday notions such as those of a collective preference.[12] A joint commitment is a commitment of two or more persons. In order to clarify what this amounts to I first say something about commitment in general and another species of commitment, namely personal commitment.

With respect to commitment in general, I focus on a particular example. I take a personal decision to do A to involve a commitment. That is, if I have decided to do A, I am subject to a commitment to do A. In contrast to this, inclinations and enthusiasms, for instance, do not yet involve commitments. I can be inclined to do A but not yet subject to a commitment to do A.

A personal decision can also serve to exemplify what I call a personal commitment. This is, by definition, the commitment of a single person who created it and who has the authority unilaterally to rescind it. One only has to change one's mind, as we say, and one is no longer committed.

It is now possible to clarify the concept of a joint commitment by distinguishing it from a set of personal commitments. A joint commitment is not a conjunction of personal commitments of the different parties. Each of the parties plays a part in the creation of a joint commitment, not by creating an appropriate personal commitment, but by expressing to the others his or her willingness to be jointly committed with them.

Each one understands that the parties will be jointly committed once all have made such expressions in conditions of common knowledge. Once in place, a joint commitment can only be rescinded by appropriate expressions of the parties in conditions of common knowledge. I alone cannot change *our* mind.[13]

Given that we understand ourselves to be jointly committed in some way, we do of course understand that each of us is subject to a commitment, but it is not a personal commitment in the sense defined above. I cannot rid myself of my commitment here just by changing my own mind.

---

preferences that gives the lie to the common assumption among social choice theorists that "no sense can be given to the notion of a social preference (or a group's preference) except in terms of (some function of) the personal preferences of the individuals concerned" (Gilbert, 1996, p. 211). See also Gilbert, 1989, pp. 361–2, discussed briefly in section 7 below.

[12] In Gilbert, 1987, I wrote of "commitment as a body." In Gilbert, 1989, pp. 198f., I began to write of "joint commitment." Gilbert, 1996, Introduction, pulls together some key features of joint commitment as I understand it. See also the Introduction, this volume. Historically the use of such phrases as "common will" and "unity of wills" by political philosophers and contract theorists may well relate to this phenomenon.

[13] Special background understandings may sometimes suggest that a joint commitment can be created or rescinded by just one of the parties. On such understandings see, for instance, Gilbert, 2000, p. 67 n13. On the meaning of default, see Gilbert, 1996, pp. 14–16, 381–3, and elsewhere.

As to its content, a joint commitment is a commitment to do something *as a body*, where "do" is interpreted broadly enough to include beliefs and preferences among other broadly speaking psychological states. The qualifier "as a body" is important. To be jointly committed to believe something as a body, for instance, is not to be jointly committed *each to believe that p*. Rather it is to be jointly committed to emulate—in relevant respects—a single body that believes that p. In order to have a compact phrase with which to refer to those who are jointly committed to do something as a body, I say that they constitute a *plural subject*.

As noted, mutual expressions of willingness to be jointly committed, in conditions of common knowledge, suffice for a joint commitment of the parties in question. A standard way of expressing such willingness is the use, without irony, of the first-person plural pronoun, as in Jake's "Our objective is to…"[14]

5. Collective Preferences and Obligations

I have argued at length elsewhere that the parties to a joint commitment are in an important and special sense obligated to one another.[15] For now the following remarks must suffice.

If I fail to act according to our joint commitment, you—as one of us—have the standing to rebuke me—as one of us. You have this standing because the commitment I have failed to honor is, precisely, a joint one. It is not a personal commitment. It is not mine and mine alone. Nor is it a conjunction of personal commitments, mine and yours. It is ours.

Your standing to rebuke me may appropriately be said to correspond to an *entitlement* or *right* to my acting in conformity with our commitment. I have a corresponding *obligation to you*, an obligation to conform. If I fail to fulfill this obligation, your right—which is a right against me—has thereby been violated, and you have the standing to rebuke me.

Of particular importance here is the fact that all this is so simply by virtue of what a joint commitment is. No moral principle need be appealed to. If you

---

[14] See Gilbert, 1989, chapter 4, on the first-person plural pronoun; also Gilbert 1999a, cited by Sugden.
[15] See e.g. Gilbert, 1993, and, more fully, Gilbert, 1999b. In this volume, see chapters 1 and 13.

like, the obligations in question here are not moral obligations. They may be referred to as obligations of joint commitment to avoid misunderstanding.[16]

Surely conscripts and teenagers can have such obligations. As long as they express their willingness to be jointly committed, and thus enter a joint commitment, they will have the obligations that attach to all such commitments. *Particularly* when one has no option, one may be willing in the relevant sense. Clearly this is not a sense of "willing" that implies this is something one would want outside one's particular circumstances.[17]

My plural subject account, then, entails that collective preferences provide group members with obligations of the appropriate sort, that is, obligations to a person or persons who have corresponding rights. At the same time, it implies that collective preferences are not constituted by a set of personal preferences. As I argue below it also respects the observations that a collective preference provides members with sufficient reason for acting, and that in some circumstances a member may without irrationality act contrary to it.

6. Collective Preferences as Providing Sufficient Reason for Action and Allowing for Rational Deviation

With regard to the point about sufficient reason, a joint commitment will be akin to any commitment as such. In everyday thought, the personal commitment derived from a personal decision would normally be judged to make it the case that, all else being equal, one ought to conform to it rationally speaking. Thus, suppose I decide to go to France tomorrow, and do not subsequently change my mind. When tomorrow comes, however, I start off for Alaska. Given my decision, this action will seem questionable: I am apparently not doing what I rationally ought to do.[18]

With regard to the point about the possibility of rational deviation, this is something my account can accommodate. One can sometimes validly excuse

---

[16] The obligations in question can be described as "obligations to" a particular person or persons, or, as in the literature of deontic logic, "directed obligations." I am not arguing that all directed obligations are obligations of joint commitment. I argue rather that obligations of joint commitment constitute at least an important species of directed obligation, a species I conjecture to be associated with collective preferences and the like. For discussion of the contrast of the obligations of joint commitment with obligations of another important type see e.g. Gilbert, 1993. For the conjecture that all directed obligations *are* obligations of joint commitment see ch. 13, this volume, and, more fully Gilbert, 2018, chs. 11–12.

[17] See Gilbert, 1993.

[18] On personal decisions as providing sufficient reason for action see also e.g. Gilbert, 2018 ch. 2, esp. secs 4.1 and 6.

oneself from violating a commitment, joint or not. What counts as a valid excuse in such a case, as in any other, will ultimately be a matter of judgment, that is, a matter of assessing the way in which reasons of various kinds play off one against the other.

7. Collective Preferences and Rational Choice Theory

I have argued for a particular account of the collective preferences of everyday understanding, an account according to which such preferences involve obligations of a specified type. I take such preferences to be possible, and indeed to be prevalent, and importantly to affect the course of human life.

Though at the outset of "Team Preferences" Sugden implicitly invokes the collective preferences of everyday understanding, informally discussing various preferences of his family as a group as opposed to the individual members, he doubts that such collective preferences involve obligations, and proposes a definition of "team preferences" that does not have this consequence. Of course one is at liberty stipulatively to define a technical notion of team preference for theoretical purposes. It would be unfortunate, however, if acceptance of Sugden's definition led one to overlook collective preferences in the everyday sense.

In this concluding section I wish briefly to note two issues on which there is accord between Sugden and myself.

I argued in *On Social Facts* that given the existence of collective objectives in the everyday sense it evidently makes sense to talk, in the terms of rational choice theory, of a collective's *utility function*, where this is not logically derivable from the personal utility functions of the group's members and may differ qualitatively from any of them.[19] Insofar as one of the central aims of Sugden's "Team Preferences" is to recommend the idea of such a collective utility function to rational choice theorists he evidently agrees with me on this point.[20]

Sugden sees the idea of a collective utility function as helpful to understanding human reasoning in a group context. He focuses on his "footballers' problem" in which both of two particular players moving to the right rather than to the left is what will most likely lead to a goal for their team.

---

[19] Gilbert, 1989, ch. 6, section 6.3: "On the limitations of game-theoretical approaches to social convention and social phenomena in general," pp. 361–3.

[20] See Sugden, 2000, p. 176.

He first describes this situation as it might be represented in classical game theory. Each player—wanting his team to win—personally ranks their both moving to the right highest, both moving to the left next highest, and the other combinations of actions tie for worst outcome.

Sugden argues that were each player to look at the situation so represented in terms of maximizing personal utility and ask "What should I do?" there would be no conclusive answer. He would know he should do his part in the unique optimal outcome if his opposite number does, but he has no basis for inferring that his opposite number will. For his opposite number will have the knowledge he has, *mutatis mutandis*, and no more. I am not sure that there is indeed no conclusive answer in this particular case, but let that pass here. It is certainly true of many of the situations that game theorists refer to as coordination games or problems, of which this is one.[21]

Sugden then considers how the footballers' problem would be represented as a "team-directed decision problem": "There are still two players, each of whom has to [choose] between moving left and moving right, but now there is only one scale of preferences on which outcomes are ranked, the scale of team-directed preferences."[22] Sugden goes on to contrast the situation in which agents consider what will maximize collective utility with a standard-issue coordination problem.[23]

These points are consonant with the discussion in Gilbert, 1989, where I argue among other things that to consider "What shall we do in order to reach our collective goal?" is not to participate in a coordination problem in the game theorists' sense.[24]

I am glad that Sugden, a distinguished rational choice theorist, finds these ideas important. Precisely how they are best applied to the understanding of human actions is a further topic there is no space to engage with here. Suffice it to say that in any fine-grained analysis of actions in the context of collective preferences the obligating character of these phenomena will doubtless play a role.[25]

---

[21] Against the assumption of various others, I have argued that rationality does not always dictate that a given agent does his part in a combination of actions that is uniquely optimal according to the utility functions of all the parties. See Gilbert, 1981 (pp. 136–8 in Gilbert, 1996) and Gilbert, 1990 (pp. 44–6 in Gilbert, 1996). On why I am not sure about Sugden's footballers' problem see Gilbert, 1981 (Gilbert, 1996, pp. 150–2). The case I discuss there is not the same, but similar reasoning may be plausible.

[22] Quotations from Sugden, 2000, p. 193.   [23] Sugden, 2000, p. 193.

[24] Gilbert, 1989, pp. 361–3.   [25] Gilbert, 1999 ms. further develops this topic.

References

Aumann, R. 1976. Agreeing to disagree. *Annals of Statistics*, 4:16–28.

Gilbert, Margaret. 1981. Game theory and *Convention*. *Synthese*, 46:41–93. (Reprinted in Gilbert, 1996.)

Gilbert, Margaret. 1987. Modeling collective belief. *Synthese*, 73:185–204. (Reprinted in Gilbert, 1996.)

Gilbert, Margaret. 1989. *On Social Facts*. Routledge and Kegan Paul.

Gilbert, Margaret. 1990. Rationality, coordination, and convention. *Synthese*, 84:1–21. (Reprinted in Gilbert, 1996.)

Gilbert, Margaret. 1993. Agreements, coercion, and obligation. *Ethics*, 103:679–706. (Reprinted in Gilbert, 1996.)

Gilbert, Margaret. 1994. Me, you, and us: distinguishing egoism, altruism, and groupism. *Behavioral and Brain Sciences*, 17:621–2.

Gilbert, Margaret. 1996. *Living Together: Rationality, Sociality, and Obligation*. Rowman and Littlefield.

Gilbert, Margaret. 1999a. Reconsidering the 'actual contract' theory of political obligation. *Ethics*, 109: 236–60. (Reprinted in Gilbert, 2000.)

Gilbert, Margaret. 1999b. Joint commitment and obligation. *Utilitas*, 11:143–63. (Reprinted in Gilbert, 2000.)

Gilbert, Margaret. 1999 ms. *Reasoning about Us*. Presented at an expert seminar on rationality and intentions, University of Amsterdam, 1999.

Gilbert, Margaret. 2000. *Sociality and Responsibility: New Essays in Plural Subject Theory*. Rowman and Littlefield.

Gilbert, Margaret. 2018. *Rights and Demands: A Foundational Inquiry*. Oxford University Press.

Lewis, David. 1969. *Convention: A Philosophical Study*. Harvard University Press.

Sellars, Wilfrid. 1963. Imperatives, Intentions, and the Logic of "Ought." In *Morality and the Language of Conduct*. G. Nakhnikian and Hector-Neri Castaneda (eds.). Wayne State University Press.

Sugden, Robert. 2000. Team preferences. *Economics and Philosophy*, 20:175–204.

10

Corporate Misbehavior and Collective Values

"Our merely social intolerance kills no one, roots out no opinions, but induces men to disguise them or to abstain from any active effort at their diffusion."[1]

I. Introduction

In recent years there have been many scandals in which highly paid corporate executives have apparently acted in morally unacceptable ways. Why is this? Is it a matter of a few "bad apples" or is there some other, or some additional, explanation? In order to answer such questions, one needs to know what the possibilities are: what, generally, goes on in the life of a corporation and its members? What factors might influence the behavior of a given executive or other member of the corporation?

It is plausible to suggest that collective value judgments or, for short, collective values, are important components of corporate life and must be considered in examining immoral behavior within corporations. This article carefully articulates a particular interpretation of this idea.

It is argued, first, that considerations of our everyday ascriptions of beliefs and value judgments to groups of people point away from an account of collective values that might initially be proposed. A different account is then offered.

The likely influence of collective values according to this account, and phenomena akin to them, is discussed. It is argued that they are indeed likely to be influential. To echo Mill in the above quotation, collective values are apt to induce people to abstain from any active effort to counter them. Some practical consequences for corporations and those concerned with them are then sketched.

---

[1] J. S. Mill, *On Liberty* 37 (John Gray ed., 1991).

Life in Groups: How We Think, Feel, and Act Together. Margaret Gilbert, Oxford University Press. © Margaret Gilbert 2023.
DOI: 10.1093/oso/9780192847157.003.0011

II. Group Belief Statements

Among the possible sources of malfeasance that one finds informally proposed are a climate of opinion or corporate culture in which "anything goes" as long as the corporate bottom line—the maximization of profit—is served. Most people have a rough idea of what is at issue when a climate of opinion or a culture is mentioned. It is harder to say exactly what phenomena are in question. If we are to make more of this explanation of behavior, we need to go further.

If pressed, many would most likely propose the following: the judgment that "anything goes" is part of the climate of opinion or corporate culture in a given corporation if and only if most of the people working for that corporation personally endorse that judgment. This accords with philosopher Anthony Quinton's statement that "[i]n some cases, which may be called summative, statements about social objects are equivalent to statements otherwise the same that refer explicitly, if at some level of generality, to individual people. To say that the French middle class is thrifty is to say that most French middle-class people are."[2]

It can be argued, however, that everyday statements about the beliefs and attitudes of social objects, to use Quinton's phrase, are not always summative in his sense. That is, they are not always equivalent to statements "otherwise the same" that refer to individual people generally described.[3] Consider some further statements about the beliefs and attitudes of social objects: "The union believes management is being unreasonable," "In the opinion of the court, this law is unconstitutional," "Corporations value nothing but profit," "Our family favored Bush," "We"—said by an unmarried couple—"want to get married." If it is sometimes appropriate to take these as summative statements, it is surely not always so.

After all, in many cases, a formal voting procedure determines what the social object or group believes. What counts as far as any individual group member goes, then, is his or her vote—not what he or she personally believes. Evidently, one's voting in favor of the proposition that, say, Arthur was the best candidate for the position does not logically entail that one personally takes this proposition to be true.

---

[2] Anthony Quinton, "Social Objects," 75 *Proc. Aristotelian Society* 9.
[3] See Margaret Gilbert, *On Social Facts* 257–88 (1992) [hereinafter Gilbert, *On Social Facts*]; see also Margaret Gilbert, *Living Together: Rationality, Sociality, and Obligation* 195–214 (1996) [hereinafter Gilbert, *Living Together*]. The text below draws on these and related discussions.

Less formal processes are also taken to determine what a group believes. These can be argued to be analogous to the case of voting insofar as public expressions as opposed to private thoughts are what matter. Thus, after some discussion, a literary discussion group may reach a point of quiescence after which no one would dispute that "We thought Plath's poem a very strong one."

It appears, then, that there is an important sense in which for a group to believe something (or value it in a certain way or want it, and the like) it is not necessary that all or most of the members believe it. Were group belief statements always summative statements in Quinton's sense this would not be so.

Given this sense of group belief (and so on), is it *sufficient* for a group to believe something that all or most of the members do? Apparently not. Consider a court. A certain matter may not yet have come before it. It would then seem right to say that, as yet, the court has no opinion on the matter. The individual justices may, at the same time, have definite personal opinions about it. What they think, however, does not determine what the court now thinks. This is true even if the court is in session and the matter in question is before it. All may be of the same personal opinion but before a vote is taken, the court itself has none.

The same goes for less formal groups as well. Asked what her discussion group thought of a particular poem, someone might respond, with some emphasis, "The group has no opinion: we've not discussed it!" At the same time, she would acknowledge it to be perfectly possible that all of the members have the same personal view of the poem.

In sum, everyday group belief (value, goal, and other) statements are not always interpretable as summative statements. In other words, when we talk of a group's belief, we may well be talking about something other than what all or most of the members believe. What, then, are we talking about?

In what follows I refer to the phenomenon in question simply as group belief.

III. Observation: The Standing to Rebuke

One clue as to what defines a group belief has to do with informal rebukes or reproof. A rebuke is a form—albeit a mild form—of punishment.[4] I take it that although one can cause pain to someone without any special standing,

---

[4] Cf. H. L. A. Hart, *The Concept of Law* 11 (1961).

one cannot punish them without such standing.[5] Similarly, one can speak harshly to a person without any special authority, but one cannot rebuke them without such authority. This is supported by the fact that people sometimes respond to purported rebukes in such terms as, "What's that to you?" or "What business is that of yours?"

In contexts where group members believe their group to have a particular belief, they understand that they have the standing to rebuke any member who bluntly expresses the opposite belief. Opposed to a "blunt" expression is one that makes it clear that the speaker is "speaking personally." That the other parties have the standing to rebuke the member in question appears to be a function of the collective belief itself.[6]

This clue is, perhaps, little more than a provocation or a question. What is it about group belief that gives the group members the standing to rebuke each other for blunt expressions of a contrary opinion? An adequate account of group belief should give a plausible answer.

IV. The Plural Subject Account of a Group's Belief

The foregoing discussion suggests three criteria of adequacy for an account of a group's belief. Such an account should explain how the existence of such a belief gives the group members the standing to rebuke each other for bluntly expressing a view contrary to that belief. It should neither logically entail that all or most of the parties personally have the belief in question nor should it suppose that if all or most of the members have a given belief then the group believes it. For the former is not necessary for group belief and the latter is not sufficient for group belief.

The following account of group belief—whose terms will be explained—meets all of these criteria.[7] Here the letter p stands for any particular proposition.

A group, G, believes that p if and only if its members are jointly committed to believe as a body that p.

---

[5] Perhaps it should be said that "one cannot punish someone *in the strict sense* of 'punish' without a special standing," since at this point the term "punish" would appear to have both a broader and a narrower (the so-called "strict") meaning.

[6] For extended discussion on this point see Gilbert, *Living Together*, 200–3.

[7] This account was introduced in Margaret Gilbert, "Modeling Collective Belief," 84 *Synthese* 185, 185–204, reprinted in Gilbert, *Living Together*, 195–214, and has been further elaborated in subsequent publications.

Two aspects of this account need to be explained: what is a joint commitment, and what is it to be jointly committed to believe something as a body? These will now be discussed in turn.

What is joint commitment, as understood here? The answer to that question can usefully be broken down into two parts, one concerning the commitment side of things, the other relating to jointness.

The relevant general concept of *commitment* is illustrated, for example, in the following judgment: if Sandra decides to read the newspaper this evening, then she is committed to doing so. In the case of a personal decision such as Sandra's, the commitment is *personal*. That is, the one whose commitment it is creates it unilaterally and is in a position unilaterally to do away with it. I take it that, once committed, Sandra has reason to read the newspaper and will continue to do so unless and until she rescinds her decision.

The concept of a *joint* commitment is the concept of a commitment *of two or more people as one*. It is not a conjunction of the personal commitment of one party with the personal commitment(s) of the other(s).[8]

Joint commitments can be created in various ways. One such way is to informally agree that one or more of the parties to the agreement is to act in a certain way. Less explicit means are also possible. Absent special background understandings, what is needed generally speaking is an expression of readiness by all parties to be jointly committed in the relevant way, in conditions of "common knowledge." Common knowledge is intended here in roughly the sense introduced by the philosopher David Lewis.[9] Rather than going into the details of that here, suffice it to say that the expressions in question must be "out in the open" as far as the parties are concerned. In parallel with the conditions of its creation, the more or less explicit concurrence of all is required for the dissolution of a given joint commitment.

There may be special background understandings that impact upon how joint commitments are formed. For example, people may jointly commit to believe as a body whatever a certain person says about the group. Thus the members of the board of a corporation may be jointly committed to believe as a body whatever the chairman of the board says about the corporation. As a consequence of this background commitment, if the chairman says that the

[8] For more detail see generally Margaret Gilbert, "The Structure of the Social Atom: Joint Commitment as the Foundation of Human Social Behavior," in *Socializing Metaphysics* 39 (Frederick Schmitt ed., 2003); Margaret Gilbert, "A Theoretical Framework for the Understanding of Teams," in *Teamwork: Multidisciplinary Perspectives* 22, 29–30 (Natalie Gold ed., 2005) (responding to some queries about joint commitment).

[9] David K. Lewis, *Convention: A Philosophical Study* 52–60 (1969). See also Gilbert, *Social Facts*, 188.

corporation is doing fine, then the other members of the board are jointly committed to believe as a body that the corporation is doing fine. Given this background, the chairman need not heed to what anyone else does or thinks: the board will believe whatever he says about the corporation.

A given joint commitment can always be described in a sentence of the following form: the parties are jointly committed to x as a body. Acceptable substitutions for x are psychological verbs such as "believe," "value," "intend," and so on. What is it to be jointly committed to x *as a body*? This can be spelled out further roughly as follows: it is to be jointly committed to constitute, as far as possible, a single body that *x*s.

Note that the guiding idea of *a single body that xs* includes nothing about the intrinsic nature of the single body in question. In particular, it does not imply that it is in some way made up of two or more distinct bodies who are its members. Thus there is no circularity in the proposed account of group belief. It does not say that *a group believes that p* if and only if its members are jointly committed to constitute, as far as possible, *a group that believes that p.* The point is, rather, that if and only if they are jointly committed to constitute, as far as is possible, *a single body* that believes that *p*, they will then constitute a *group* that believes it.

V. Joint Commitment and the Standing to Rebuke

It can be argued that by virtue of their participation in a *joint* commitment, the parties gain a special standing in relation to one another's actions. To put it briefly, each can call on the other in the name of the joint commitment. If one violates it, for instance, he has not violated a commitment that is his alone, but a commitment to which others can lay claim. Each can say: "You violated *our* commitment."

Important aspects of the special standing of the parties in relation to one another are as follows. The parties to a joint commitment are *answerable* to one another with respect to their conformity. Further, one who violates a joint commitment has *offended against* all of the parties to the joint commitment, as such. The offense in question can plausibly be characterized in terms of a *violation of right*. In other words, when I am subject to a joint commitment requiring me to do certain things, all of the parties to the commitment have a right against me to the relevant actions. Correlatively, I am *under an obligation* to all of them to perform these actions. These obligations and rights are derived directly from the joint commitment.[10] They are not a matter of moral principle.[11] Once it exists, they exist also, irrespective of the surrounding circumstances.[12]

In consequence of the existence of these rights and obligations, failing special background circumstances, those who are party to a joint commitment have the standing to demand that others conform to it, if nonconformity is threatened. They also have the standing to rebuke one another for defaults that have taken place.

The present author uses the phrase "plural subject" as a technical term to refer to those who are jointly committed to x as a body, for some x.[13] Those who are jointly committed to x as a body constitute, by her definition, the *plural subject* of x-ing. Accordingly, one can label the above account of group belief *the plural subject account*.

There are some important aspects of that account that have not yet been discussed. A joint commitment to believe as a body that p does not require each participant personally to believe anything. The requirement at issue is rather to constitute, as far as is possible, a single body that believes that p. It does not concern any other bodies that may bear some relation, however close, to the body in question.

More positively, the joint commitment will be fulfilled, to some extent at least, if those concerned say that p in appropriate contexts, with an appropriate degree of confidence, and do not call p or obvious corollaries into question. Their behavior generally should be *expressive of the belief that p*, in the appropriate contexts. That does not mean that they must personally have that belief. In other words, this expressive behavior need not connote or be the expression of *a personal belief that p*.

Certain contextual conditions are likely to be understood. Thus, for example, members of a seminar on rights may form a joint commitment to believe

---

[10] For amplification see Margaret Gilbert, *Sociality and Responsibility: New Essays in Plural Subject Theory* 50–70 (2000) (discussing obligation in relation to joint commitment).

[11] I have in mind a general moral principle such as philosopher Thomas Scanlon's Principle of Fidelity. See Thomas M. Scanlon, "Promises and Contracts," in *The Theory of Contract Law* 86, 95 (Peter Benson ed., 2001) (discussing the principle as "Principle F"). For a critique of Scanlon's account of promissory obligation, see Margaret Gilbert, "Scanlon on Promissory Obligation: The Problem of Promisees' Rights," in *The Journal of Philosophy* 101 (Feb. 2004) (arguing that one cannot account for the rights of a promisee by reference to a moral principle such as Scanlon's).

[12] See Gilbert, *Living Together*, 305 (stating that coercive circumstances do not affect the obligating quality of joint commitments). See also Margaret Gilbert, *A Theory of Political Obligation* (2006) (stating that joint commitments with immoral content obligate in the usual way; it may well be that one ought not to fulfill such an obligation, all things considered).

[13] See generally Gilbert, *On Social Facts*.

as a body that the notion of a group right is a viable one. This would involve a requirement to express that belief *when acting as a member* of the seminar. Presumably the parties are not always so acting. If a friend who is not a member of the seminar engages one of them on the topic in the middle of a picnic, it would presumably be appropriate for each to speak *in propria persona*, without preamble.

Suppose, however, that one is in a context where it is appropriate to act in accordance with a given joint commitment. It is then open to one to use such qualifiers as "Personally speaking," to preface the expression of a belief contrary to the collective one. This makes it clear that one is indeed now speaking for oneself and not as a member of the relevant group. One makes it clear that one's utterance is not a violation of the joint commitment in question. This is one way in which the plural subject account of group belief accords with the logic of "Our group believes that *p*" and so on, as this is understood in everyday life. It allows for the possibility that a party to a supposed group belief aver without fault—though not necessarily without danger—that he *personally* does not believe that *p*.

What danger might there be in making such an avowal? Other members may subsequently regard one with suspicion, thinking one more liable to default on the joint commitment, either inadvertently or deliberately. If one does default, they have the standing to rebuke one for doing so. They may also begin to think of one as an "outsider." To be regarded with suspicion, to be thought of as "not one of us," to risk inadvertently incurring rebukes, are things that most people would prefer to avoid. It is clear then that group beliefs according to the plural subject account are likely to suppress the development of contrary ideas at both the individual and the collective level.

VI. Collective Beliefs, Values, Goals

The plural subject account of a group's belief that *p* may well articulate a central everyday conception. Among other things, it meets the criteria noted earlier: it explains the standing of the parties to rebuke each other for bluntly speaking as if *p* were false, and it is neither necessary nor sufficient for group belief, on this account, that most members of the group personally believe that *p*. It is necessary and sufficient only that they are jointly committed to believe that *p* as a body. Whatever its relationship to everyday conceptions, if there are group beliefs in the sense of the plural subject account, they will be an important aspect of the lives of the parties to them.

In what follows group beliefs as these are understood on the plural subject account will be referred to as collective beliefs. Members of a given population— members of the board of a certain corporation, for instance—will be said *collectively to believe* that *p*, by definition, if they are jointly committed to believe as a body that *p*.

Analogous plural subject accounts can be given collective values, collective goals and intentions, and so on. As to collective values, the relevant account would run along the following lines:

Members of population P *collectively value* item *I* in a certain way if and only if they are jointly committed to value item *I* in that way as a body.[14]

Evidently, in relation to the ideas about corporations mentioned at the outset of this discussion, one might interpret the idea of a climate of opinion or corporate culture in such terms. If members of a given corporation were jointly committed to value as a body the maximization of the corporation's profits above everything else, one could reasonably say that such valuation of the maximization of profit was part of that corporation's culture. Important parts or accompaniments of this culture would be collective beliefs of a factual nature, such as beliefs about the capabilities and temperament of various corporate executives, and collective goals and plans.

It is plausible to hypothesize that there are collective values and beliefs according to the definitions given. That is, it is plausible to hypothesize that in the world as it is there are a variety of such phenomena. This hypothesis, like the plural subject account of group belief, is based on observation of the judgments people make in the context of their ascriptions of beliefs to groups and so on. On the assumption that such phenomena abound among those living and working together, in corporations and elsewhere, the concluding sections of this discussion briefly discuss their nature as rational motivators, and some practical implications for those who are concerned about morally unacceptable behavior in the corporate realm.

---

[14] For a different version, still in plural subject terms, see generally Margaret Gilbert, "Shared Values, Social Unity, and Liberty," 19 *Pub. Affairs Q.* 25, 33 (2005). For present purposes the precise details of the account are not important.

VII. Collective Beliefs, Values, and
Goals as Rational Motivators

Something may be considered a rational motivator if the behavior of a perfectly rational agent would be influenced by it, all else being equal. A perfectly rational agent, for purposes of this idea, is one who always acts as reason dictates he should act.[15] Thus, he does whatever he has reason to do, all else being equal.

I take it that perfectly rational participants will be motivated by their joint commitments. That is, all else being equal, a perfectly rational agent who is party to a joint commitment will conform to that commitment. If he is jointly committed with other members of the firm to assigning as a body the highest possible value to the maximization of his firm's profits, then all else being equal, he will act in ways expressive of such valuing. Insofar as human beings are at least imperfectly rational agents, their joint commitments are liable to motivate them in a similar way. This does not mean that, all things considered, it would be rational to pursue the corporate bottom line come what may. All else being equal, one is rationally required to conform to a commitment, but all else may not be equal. Morality, many would say, is an external consideration— one not founded in the corporation, at least—that may change the picture.

Of course, if you violate a standing joint commitment for moral reasons, you will be liable to the rebukes of at least your less morally aware colleagues. Your preference to avoid such rebukes, or worse, may lead you not to violate the commitment. Depending on one's colleagues and one's circumstances, it may be little short of heroic for one to violate the commitment. It may then be that even morally speaking it is permissible for you not to take a moral stand. Evidently, much depends on the case.

VIII. Practical Implications

Collective values and factual beliefs make a difference. If one wishes to understand the pressures on corporate executives and other members of corporations to behave in a manner contrary to central moral principles, one must be aware of the collective values, beliefs, and goals to which they are party.

---

[15] I take it that one may have reason to do something irrespective of one's own preference ranking of the various possible outcomes of one's action. The conception of the dictates of rationality at issue here, then, is different from that employed in the mathematical theory of games.

These may work to stifle the expression of moral concerns. To echo my opening quotation from J. S. Mill, collective beliefs, values, and goals are apt to induce people to disguise their contrary opinions—however morally perspicacious—and to abstain from any active effort at their diffusion. Indeed, contrary to the suggestion in the quotation, they may tend to root out opposing opinions themselves. Forced regularly to couch their arguments in terms of profit maximization, or other corporate goals, executives and other members of a corporation may simply lose sight of moral constraints and values they previously held. At first, executives may cease to understand fully the constraining maxims they previously endorsed, and gradually they may cease to entertain them.

How might a situation of this kind be rectified? If in a corporate context adherence to central moral norms is highly valued collectively, then this will encourage the critique of other collective assumptions. If the members of corporation C collectively accept that certain moral constraints must rein in the pursuit of corporate profit, respecting such constraints will be collectively understood as part of being a good corporate citizen. The same goes, of course, for any other type of citizenship.

11

Can a Wise Society Be a Free One?

1. Introduction

This chapter invokes something that is not generally appealed to in contemporary philosophy: the idea of a wise society. One of its aims is to stimulate exploration of this idea, which is pertinent to several branches of the subject. These include both political philosophy and epistemology, in particular social epistemology.[1]

The idea of wisdom, in general, is a longstanding part of the philosophical repertoire. The very word "philosophy," as is well known, comes from the Greek for "love of wisdom." That is not to say that there is general agreement on what wisdom is. Nor is it to say that latter-day philosophical discourse is peppered with references to "wisdom." Paradoxically perhaps, it isn't.[2]

It is even less common to find references in this discourse to the wisdom of a society as opposed to that of an individual person. The same is true of the frequent contemporary philosophical references to knowledge, belief, and other close cousins of wisdom. There are incomparably more discussions of the knowledge and beliefs of individuals than of the knowledge and beliefs of societies.[3]

Outside the circle of professional philosophers—and, indeed, within it—discussion of the latter topic may recently have been stimulated by a popular work in which James Surowiecki argues that the *wisdom of a crowd*—"loosely defined"—may be superior to that of an expert on a given subject.[4] As will emerge, a society, as I understand it, is a subtype of "crowd" in Surowiecki's sense.

I take it that if a society can be wise, it will be better for being so, all else being equal. It is therefore important to consider both whether a society can be wise, and, if so, what that wisdom entails. For instance, given what it is,

---

[1] Within the relatively broad field of social epistemology it relates, as will be seen, to a branch that can be referred to as *collective* epistemology. See e.g. Gilbert 2004.

[2] For interesting observations on this score, see Conway 2000, ch. 1.

[3] For references to some philosophical work on the latter topic, see note 16 below.

[4] See Surowiecki 2004, 286.

Life in Groups: How We Think, Feel, and Act Together. Margaret Gilbert, Oxford University Press. © Margaret Gilbert 2023.
DOI: 10.1093/oso/9780192847157.003.0012

does a society's wisdom militate against its having some other valuable feature or features?

This paper addresses one aspect of the question just mooted: Can a wise society be a free one? One's first response to this question is likely to be "Of course!" or at least "Why on earth not?" My main aim in this paper is to show how one can argue for a negative answer. More precisely, it is to show how one can argue that, in plausible senses of the pertinent terms, the *wiser* a society is, the *less free* it is.

For the sake of a label, I call the argument I present the *negative argument*. It is essentially conceptual. It raises various evaluative questions but does not itself proceed at the level of evaluation. Given its focus, the paper might be categorized as an essay in political philosophy. Given that a good deal of time is spent elaborating an account of a wise society, however, it might also be categorized as an essay in social (or more specifically collective) epistemology.

2. Key Terms

Before setting out the negative argument I must explain how I am interpreting its key terms. They are all open to, and have received, a variety of interpretations. Thus some degree of clarification is necessary. It is possible that the negative argument works for interpretations other than those I offer here. It is also possible that it fails to work for one or more plausible construals. For present purposes I set these possibilities aside.

2.1 A Society

I take a society to be a kind of social group, where paradigmatic social groups include informal discussion groups, army units, sports teams, and labor unions. To give a rough and partial characterization of such a group one might say, echoing Rousseau, that its members are *unified* in such a way that they constitute *more than a mere aggregate* of persons.[5]

Typically a society, in particular, includes many smaller social groups. Thus within a given society there may be many families, labor unions, sports teams,

---

[5] This brief account is enough to show that societies as I understand them are a subtype of Surowieckian "crowds." I have nothing to say about such crowds in general here.

and so on. A society is therefore relatively large, in contrast with a family, say, or a sports team. For now, this brief characterization of societies will suffice.

2.2 Personal Freedom and a Free Society

The freedom of a society, as I shall construe that, is closely tied to the *personal* freedom of the individual members of that society, understood in a certain way. A concern for personal freedom in some sense of the phrase is central to a number of evaluative stances in political philosophy.

Thus, on one account of it, *anarchism* involves "a concern for preserving individual freedom and a distaste for the coercive measures of governments," while a government coerces by "threatening to use force or impose punishments if a person does not follow its laws" (Nathanson 1992).

Now, in what I take to be the central sense of the term, *punishment* requires a special standing or authority.[6] As I understand it, to have the *authority* to punish is not necessarily to be *justified* in doing so, but it does away with a possible objection to its use by a given agent. It cannot be objected "It is not for *you* to do that."

Indeed, anarchism is often characterized in terms of distaste, not so much for the *coercive measures* governments take but rather for *government* itself. Here government is construed as a matter of the authority to command, to demand or insist on compliance when noncompliance is threatened, and, where appropriate, to punish. The problem of government is posed in terms of *the loss of personal autonomy inherent in the authority of one person over another*, whether they command, demand conformity, or punish. That is the tenor of the well-known brand of philosophical anarchism that was advocated by Robert Paul Wolff (1970), for instance.[7]

The anarchist's concern is often couched in terms of the authority of one person, or of a body of persons smaller than the society that is in question. I take it, meanwhile, that there can be whole societies—even societies reasonably thought of as *political* societies or *polities*—without such a ruling person or body (Gilbert 2006, ch. 9).

---

[6] That is not to deny that people often speak of "punishment" in contexts where the appropriate kind of authority seems to be lacking. Clearly, they do. The authority sense can still be central in that the broader sense derives from it.

[7] *Philosophical* anarchism has been distinguished from anarchism of a more practical kind. See, for instance, Horton 1992.

Even in such "acephalous" societies, there are issues of personal autonomy. Such societies are likely to have a variety of rules. Each member will then have the authority to insist on any other's conformity to a given rule and to rebuke any other for not conforming to it.[8]

Evidently, I take it that one cannot *rebuke* someone without a special standing or authority. One can, of course, speak in a rebuking *manner* without such authority, just as one can speak in a demanding manner, without the authority actually to demand.

Rebukes and demands may be unaccompanied by physical force or by threats that such force will be applied unless what is demanded is done. There is, nonetheless, something *forceful* about any rebuke, just as there is something forceful about demanding. Indeed, in *The Concept of Law*, Hart suggests that rebukes lie at the informal end of a spectrum at the formal end of which lie punishments imposed through due process of law (1961, 10–11).[9]

Penal sanctions may sound—and may be—worse than informal demands and rebukes, but most people do not relish such forceful interventions from others. Most would prefer not to incur the reproofs of strangers, the rebukes of colleagues, or the reprimands of friends and intimates. Mill, the great philosophical champion of liberty, saw this clearly. And verbal chastisement can be the precursor of physical violence.

Suppose, now, that there is a rule in my society that women are not to contradict men. I know that if I, a woman, contradict a man on some point, the other members of my society have the authority to rebuke me for doing so. Accordingly, I may regularly decide not to make some point though I desire to do so. In other terms, my freedom is limited in an important way: there is something I want to do, but I risk an *authoritative forceful negative response* should I do it.

The account of a society's freedom that I shall make use of in developing the negative argument reflects the idea that the standing threat of such a response is an important limitation on personal freedom. In speaking of a "threat" here I do not mean to imply that the response is imminent, or even probable, but rather that it is "in the cards." If someone has the standing to rebuke me for doing something, I know that, should he speak to me in a rebuking manner, I cannot dodge the issue by saying "It's none of your business." If he has the standing to rebuke me, it is his business.

---

[8] Cf. Hart 1961. For discussion of Hart's account of social rules, see Gilbert 2000, ch. 5.
[9] See also the discussion of punishment in Gilbert 2006, ch. 11.

I shall say that a given member, M1, of a society S, is *personally free to perform a given action*, A, in face of another member, M2, if and only if M1 is under no threat of an authoritative forceful negative reaction from M2 should M1 perform A or, indeed, should M1 propose to perform A.[10] For the sake of brevity, I shall generally refer in what follows to being under no threat of a *rebuke*. It should be understood that all forms of authoritative forceful negative reaction are included under this heading.

Now, a given member, M1, of a society S, may be under a threat of rebuke from another member, M2, where these rebukes are not grounded in M1's membership in S as such. For instance, M1 promised M2, and no one else, that he would not do A. I am not concerned with such grounds here. The definition of *personal freedom* just given should be interpreted accordingly. What is at issue is rebukes whose ground is some aspect of *the membership of M1 and M2 in society S*.

I take it that a society itself can be "personally free" in the defined sense, insofar as it can be a member of a society of societies.[11] Meanwhile, the type of *societal freedom* with which this essay is concerned relates to the personal freedom of a society's members as just defined. This might be referred to as the society's *internal* freedom. My focal case continues to be a society whose members are individual human beings as opposed to other societies.

I shall assume that, as a matter of definition, a society becomes *less free* as particular personal freedoms are subtracted from those its various members already have. This is clearly only a partial account of societal freedom. It concerns only a single condition under which a society can be said to become less free than it was. Nonetheless it is of interest to ask whether a society's relative freedom in the respect at issue is altered by one or another factor.

I shall not attempt to offer a full account of a *free society*. Given the notion of personal freedom with which I am operating, however, a plausible account will not allow that a society is free when its members have little personal freedom. Nor will it demand that a free society be maximally free, where a

---

[10] A stronger notion would add that M1 is only *free to perform* A if he is not under threat of an authoritative forceful negative reaction *should he fail to perform* A. For present purposes the weaker notion offered in the text will suffice. I do not say that either notion is "correct." The weaker notion is, one might say, concerned with what one is permitted to do: if no one is in a position to insist that one not do A or to reprimand one for doing A, one's doing A is *permissible* as far as "the authorities" go. Clearly, if one is under threat of an authoritative forceful negative reaction should one fail to perform A, that does not take away from the *permissibility* of one's doing A. This note was added in response to Philip Pettit, personal communication.

[11] As in the case of individual human beings, one can distinguish between a society's freedom from the threat of *authoritative* forceful reactions and its freedom from the threat of force, authoritative or not. On the more general question, see Gilbert 2000, 149–50.

maximally free society is one in which, for any action whatever, each member of the society is personally free to perform that action in face of any other member. It may reasonably be questioned whether a maximally free society, as just defined, is possible. As will emerge, it can be argued that it is not, given what a society is.

2.3   A Wise Society

Some may be inclined to deny that there is such a thing as a society that is *wise* to any degree. They may point to the fact that wisdom involves or is closely connected to knowledge or, at least, good judgment and argue that a society is not *the kind of thing* that can be wise. Individual human beings can be wise but societies are not sufficiently like them for a wise society to be possible.

When it is presented, this argument may look plausible. Yet people regularly talk about a society's beliefs, judgments, decisions, and knowledge. Thus a particular society may be said to have made a wise (or unwise) decision, wrongly to consider itself superior to other societies, and so on.

When people talk about the belief of a society or other social group, they think of themselves as speaking literally rather than metaphorically. Rather than assuming that they are misguided, one might do well to consider what phenomenon on the ground, so to speak, they have in mind.

Perhaps because they think along the skeptical lines mentioned above, contemporary political philosophers have not paid attention to the idea of a wise society. Following John Rawls (1971), they have considered the key quality of a good society to be its justice and focused on that.[12]

In the *Republic*, Plato also focused on a society's justice. This did not lead him to neglect the idea of a wise society. Indeed, he thought of a society's wisdom as necessary to its justice. Notoriously, he did not think this way about its freedom. Plato does talk about freedom. His picture of what he called "democracy" in Book 8 of the *Republic* is perhaps the closest to true anarchy—and maximal personal freedom—that one can imagine. It is not clear, indeed, how consistent a picture this is. There is some talk of "laws" and "courts" of law, yet—he says—*one can do anything one pleases* (Plato, 1974,

---

[12] John Rawls (1971, 3) says that justice is the "first virtue" of social institutions. "Virtue," of course, may mean little more than "good quality." There is, meanwhile, a narrower sense of "virtue" such that only beings of particular kinds—those possessing broadly speaking qualities of mind—can be virtuous. Cf. Beggs 2003.

557b). Those condemned to death or exile walk about as if they are heroes and nobody cares (Plato, 1974, 558a).

This is not Plato's favored scenario. In the type of political society he favors, the laws are taken seriously. Most important for present purposes, the rulers are few in number and carefully selected and trained. Those with the right natural aptitudes go through the rigorous training necessary for one who loves wisdom—a philosopher—to reach his goal, knowledge of the Good.

Before the details of this training have been developed Plato considers what it is for a political society to be wise (Plato, 1974, 428b ff.). What he says is open to different interpretations, and I shall not attempt carefully to probe it here. At a minimum, it seems fair to characterize his opinion as follows. The judgments of the rulers, in making rules and decisions for the society, must, in a phrase, *track the Good.*

I shall work with an account of a wise society that has something of the same spirit. I shall not require that such a society is ruled by a particular person or body of persons, however—let alone a body of persons trained from birth for the purpose. Thus I shall allow that in principle an acephalous society can be wise.[13]

I shall not attempt carefully to explore either the idea of wisdom in general or the idea of a wise society in particular. The account of the latter that I shall work with has something to be said for it, but it may well be that an alternative account is more plausible. I hope that my discussion will help to stimulate consideration of precisely this issue. In the meantime, it is important to see that *on the account of a wise society proposed, the negative argument is sound.* A wise society, on this account, is a society possessed of features that, whatever their relation to wisdom in particular, would appear to be desirable, all else being equal.

The working account I shall adopt appeals, simply, to a society's *true value judgments,* in particular those relating to the goodness and badness of human and societal features and actions. Such judgments may be very general—as in the judgment that wantonly destroying a human life is a very bad thing—or quite specific—as in the judgment that Hitler was an evil man. They may not lead to specific decisions or actions or they may. If one judges that wantonly destroying another's life is a very bad thing to do, for instance, one is likely to avoid such destruction.

---

[13] Possibly Plato could allow this. The tiny acephalous society he first describes, though lacking fully fledged philosophers, may be wise enough for its own practical purposes. It may be, though, that he thinks its limited needs and purposes do not call for wisdom as opposed to some other capacity.

A true value judgment evidently tracks the Good at least to some extent. It may be plausible to argue that if a value judgment *fully* tracks the Good it must not only be true but it must also have been made on good grounds. It is not, then, "fortuitously" true. That said, I focus here on the simpler condition.[14]

I shall assume that, by definition, the true value judgments of one who is wise will be relatively numerous. This, along with the following points, is intended to apply both to individual human beings and to human societies. I shall assume one who is wise, as a matter of definition, does not make false judgments. If the truth on some matter of value is hard to discern, one who is wise will if necessary act on working assumptions understood to be such. These are relatively stringent conditions. They are not, however, as stringent as they might be. At the upper limit of wisdom, one would get *everything* right. I shall take the stated conditions to be both necessary and sufficient for one to be wise.

I shall make the following comparative judgment about one who is wise on the above account. Any new true value judgment one makes in addition to those one has already made amounts, by definition, to an increase in one's wisdom. This is only intended to be a partial account of what makes for an increase in wisdom, but it suffices for presentation of the negative argument.[15]

It is now time to turn to the core of the negative argument. This is the pertinent account of what it is for a society to endorse a particular value judgment.

2.4 A Society's Value Judgments

I have elsewhere developed an account of what it is for a group to believe that such-and-such.[16] I have also proposed a related account of what it is for a group to make a particular value judgment (see Gilbert 2005). Here I shall do

---

[14] Though I shall not argue this here, one can understand what it is for a society to judge that such-and-such *in light of certain considerations* in terms similar to those in which I explain what it is for a society to make a particular judgment. For further discussion see Gilbert 2002.

[15] It avoids such matters as the relative importance of different particular value judgments. It could be that some are more central, and a switch from a less to a more central judgment, or even from a few less to a single more central judgment must count as an increase in wisdom. Think of someone who knows that lying always has something to be said against it but ceases to see that is so, while coming to appreciate that killing a human being has much to be said against it.

[16] Initially in Gilbert 1987 and Gilbert 1989, ch. 5. See also Gilbert 2000 and elsewhere. There have been discussions of this work in articles and chapters by, among others, Alban Bouvier, Angelo Corlett, Christopher McMahon, Anthonie Meijers, Gianguido Piazza, Frederick Schmitt, Raimo Tuomela, and K. Bradley Wray. I respond to some of these discussions in "Belief and Acceptance as Features of Groups" (Gilbert 2002).

little more than sketch the account, saying only what I take to be needed to make the negative argument.

I proceed in terms of an illustrative value judgment, which may or may not be true: marriage is a valuable social institution. I shall refer to this judgment as V. Obviously any other particular judgment might stand in its stead. According to my account of such matters, in terms that will be explained,

A society judges that V if and only if its members are jointly committed to judge as a body that V.

I have argued at length elsewhere that the concept of a joint commitment is a fundamental part of human life, embedded in many of those central concepts with which human beings approach their interactions with one another.[17] I now say something about what a joint commitment amounts to.

A *joint commitment*, as I understand it, is a commitment *of two or more parties*. It is *not* a combination of commitments, one of one party, one of another, and so on. Given their joint commitment, each party has sufficient reason to act accordingly, just as one has sufficient reason to act according to a personal decision one has made. As I understand the phrase, if one *has sufficient reason* to do something, then one is rationally required to do it, all else being equal.[18]

Any joint commitment is a joint commitment to "do" something as a body, in a broad sense of "do" that includes *judging that* V. To say that certain people are jointly committed to judge that V *as a body* means something like this. They are jointly committed as far as is possible together to constitute a single body—or person—that judges that V. I say more about this shortly.

How do people become jointly committed? Failing special background understandings—in the *basic case*—a given joint commitment can only be created by all of the parties together. The same is true of its rescission. Here is a rough account of the conditions under which such a commitment is created in the basic case. Each of the would-be parties must express his readiness to be jointly committed with the others in a particular way, and the fact that these expressions have taken place must be open to all or, in something like David Lewis's (1969) sense, common knowledge.[19] Though I shall not

---

[17] This was the gist of Gilbert 1989. Longer treatments are to be found in Gilbert 1996, Gilbert 2003, Introduction, Gilbert 2006, ch. 7, and elsewhere.
[18] See Gilbert 2006, ch. 2. I distinguish between having (sufficient) reason and having *a* reason, or reasons, for doing something.
[19] For another version see Gilbert 1989.

attempt to elaborate on this point here, this account does not rule out joint commitments on a large scale.[20]

I take it that people can enter joint commitments in situations of strong pressure. Just as you can make a decision under pressure to do so, you can enter a joint commitment in such circumstances (see Gilbert 1993). To say that is not, of course, to contest the desirability of one's making decisions and entering joint commitments in the absence of such pressures.

Special background understandings allow for non-basic cases. Thus all of the members of a given population, large or small, may create an open-ended joint commitment such that one person or a smaller population of persons is in a position to create new joint commitments for the population as a whole. For example, the members of a labor union may jointly commit to endorse as a body any fiats issued by Jones under certain conditions. In that case when Jones issues a fiat under the relevant conditions, the union members are jointly committed to endorse, as one, that fiat. To keep things simple here, I am going to focus on societies where no such special background understandings prevail.

For the purposes of the negative argument the most important feature of a joint commitment is this. If I am jointly committed in some way with another person, I am answerable to him with respect to my proposed or actual nonconformity to the commitment. Not only do I owe him an *explanation* of any proposed or actual nonconformity, I also owe him *actions that conform to the commitment*. I owe these to him insofar as he participates in the joint commitment.

I have said that the negative argument is essentially conceptual rather than evaluative. The point just made may seem to refute that. However, it relates to what a joint commitment is, as opposed to its value or the value of any related actions.

One way of amplifying the point is as follows. There is a sense in which, by committing each party to act in certain ways, a joint commitment in and of itself creates in each party ownership of the actions in question. Being in the future, the actions are *owned* but not currently *possessed*: in that sense they are *owed*.[21]

Evidently this puts each of the other parties in a special position in relation to me. If I propose not to perform an action the commitment requires, he has the standing or authority required in order that he *demand* it. He can say, in

[20] For further discussion of large-scale joint commitments, see e.g. Gilbert 2006, ch. 8.
[21] For further discussion see, e.g., Gilbert 1999 and also Gilbert 2006, ch. 7.

effect, "Give me that! It's mine—qua party to the joint commitment!" He also has the standing to *rebuke* me. After the fact, he can say, in effect, "How could you not have given me that! It was mine!" Thus those who either propose to violate a standing joint commitment or who do violate one lay themselves open to the authoritative forceful negative reactions of the other parties.

So much, then, for the nature and implications of joint commitment. I turn now to the relationship of joint commitments to social groups.

I have argued elsewhere that those who are jointly committed in some way constitute a social group in a central sense of the phrase (Gilbert 1989, especially ch. 4). This accords with the rough characterization of a social group offered earlier in this article: its members are unified in such a way that they constitute more than a mere aggregate of persons.

Given this amplification, if certain persons are jointly committed to judge that V as a body then they constitute a social group. Indeed, they constitute a social group that judges that V. As I have argued elsewhere, to say that under these conditions people constitute a social group that judges that V answers to a standard everyday concept of a social group that judges that V (see, e.g., Gilbert 1989, ch. 5). In sum, the present account of a society's value judgment is not merely stipulative. It accords with entrenched, everyday understandings of the component ideas.

On the account proposed, then, *a society judges that V* if and only if the members are jointly committed to judge that V as a body. That is, they are jointly committed as far as possible to constitute a single body that judges that V. How might this commitment be fulfilled?

When people are acting in conformity with the commitment, they might confidently state that V when talking to one another. They would refrain from calling V or obvious corollaries into question without preamble. In short, they would suggest by their actions and emotional expressions that V. They would refrain, therefore, from acting contrary to V and from reporting contrary actions with bravado. Thus one would not say out loud, with an air of bravado, "I've managed to avoid getting married again!" or, critically, "Marriage? That's for the birds!"

I do not say that in order to act in conformity with the commitment people must personally judge that V. There are several reasons for this, but for now I simply state my understanding that a joint commitment to judge that V as a body does not require the parties personally to judge that V. Should one judge that not-V, however, he is committed not to say this *without preamble.* Rather, he must say, for instance, "Personally, I don't think marriage is such a wonderful thing." This indicates that he is speaking not from the perspective of the group as a whole but from his personal perspective (see Gilbert 1987; also 1996, ch. 14).

3. Can a Wise Society Be a Free One?

So much for the definitions and assumptions in terms of which I shall present the negative argument. They all have some plausibility, and it is worth considering what follows from them for the question: Can a wise society be a free one?

I am supposing that, by definition, a wise society endorses a fair number of true value judgments and eschews false ones, and that a new true value judgment added to its current stock of such judgments increases its wisdom. The negative argument can be put as follows.

Suppose that society S is wise. Suppose now that it adds a new true value judgment J to its current stock of true value judgments. By definition, it becomes wiser. Given the nature of societal value judgments in general, J provides the members of S, as such, with a ground for rebuking one another for a new range of possible actions, R. R includes speech acts as well as actions that do not involve speech. Thus S becomes less free.

A query may arise as to this conclusion. What if there was already a joint commitment in S—one distinct from that underlying S's new value judgment J—such that members of S have a ground for rebuking one another for the very same range of actions R covered in the case of J? Assuming for the sake of argument that this is possible, it is still fair to say that S becomes less free on making J, for now there is a new *ground* for rebukes in relation to R.

People can certainly have the standing to rebuke one another for performing a given action on more than one ground. Perhaps, for instance, several of us agreed not to do something, and I made a special promise to you that I would not do it. Then you can upbraid me both on the ground that we agreed not to do it and on the ground that you promised me not to do it. It seems fair to say, generally, that the more grounds for rebuke there are for one's performing a given action, the less free one is.[22]

Now it is true, of course, that if S were to add a *false* value judgment to its current stock of value judgments, it would also become less free. The striking thing about the negative argument, however, is this: something that on the

---

[22] I discuss a situation in which there may be multiple grounds for rebuking one and the same type of action later in this paper.

face of it is a *bonus*—S's increasing wisdom—turns out to have a specifiable *cost*—a corresponding loss in S's freedom. That assumes, of course, that a lessening of societal freedom, in and of itself, is a bad thing, while an increase in societal wisdom is a good thing. As said, at least on the face of it, this is so.

I should emphasize that the negative argument does not render problematic the idea that, all else being equal, it is better for a society to replace a false value judgment with a true one, if these are the alternatives. It implies, however, that it would make for more freedom in a society with a false value judgment if that judgment were simply abandoned—if the society were left with no view on the matter—rather than replaced by the corresponding true judgment. True judgments, just like false ones, reduce the freedom of society.

The negative argument raises or highlights several important questions. Before concluding I note and discuss a number of these without attempting fully to answer any.

4. Questions Arising

4.1 What If Everyone was Happy to Enter the Relevant Joint Commitment?

It may be proposed that the loss of personal freedom entailed by a wise society's increasing wisdom will make no practical difference if each member was happy to enter the relevant joint commitment. It may be added that it will matter even less if at the time they happily entered the joint commitment they personally endorsed the society's value judgment.

This seems not to be so. Suppose Qiong was happy to enter the joint commitment at issue in my focal example, personally believing that marriage was an excellent social institution. Suppose that through personal or vicarious experience she later changes her mind. Her change of mind is one thing; her society's change of mind is another. The joint commitment may still stand. She is then still subject to it.

At this point Qiong may well find none of her choices attractive. She can baldly make concordant statements she believes to be false and act in ways she takes to express a false value. She can cause herself to stand out from the crowd by saying, as the joint commitment permits, "Personally, I think marriage as an institution is problematic." She can publicly violate the commitment by omitting the qualifier "Personally," and lay herself open to authoritative forceful responses. One may well shrink from any of these options, and from others that might be available—such as giving up one's membership in the society in question.

Knowing all this, one who is simply contemplating *a personal change of mind* may turn away from that option. Or the very movement toward such contemplation may itself be suppressed.

Note that Qiong's option of prefacing her antimarriage statement with "Personally" may do more than make her stand out from the crowd. (Some people might find that outcome relatively attractive.) Another possible outcome is likely to be less attractive. Though the joint commitment does not require her personally to endorse the value judgment in question, when she says or implies that she personally doesn't endorse it, she puts herself in a problematic position. People have reason to wonder if she can be relied upon to fulfill the commitment in the future. Might her contrary opinion not soon break out untrammeled? Might she be a spoiler? She may find herself shunned, though she did not violate the commitment.

In sum, even if each one of a number of people is happy to enter a given joint commitment, and each one's personal judgment at that point accords with the societal value judgment thus created, its providing a basis for rebuke makes a practical difference. It allows, in general terms, for a tension to arise between a given member's joint commitment, on the one hand, and his personal judgment on the other.

4.2 How Important in Practical Terms Is a New True Societal Value Judgment?

Some are inclined to think that if any human being violates a moral rule, any other human being has the standing to rebuke him for this. Moral rules, in turn, may be conceived of as existing independently of all actual societies, and as corresponding to the subset of true value judgments at issue in the present discussion.

It may then be argued that the standing to rebuke another member of one's society that one gains from a new, true value judgment of that society does not make much practical difference to anyone's situation. Irrespective of our status as members of one or another society, we are all always open to rebukes from others for the violation of any moral rule. The fact that with an increase in a society's wisdom some people have a new ground for some such rebukes is of interest, to be sure. However, it would not seem to make much difference from a practical point of view.

I have argued elsewhere against the idea that human beings as such have the standing to rebuke one another for violations of moral rules (Gilbert 2005, 29–30). If they do not then the argument in the previous paragraph must be rejected: its central premise is false.

At the least, the truth of its central premise is not immediately obvious. Given that this is so, people who attempt to rebuke others "because what you are doing is morally wrong" may be given short shrift by those to whom they speak. These latter may simply, and sincerely, respond that "It's none of your business."

Thus even if rebukes were automatically in order by reason of the existence of moral rules as such, the practical impact of an increase in societal wisdom could be considerable. "This runs counter to our values" may well be received as a more pertinent explanation of rebuke than "What you are doing is morally wrong."

4.3 Can the Impact of a Society's Wisdom Be Mitigated?

Rather than attempting to curtail a society's wisdom—perhaps by making sure it does not address particular issues—is there a way of keeping its wisdom intact, and, indeed, increasing it, while reducing its impact on the society's members? The full spectrum of true value judgments may, indeed, include some that will lead a society that makes them to minimize the impact of its own value judgments.

I have in mind here value judgments associated with *when and how to tell people off* for violating a given joint commitment.[23] It may be that it is best to start in a kind and non-forceful manner. A maximally wise society, at least, will take this value judgment on board. It will then be incumbent upon its members to act appropriately if someone baldly says something contrary to a value judgment of the society. For instance, one might mildly observe, "That's not a very democratic sentiment!" or "I'm surprised to hear someone from these parts saying that!" or "I take it that you are simply expressing your personal opinion?" If the person addressed answers the last question affirmatively, the joint commitments to which he and his interlocutor are parties will offer little basis for rebuke.

A society's embracing the value judgments currently under consideration— those advocating an initially kindly approach—will most likely reduce the

---

[23] For a highly detailed discussion of the general problem within one religious tradition see Cook 2000.

frequency of rebukes. If a rebuke is considered acceptable in face of a recalcitrant interlocutor, however—one who will not say the expressed opinion is his personal one, or take it back in the light of gentle suggestion—they may well sometimes occur.

Moreover, as all will understand, the members of the society will at all times have the *standing* to rebuke provided by the joint commitment that underlies any of that society's value judgments. Thus should one forego an initially kindly approach and immediately offer a rebuke, the person rebuked will not be able to respond, "It's none of your business." The parties, then, are still *threatened* with rebuke, in the sense in question here.

4.4 How Is Societal Wisdom to Be Preserved?

What if forceful responses, though authoritative, never occurred? What might the effects of this be? How necessary to the very existence of a society's wisdom is the imposition, at least after gentler responses, of rebuke?

This question recalls Patrick Devlin's argument for the very strong thesis that a society risks disintegration if at least its core value judgments are not supported with the weight of the criminal law. His idea was, roughly, that the very existence of the society depends on the persistence of those core judgments as its judgments. If action contrary to those judgments was permitted by law, this would be liable to increase such action and would lead, eventually, to *the demise of the society's value judgment as such.*[24]

The general question is: What is necessary to ensure that a given true societal value judgment will persist? I shall not attempt to answer this question here. That it can be raised suggests, at least, that *there may be a cost to mitigating the effects of a society's wisdom to the point that even informal rebukes are disallowed.* The cost in question is the loss of the society's wisdom.

4.5 Evaluative Questions

Many evaluative questions arise. How good a thing is it that a society makes true value judgments as these have been understood here? Is it better, all things considered, that a society minimize its evaluative judgments or sticks only to certain areas of value judgment? Is a society that is good overall one

---

[24] See "Morals and the Criminal Law" (originally "The Enforcement of Morals") in Devlin 1965. The most famous commentary is Hart 1963. For discussion of Devlin's social theory see Gilbert 2005.

that looks the other way as far as values, or some kinds of value, are concerned—irrespective of its capacity to get things right? If so, why is that? Personal freedom is likely to be invoked at this point. Invocation alone, however, is not enough.

Given that a diminution in personal freedom is always a loss, how is it to be weighed against an increase in the wisdom of a given society? All else being equal, is it indeed better for a society to make a true value judgment rather than no judgment on the topic or a false one? These questions are important and timely. They press us to think further about the wisdom of a society, its implications, and its value.[25]

References

Beggs, Donald. 2003. The idea of group moral virtue. *Journal of Social Philosophy* 34: 457–74.

Conway, David. 2000. *The rediscovery of wisdom: From here to antiquity in quest of Sophia.* New York: St. Martin's Press.

Cook, Michael. 2000. *Commanding right and forbidding wrong in Islamic thought.* Cambridge: Cambridge University Press.

Devlin, Patrick. 1965. Morals and the criminal law. In *The enforcement of morals.* Oxford: Oxford University Press.

Gilbert, Margaret. 1987. Modeling collective belief. *Synthese* 73: 183–204.

Gilbert, Margaret. 1989. *On social facts.* Princeton: Princeton University Press.

Gilbert, Margaret. 1993. Agreements, coercion, and obligation. *Ethics* 103: 679–706, reprinted in Gilbert 1996.

Gilbert, Margaret. 1996. *Living together: Rationality, sociality, and obligation.* Lanham, MD: Rowman and Littlefield.

Gilbert, Margaret. 1999. Obligation and joint commitment. *Utilitas* 11, 143–163, reprinted in Gilbert 2000a.

Gilbert, Margaret. 2000. *Sociality and responsibility: New essays in plural subject theory.* Lanham, MD: Rowman and Littlefield.

---

[25] Versions of this chapter were presented to the Philosophy Department at the University of Connecticut, fall 2003, and to the 2005 Spindel conference in Memphis. I thank the discussants on both of these occasions. Particular thanks go to Christopher McMahon for his thoughtful comments in Memphis and to Austen Clark and Len Krimerman. The chapter is a somewhat fine-tuned version of the Memphis version. A full treatment of its topic would have to be far longer than the present one.

Gilbert, Margaret. 2002. Belief and acceptance as features of groups. *Protosociology* (online journal) www.protosociology.de.

Gilbert, Margaret. 2003. The structure of the social atom: Joint commitment as the foundation of human social behavior. In *Social metaphysics*, ed. Frederick Schmitt. Lanham, MD: Rowman and Littlefield.

Gilbert, Margaret. 2004. Collective epistemology. *Episteme* 1, 95–107.

Gilbert, Margaret. 2005. Shared values, social unity, and liberty. *Public Affairs Quarterly* 19: 25–49.

Gilbert, Margaret. 2006. *A theory of political obligation: Membership, commitment, and the bonds of society*. Oxford: Oxford University Press.

Hart, H. L. A. 1961. *The concept of law*. Clarendon Press: Oxford.

Hart, H. L. A. 1963. *Law, liberty and morality*. Stanford: Stanford University Press.

Horton, John. 1992. *Political obligation*. Atlantic Highlands, NJ: Humanities Press.

Lewis, David K. 1969. *Convention: A philosophical study*. Cambridge, MA: Harvard University Press.

Mill, J. S. 1976. *On liberty*. Indianapolis: Hackett.

Nathanson, Stephen. 1992. *Should we consent to be governed?* Belmont, CA: Wadsworth.

Plato. 1974. *Republic*, trans. G. M. A. Grube. Indianapolis: Hackett.

Rawls, John. 1971. *A theory of justice*. Cambridge, MA: Harvard University Press.

Surowiecki, James. 2004. *The wisdom of crowds*. New York: Anchor Books.

Wolff, R. P. 1970. *In defense of anarchism*. New York: Harper Torch Books.

PART V

RIGHTS AND OBLIGATIONS IN GROUP LIFE

12

Regarding *A Theory of Political Obligation*

Everyday references to what we, collectively, think, do, feel, and so on, are standardly applied to groups of all sizes, from married couples to whole nations. Hence we find such language as "We, the People of the United States of America . . . do ordain and establish this constitution for the United States."[1]

One might think that in the case of extremely large groups such language has to be used in a tendentious or aspirational way. In some cases, it may be so used. But could the collective "we" ever appropriately be used in a full-blooded way in such contexts? In other words, could the collective "we" ever appropriately be used with the intention to refer to a whole people?

This is a compelling question, both theoretically and practically, particularly when political or other divisions within a given country are salient, and it may be unclear what kind of unity that country as a whole could possess.

I addressed this and related questions in my book *A Theory of Political Obligation: Membership, Commitment, and the Bonds of Society*—henceforth *TPO* for short.[2] In what follows I respond to some of the comments it has received, hoping thereby to clarify central aspects of my approach.[3]

I begin with a brief outline of the book.[4]

Outline of *A Theory of Political Obligation*

I first envisaged the theory of political obligation presented in *TPO* when completing my book *On Social Facts*.[5] I saw that the account of social groups proposed there had the makings of a positive solution to one version of the

---

[1] From the Preamble to the United States Constitution.

[2] As noted in that volume, the paperback version (Gilbert 2008) contains some clarifying revisions to the hardback (Gilbert 2006a) without any changes to the pagination.

[3] I draw here on Gilbert (2013), which replies one by one to four commentators: Diane Jeske, John Horton, Fred Stoutland, and Jan Narveson. The discussion here is more streamlined, focusing on issues rather than particular commentators. It discusses some central issues further, and makes new points. In *TPO* ch. 11.3, pp. 266–74, I respond to a set of objections from Simmons (1996) and others that were directed to earlier work of mine on political obligation, including Gilbert (1993).

[4] For a fuller summary, see *TPO* ch. 12.   [5] Gilbert (1989: 411; 415–16).

Life in Groups: How We Think, Feel, and Act Together. Margaret Gilbert, Oxford University Press. © Margaret Gilbert 2023. DOI: 10.1093/oso/9780192847157.003.0013

much-debated problem of political obligation, a version I refer to as *the membership problem*: Are members of a political society, as such, obligated to uphold its political institutions and, in particular, to conform to its laws?[6]

The main claims for which I argue in *TPO* are as follows.

There is a central everyday concept of a *social group* that has a particular notion of a *joint commitment* at its core. This point is introduced by way of an extensive discussion of *what it is to do something with another person or persons*, on the understanding that when people do something together they form a social group, albeit in some cases a small and transient one.[7] It is argued that one needs to appeal to a joint commitment of the parties in order to understand what it is for people to act together.

There are both basic and non-basic cases of joint commitment. In the *basic* case, those who are jointly committed in some way are committed, as one, by virtue of *expressions of readiness on the part of each* to be jointly committed with the others in the relevant way. In a *non-basic* case, the joint commitment is established by some person or body of persons who have been authorized to do so by a basic joint commitment of the committed persons.[8]

There are several ways in which a basic joint commitment may be concluded prior to fulfillment, given that all of those subject to the commitment are involved in its conclusion.[9] The concluding parties need not be identical to the creating parties, but just as whoever is to be jointly committed in the first place must partake in its creation, whoever is there at the finish must partake in its conclusion in one way or another.

To be jointly *committed* in the sense in question is to be subject, as one, to a *normative constraint*. More precisely, the parties *ought* to conform, all else being equal. This "ought" is not a moral "ought." It does, however, exclude from consideration such countervailing factors as the parties' personal inclinations and desires as such.[10]

Given their status as co-creators of the joint commitment, those who are jointly committed in some way have *obligations to one another* to comply with the commitment.[11] These *directed obligations* of joint commitment are

---

[6] *TPO*, p. 14. In ch. 1.2 of *TPO* I distinguish four different questions that represent other understandings of the problem of political obligation, including some that do not mention "obligations" specifically.

[7] See *TPO* ch. 6 (offering observations on acting together (6.2 and 6.3) that call for a theory of this phenomenon) and ch. 7 (introducing joint commitment (7.1–2), relating it to acting together (7.3), and arguing (7.4) that the parties have obligations to one another to conform to it).

[8] For further discussion of basic versus non-basic cases see e.g. *TPO*: 140–1, and the Introduction, this volume.

[9] See *TPO*: 141–4.   [10] See *TPO*: 131–2.   [11] See *TPO* ch. 7, sec. 4.

genuine in the sense that, by my definition, those who have them ought to comply with them, all else being equal.[12]

An important aspect of the directed obligations of joint commitment is that the person to whom the obligation is directed has a *right* to its fulfillment, and the standing, in the sense of authority, to issue related demands and rebukes should the object of these rights not be forthcoming.[13]

I emphasize that there is no barrier in principle to social groups constituted by joint commitments being *very large* or *hierarchical*. They may also be *anonymous* in the sense that, generally speaking, individual parties to the commitment are not personally acquainted with one another. They may, indeed, be *impersonal* in the sense that, generally speaking, the individual parties do not *know of* one another as individuals.[14]

Understanding a *political society* as a social group in the sense just referred to, and allowing that its political nature is a matter of its members being jointly committed to uphold or in other terms accept as a body certain *governing rules*—where behavior appropriate to accepting such rules includes conforming to them—one can conclude that a political society's members have genuine obligations to one another to conform to the governing rules of that society.[15] Insofar as *political obligations* are understood to be obligations to accept the political institutions of one's society, then, the obligations just mentioned are apt to be labeled "political obligations."

I labeled my theory of political obligation the *plural subject theory* because, in my technical terminology, a *plural subject* is equivalent to that of a population of persons who are jointly committed in some way. It might also have been labeled the *joint commitment theory*. My point in adopting the label "plural subject" for any set of jointly committed persons was my sense that the full-blooded use of the first-person plural pronoun—in its collective sense—implied the existence of a joint commitment of the relevant parties.[16]

I turn now to some of the questions and concerns that commentators have raised about *TPO*. In responding to these I expand, as necessary, on points in

---

[12] Contrary to what some commentators have assumed, this is not to say that one has a genuine obligation, let alone a genuine directed obligation, to do something just in case one *ought* to do it. It is also not to say that any genuine *obligation* always determines what one ought to do, *all things considered*.

[13] See *TPO*: 148ff.   [14] On these points see ch. 8 of *TPO*.

[15] In my technical terminology, a joint commitment to accept certain rules *as a body* is, roughly, a joint commitment to emulate, by virtue of the actions and utterances of each of the parties, one who accepts those rules. Each of the parties is thereby committed—and obligated to the others—to do his (or her) part in such emulation, coordinating as appropriate with the rest. I take it that in the case of accepting certain rules as a body, each party is obligated, among other things, to conform to those rules.

[16] See Gilbert (1989: ch. 4).

this outline, offering, in effect, a more comprehensive view of the book. I begin with some of the most general questions, going on to those focused more specifically on political societies, and their members' obligations.

1. Concerning Commitments: Personal, Individual, and Joint

1.1 On Personal Commitments
(with Special Reference to Decisions)

In *TPO* as in other places I introduced the idea of a *joint* commitment by reference to another kind of commitment, which I refer to as a *personal* commitment.[17]

I take a personal commitment to issue from a person's decision, among other things.

My reference to personal commitments was intended to introduce the less familiar—joint commitment—by reference to the more familiar—personal commitments. As I just did, however, one can introduce joint commitment without reference to personal commitments. One can also argue that the parties to a given joint commitment have associated rights and obligations without such reference. Nonetheless, personal commitments are of independent interest, and since several commentators have questioned what I have said about personal decisions in particular, I shall say something here about my position on these matters.

In saying that someone is personally *committed* by virtue of having decided on some course of action I mean that person is subject to a *normative constraint*. In my technical terms, he (say) has *sufficient reason* to conform.[18] By which I mean, he ought to conform, all else being equal. All this assumes, of course, that the decision stands—it has not been rescinded by its maker.

My central point can be put this way: there is *something wrong* with contra-decisional action *as such*. More precisely, it involves a kind of *error in action*. To say this, as I see it, is not yet to say anything about reasons with an "s."

Let me try to spell this out a bit. One way in which there could be something wrong with my action—and, indeed, my decision—is that it does not

---

[17] In addition to *TPO* see, for instance, chapter 1, this volume.
[18] The notion of commitment that I employ, then, is normative rather than psychological: to say that "I am committed" in the sense in question is not to refer to a particular state of my mind. It relates, rather, to what I ought to do.

appropriately reflect the reasons for and against that action that existed before the decision is made.

Another way in which my action could be wrong, all else being equal, is that I act contrary to a decision of my own that I have not rescinded. There is, I take it, something wrong about this, *irrespective of any reasons I had for or against the action, prior to my decision*. Perhaps, indeed, my decision was, to all intents and purposes, unreasoned.[19]

In a thoughtful discussion of my treatment of decisions in *TPO*, Diane Jeske suggests that "there is something odd about supposing that reasons are grounded or constituted by decisions considered in and of themselves."[20] That may be so. As I have just made clear, however, I do not start from any such supposition about *reasons*.

Jeske is unhappy with another point I make about decisions, a point I take to apply to all commitments of the general kind I take them to impose— commitments of the will, as I call them. I suggest that a standing decision *trumps countervailing desires and inclinations* with respect to what rationality requires, unless these inclinations and desires meet some very strong conditions.[21]

I have in mind, in particular, that it might be arguable in some cases that it would be morally wrong not to follow one's inclination in a given case, in which case the decision is trumped by that consideration. Of course, given one's usual ability to change one's mind or, in other words, rescind one's decision, it is generally easy enough to do so and follow one's desires and inclinations without contravening any requirement of rationality deriving from a prior decision.

To illustrate her concern, Jeske discusses an example much like this: Jill decides to forgo sugary pastries. Then, in a coffee shop, she feels a strong inclination to order a Danish pastry, orders one, and eats it with her coffee— without at any point rescinding her decision.[22] Jeske suggests that it would be wrong to assume that in all cases falling under this description Jill would be acting contrary to what reason requires: everything depends on the reasons for which Jill's decision to forgo sugary pastries was made.

That suggests that Jill's decision has no role in the rationality or otherwise of Jill's action—no role in deciding the question whether she acted contrary to what reason required of her.

---

[19] See Gilbert (2012b).   [20] Jeske (2013: 274).   [21] See *TPO*: 131–2.

[22] Someone might wonder whether Jill's ordering the Danish doesn't constitute her rescission of her earlier decision. I think not. Rescission of a decision must be intentional, as when one thinks, "I've changed my mind, I don't have to forgo sugary pastries *entirely*." A decision can, of course, be forgotten, and then from the decider's point of view it is as nothing. Should it later be remembered, it would be appropriate to rescind, revise, or conform to it, depending on the circumstances.

252 LIFE IN GROUPS

Of course it could be that Jill took what is objectively the best course for her, all things considered. I take it, however, that that is not what is at issue here. Nor does Jeske suggest that it is.

She does suggest, however, that the rationality of Jill's eating the pastry is not affected by her having previously decided to forgo such pastries. What is needed, the suggestion runs, is to see how things stack up in light of the considerations Jill acknowledged as bearing on her decision. If those reasons make it clear that she ought not to have taken the pastry, then she acted contrary to reason. If they do not—if they allow for the occasional lapse—then she did not.

Now, in addition to asking if Jill took the objectively best course, one can of course also ask whether she took the best course given her own reasons for deciding to forego sugary pastries. One can also ask whether her decision, as such, trumps her inclinations, as such, in this situation. My point is that this is, intuitively, the case, and indicates the exclusionary normative impact of a decision as such.

Imagine that Jill has told her friend Pete of her decision. Seeing her ordering the Danish with evident anticipation of gustatory delight, he well might say: "I thought you decided to forgo sugary pastries!" I take it that he would then be suggesting that something is wrong with her ordering the Danish, whatever its expected pleasures, *given the decision in question*.

Jeske might propose that in this scenario Pete must have Jill's *reasons for her decision* in mind, either the specific reasons, or the reasons, whatever they are, that he presumes she has. On the face of it, however, he has in mind only *the fact that she made the decision in question*. In sum, he suggests that there is something questionable about Jill's contra-decisional action, as such, in spite of her evidently strong inclination to act contrary to it. More precisely, she ought to conform to her decision, in spite of her inclination. Though it may be unclear exactly why this is so, I propose that this suggestion is correct.[23]

1.2 On the *Individual* Commitments Deriving from a Joint Commitment

In *TPO* and elsewhere I distinguish between the *personal* commitments I take to be engendered by personal decisions and related phenomena and the

---

[23] For further discussion of this case, referencing some proposals from John Broome and others regarding the relation between decisions and "oughts," see e.g. Gilbert (2018: 38, 43–5).

individual commitments I take to be engendered by the process of joint commitment. I take it, that is, that by virtue of us all being committed as one, each of us, individually, is committed to promote the conformity of each with the joint commitment.[24]

I see these individual commitments as being of the same genus as personal commitments: they are both "commitments of the will." Importantly, however, the individual commitments that ensue from a joint commitment are *interdependent* in the sense that there cannot be a single such commitment, deriving from a given joint commitment, in the absence of two or more other such commitments. The derived joint commitments of those creating a joint commitment come into being simultaneously, at the time of the creation of that joint commitment.

1.3 On Joint Commitment versus Mutual Promises or Agreements as Sources of Obligation

Jeske has suggested that an appeal to mutual promises would be better than an appeal to joint commitment in the search for a potential source of political obligations.[25] She makes this suggestion in part because she takes it that no commitment of the will, as such, gives the committed person a reason for action.

Granting that point, I disagree with an inference that Jeske and others may make from it: that no species of commitment of the will can, in and of itself, be a source of genuine obligations and rights. Rather, as I argue in *TPO*, I take it that a commitment of a certain type—namely, a joint commitment in my sense—is such a source, on account of the way it is brought into existence.

I also believe, as I argue in *TPO*, that a promise, like an agreement, is best understood as constituted by a joint commitment.[26] Against this proposal about promises, Jeske says that if, for example, she promises Todd to go to spin class on Sunday her reason for doing so "supervenes on *my act* of promising. There just does not seem to be any motivation for having my reason supervene on a state of affairs that also involves Todd's will" (emphasis mine).[27]

Certainly, the way Jeske describes the case in question has nothing untoward about it: she is the one who—as we put it—*promises* something to Todd. The promise is in that sense *hers*. She may well think of it that way if she is

---

[24] See *TPO*: 136.   [25] Jeske (2013: 273-4).   [26] See *TPO* ch. 10.
[27] Jeske (2013: 278).

wondering whether to go to spin class. It could yet be that, in the paradigm case at least, it takes two to promise. What suggests that this is so is the role of *acceptance*, a particular kind of "uptake," as when Todd says "Okay," "Great," or whatever. In short, Todd's acceptance of Jeske's promise seems to seal the deal.[28]

The proposed joint commitment account of promising makes sense of this. Given that, in the example, Jeske has already openly expressed her readiness together with Todd to commit them both in the relevant way, a matching expression of readiness is needed from him. Once both expressions are in place, in conditions of common knowledge, Jeske and Todd are jointly committed.[29] That is, they are jointly committed to endorse as a body the decision—in the sense of plan or scheme of action—that she will go to spin class on Sunday.[30]

Evidently, if promises are a kind of joint commitment, then invoking mutual promises, as Jeske suggests, is not to take joint commitment out of the picture. Rather, it is to invoke it twice.

Jeske's invocation of mutual promises may reflect the view that bilateral executory agreements are exchanges, or pairs, of promises. As I explain in *TPO*, there are good reasons for rejecting this view in favor of an account in terms of joint commitment.[31]

Jeske does not propose an account of promising but does offer a stance on promissory obligation, which she describes as "a broadly Rossian intuitionist account." On this account, she says, promises "by their very nature ground prima facie reasons for action," something we can know by reflection on the nature of a promise.

For present purposes the problem with this is that we do not need an account of how promises give reasons or even obligations in *some* sense of the term. We need an account of how promises give obligations of the particular sort to which promises and agreements give rise, namely, *directed* obligations

---

[28] See *TPO*: 221-2. See also Gilbert (2018: ch. 6, sec. 3.2).

[29] "In conditions of common knowledge": roughly, these expressions are "out in the open" as far as Jeske and Todd are concerned. For a note on common knowledge see the Introduction, this volume. I discuss common knowledge in most detail in Gilbert (1989), where I distinguish between "individual" and "population" common knowledge: the latter, roughly, is common knowledge within and with respect to members of a given population considered as such. See *TPO*: 176.

[30] In *TPO* ch. 10 I argue that both agreements and promises are constituted by a joint commitment, in which case the obligations most closely associated with them are obligations of joint commitment. See also Gilbert (2011), (2018: ch. 10). For extended critical discussion of moral principle accounts of promissory obligation, with special reference to Scanlon (1998), see Gilbert (2004), and (2018: ch. 7).

[31] See *TPO* 217-220 and references therein.

that correlate with *rights* and the *standing to demand* what one has a right to, and rebuke for refusal to provide.

Joint commitment accounts of promises, mutual promises, and agreements are attractive in part because they do this. It is not clear that the promisor or the parties to the agreement accrue the right kind of obligation on any other type of account.[32]

In the context of a discussion of political obligation there is good reason to appeal to joint commitments as opposed to promises, mutual promises, or agreements specifically. In the clearest cases promises and agreements are entered into explicitly. Any account of political obligation that appeals to promises or agreements is going to be quickly met with such claims as "I never made such a promise."[33]

This is one of the reasons that contemporary political theorists have rejected the classical theory of political obligation according to which—in a standard formulation—a political society is founded in an agreement or contract of the would-be citizens.[34]

The process of establishing a joint commitment need not reach the level of explicitness required for a promise or agreement. For this and other reasons the concept of a joint commitment is a much more auspicious starting point for a theory of political obligation than the concept of a promise, an agreement, or some combination of promises.

1.4 Regarding the Standing to Issue Demands and Rebukes to Others

As mentioned earlier, one with a right of the kind possessed by the parties to a joint commitment has the *standing to demand* the object of his right from the right's addressee, and the *standing to rebuke* that person for failure to accord him that object. One might wonder at the suggestion that some kind of "standing" is needed in order to make a demand of someone or issue a rebuke to them. That depends on one's interpretation of "demand."

I take there to be at least two different senses of "demand" and "rebuke." Focusing on demands: one needs a special *standing* or, in other words, *authority* in order to make a demand in the relatively narrow sense associated with

---

[32] See Gilbert (2018: esp. chs. 6–9).   [33] Cf. Simmons (1979: 79); Klosko (1992: 142).
[34] I discuss both the attractions of, and common objections to, that theory in chs. 3 and 4 of *TPO*. I reconsider the theory in ch. 10 in light of my discussion of joint commitment and its attendant obligations.

rights. Importantly, the standing to make a demand in that sense is not to be confused with *justification*.[35]

Thus suppose Tess is beating her child, something she has a moral duty not to do. Suppose, further, that Mark, a stranger to her, is justified in attempting to get her to fulfill that duty by saying, for instance, "Stop beating that child!" As I understand it, it is not yet clear that Mark has the standing to *demand* of Tess that she fulfill the duty *in the authority-supposing sense*, nor that he has a corresponding *right* to her doing so. It is possible that he does have this standing—but it does not come from the justified nature of his "demanding" speech.[36]

Similarly, his standing to rebuke her, in the authority-supposing sense, is unclear. I take it that such standings exist only in the context of her obligation *to* him not to act as she is acting, or in other words, his right (in the relevant sense) to her not so acting.[37]

2. Some Questions about Acting Together

2.1 Is There a Concurrence Condition?

On the way to offering an account of social groups and, ultimately, political societies, in *TPO*, I focus on what I take to be a small-scale, relatively ephemeral social group—two people going for a walk together—and argue for a joint commitment account of such activity.[38]

In responding to comments on this part of my discussion I should emphasize that my central example is indeed two people who are *going for a walk*

---

[35] Distinguishing between two related *senses* of "demand" is not strictly necessary to make the point at issue here. One might instead distinguish between, say, demands *simpliciter* and *authoritative* demands, keeping the sense of "demand" constant. Compare Feinberg (1970), who speaks of "righteous" demands in the context of rights. That said, I shall continue in the present vein in what follows. This note responds to a comment from Kory DeClark.

[36] Contrary to the suggestion in Jeske (2013: 278). See also Frederick Stoutland's suggestion (Stoutland 2013) that insofar as his wife has the standing to rebuke him for stopping just because he feels like it, while he is out on a walk with her, bystanders have such standing also. Some indication of the supposed grounds of the bystanders' standing is needed in order to evaluate this, whereas, in my view, his wife's being his walking partner suffices for her having the standing in question. See my discussion of acting together in the next section. For an extended discussion of demands and the standing to demand, including the situation of "members of the moral community," see Gilbert (2018: chs. 4ff.).

[37] In *TPO* at p. 105, I emphasize the *sufficiency* of a pertinent directed obligation for the standing to make demands and rebukes. That is not to deny that it is also *necessary* for such standing. See e.g. Gilbert (2018) for discussion focused on the standing to demand an action of someone.

[38] In doing so I draw on and further develop work on acting together begun in Gilbert (1989: ch. 4) and (1990).

together—and so constituting, as one might say, a two-person "walking party," as opposed to various other possibilities that might also be referred to in the vernacular as "walking together." For instance, it is distinct from the case of two people who understand that they are (intentionally) sharing part of separate walks because, as we say, their paths have crossed for a while. These people may then characterize what they are doing as "walking along together for as long as it suits us both."

I take it as a background assumption that, roughly, people who are *going for a walk* together understand that, if what they are doing proceeds appropriately, they will walk alongside each other for some period of time, returning together to their starting point.

Given these background understandings and assumptions, suppose that Pam and Sam are out on a walk together. Assume there are no special background understandings between Pam and Sam relating to their walk. Some commentators have suggested that, even then, Pam is free to stop walking alongside Sam at any time without any "by your leave."[39]

I doubt this. Of course, Pam is in a position to change her mind about anything she herself is doing. She can simply decide to act in a way that is not appropriate given that she and Sam are walking together. She may, indeed, have a good reason so to act, with or without Sam's concurrence. That, however, is not to say that nothing will be amiss if she goes ahead without it.

That she needs his concurrence is suggested by the typical way people disengage from a joint walk. Perhaps Pam says, "I don't want to walk any further" or even "I'm stopping here!" and Sam replies "Okay." In the type of exchange I have in mind, Sam's "Okay" is not merely a matter of acknowledging his receipt of Pam's message. Rather it expresses his concurrence with the idea that she stops at the place in point.

Sam might in some cases ask Pam why she doesn't want to go on, before offering his concurrence with her stopping. As the other party to their walk, he may well be entitled to such an explanation. That, however, does not seem to be his sole entitlement with regard to his walking partner.

It has been suggested that one might have serious doubts about the conjectured concurrence condition on acting together because "it would appear to bestow something like a veto on each and every member of a plural subject in determining not only its action, but the terms on which it can be dissolved,

---

[39] Some authors qualify this somewhat. Thus Horton (2013: 283) suggests that, though she need not seek Sam's concurrence, it may be incumbent upon Pam to explain why she is stopping if she does stop. Others have suggested that she must at least notify him that she is about to leave their walk.

within its conventional duration."[40] Such doubts could arise because one finds it discomfiting explicitly to acknowledge that, absent special background understandings, there is such a veto. That there is such a veto, however, is further suggested by the fact that such special understandings are often explicitly introduced.

Thus, knowing that Ben is reluctant to come on a projected joint walk because he prefers solitary walks, Anne might say "Look, if at any time you want to go off on your own, just say so, and that will be fine." If his say-so was always enough, why would such things be said?

It may be noted that people often do something together as the result of an informal agreement. It is generally acknowledged that such agreements cannot be rescinded unilaterally, absent special background understandings. Could this be driving the thought that there is a concurrence condition on exit from a joint action? I think not: those who are acting together may well not allude to an initial agreement, if there is one, in objecting to attempts unilaterally to force issues relating to their joint action. They may allude, rather, to the fact that they are, say, taking a walk together.

This suggests that, in and of itself, acting together involves a concurrence condition. That may be a good thing from a practical point of view insofar as it will tend to keep the parties on track even when an initial agreement has faded from view.

This is all that I shall say, here, in defense of a concurrence condition on exit from a joint activity.[41] Suffice it to say that I have not found the objections that have been made to it compelling.[42]

The most important point for the purposes of *TPO* is that those who are acting together have *rights* against one another to the performance of appropriate actions, and corresponding *obligations* to one another. As I argue, this point is well explained by a joint commitment understood as, at a minimum, a commitment of all imposed by the actions of each.[43] It is this feature of joint commitment that is crucial for the plural subject theory of political obligation.

2.2 The Place of Acting together in the Argument of *TPO*

There are several reasons one might want to approach an account of political societies through a discussion of acting together as I do in TPO. Prominent

---

[40] Horton (2013: 283).

[41] My discussion of the concurrence condition in *TPO* runs from p. 106 to p. 115 and considers a variety of kinds of acting together and ways in which a case of acting together may conclude.

[42] In addition to Horton's discussion, see also e.g. Bittner (2002) and Stoutland (2013).

[43] See, in particular, *TPO*: 103–6, 115.

political philosophers have assumed that political societies are joint enterprises of a particular kind.[44] And those who engage in joint enterprises of any kind are apt to be deemed social groups, of whatever scale or duration.

Be that as it may, the plural subject theory of political obligation can be explained without reference to acting together. Its core idea is the concept of joint commitment. Joint commitments may have a wide variety of contents. We may be jointly committed to espouse as a body a certain goal, as I proposed is the case when people act together. We may also be jointly committed to believe or to accept as a body that such-and-such is the case, and so on. For us to constitute a social group in the plural subject sense, then, we do not need to be jointly committed specifically to espouse as a body a certain goal.

According to the understanding of a political society I adopt in *TPO*, the members of a given population constitute such a society if and only if there are social rules of a certain type in that population—rules of the type I call *governing rules* or rules of governance. My account of social rules takes off from the influential though debated account of H. L. A. Hart.[45] I explain why an alternative is needed and offer a joint commitment account: a social rule, as I understand it, is constituted by a joint commitment to accept as a body a given requirement or fiat concerning the conduct of the people in question.[46] This accords with central contentions of Hart's, though it differs radically from the account he proposed.

One can, then, state the essence of the plural subject theory of political obligation without reference to acting together. It is a joint commitment account of social rules, rather than a joint commitment account of acting together, that lies at the heart of the theory.[47]

3. Political Societies as a Matter of Joint Commitment

3.1 Political Societies—A Particular, Common Conception

In a probing discussion of *TPO*, John Horton, a major theorist of political obligation, says I believe "membership in a political society should be understood in terms of joint commitment."[48] I believe, rather, that *on one*

---

[44] See *TPO*: 100–1.   [45] See Hart on "rules of obligation" in Hart (1961: 84–88).

[46] See *TPO*: 197.

[47] For discussion of the plausibility of a joint rescission condition on joint commitment *qua* commitment with the etiology in question, see *TPO*: 155–6.

[48] Horton (2013: 307). Horton's publications on political obligation include Horton (1992) and (2010), a revised and extended version of the former.

natural interpretation of the phrase "political society" (or "polity" for short) membership—or fully fledged membership—is implicitly so understood. By "natural" I mean that the interpretation accords with common understandings of the component terms, allowing that other such understandings may exist.[49]

Other notions of membership in a polity surely exist and one of these in particular may come to the fore in discussions of political obligation. I have in mind the notion according to which anyone who is a citizen of a nation-state such as the United States, legally speaking, is the member of a polity. Some who are members according to this notion cannot be fully fledged members of a polity according to the plural subject notion operative in *TPO*, since they will lack the capacities to be parties to the constitutive joint commitment(s). Think, for instance, of infants born within the confines of the state. I take it that as a child develops the relevant capacities it may become a fully fledged member though it was officially a citizen from birth onwards.[50]

Legal citizenship and membership in a political society on the plural subject account can come apart in other ways as well. Both citizens and, say, non-citizen permanent residents, may clearly express their understanding that both of these groups are members of one "we." In short, some citizens may not be fully fledged members of a given polity while some non-citizens are.[51]

That does not mean that the plural subject notion can have no relevance to the situation of most citizens of a given nation-state. As the line of argument begun in *On Social Facts* and continued in *TPO* suggests, such expressions as "We hold these truths…" are likely to be interpreted in plural subject terms by speakers and hearers alike. By virtue of processes of the kind described in *TPO*, including but not restricted to the making and accepting of statements involving these expressions, a large multitude *approximating* the citizenry of a nation-state may come to constitute a genuine plural subject.[52]

It is worth noting that one can contribute to such processes without having much choice in the matter—having no option to emigrate, for instance. One can still express one's (genuine) readiness to participate in the established joint commitment. Even strong external pressure to do so need not prevent such expression: one may be ready to participate failing any viable alternative.[53]

---

[49] See the outline of *TPO*, above.   [50] *TPO*: 239, first para.
[51] I thank Itzel Garcia for emphasizing this point to me in discussion, March 2022.
[52] For extended discussion see Gilbert (*TPO* chs. 8 and 9).
[53] For related discussion see TPO: 75–82, discussing a standard objection to "actual contract" theory. See also the discussion of "acceptance" in section 3.3 below.

One way of conceiving *nation-building* is as the gradual creation of a plural subject—a genuine collective "we"—of the appropriate type. Nor need the scale of such a "we" be restricted to single nations in principle. In addition to such associations as the European Union, global government has been envisaged and there could in principle be a "we the people" of the earth.[54]

A given political society on the plural subject model can be expected to include many smaller plural subjects, from families to trades unions and so on. Notably the existence of such a society does not preclude uprisings that involve one or more of these smaller plural subjects. These may protest specific features of established political institutions, they may object to the continuance in power of particular individuals, and so on. They may foment revolution in the sense that they think the whole existing constitution should be overturned. Of those who constitute the initial plural subject, including themselves, the revolutionaries may be saying, in effect, "We who have this constitution need to change it."[55]

3.2 The Constitutive Joint Commitment: Some Observations

As I have explained, in *TPO* I understand a political society as founded in a joint commitment to accept as a body a particular set of governing rules, a joint commitment that obligates the parties to one another to act in ways that include conforming to these rules. These obligations are their *political obligations*. In this section I first make some clarificatory points about this proposal. In the next section I consider one concern about it.

First, the joint commitment is to accept *as a body* the pertinent rules. In order to conform to this commitment, as I understand it, it is not necessary that the individual parties have any particular *personal attitude* towards the rules—they need not think well of them, for instance. However, they should not—as far as their joint commitment goes—speak badly of the rules unless it is clear that they are speaking personally.

Second: in order to *accept* as a body a particular set of governing rules, the parties do not have to act as if, as a body, they *approve* the rules in question in the sense of thinking them good.[56] Their individual or collective approval of

---

[54] Gilbert (2009) discusses the European Union in this connection.

[55] For further discussion of protest in the context of a joint commitment see *TPO*: 281–2, and Gilbert (2010: 337).

[56] Cf. Gilbert (2010: 337).

these rules is not of course *precluded* by the fact that they are jointly committed to accept them as a body. It is, simply, a different matter.

As I understand it, then, accepting as a body a particular set of governing rules requires quite a lot of those involved, in terms of their behavior, though not in terms of their innermost appraisals of those rules. That said, if we are looking to ground an obligation to conform to a set of governing rules, we need something like a joint commitment to accept those rules as a body, interpreted roughly as I have done. It seems, further, that such a joint commitment is feasible. The presence of such a joint commitment at some particular point in space and time is of course an empirical matter.

There is more than one possible joint commitment relating to a set of governing rules, and, as Jeffrey Helmreich has emphasized, not all of these will entail obligations of conformity among the populace.[57] For instance, people might be jointly committed to acknowledge, as a body, that "these are the rules that are enforced around here"—they are "the law" in that sense—but not jointly committed to accept those rules as rules, as one might put it, *for them.*

All else being equal, then, their motives for compliance will not include an appropriate sense that they are obligated to their fellows to comply with the rules. Nor will they appropriately express rebukes for non-compliance as such. What they are obligated to their fellows to do is, rather, to acknowledge that, for instance, the rule they have just broken is one for which they are likely to receive some sanction. So someone's "That's against the law!" would not be construed as a rebuke for breaking it so much as a rebuke for doing something that is likely to attract some sanction to oneself.

3.3 Knowledge of the Constitutive Joint Commitment

Horton expresses concern regarding my theory's requirement that there be widespread "knowing and intentional" participation in a joint commitment to accept as a body a particular set of governing rules. This recalls a discussion of H. L. A. Hart's in *The Concept of Law* in which the central issue is this: Assuming that a legal system of any degree of complexity exists in a given population in part on account of attitudes of members of that population, *whose* attitudes are in question?[58]

---

[57] Helmreich (forthcoming).
[58] Hart (1961: esp. 110–14). In addition to attitudes, there are supposed to be mostly conforming actions.

Hart believed that any legal system proper included a fundamental social rule that, in effect, selected a particular set of other rules or potential rules as, also, rules of the population.[59] Hart called any such fundamental rule a "rule of recognition." He worried that it was too much to expect "knowledge and acceptance" of a given rule of recognition by "the bulk of society" except in the simplest of cases.

Thus he appealed only to the attitudes of a relatively small group of officials as far as the existence of a given rule of recognition went. The main point for present purposes is that Hart ends up with a radical disjunction between officials and the bulk of the population with respect to what makes it the case that a legal system exists in that population. The existence of the system depends only on the attitudes of the officials.

Horton's concern may be analogous to Hart's worry. What can we expect by way of participation in a joint commitment of the relevant kind from the "bulk of society" when the political institutions in question are at all complex?

It is not clear that we need a detailed understanding of these institutions in order to be jointly committed in the relevant way. What we need is a joint commitment that suffices to *pick out* a particular set of political institutions, without necessarily *specifying* them in any detail. If we are jointly committed to accept as a body a particular set of political institutions thus picked out, we have the corresponding obligations of joint commitment.[60]

3.4 On "Expressions of Readiness"

Jan Narveson raises the question: Are those in relation to whom the laws of a nation-state are enforced—call them *the populace*—jointly committed to accept as a body the authority of the law-makers and enforcers, *whether they think so or not?*[61]

Here two questions should be distinguished. First, can members of the populace be jointly committed in the relevant way whether or not they have ever consciously attended to the question? Second, can they be jointly

---

[59] Cf. Hart (1961: 110): "the ultimate rule of recognition specifying the criteria in terms of which the validity of laws are [sic] ultimately assessed."

[60] Cf. Hart on how one who is part of the bulk of society may think about the complicated legal system in question (1961: 111): "The law which he obeys is something which he knows of only as 'the law.'"

[61] Narveson (2013).

committed even though they have never done anything from which it can be inferred that they are ready jointly so to commit themselves?

I would answer the first question in the affirmative, the second in the negative. In any basic case of joint commitment—such as a basic case that sets up the authority of law-makers and enforcers—it is necessary that the parties be ready to be jointly committed with the pertinent others in some way, *and* have openly expressed that readiness. They need not be focusing on the fact that this is what they are doing or at some level saying to themselves that this is what they are doing.

To say that their authority to make and enforce the law may have been established by a joint commitment of the populace does not, of course, mean that the law-makers and law-enforcers for whom such authority has been so established are not open to criticism on moral or purely practical grounds.

Authority can be misapplied—as it can be mistakenly granted. Consequently, it may be useful, if not urgent, to question and even rebel against its dictates, in certain circumstances.[62]

3.5 The Persistence of Political Societies on the Joint Commitment Account

John Horton has questioned whether political societies in the sense of *TPO* are capable of persisting over time and through many generations. The answer is that they are.

That is because people who find a polity-constituting joint commitment in place around them as they emerge from childhood may be able, in effect, to "sign on" to this already established commitment. Whether or not they *are* so able will depend on aspects of the established commitment.

It could in principle deny this possibility to certain persons or persons of certain types. Thus, for example, it could be understood that those who are eligible as parties to the commitment have a certain skin color or a particular ancestry, something that a would-be entrant has no control over. Again, particularly in small-scale cases, the parties to a polity-constituting joint commitment could be specified as particular individuals, irrespective of the qualities that characterize them.

---

[62] Thanks to Itzel Garcia for prompting me on this point. Cf. Gilbert (2010) on the different forms that patriotism may take.

Generally speaking, joint commitments can either be between particular persons as such—John, Phyllis, and Jimmie, say—or between persons with specified features—those who live on a certain island, those with a particular further feature, and so on. Given the latter possibility, the way is open for those with the specified features to sign on over many generations.[63]

Members of a given political society can also, of course, be jointly committed to accept as a body a set of rules that determine who is, and who is not, eligible to join that society, perhaps after engaging in certain rituals such as reciting a particular pledge in a public forum. These members, then, can be understood to have expressed their readiness jointly to commit to accepting as a body the governing rules of their society *with whoever has satisfied the relevant criteria*, that person having in their turn indicated a readiness to join with them in doing so.

4. The Obligations in Question

4.1 The Wrong Kind of Obligation?

Several political theorists share John Horton's concern with my "distinctive but highly controversial claim...that...obligations of joint commitment...although genuinely obligatory...need not be understood as *morally* obligatory."[64]

One reason they find this claim troubling is that it does not sit well with the standard approach to political obligation: "at least in the philosophical literature, the central question about political obligation has been precisely that of whether or not we have any moral obligations by virtue of our membership in a particular political society."[65] Horton suggests that, if that is not my question, I am talking past almost all theorists of political obligation.

Now, not all theorists address precisely the problem of political obligation that Horton mentions. Not all pose the problem in terms of obligations at all.[66] Certainly, though, it is standard to see the question of political obligation as concerning a moral obligation in the sense of a moral requirement, however it is spelled out.[67]

[63] See Gilbert (2006b).
[64] Horton (2013: 13). Miller (2008) and Narveson (2013) make similar points.
[65] Horton (2013:13).   [66] For a variety of formulations of the problem see *TPO* ch. 1.
[67] In TPO: 159–61 I note an important difference between obligations of joint commitment and moral requirements as I understand these: only the latter are "context sensitive." On some conceptions of the moral realm both moral requirements and obligations of joint commitment will be considered

Going against the grain in this respect could be a blessing rather than a curse. Here are three independently plausible reasons for thinking that a new approach should be welcome.

First, in what has long been the reigning discussion of the subject—*Moral Principles and Political Obligations*, published in 1969—A. John Simmons arrives at a skeptical position with respect to the observations he uses to motivate his inquiry—observations taken from everyday thought and experience. I have in mind the kind of experience Simmons refers to when he mentions a common sense of one's "political bonds," which he interprets in terms of moral requirements. One might, then, be forgiven for wondering whether theorists of political obligation, including Simmons, have been pursuing what is in at least some respects the wrong question. Perhaps the everyday experiences, the sense of one's "political bonds," do not relate to moral obligation, as understood by these theorists, but to obligation of a non-moral kind.

Second, if there *are* genuine non-moral obligations associated with membership in a polity, this is something someone concerned with the *moral* obligations associated with such membership must surely take into account. The non-moral obligations in question will surely be *morally relevant*. Quite likely one is morally obligated or, in other terms, required to conform to such obligations, *all else being equal*.

Third, the question I address in *TPO* concerns genuine obligations—obligations of a type that one ought to conform to, all else being equal. It is reasonable to propose that a given theory should primarily be judged by the answer it gives to the question it sets itself. If the question it sets itself is significant, why worry if few, if any, others have pursued it? Indeed, any significant question that has generally been ignored is a particularly pressing one.

4.2 The Obligations of Joint Commitment: Their Scope

Horton expresses his deepest concern regarding the obligations of joint commitment as follows:

> …it seems that there cannot be a plural subject in which the participants who constitute it are without associated obligations. And this is as true of

---

moral. In that case what is crucial from an analytical point of view is to notice the important distinctions among moral obligations according to the conception in question.

plural subjects constituted by a commitment to nefarious, or indeed evil, activities as it is of innocuous or benign forms of joint commitment.[68]

Given the above, Horton finds the normative force of such obligations to be opaque. Let me see if I can go some way to clarify my position.

Suppose you and I do everything that is in our power with respect to jointly committing ourselves to accept as a body a given legal system where— possibly unknown to us—the ensuing joint commitment would have associated obligations to do evil. Normally this would suffice to effect our joint commitment. So: Do we succeed in jointly committing ourselves in this case? In particular, is each of us now *committed* in the way intended?

The question can be expanded thus, assuming my understanding of commitment: Can we fail to make it the case that—*without reference (yet) to the content of the putative commitment*—each of us now ought to act accordingly, all else being equal?

Note that I have not yet referred to obligations. Before one can argue that the parties are *obligated* to conform to their joint commitment, one needs to establish that the joint commitment is possible. Once that has been established, the point about obligation follows. In other words, if there *can* be a joint commitment conformity to which requires evil actions, then there can be *obligations* of joint commitment to perform evil actions.

Is there some way to block the connection between a given joint commitment and obligations of the parties to conform? I do not see that there is. Nor do I see that as problematic. I see my obligation *to you*, in this case, as a matter of your having played the role you did *in committing me*. If you and I are *jointly committed* in some way, then, I am obligated to you to conform to the commitment. This does not mean that I ought so to conform *all things considered*.[69]

Suppose for a moment that a joint commitment requiring performance of evil actions is *not* possible. Suppose, that is, that whatever each expresses to the other in conditions of common knowledge, no such joint commitment ensues. That does not affect the point that a joint commitment, *when it occurs*, obligates the parties one to another to act accordingly. So—failing some other possible qualification—it will still be true that members of political societies constituted by appropriate joint commitments have associated obligations to conform to those political institutions of their polities that do *not* mandate

---

[68] Horton (2013: 13).
[69] Paragraph added in response to a comment by Kory DeClark.

evil actions. The plural subject theory of political obligation will then be on a par with more clearly morally oriented theories, such as Horton's own, which, as he puts it, limit the kinds of association that can give rise to binding obligations, through accepting they have to meet some minimum moral threshold.

Such theories have a disadvantage, however, insofar as an intuitive link between membership in a polity—as such—and obligation is not maintained.[70] One may of course choose to focus on a particular kind of polity, as does John Rawls in A Theory of Justice. Rawls, who invokes a "natural duty of justice," is explicitly concerned with the duties of citizens of a *just* society.[71]

As such, this concern is fine, but *restricting a whole field of inquiry in this way risks ignoring significant aspects of political life as such*—as does the standard focus on political obligations understood as moral requirements.

The plural subject theory of political obligation does not restrict its purview to just or otherwise admirable polities, and in so doing is able to offer an explanation of the felt tug of "political bonds" in polities generally that was the starting point for Simmons's classic treatise on political obligation.

4.3 The Obligations of Joint Commitment: Their Nature

It is crucial to note in this context that the obligations of joint commitment are primarily a matter of *relationship*. Yes, one who is committed jointly with another ought to conform to that commitment, all else being equal, where one's personal desires and inclinations are excluded from consideration. In addition, however, the relationship of parties is altered in significant ways, on account of the way their joint commitment came about, with their being, one might say, co-authors of the commitment.

In particular: each *owes* the other conforming actions or (in other terms) is *obligated to* the other to conform, with a correlative *right* to conformity. Each, accordingly, has the *standing* to demand compliance of the other, and to rebuke the other for non-compliance.[72] These are not trivial changes in the normative landscape.

Given these considerations, one's reneging on one's political obligations, in the plural subject sense, is a matter of failing to give one's fellow members what one owes them, *qua* members of the polity in question. It is to put them

[70] Cf. Dagger (2000).   [71] Rawls (1971: 51).
[72] This line of thought, as presented in Gilbert (2006a: ch. 7), is further developed Gilbert (2018), which focuses on the corresponding rights. See also chapter 13, this volume.

in a position to make relevant demands of you and to rebuke you. It is, in sum, to offend against them—whether or not one's action is otherwise sanctioned, all things considered.

All of this is perfectly consistent with the point that one may sometimes be morally obligated not to conform to a particular joint commitment—either because of its content or as a result of external factors. One will then properly default on genuine obligations of joint commitment, risking the rebukes of one's fellows.

4.4 The Distinctiveness of the Obligations of Joint Commitment

It was never my intention in *TPO* to insist on a particular account of moral obligation. I do distinguish the obligations of joint commitment from moral obligations conceived of in one standard way. I call the latter *moral requirements*. I note that, unlike the obligations of joint commitment, these are *context-sensitive*.[73]

Possibly both moral requirements so conceived and obligations of joint commitment will count as *moral* on one or more broad conceptions of the moral.

In that case what is crucial from an analytical point of view is to notice the important distinctions among moral obligations according to the conception in question.

5. Standing versus (Moral) Justification: The Case of Punishment

Philosophical discussions of punishment tend to be silent on the question of who has the standing or authority to punish in a given case, and how one can accrue such standing. Perhaps this is because most people are primarily interested in questions of moral justification.[74] Such questions are undoubtedly compelling. It is important, however, to see that there are two kinds of question to be answered about punishment, whether one is talking about the verbal punishment of a rebuke, or the "jail terms, fines, or physical punishment

---

[73] See Gilbert (2006a: 159–61).
[74] Cf. Gilbert (2006a: 251). The standard theories of the justification of punishment are briefly discussed at pp. 251–2.

including the death penalty" that are at issue in the political realm—physical sanctions, for short.[75]

The standing to rebuke or otherwise punish a person and the justification for so doing must be sharply distinguished. Importantly, one may have the standing to rebuke someone for performing some action yet not be morally justified in doing so.

Thus suppose you promised me to perform some small service, but forgot to do so. You are very well-meaning and have helped me many times in the past. I take it that I have the standing to rebuke you for failing to perform your promise. Yet I could reasonably be considered churlish should I in fact rebuke you. To say that I am being churlish is a moral criticism. Thus one may be morally criticized even for a verbal rebuke, and in spite of having the standing to issue one.

There is a significant contrast between one's being morally justified in punishing someone and one's having the standing to punish him. The standing to rebuke or engage in punishing behavior of one or another kind *does not come in degrees*. Either you have it or you don't, and you cannot have more or less of it.

This suggests something that is otherwise plausible for the obligations of joint commitment, insofar as these are correlated with such standing: one such obligation cannot be more or less weighty, or important than another, *qua* obligation.

Moral justification is different. With respect to punishment of a given degree of severity you can be more or less justified in imposing that punishment, and there may be a threshold below which you have no justification for imposing it. As potential punishments become more and more severe, the minimum threshold will rise accordingly.

From an analytical standpoint I take it to be more important to understand the differences between standing and justification, like the differences between the context-insensitive directed obligations of joint commitment and context-sensitive requirements on behavior, than to know whether one or another counts as moral on one or more prevailing conception. Once a given conception of morality is articulated relatively clearly, the question whether the obligations of joint commitment and the related standings are moral or not should be settled easily enough, one way or the other.

---

[75] The quoted words are from Narveson (2013). Hart (1961: 10–11) sees "informal reproofs" as the non-legal analogues of legal punishment. Though it may primarily be used to refer to a form of verbal behavior, the term "rebuke" is sometimes used more broadly, as in "He was rebuked for this behavior by being posted abroad."

6. Old Wine in—at Least—a New Bottle?

At one point Jan Narveson links my theory of political obligation with that of a host of illustrious philosophers from the past: Aquinas, Hobbes, Locke, Hume, to name a few. He writes: "What they/we all say is that political authority is somehow derived from the people being ruled."[76] So: Does my theory advance the discussion at all? Does it go beyond the generality Narveson expresses here; or, more specifically, beyond the idea of a polity-sustaining contract?

The three chapters on what I refer to as "actual contract theory" in *TPO* are integral to my purposes in the book.[77] Actual contract theory makes a more specific claim than Narveson's, and tends to be dismissed in the contemporary literature with quick observations as to how the discussant and others "never agreed to obey the laws."

Narveson could now say that he "never expressed his readiness jointly to commit with such-and-such others to accept, as a body, the laws" but that is less easy for him to be sure about. Thus consider a United States citizen who is highly critical of the United States, its government, and its edicts. Yet he constantly, when referring to the United States, refers to what "we" are doing and about how wrong "we" are.

As I have argued, there is reason to see these references as indicating his understanding that he participates in the kind of joint commitment I have been writing about.[78] This is so even though—as he might possibly aver with some emphasis—he never, ever actually *agreed* to support and uphold its laws.

He could, of course, be wrong in thinking he participates in such a joint commitment: he may be using the language of the collective "we" without warrant. Suffice it to say that *even if he never, ever actually agreed*, he could still be right.[79]

---

[76] Narveson (2013: 298).

[77] Chs. 4 and 5, which characterize the theory to be discussed and review the standard objections to it; and ch. 10, which reconsiders it in light of the exposition of my plural subject/joint commitment theory.

[78] Again, see the arguments in Gilbert (1989: esp. ch. 4).

[79] Narveson aptly quotes Hobbes on "government by institution"—aptly, insofar as a "real Unity of them all" is supposed to be engendered in the process envisaged; inaptly, insofar as Hobbes does not distance himself from the idea of a single event in which everyone explicitly expresses his readiness (as I would say) jointly to commit with the others. Gilbert (1990) briefly discusses the relation of my account of social groups to that of "actual contract" theorists Hobbes and Rousseau.

Concluding Note

I thank all of those who have commented on *TPO* both formally and informally for their stimulating questions and comments. Though I have not been able to give anything like a complete response even to those comments and questions to which I've responded here, I hope that what I have said has helped to clarify important aspects of *TPO*, while offering something of an introduction to it to those who are unfamiliar with it.[80]

Bibliography

Bittner, Rudiger (2002) "An Action for Two," in Georg Meggle, ed., *Social Facts and Collective Intentionality*, Frankfurt: Dr. Hansel-Hohenhausen AG.

Dagger, Richard (2000) "Membership, Fair Play, and Political Obligation." *Political Studies* 48: 104–117.

Feinberg, Joel (1970) "The Nature and Value of Rights." *Journal of Value Inquiry* 4: 243–260.

Gilbert, Margaret (1989) *On Social Facts*. London: Routledge and Kegan Paul; 1992: Princeton: Princeton University Press.

Gilbert, Margaret (1990) "Walking Together: A Paradigmatic Social Phenomenon." in vol 15, *The Philosophy of the Human Sciences,* ed. P.A. French, T. E. Uehling, Jr. and H.K. Wettstein, eds. Notre Dame: Notre Dame University Press.

Gilbert, Margaret (1993) "Group Membership and Political Obligation." *The Monist* 76: 119–133. Reprinted in Gilbert (1996).

Gilbert, Margaret (1996) *Living Together: Rationality, Sociality, and Obligation*. Lanham, MD: Rowman and Littlefield.

Gilbert, Margaret (2004) "Scanlon on Promissory Obligation: The Problem of Promisees' Rights." *Journal of Philosophy* 101: 83–109.

Gilbert, Margaret (2006a) *A Theory of Political Obligation: Membership, Commitment, and the Bonds of Society*. Oxford: Oxford University Press (hardback).

Gilbert, Margaret (2006b) "Who's To Blame? Collective Moral Responsibility and Its Implications for Group Members." *Midwest Studies in Philosophy*, ed. Peter French, 30: 94–114.

[80] Warm thanks to John Broome, Matthew Dean, Kory DeClark, Itzel Garcia, Jeffrey Helmreich, Daniel Pilchman, and Maura Priest for valuable comments on related material.

Gilbert, Margaret (2008) *A Theory of Political Obligation: Membership, Commitment, and the Bonds of Society.* Oxford: Oxford University Press (paperback).

Gilbert, Margaret (2009) "A Real Unity of Them All?" *The Monist* 92: 268–85.

Gilbert, Margaret (2010) "Pro Patria: An Essay on Patriotism." *Journal of Ethics* 13: 319–40.

Gilbert, Margaret (2011) "Three Dogmas about Promising," in *Promises and Agreements: Philosophical Essays*, Oxford: Oxford University Press.

Gilbert, Margaret (2012a) "Giving Claim-Rights Their Due," in B. Bix and H. Spector, eds., *Rights: Concepts and Contexts*, Farnham, Surrey: Ashgate.

Gilbert, Margaret (2012b) "Commitment," in Hugh LaFollette, ed., *International Encyclopedia of Ethics*, 1st edn, Oxford: Blackwell.

Gilbert, Margaret (2013) "A Theory of Political Obligation: Responses to Horton, Jeske, Narveson and Stoutland" *Jurisprudence* 4. 301–321.

Gilbert, Margaret (2018) *Rights and Demands: A Foundational Inquiry.* Oxford: Oxford University Press.

Gilbert, Margaret (2022) "A Simple Theory of Acting Together." *Journal of the American Philosophical Association.*8: 399–408.

Jeske, Diane (2013) "Reasons and Decisions." *Jurisprudence* 4: 273–9.

Hart, H. L. A. (1961) *The Concept of Law.* Oxford: Oxford University Press.

Helmreich, Jeffrey (forthcoming) "Legal Rights and Joint Commitment." *Philosophy and Phenomenological Research.*

Horton, John (1992) *Political Obligation.* Humanities Press. Atlantic Highlands, NJ.

Horton, John (2010) *Political Obligation*, 2nd edition. London: Palgrave Macmillan.

Horton, John (2013) "Plural Subjects and Political Obligations." *Jurisprudence* 4: 280–6.

Klosko, George (1992) *The Principle of Fairness and Political Obligation*, Lanham, MD: Rowman and Littlefield.

Miller, David (2008) "Margaret Gilbert, *A Theory of Political Obligation.*" *Philosophical Quarterly* 58: 755–7.

Narveson, Jan (2013) "Gilbert on Political Obligation." *Jurisprudence* 4: 295–300.

Rawls, John (1971) *A Theory of Justice.* Cambridge, MA: Harvard University Press.

Scanlon, Thomas (1998) *What We Owe to Each Other.* Cambridge, MA: Harvard University Press.

Simmons, A. John (1979) *Moral Principles and Political Obligations.* Princeton: Princeton University Press.

Simmons, A. J. (1996) "Associational Obligations." *Ethics* 106: 247–273.

Stoutland, Frederick (2013) "Gilbert on Commitment and Intention." *Jurisprudence* 4: 287–94.

13

Giving Claim-Rights Their Due

Introduction

"Rights" are so often appealed to in contemporary moral, political, and legal discourse that it is of great importance to clarify our ideas on the subject.[1] Much clarification has already been achieved, most famously by the jurist Wesley Newcomb Hohfeld at the beginning of the twentieth century. Hohfeld noted four distinct referents for the phrase "right" in legal parlance. Using different labels to distinguish them one from another he called these referents "rights," "privileges," "powers," and "immunities." To avoid further ambiguity he also used the word "claim" as equivalent to "right" in the above list. Claims, he opined, were rights "in the strictest sense." There are reasons for thinking that he was right about this but this aspect of the matter will not be pursued here. This paper focuses on claims or, as they are now often called, "claim-rights."

As I explain later, Hohfeld had something, though not a great deal, to say about claims, as he did about privileges, powers, and immunities. Indeed, he bequeathed to later rights theorists a problem that continues to compel their attention: how to advance our understanding of claims beyond what he says.

I take it that, at a minimum, the existence of a claim-right—at least in the paradigm case—involves at least two people, and that the appropriate form of ascription of such a right, where just two people are involved, is:

A has a right against B to B's phi-ing.[2]

---

[1] Earlier versions of this paper were presented as a Humanities Center lecture at the University of Connecticut, Storrs, 2003, at the Melden workshop on claim-rights at the University of California, Irvine, 2008, at the Georgetown Law and Philosophy Seminar, 2008, at the Rocky Mountain ethics conference in Boulder, Colorado, August 2009, at Leif Wenar and Rowan Cruft's workshop on claim-rights, King's College London, May 2010, and as part of a series of four lectures at the University of Palermo, June 2010. I am grateful for all of the comments received on this and related material. Special thanks go to Gopal Sreenivasan and Peter Jones, official commentators in Colorado and London, respectively, and to Sreenivasan, Aaron James, Joseph Raz, Frank Stewart, and Leif Wenar for extended informal conversations on claim-rights and my ideas about them. Daniel Pilchman and Frank Stewart made helpful comments on the penultimate draft of this version. Responsibility for the final version is mine alone.

[2] Some prefer "A has a right against B *that* B phi." I am not aware of anything that hangs on the difference. A less expansive form, more common in the vernacular, would be "A has a right to B's

Life in Groups: How We Think, Feel, and Act Together. Margaret Gilbert, Oxford University Press. © Margaret Gilbert 2023.
DOI: 10.1093/oso/9780192847157.003.0014

At a minimum, then, the existence of a paradigmatic claim-right in the broadest sense concerns at least one party (the claim-right holder), the performance of an action by another party, and a relation between the first and the second party, which is referred to by saying that the first holds the right "against" the second party or, in other familiar technical terminology, that the right is "addressed to" him.[3]

That much is uncontroversial. It does not yet tell us very much about claim-rights. What is the substance of the relationship between a right holder and the right's addressee?

The question assumes that there is but one such relationship. This assumption may be challenged. A claim-right has so far been characterized by reference to an essentially formal criterion: the appropriate linguistic form for referring to such rights. Those who make rights-ascriptions of this form may well construe them in different ways.[4] Be that as it may, something like the question posed has been the motivation for much contemporary theorizing about claim-rights.

The standard approach to such theorizing is generally agreed to have resulted in a stalemate between two opposing positions. In the first part of this paper I review this approach in a way that brings out some questionable, though deeply entrenched, assumptions of both positions and some others as well. Looking once again to Hohfeld, I propose and develop a different approach to claim-rights. This takes seriously his proposed nomenclature and homes in on a particular, significant relationship that is closely associated with claim-rights of an important sort.

I. Understanding Claim-Rights: The Standard Approach

The Aim

The standard approach to understanding claim-rights involves, explicitly or implicitly, the aim of producing a unitary account of claim-rights *that respects a certain canonical set of claim-right ascriptions.*

---

phi-ing" (or "A has a right that B phi)," where the idea incorporated in the phrase "against B"—whatever precisely that is—is not made explicit.

[3] On this account, then, less than paradigmatic cases, if cases at all, will include rights against oneself and rights not held "against" anyone. The account is supposed to allow that rights may be held against people qua members of a certain class as well as qua particular persons.

[4] Kagan (1998) writes of actual (claim-) rights language in the moral sphere as "horrendously ambiguous" and offers a series of increasingly narrow definitions that he suggests have been explicitly or implicitly adopted by different authors.

Here a *unitary* account is, roughly, one intended to articulate a single concept rather than a disjunctive set of concepts. To *respect* the set of ascriptions in question is to provide an account of claim-rights such that these ascriptions, when interpreted as the account suggests, are *true*.

The canonical set of claim-right ascriptions includes the ascription of rights to those who make unimpeachable *everyday agreements*—rights to the actions specified in the agreement.[5] This canonical set of claim-right ascriptions is also generally taken to include the ascription of rights understood to exist independently of agreements and the like: among these is a right ascribed to each human being, at least from infancy onwards, not to be physically assaulted in the absence of special justification.[6]

Although many of the central texts in rights theory come from legal theorists, the canonical claim-rights I have just mentioned are both generally thought of as moral as opposed to legal rights. I say more about the idea that rights are either legal or moral in due course.

The rights of the parties to an agreement are rights against each other only—thus sometimes referred to as *special* rights. The right not to be physically assaulted, more fully described above, is at least a right against every other human being capable of respecting that right, thus sometimes referred to as a *general* right.[7]

The Central Debate

For those taking the standard approach, the central debate has been between two opposing classes of theory. Not all prominent theories of claim-rights fall into one of these classes, but these, and their opposition, have garnered much attention in the literature. I write here of "the" will theory and "the" interest theory on the understanding that these come in different versions.

In generalized versions offered by Gopal Sreenivasan, the will theory runs thus:

---

[5] The qualifier "everyday" is supposed to indicate that what is at issue is not a specifically legal agreement or contract in law. I refer to "unimpeachable" agreements insofar as some everyday agreements may be thought not to result in rights, e.g., agreements to participate in an immoral enterprise. I discuss immoral and coerced agreements in, e.g., Gilbert (2006a: ch. 10).

[6] What counts as a canonical claim-right ascription may change over time, and that may affect which accounts of claim-rights will be deemed to fall within the pale of acceptability. For present purposes that need not concern us.

[7] See, e.g., Hart (1955).

Suppose X has a duty to phi. Y has a claim-right against X that X phi just in case Y has some measure of control over X's duty.[8]

The interest theory, in contrast, runs thus:

Suppose X has a duty to phi. Y has a claim-right against X that X phi just in case Y stands in a sanctioned relation to benefiting from X's phi-ing.[9]

I set aside for now the further elaborations that have been associated with these brief descriptions—in particular the "measures of control" or "sanctioned relationships" that have been contemplated.

Each of these theories has been held to have serious problems from the point of view of the aim in question. Accordingly, further theories have been and surely will be proposed by those engaged in this project, both versions of the will and interest theories and new theories altogether.[10]

Even if one of these theories succeeds in terms of the standard project, there is reason for theorists of the claim-right—indeed, of rights generally—not to neglect a different approach. Or so I shall argue.

The Method: Starting with Duties

Sreenivasan's generalized versions of the will and interest theories make clear the method that has generally been used within the standard approach. Both of these formulations start with someone's "duty to phi." This is not surprising. Most contemporary rights theorists would probably agree with Peter Jones that "the existence of a correlative duty is part of the very definition of a claim-right."[11] Most would also agree that not all duties are correlated with rights, and that something must be said about the duties that are so correlated.[12]

---

[8] Sreenivasan (2005: 261).   [9] Sreenivasan (2005: 261).

[10] See, e.g., Sreenivasan (2005) for a "hybrid" of the will and interest theories.

[11] Jones (1994: 16). References to "correlative duties" are rampant in discussions of rights in a variety of contexts. For a conjecture as to why this is so, see the text below.

[12] Cf. Jones (1994: 26): "What distinguishes duties that are paired with rights from those that are not?" Sreenivasan (2005: 258): "If I have a duty to pay my taxes, it may be asked who, *if anyone*, holds the correlative claim-right," my emphasis. The existence of duties not correlated with rights was emphasized in two classics of rights theory: Hart (1955) and Feinberg (1970). Hart emphasizes the possibility of a moral code involving duties but not rights.

Those duties that have correlative rights are said to be the *directed* duties: duties directed *toward* the right holder or, as it is often said—somewhat awkwardly, it seems to me—*duties that are owed* to the right holder.[13]

According to the will and interest theories among others, then, directed duties are still duties; they are, if you like, "duties—plus." Thus one might say that the duty in question is *conceptually independent* of whatever else is at issue.

In sum, the standard method, given the standard aim of rights theory, is to take up the following question: *Given that X has a duty to phi, what must be true of Y in order that the duty in question be directed towards Y?*

Why Start with Duties?

Hohfeld may be at least in part responsible for the prevalence of this method, though he does not regard himself as the source of the idea that claim-rights have correlative duties.

In the first decades of the twentieth century he famously wrote:

> ...if X has a right against Y that Y stay off his land, the correlative (and equivalent) is that Y is under a duty toward X to stay off the place.[14]

This is commonly referred to as Hohfeld's "equivalence."

Hohfeld tells us that the reason he thinks that rights as characterized above are rights "in the strictest sense" or, as he also says, rights in the "limited and proper meaning" of the term is that:

> ...it is certain that even those who use the word and conception "right" in the broadest possible way are accustomed to thinking of "duty" as the invariable correlative.[15]

Note that, here, "duty" is detached from any type of direction.

---

[13] See, e.g., Jones (1994: 13): "To have a claim-right is to be owed a duty by another or others." In at least one place elsewhere in that book Jones writes of an *action* (rather than a duty) being owed. What is owed is, surely, an action rather than a duty. Perhaps "owed a duty" is to be parsed as "owed an action which it is the duty of the person who owes it to perform."

[14] Hohfeld (1964: 38). Cited in, e.g., Thomson (1990), Sreenivasan (2010).

[15] Hohfeld (1964: 38).

As mentioned above, Hohfeld used the term "claim" as a synonym for "right" in its "limited and proper meaning." His discussion as a whole has surely helped to sustain the assumption that claims or claim-rights have correlative, conceptually independent, duties, duties that are for some reason to be referred to as duties "toward" the claim-right holder.

There are other reasons why appeals to duties may have become entrenched. One is that, as I explain in the next section, there is a relatively easy way of situating duties in the context of law on the one hand and morality on the other. I also explain why that is important in the context of contemporary rights theory.

What Are Duties?

Despite the major role duties play in contemporary rights theory, little attention has been paid to the nature of a duty in this context.[16] I shall not be focusing on this issue here myself but the following related considerations are pertinent to the discussion that follows.

The terrain of rights is generally considered to be exhaustively divided into two domains: the legal and the moral. Some—Bentham, in particular— thought that the only domain of rights was the legal or more broadly speaking *institutional* side. Others, including Judith Thomson, as I understand her, see all rights as falling on the moral side.

I take it that Thomson's gist is this: rights proper have normative significance; a given legal right as such lacks normative significance; therefore so-called legal rights are not rights proper.[17]

One will reasonably take the view that legal rights as such lack normative significance if one thinks of a legal right as a right *according to a particular legal system*, which is an abstract object. Any such system must bear a particular kind of relation to the world and, indeed, to me in particular, in order for your right against me according to that system to make any difference to what I have reason to do.

As moral rights are generally conceived of, meanwhile, a given moral right will have normative significance just by virtue of its existence. To put it in a way that brings out the distinction between the two kinds of right: if you have

---

[16] One exception is Thomson (1990). After some discussion she rejects the word "duty" in favor of "constraint." Most rights theorists continue to write of "duties."

[17] See Thomson (1990: 2).

a moral right against me according to "the morality system," that does make a difference to what I have reason to do.[18] In particular, I have reason to act in a way that respects your right.

Accepting this difference between legal and moral rights does not mean that one cannot meaningfully talk of legal rights, and I shall feel free to do so.

The terrain of *duties* is generally considered to be exhaustively divided into the same two domains. For present purposes I shall take one's legal duty, if any, given considerations C, to be whatever the law requires one to do given C, where C may be "all pertinent matters." As to one's moral duties, I shall assume that they are analogous to legal duties insofar as they are *requirements*, with respect to specified considerations. As is standard, I shall take the requirements in this case to be in principle independent of human laws and institutions, as to their source, and, indeed, to be independent in that way of all contingent human arrangements, allowing that in particular cases, such as the case of an everyday agreement, they may be predicated on such arrangements.[19]

The Position of the Right Holder in Contemporary Theories of Directed Duties

Looking only at the will and interest theories one can see that different accounts of directed duties will have very different consequences in terms of the position accorded to the right holder.

Thus consider again the generic version of the will theory deployed by Sreenivasan: Suppose X has a duty to phi. Y has a claim-right against X that X phi just in case Y has some measure of control over X's duty.[20] I detail the particular measures of control that Sreenivasan mentions shortly. Suffice it to say, here, that having some measure of control over another's duty looks like a relatively powerful position in relation to the person with the duty. Now take Sreenivasan's generic version of the interest theory: Y has a claim-right against X that X phi just in case X has a duty to phi and Y stands in a sanctioned relation to benefiting from X's phi-ing. The sanctioned relations in question are "standing to benefit from X's phi-ing" and "being intended to benefit from X's phi-ing." In either case, though it might be nice to have a claim-right, once

---

[18] Rights theorist Carl Wellman refers to "the morality system" in Wellman (1985).
[19] Evidently more could be said as to what a requirement is. For now I leave this to be understood at an intuitive level.
[20] Sreenivasan (2005: 258).

he has it the right holder is not—or not obviously—in any particularly powerful position in relation to the duty holder.

Under Sreenivasan's own hybrid theory, some claim-right holders have
more power over their right's addressee than other such right holders. There
may be nothing wrong with that—perhaps it is all to the general good—but it
is worth noting. And it is striking.[21]

One might have thought, off the cuff, that if I *have a claim* against you, I am
in a position to *claim* something from you. This is presumably a relatively
powerful position for me to be in, a position that differs from that of anyone
who lacks an equivalent right. That depends, of course, on what precisely it is
to claim something from another person. I say more about this shortly.

II. A Different Approach

Two Differences from the Standard Approach

My own approach differs from the standard one in at least the following two
ways. First, its *aim* is not a unitary account of claim-rights such that all members of the canonical set of claim-right ascriptions turn out true. Second, it
differs *procedurally or methodologically* in that it does not start from the question: Given that X has a duty to phi, what must be true of Y in order that the
duty be directed towards Y? In other terms, it does not start with duties.

As to the first difference, the longstanding debate between the will and
interest theories makes it clear that it is hard, at best, to produce a unitary
account of claim-rights even when limiting one's purview to the canonical
set.[22] Even if it is possible to arrive at a generalization that offers some edifica-
tion, it may well fail to explain what is distinctive about some important class
of claim-rights. At some point any such class should be singled out for special
attention. Indeed, a more general theory may find itself with a good *starting
point* in face of such a class. There are different ways of being systematic, and
one is to start with such a class and later show how other classes relate to it,
explaining what the similarities and differences are.

In this paper I discuss an important, distinctive class of claim-rights. I shall
refer to claim-rights that fall into this class as *claim-rights** or, more briefly,

---

[21] Does Sreenivasan offer a unitary account? I think so: it purports to capture a single concept not a
disjunctive set of concepts.
[22] Cf. Spector (2005: 793).

rights*, in order to make it clear that there may be claim-rights in the broad sense previously in play that do not fall into this class. An important context in which rights* arise is an everyday agreement. Indeed it is partly my sense of the nature of the rights created when agreements are made that drives my characterization of rights*—along with a prompt from Hohfeld, to be mentioned below.

Hohfeld's Further Remarks

Why did Hohfeld choose the term "claim"? In his text he cites as its virtue that it is a monosyllable. He also finds the language of Lord Watson "instructive" when he refers to the creation of a "right *or claim* in favor of an executor" (I presume the emphasis is Hohfeld's rather than Watson's).

He says a little more in a footnote to his "monosyllabic" justification of the label, quoting with approval Mr. Justice Stayton's statement that:

> a right has been well defined to be a well-founded claim, and a well-founded claim means nothing more nor less than a claim recognized or secured by law...[23]

and the following further statement from the same source:

> ...it must necessarily be held that a right, in a legal sense, exists, when in consequence of given facts the law declares that one person is entitled to enforce against another a claim.[24]

This suggests a particular way of filling out Hohfeld's spare account of claims as equivalent to "duties toward." Before filling it out in the way I have in mind, two preliminary points should be noted.

First, Stayton's discussion—like Hohfeld's—is about rights "in a legal sense." My discussion focuses outside the legal context, allowing for that context to be considered separately. Second, I take it that outside the legal context verbal acts, such as demanding performance and rebuking someone for non-performance, count as a kind of *enforcement* of claims.[25] Indeed, these things constitute an important special class of non-legal enforcement mechanisms.

---

[23] Hohfeld (1964: 38, note 32a).   [24] Hohfeld (1964: 71, note 16).
[25] Cf. Hart (1955).

One of their important aspects is that they do not in and of themselves involve more than verbal address. I say more about demanding, in particular, shortly.

Claim-Rights*: Several Equivalences

I now characterize rights* in terms of a set of equivalences along the lines of Hohfeld. Following Hohfeld I allow that to each right* there is a directed duty that is equivalent to it. I do not assume, however, that a *directed duty* can be broken down into a duty *simpliciter* plus something else. That said, I start with an equivalence corresponding to Hohfeld's, regimented somewhat for present purposes:

(1) Y has a right* against X to X's phi-ing if and only if X has a duty to Y to phi.[26]

I proceed to add to this in a number of ways.

Taking my cue from Hohfeld quoting Stayton, and various others, I shall take it that if and only if one has a right*, one is entitled *to claim* something from the right's addressee—the person "against" whom one has the right.[27] More precisely, one is in a position to or, as I shall tend to put it, *has the standing to* claim fulfillment of the relevant directed duty from the right's addressee—or, if it is too late for that, to claim something that, as we say, "does duty" for it.

I understand *claiming*, here, as a matter of *demanding*.[28] Here and in what follows I use what I take to be a central, relatively narrow sense of "demand." It is not enough seriously to "issue an imperative" in face of someone, or in that sense "tell him what to do," in order to demand, in this sense, that he do some particular thing.[29] Nor, I take it, is it enough to threaten some undesired

---

[26] Here and in what follows it may be more perspicuous to formulate things as follows: For Y to have a right* ...is for X to have a duty.

[27] Stayton says a right exists "when" the stated conditions obtain. Though this could be interpreted as stating a sufficient condition only, a stronger interpretation in terms of a condition both sufficient and necessary is probably the more natural one.

[28] Given standard everyday understandings of the terms, instances of *claiming* may include a milder kind of approach than demanding allows for. So "I've come for my ticket" may count as *claiming* but not as demanding. Compare "Give me my ticket!" For present purposes these nuances do not matter since, I take it, one with the standing to claim in the manner of these examples has the standing to demand if necessary, and vice versa.

[29] Doubtless a broader sense of "demand" exists. See Gilbert (2006a) on a range of similar terms for which in their broadest meaning the main thing remaining of a narrower—and perhaps prior—meaning is the behavioral component. Perhaps it would be more accurate to talk about different *types*

consequence should he not do it. Nor, again, is it enough to be *justified* in attempting by means of issuing an imperative to get him to do it—in case that will work.

The main point for present purposes is that in order to demand—in the sense in question—that someone act in a particular way one must have a particular *standing* or *authority*. Without this standing one may purport to demand some action but one is not in a position genuinely to demand it.

I take it that most people have some sensitivity to the conditions under which someone has this standing in relation to them and some action of theirs. Typical reactions denying this status to one who purports to demand something include "Who are you to tell me what to do?", "I don't have to listen to you!", and "That's none of your business!"

Suppose Y has the standing to demand that X phi. I take it that Y does not *thereby* have a "right to demand" of X that he phi, if that is equivalent to his having no duty to X not to demand of X that he phi.[30] Again, Y may have the standing to demand that X phi though, all things considered, he ought not to make this demand. Perhaps X is a sensitive soul who will collapse mentally if this demand is made. All things considered it may then be wrong to make it.

I say more about demanding in due course. For now I offer the following equivalence, which I take to be central.

(2) Y has a right* against X to X's phi-ing if and only if Y has the standing to demand of X that X phi.

A third equivalence derives from suggestions of H. L. A. Hart in a famous essay, and from concordant discussion by other authors.[31] They indicate that the concept of *owing* is pertinent here—not owing a *duty* but owing an *action*. In terms of the equivalence I have in mind:

(3) Y has a right* against X to X's phi-ing if and only if X owes Y X's phi-ing.

Note that it follows from the first equivalence and this one that for you to have a duty toward someone is for you to owe him performance of the action

---

of demand as opposed to different *senses of "demand."* For present purposes the distinction will not matter, and I shall continue to talk of senses of "demand."

[30] An example may be helpful: Y promises X that should X promise Y to phi, Y will not demand of X that he phi. X then promises Y to phi. It may be, of course, that generally speaking someone with the standing to demand someone's phi-ing has no duty to him not to demand that he phi.

[31] Hart (1955): Hart later repudiated much of the substance of this article. In my view that does not detract from any of the points I adopt here.

that constitutes fulfillment of the duty. In other terms, that action is *due to him from you*. In the form of another equivalence:

(4) X has a duty toward Y to phi if and only if X owes Y his, that is X's, phi-ing.

In the context of rights*, then, we can *dispense with talk of directed duties* and speak instead of owing.

One must be careful with talk of owing, however, since nowadays at least to say that one owes someone an action is ambiguous.[32] The previous equivalences allow us to say more about owing in the context of rights*. In particular,

(5) X owes Y X's phi-ing if and only if Y has the standing to demand of X that he, X, phi.

In what follows I shall take the listed equivalences and any others that follow from them for granted. The un-asterisked terms "owing" and "demanding" and cognate terms should be understood in terms of the equivalences above.

I do not say that these equivalences answer all questions about rights*. On the contrary, they leave important questions open. Is it possible, for instance, to say something more about the standing to demand of someone that he act in a certain way?

With respect to the question just posed: Joel Feinberg refers in various places to a claim-right holder as being in a position to demand *as his* what he has a right to.[33] Irrespective of Feinberg's intent, the following idea has some intuitive pull: Y's demanding of X that he phi is, more fully, Y's demanding X's phi-ing as in some sense his.[34] It suggests, indeed, that what gives Y the standing to demand of X that he phi is that X's phi-ing is Y's in the relevant sense. Without an appropriate articulation of that sense, however, these suggestions are not very helpful in the current context. Evidently, one way to elaborate them, if they can indeed be elaborated successfully, is to understand how particular rights*—understood in terms of the equivalences set out so far—come to be.

---

[32] Thus, e.g., Kamm (2002) argues regarding Scanlon (1998) that in writing of "what we owe to each other" his is a special sense of "owe," such that I may owe you an action without your having a *right* to it.

[33] See, e.g., Feinberg (1970: 251).

[34] For some discussion of this pull see Gilbert (2004: 89–90).

The Interest Theory, the Will Theory, and Claim-Rights*

Can either the interest or the will theory help us here? That is, if one has a claim-right according to these theories, does one thereby have a right*? Using Sreenivasan's descriptions of the theories, I argue in this section for a negative answer on both counts.

Consider first the interest theory: Y has a claim-right against X if and only if X has a duty to phi and Y stands in a sanctioned relationship to benefiting from X's phi-ing.[35] As noted earlier, the two "sanctioned relationships" that Sreenivasan has in mind are "standing to benefit from X's phi-ing" and "being intended to benefit from X's phi-ing." The latter is particularly relevant, presumably, when we are talking about stipulated duties such as those of the law and other institutions, which have individual or collective intentions behind them. I focus here on the former relationship.

I propose that *Y's standing to benefit from X's phi-ing*, when X has a moral duty to phi, and so on, does not in itself suffice, intuitively, to make it the case that Y has the *standing to demand of X that he phi*.[36] Hence he does not on that basis have a right* that X phi, and X does not owe Y his phi-ing.

The following example makes the point more vivid. Suppose Jill, who has every reason to live, is in grave danger of drowning in the middle of a lake. A stranger to her, Jack, is passing by on a leisurely walk. I take it to be plausible to think that Jack, a strong swimmer, has a moral duty to rescue Jill, a duty whose fulfillment will greatly benefit Jill—to put it mildly. Imagine now that Jill purports to demand of Jack that he rescue her. Having done so as a result of the promptings of his own conscience, Jack engages Jill in some rights-theoretical debate.

"What made you think you were in a position to *demand* of me that I rescue you?" he asks. "Well," says Jill, "Not only was it your moral duty to do so—that may or may not put everyone in a position to make such a demand—but your doing so was going to be of the greatest benefit to me." "I agree on both counts," says Jack, "but I do not see how the fact that you would so greatly benefit gives you the standing to demand that I rescue you." Jack's failure to see this, I take it, is a matter of his accurate assessment of the implications of the points on which they both agree.

---

[35] The discussion in this section also applies to the version of the interest theory proposed in Raz (1984).

[36] Putting the point this way allows one to sidestep the question whether for every moral duty everyone has the standing to demand of the duty holder that he conform to it—as some philosophers (for instance Stephen Darwall) have claimed. That is a question best set aside here.

That, in the example, Jill lacks this standing to demand of Jack that he rescue her *on any basis* is suggested by the way in which people typically communicate with others in situations like hers. What we understand to be a *cry for help* is not best construed by its utterer or its receiver as a demand. Rather, it is a plea, and might be couched accordingly: "Help me, please!"[37]

Of course, the interest theorist is entitled to interpret *the directionality of a duty* as he wishes, for his own purposes. Nonetheless, it is worth drawing his attention to one particular implication of the present discussion: directionality in the sense of the interest theory, as such, does not bring with it the right holder's standing to demand that the duty in question be fulfilled.

That this is so is not always apparent to those who espouse a form of interest theory—having made such espousal clear, they sometimes simply assume the demandability of what one has a right to. Something similar is true of some other rights theorists also: the demandability of what one has a right to, on their account, is assumed without argument.[38]

Quite generally, one should not think that all "comprehensible" interpretations of directionality imply demandability or, more generally, have the same practical implications.[39] The interest theorist may well have provided a comprehensible interpretation, but he has not captured the idea of a right*— whether he intended to capture this idea or not.

The will theory may seem more promising in this respect, and to some extent it is. It says that Y has a claim-right against X if and only if X has a duty to phi and *Y has some measure of control over X's duty*. Somewhat following Hart (1982), Sreenivasan explains what measures of control are in question in terms of the following three powers: (i) to waive X's duty or not; (ii) to enforce X's duty or not, given that X has breached it (which includes the power to sue X for compensation and the power to sue for an injunction against X); (iii) to waive X's duty to compensate, which is consequent upon his original breach.[40] In order to have *some* measure of control over someone's duty, I take it, one should have at least one of the powers just listed.

Is one who has a claim-right according to this theory the possessor of a right*? Several key terms in the above list of powers are not defined, and the context envisaged is clearly a legal one.[41] That said, it seems that the most that

---

[37] Possibly the explanation of this observation is that most people do not think there is a generic "duty to rescue." Suffice it to say that it is intended to be suggestive rather than probative.

[38] See, e.g., Thomson (1990), discussed below.

[39] "Comprehensible": Sreenivasan (2005: 261).   [40] Hart (1982), Sreenivasan (2005: 259).

[41] Indeed, it is hard to know how to interpret "suing for an injunction," in particular, outside a legal context.

can be argued is that *were* Y to have a right* to X's action, *then* absent special background understandings, Y would have powers describable, in less legally tinged terminology, along the lines of (i) to (iii) above—assuming that one who owes someone his phi-ing thereby has a duty to phi.[42]

Consider, in this respect, the power of waiver: suppose X owes his phi-ing to Y. X then says to Y, "Do you mind if I don't phi?" and Y responds, "No, I don't mind." Y would then have done something that could be described as waiving X's duty to him. For it would seem that Y has made it the case either that X no longer owes him X's phi-ing, or at least that X may ignore the fact that he owes it to him.

In sum, *if* X owes his phi-ing to Y, *then* Y will have the pertinent measure of control over X's associated duty. This is a "one-way" conditional statement. It concerns what *follows from* the fact that one person, X, owes his phi-ing to another, Y. The truth of this statement does not entail that its converse is true.

Is its converse true? That is, if Y has the power to waive X's duty to phi, does X owe his phi-ing to Y? Suppose we allow that if X has a duty to phi and (for some unspecified reason) this duty will cease if and only if Y says to X "I don't mind if you don't phi," Y then has the power to waive X's duty to phi. It is hard to argue that these conditions suffice for X to owe Y his phi-ing. Surely they do not suffice, intuitively, to give Y the standing to demand that X phi given only the conditions stated.[43]

This suggests the following general point about the will theory. If, in appealing to the *power of waiver* in attempting to say what a directed duty is, the will theorist is *presupposing* that the right holder is owed the action he has a right to, then he might as well bring the owing relationship to center stage. He should say, simply, that X has a duty to phi that is directed toward Y if and only if X owes Y his phi-ing, drawing out the implications of the right side of the equivalence as I have done, and beyond that as far as possible. If he is *not* presupposing that the right holder is owed the action he has a right to, his account of claim-rights may be comprehensible but most likely fails, like the interest theory, to capture the idea that the right's addressee owes the right holder an action.

---

[42] I do not say that this assumption is correct. The duty in question must, of course, be a non-directed duty of some kind.

[43] The same goes, with relevant changes, for the type of conditional duty that is found in the apodosis of Thomas Scanlon's "Principle F," and which he sees as accounting for the obligation of a promisor to act as promised (Scanlon (1998: ch. 7). Thus suppose X has this duty: to phi unless Y says it is fine with him that X not phi. If this is counted as a case in which Y has the power to waive X's duty to phi, it is hard to argue that it is a case in which X owes Y his phi-ing. For my reasons for construing Scanlon's "consent" clause along these lines see Gilbert (2004).

I am not saying that either the will or the interest theory's aim is to capture this idea—though some proponents of either theory may have had that aim. The common aim of respecting all of the canonical set of claim-right ascriptions is certainly a distinct one, and the interest or will theorist who adopts the latter aim may not be concerned with owing at all. That, however, is a concern that one should at some point address, if one is interested in rights generally. I now revert to rights*.

III. Joint Commitment as a Source of Claim-Rights*

I have offered a set of equivalences that are together intended at least partially to characterize rights*. One question arising was how rights* come to be. In this section I pinpoint one source of rights*—a *joint commitment*.

I have argued elsewhere that many central social phenomena are constituted by joint commitments of various sorts.[44] I say something about this in the next section of the paper. In this section I argue simply that wherever it is found, joint commitment is a source of rights*.

Joint Commitment

I first explain what I mean by "joint commitment," with an eye to the matter at hand.[45] What general kind of *commitment* is at issue?[46] I call commitments of this kind "commitments of the will." The personal decision of an individual human being is a case in point. In the relevant sense, one who has decided to phi at time t is from now until t *committed to phi at t*—unless and until he rescinds his decision. He has, indeed, *committed himself*.

But what is it to *commit* oneself in this context? At a minimum, it is to make it the case that one is now, as I shall put it, *rationally required* to act in a certain way, all else being equal. *Rationality* is here understood in a broad sense: it is a matter of responding appropriately to relevant considerations. In short, it is a matter of *reason-responsiveness*.

---

[44] See, for instance, Gilbert (1996), (2000), and this volume.

[45] I have written about it at length elsewhere, initially in Gilbert (1987 and 1989), later in, e.g., Gilbert (2006a: chs. 2 and 7). See also Gilbert (2003). In order that this chapter be relatively free-standing I briefly review what is necessary for present purposes.

[46] Conceptions of commitment vary, so some may not see "commitment" where I see it here. For present purposes I take this to be simply a matter of labeling.

I deliberately say "*reason*-responsiveness" here rather than "*reasons*-responsiveness." I mean to indicate that in the case of a commitment of the will as such we are not concerned with *reasons* for acting in the sense of considerations relating to the intrinsic goodness of an action or of its consequences. The fact that you have decided to perform some action does not, of course, make that action better in itself or in its consequences. Yet, all else being equal, one who is responding appropriately to relevant considerations will, I take it, act according to his standing decision.[47] I take this to be a matter of what a decision, as such, amounts to, as opposed to its relationship to independent matters.[48]

I shall say that one who is rationally required to phi, all else being equal, on whatever basis, *has sufficient reason* to phi. I shall also say, equivalently, that he *ought to phi, all equal.* I take the "ought" in question—the *rational* "ought," if you will—to be broader than the moral "ought." I shall not attempt to say much here about when all else is equal. To some extent this will be a matter of judgment. That said, I assume that commitments of the will, generally, can be trumped by at least some moral considerations in terms of what rationality requires, all things considered.

The personal decision of an individual human being creates what I call a *personal* commitment. Such a commitment, by definition, is created by a single person who is in a position unilaterally to rescind or abandon it.

A *joint* commitment is not the conjunction of two personal commitments. In explaining what it is I focus on a *basic* case in which there are no special background understandings. A basic case contrasts with a *non-basic* case created by virtue of a joint commitment that, in effect, authorizes a given person or body to create new joint commitments for the parties.[49]

A joint commitment is a commitment of two or more people *as one*. Each of the parties is committed through a given joint commitment to promote its fulfillment in conjunction with the others, but this commitment of his is not *personal* in the sense just noted.

In order for the people in question to be jointly committed in some way, each must express to the others, in conditions of common knowledge, his readiness for the establishment of the joint commitment in question—perhaps under

---

[47] There is argument for the point that personal decisions commit the decider in e.g., Gilbert (2006a: 127–132). A similar position is taken by, e.g., Shapiro (2011).

[48] Gilbert (1999), citing Kenny (1963), discusses the conjecture that decisions commit by virtue of constituting self-commands—where this type of command differs from standard interpersonal types in important ways.

[49] For the importance of non-basic cases see Gilbert (2006a), and, for further discussion, see e.g. the Introduction, this volume.

some general description, such as "member of this committee."⁵⁰ Absent special background understandings, each party to a joint commitment must participate in like manner in rescinding or otherwise concluding the commitment.

The expressions of readiness may be verbal or not, clear as the day or quite subtle. They may take place either in a single interaction or over a longish period of time.⁵¹ The latter process is most likely in a large population.⁵² I give an example of the creation of a joint commitment shortly below.

There is a variety of possible contents to a joint commitment. What one might call the *general form* of a joint commitment is as follows: people jointly commit to *phi as a body*, where substitutes for "phi" include a variety of "actions" broadly speaking—"mental actions," speaking more narrowly. Thus, for example, people can be jointly committed to *accept*, as a body, *a certain principle of action*, or to *believe*, as a body, *a certain proposition*, or to *pursue*, as a body, *a certain goal*. As to phi-ing *as a body*, this is a matter, roughly, of their representing a single phi-er—for instance, one who accepts a certain principle of action—by virtue of the combined actions (including the refrainings) of each.⁵³

Here is a two-person case of the creation of a joint commitment. Jack approaches Jill as she stands on the edge of the dance floor. He holds out his hand and addresses her: "Would you like to dance?" Smiling, she takes the hand he has proffered and begins to move, alongside him, on to the dance floor. In conditions of common knowledge, each has expressed his or her readiness to be jointly committed with the other to accept as a body the goal of their (immediately) partnering each other in a dance. This suffices to make it the case that they are now thus jointly committed.⁵⁴

I take the concept of a joint commitment to be a fundamental everyday concept. That does not mean, of course, that ordinary discourse has or needs a single word or phrase that expresses it. It is perhaps worth remarking that there is nothing obviously unacceptable about it from a philosophical

---

⁵⁰ "Common knowledge" in roughly the sense introduced in Lewis (1969). Here the informal "entirely out in the open" may suffice. For further discussion of my own, see Gilbert (1989: ch. 4).

⁵¹ For an example that involves a number of stages see Gilbert (1989: 398). On the role of initiatory expressions of "we" in the process of generating joint commitments generally see Gilbert (1989: ch. 4).

⁵² On joint commitments in large populations see Gilbert (2006a: ch. 8).

⁵³ For further discussion see Gilbert (2006a: 137–8, where the word "neutral" should be replaced by "negative" at 137 line–14).

⁵⁴ For the sake of a label, I say that, by definition, there a *plural subject* of the "action" in question when and only when there is a set of people who are jointly committed in some way. One reason for this label is that—as I argued in Gilbert (1989: ch. 4)—when and only when people form such a subject do they appropriately say of themselves that "we" (as opposed to "we all") are doing something, and so on.

point of view—reluctant as some philosophers have been to think in similar sounding terms.[55]

Joint Commitment and Claim-Rights*

I now argue that joint commitment is a source of claim-rights*. My argument involves several mutually supportive points.[56]

The first and central point is that, intuitively, each party to the joint commitment has the standing to demand that any other party conform to the commitment. Should his standing be questioned—should he perhaps be told that the behavior in question is "none of his business"—he can simply cite the joint commitment. Thus if Jill suddenly stops moving while on the dance floor with Jack, he might in principle say, "Hey, what about our commitment...?" implicitly demanding that she start dancing again. In reality he is likely to cite something else, on account of the joint commitment embedded therein, as in "Hey, we're supposed to be dancing together...!"

If—and only if—the parties have the standing to demand conformity do they have claim-rights* to such conformity. This is a version of equivalence (2) above. Evidently, the parties have the standing to demand conformity, hence they have rights* to it.

This argument is itself sufficient to prove the point at issue. Given that the standing to demand is present, so are rights*.

What is it about a joint commitment that gives the parties the standing to demand conformity of one another? That is a significant question that I can only address roughly here.

A central feature of a joint commitment is that, by virtue of their several expressions of readiness for the joint commitment, in conditions of common knowledge, the parties have, in effect, imposed a constraint on each one with respect to what it is open to him to do in the future, rationally speaking.[57] They have imposed this constraint in that each is now committed, through the joint commitment, to conform to it. Each therefore, at this point if not before, has sufficient reason to conform to it. That means that each *ought*

---

[55] Herman (1993), for instance, has expressed dissatisfaction with Kant's allusions to a "unity of wills."

[56] For related but distinct discussions see, e.g., Gilbert (1999), and (2006a: ch. 7).

[57] I take an applicable distinction between original creators and those who "sign on" later to make no difference in connection with the present point and shall not discuss it here. See Gilbert (2006b) for some discussion.

to conform to it, all else being equal.[58] This is so unless and until the commitment is concluded.[59]

As such, then, the co-creators of the joint commitment *have determined by their several actions how a given party ought to act, all equal.*[60] They have, indeed, *directly* determined this by the combined exercise of their several wills. I say they have done this "directly" because, in conditions of common knowledge, their several expressions of readiness for the joint commitment in question, and that alone, sufficed for the purpose.[61]

A plausible suggestion, then, is this: each party to a given joint commitment has the standing to demand of each party his conformity to the commitment by virtue of the fact that the parties have *directly determined* that each one ought to act in conformity to the joint commitment, all equal. Each has this standing in his capacity as a co-creator of the commitment. A demand he makes on the basis of this standing will be made in this capacity and addressed to another in that other's capacity as one who is subject to the commitment.

One might also put the point as follows: it is in the context of their *co-authorship* of the joint commitment that each has the *authority* to call each to order.[62]

Putting things this way suggests, indeed, that in the context of a joint commitment the specific function of the activity of demanding is precisely to allow any one of the parties to call to order any of their number in face of proposed or continuing action that is contrary to the commitment. This idea fits well with the assumption made earlier that demands—whatever else they are—are a type of enforcement mechanism.[63] What is enforced here is conformity to a joint commitment.

I now turn to some points that support the foregoing suggestion by showing its connection to a number of ideas of independent interest. First, there are some ideas mooted earlier: the idea that for me to demand an action of someone is for me to demand it as in some sense *mine*, and the related idea

---

[58] Here I invoke the sense of "ought" introduced earlier.

[59] I assume this last point without repeating it, in what follows.

[60] In many cases there will be a number of distinct sets of possible actions of the different agents that will result in such fulfillment. That does not cast doubt on the general point.

[61] Note that I do not say they have somehow willed *the fact that they are capable by severally willing of determining the other's action in this way.* Rather, given their willing, there is no longer any question that this determination has taken place.

[62] I discuss authority as such, including command authority, in relation to joint commitment in Gilbert (2006a). See also Gilbert (2014: ch. 18).

[63] I take there to be a distinction in this respect between demanding and *commanding.* For discussion of the latter see Gilbert (2006a).

that for me to have *the standing to demand* the action is for the action to be mine in the sense in question.

In the context of joint commitment, one can explain these ideas roughly as follows. Given that they have together directly determined how each of the parties *ought to act*, all equal, the co-creators of a joint commitment have, in a particular respect, directly determined how a given party *will* act, all equal, qua rational agent. In that sense, at least, the actions in question are *theirs*. As far as a given party is concerned, then, he is in a position to demand the action in the name of them all. As he might put it: it is *mine qua one of us*.

Relevant to this is the following point. One who intentionally conforms to a joint commitment acts as one of the parties or, if you like, in their name. In contrast, one who fails to conform to a joint commitment is apt to undermine whatever joint enterprise was underpinned by the joint commitment itself.

Related to the latter observation is a point concerning the important idea of *wronging* someone. Although all wronging may involve doing something wrong, not all cases of wrongdoing are cases of wronging. These things at least are common ground among theorists. It would, further, be generally acknowledged that one who fails to respect someone's right* has wronged him—at least to the extent precisely of the violation of right*.[64] Indeed, the following further equivalence may plausibly be added to the original set:

(6) Y has a right* against X to X's phi-ing if and only if X would wrong Y should X not phi.

Consider, then, the case in which one of us acts contrary to our joint commitment. In what sense has he wronged us, or any one of us qua one of us? That is, why speak of wronging here, rather than simply of doing wrong? A plausible answer is that, in brief, *he has set us, collectively, on the wrong path* from the point of view of our commitment. For, from the point of view of our commitment, *we* can be seen as going off-track—to the extent that and insofar as *he* fails to do his part in *our* acting properly from that point of view.

The main conclusion of this section is this: those who co-author a joint commitment thereby endow each other with claim-rights* against each other. These are claim-rights* to one another's conformity to the commitment.

---

[64] Cf. Hart (1955); Thompson (2004).

IV. A Conjecture and Its Implications

The conclusion that joint commitment is a source of claim-rights* was reached by reference to features of a joint commitment as such. It could be that there are other sources of rights*. That could lead one to conclude either that there are radically different sources of rights* or that there are broader considerations than those appealed to here that can bring one to the same conclusion about joint commitment.

It could be, on the other hand, that there are no other sources of rights*. In this concluding section I briefly consider whether the conjecture that this is so has any counterintuitive implications. For the sake of a label I refer to it as *the joint commitment conjecture.*

The Claim-Rights* of the Parties to Agreements and Promises

All rights theorists agree that among the canonical claim-right ascriptions are the rights of the parties to an everyday agreement: each has a right against the other to his abiding by its terms. Indeed, these are clear cases of rights*, intuitively. Is this a problem for the joint commitment conjecture? On the contrary: it is plausible to give an account of agreements in terms of joint commitment, and it falls out of such an account that the rights* most closely associated with agreements will be rights* of joint commitment.

Briefly to amplify the first point: nothing is more natural than to construe those entering a typical agreement as expressing their personal readiness to enter a pertinent joint commitment, in conditions of common knowledge. For instance, if Jack says, "Let's go up the hill this afternoon!" and Jill replies "Yes let's," they have done all that is necessary to produce *a joint commitment to accept as a body the plan* that they go up the hill this afternoon.

The explicitness of Jack's proposal and Jill's accepting response may be enough to make this particular exchange the creation of an agreement proper. A less explicit exchange or series of exchanges may still create the joint commitment in question but not quite count as an agreement proper. As far as these observations go, an agreement is the analogue, in the realm of joint commitment, of a personal decision. Less explicit processes are, rather, analogues of personal intentions.[65]

---

[65] Cf. Gilbert (2006a: 141–2). Either such process may suffice to create a joint plan or intention. See, e.g., Gilbert (2009).

Given any plausible development of the idea that those who make an agreement jointly commit one another, the parties to an agreement will have the rights* they are generally taken to have. These rights, then, pose no problem for the joint commitment conjecture.

Few philosophers have focused on agreements, but many have focused on promises.[66] It is hard to credit the central contemporary accounts of promissory obligation—as it is usually termed—as accounts of something whose correlative is a right*. Yet, intuitively, the obligation of a promisor to act as promised correlates with a right* in the promisee to the promised act.

The preceding discussion suggests that any account of promissory obligation or duty in terms of directed duties as construed by the interest theory or the will theory will be lacking, since directed duties according to these theories are not necessarily equivalent to rights*. The same goes for an appeal to Thomas Scanlon's Principle F.[67] More positively, as I argue elsewhere, the claim-rights* of promisees can also be argued to be rights* of joint commitment.[68]

Other Basic, Informal Contexts for Claim-Rights*

There are many other central social contexts in which claim-rights* are, intuitively, present. These include the contexts in which there is, according to a central everyday concept of these phenomena, a social convention, a number of people acting together, collective beliefs and values, and social groups. Indeed, given the deep involvement of such contexts in human lives, it is likely that the concept of a right*, with or without a label, has been with us pretty much from advent of humanity as we know it.

These observations are no problem for the joint commitment conjecture, for joint commitment accounts are highly plausible for the listed phenomena, and more.[69]

Claim-Rights* and the Law

According to the joint commitment conjecture there are no sources of claim-rights* other than joint commitment. Partly to shorten the discussion in this

---

[66] For an argument against the most common philosophical supposition on the relation of agreements to promises, see Gilbert (1993a). For commentary see Bach (1995), to which there is a brief response in Gilbert (2006a: 217n3).

[67] Gilbert (2004) is an extended discussion of Scanlon's approach and, more generally, "moral principle" approaches to promissory obligation. See also Gilbert (2018: ch. 7).

[68] See Gilbert (2011). See also Gilbert (2018: chs. 6–9).

[69] See, e.g., Gilbert (1996), (2000), (2006a), and (2008).

section I now further elaborate the conjecture thus: there are no sources of claim-rights* other than joint commitment *such that these rights* have, in and of themselves, normative significance for the right*'s addressee.*

Is the law such a source? Insofar as claim-rights* may be stipulated or referred to within a given legal system, such stipulations and references need have no normative force for a given person, as discussed earlier in this paper.[70] I now, therefore, set consideration of the law aside.

Claim-Rights*, "Incompetents," and the Canonical Claim-Right Ascriptions

Among the canonical set of claim-right ascriptions is the ascription of a right to human beings at least from infancy onwards not to be physically assaulted without special justification. Among such beings are tiny infants and others who, we may assume, are incapable of joint commitment with others. Following the technical terminology of rights theory I shall refer to such individuals as "incompetents." Is the idea that incompetents have claim-rights a problem for the joint commitment conjecture?

That depends on the meaning of the pertinent claim-right ascriptions— and their truth. As to their meaning, the pertinent question is: Are these claim-right ascriptions construed as ascriptions of *claim-rights**? If not, there is not even a prima facie problem for the conjecture. There is reason to think that often, at least, these ascriptions are not construed as ascriptions of claim-rights*. The rights in question are generally conceived of as moral claim-rights. Many philosophers understand such rights in such a way that they are not plausibly argued to be equivalent to a right*. This is true, for instance, of moral versions of the interest theory.

If and when these particular claim-right ascriptions are understood to be ascriptions of claim-rights*, it is not clear that there is then more of a problem for the joint commitment conjecture than for these ascriptions themselves. For the conjecture has some plausibility, and there could be an explanation of the fact that these ascriptions are commonly made other than their truth.

---

[70] Why the cautious "insofar as"? Because, though the law may stipulate that persons falling into a certain category have "rights" to certain actions, without analysis of the quoted term, such rights-ascription in the law is probably most plausibly cashed out in terms of facts about the legal system in question, such as one in a certain position being "permitted to sue." Suing someone may be the legal analogue of informal demanding, but it is hard to see it as the same thing. For an extended discussion of the relation of the "existence" of law and demand-rights of those among whom it exists see Gilbert (2018: ch. 13).

Consider in this connection that people may sometimes simply assume that one to whom they would comfortably ascribe a right against some person to some action has the standing to demand the action to which he has a right. Consider in this connection the following truncated quotation from Judith Thomson:

> [A] person's having a right has consequences. I have a right against you that you not break my nose, and much follows from the fact that I do. Other things being equal, for example, you ought not to break my nose. Other things being equal, it is morally permissible for me to defend myself against an attempt at nose-breaking by you... [A]sserting a right [that one has] is demanding that people act as these consequences say they ought to act.[71]

Assuming that the last sentence implies that when you have a right you have the standing to demand that people act as they ought to in light of it, how is the right holder supposed to come by that standing? In Thomson's discussion of what follows from the fact that I have a right against you that you not break my nose, partially quoted above, there seems to be nothing that answers that question.

Can one not simply assume that some claim-rights* are just there, outside the realm of joint commitment, yet such that their addressees ought to respect them? Is Thomson not right to assume that the claim-right she is talking about is of this kind? Perhaps so, but against this assumption the question presses: How do I come by the standing to demand of you that you not punch me on the nose? I do not say that this question cannot be answered satisfactorily. My point is that it needs to be addressed.

Moral Requirements and "the" Moral Community

It may be pointed out that little has been said here of the nature of moral requirements and suchlike.[72] I have noted only that they are generally conceived of as being independent of contingent human arrangements, with respect to their source, and I have proceeded in terms of that conception.

---

[71] Thomson (1990: 2).

[72] Darwall (2006), following Strawson (1974), is one who makes frequent use of the phrase "moral community" and, with many others, sees conformity to *moral requirements* as, by definition, demandable by all; he does not, as far as I can make out, see the moral community as formed by something akin to the usual mode of constitution of a social group. He argues for the demandability he claims without any such reference.

What if morality itself, by definition as it were, rests on a joint commitment—perhaps a joint commitment of a very special non-contingent kind? Should moral requirements be something like requirements that we humans—or most of us—are jointly committed to endorse as a body, then for every moral requirement each would have a right* against each to his conformity thereto. Each would have this right* qua party to the joint commitment.

Clearly if moral requirements are something like this, and there is a moral requirement on you not to break my nose, then I have a right* against you to your not breaking my nose. Evidently the joint commitment conjecture does not rule out "moral rights*" of this kind, if such exist.[73]

Concluding Summary

It is important to understand the nature and sources of our rights. Adopting an aim and method different from the one that is standard in contemporary rights theory, this paper focused on claim-rights according to an account that is consonant with important remarks of some prominent rights theorists beginning with Hohfeld. It has been argued that *joint commitment* is a source of these rights—and that there may be no other, at least outside the realm of stipulation.[74]

References

Bach, K. (1995). Terms of Agreement. *Ethics: An International Journal of Social, Political, and Legal Philosophy*, 105(3), 604–12.

Darwall, S. L. (2006). *The Second-Person Standpoint: Morality, Respect, and Accountability*. Cambridge, MA: Harvard University Press.

Feinberg, J. (1970). The Nature and Value of Rights. *Journal of Value Inquiry*, 4, 263–7.

Gilbert, M. (1987). Modelling Collective Belief. *Synthese: An International Journal for Epistemology, Methodology and Philosophy of Science*, 73, 185–204.

Gilbert, M. (1989). *On Social Facts*. London: Routledge.

---

[73] On this conception of a moral requirement, of course, everyone as opposed to me alone will have a right* to my not being assaulted by you.

[74] Amplification of many of the points in this chapter can be found in Gilbert (2018).

Gilbert, M. (1990). Fusion: Sketch of a Contractual Model. In R. C. L. Moffat and M. Bayles (eds.), *Perspectives on the Family* (pp. 65–78). Lewiston, NY: Edwin Mellen Press.

Gilbert, M. (1993). Is an Agreement an Exchange of Promises? *The Journal of Philosophy*, 90(12), 627–49.

Gilbert, M. (1996). *Living Together: Rationality, Sociality, and Obligation*. Lanham, MD: Rowman and Littlefield.

Gilbert, M. (1999). Obligation and Joint Commitment. *Utilitas: A Journal of Utilitarian Studies*, 11(2), 143–63.

Gilbert, M. (2000). *Sociality and Responsibility: New Essays in Plural Subject Theory*. Lanham, MD: Rowman & Littlefield.

Gilbert, M. (2003). The Structure of the Social Atom: Joint Commitment as the Foundation of Human Social Behavior. In F. Schmitt (ed.), *Social Metaphysics* (pp. 39–64). Lanham, MD: Rowman and Littlefield.

Gilbert, M. (2004). Scanlon on Promissory Obligation: The Problem of Promisees' Rights. *Journal of Philosophy*, 101(2), 83–109.

Gilbert, M. (2006a). *A Theory of Political Obligation: Membership, Commitment, and the Bonds of Society*. Oxford: Clarendon Press.

Gilbert, M. (2006b). Who's to Blame? Collective Moral Responsibility and Its Implications for Group Members. *Midwest Studies in Philosophy*, 30, 94–114.

Gilbert, M. (2008). Social Convention Revisited. *Topoi: An International Review of Philosophy*, 27(1–2), 5–16.

Gilbert, M. (2009). Shared Intention and Personal Intentions. *Philosophical Studies*, 144, 167–87.

Gilbert, M. (2011). Three Dogmas about Promising. In H. Sheinman (ed,), *Understanding Promises and Agreements*. New York: Oxford University Press. Reprinted in Gilbert (2014).

Gilbert, M. (2013). Commitment. In H. LaFollette (ed.), *International Encyclopedia of Ethics*. Malden, MA: Wiley Blackwell.

Gilbert, M. (2014). *Joint Commitment: How We Make the Social World*. New York: Oxford University Press.

Gilbert, M. (2018). *Rights and Demands: A Foundational Inquiry*. Oxford: Oxford University Press.

Hart, H. L. A. (1955). Are There Any Natural Rights? *Philosophical Review*, 64, 175–91.

Hart, H. L. A. (1982). *Essays on Bentham: Studies in Jurisprudence and Political Theory*. Oxford: Clarendon Press.

Herman, B. (1993). Could It Be Worth Thinking about Kant on Sex and Marriage? In L. Antony and C. Witt (eds.), *A Mind of One's Own*. Boulder, CO: Westview Press, 53–72.

Hohfeld, W. N. (1964). Fundamental Legal Conceptions as Applied in Judicial Reasoning. Walter W. Cook (ed.) New Haven: Yale University Press (original 1919).

Jones, P. (1994). *Rights*. London: MacMillan.

Kagan, S. (1998). *Normative Ethics*. Boulder, CO: Westview Press.

Kamm, F. M. (2002). Owing, Justifying, and Rejecting. *Mind: A Quarterly Review of Philosophy*, 111(442), 323–54.

Kenny, A. (1963). *Action, Emotion and Will*. New York: Routledge and Kegan Paul.

Lewis, D. (1969). *Convention: A Philosophical Study*. Cambridge, MA: Harvard University Press.

Raz, J. (1984). On The Nature of Rights. *Mind*, 93(370), 194–214.

Scanlon, T. (1998). *What We Owe to Each Other*. Cambridge, MA: Belknap Press of Harvard University Press.

Shapiro, S. (2011). *Legality*. Cambridge, MA: Harvard University Press.

Smith, T. (2007). Review: A Theory of Political Obligation: Membership, Commitment, and the Bonds of Society. *Mind*, 116(464), 1126–9.

Spector, H. (2005). Value Pluralism and the Two Concepts of Rights. *San Diego Law Review*, 45, 819–38.

Sreenivasan, G. (2005). A Hybrid Theory of Claim-Rights. *Oxford Journal of Legal Studies*, 25(2), 257–74.

Sreenivasan, G. (2010). Duties and Their Direction. *Ethics: An International Journal of Social, Political, and Legal Philosophy*, 120(3), 465–94.

Strawson, P. F. (1974). *Freedom and Resentment and Other Essays*. London: Methuen.

Thompson, M. (2004). What Is It to Wrong Someone? A Puzzle about Justice. In R. Wallace, P. Pettit, S. Scheffler, and M. Smith (eds.), *Reason and Value: Themes from the Moral Philosophy of Joseph Raz*. Oxford: Clarendon Press, 333–384.

Thomson, J. J. (1990). *The Realm of Rights*. Cambridge, MA: Harvard University Press.

Wellman, C. (1985). *A Theory of Rights: Persons under Laws, Institutions, and Morals*. Totowa: Rowman & Allanheld.

Wenar, L. (2005). The Nature of Rights. *Philosophy and Public Affairs*, 33(3), 223–52.

Conclusion

The Conversation Continues

The foregoing essays have addressed some central features of our life in groups. Several have focused directly on elements of our collective psychology: our intentions, our beliefs and acceptances, our preferences, values, and emotions, as these are understood in everyday life. Several have discussed related, central aspects of our life in groups, including acting together, agreements and promises, social conventions and rules, claim-rights and directed obligations. In some cases, I have highlighted specific contexts in which our collective psychological states have important effects, not always of the most desirable kind. These include the "inner life" of corporations, life in a scientific community, and the life of a political society.

In the course of these discussions, and in the Introduction as well, I have responded, explicitly or otherwise, to comments, queries, and challenges from a variety of theorists, including philosophers Michael Bratman, John Horton, Diane Jeske, Jennifer Lackey, and sociologist Annette Schnabel.

I have not said a great deal about competing views on the topics addressed. An important, related question is whether an apparently competing view is really competing at all, in the sense that two theorists' criteria for judging an account of, say, collective belief, may not be the same and may, for that reason, result in accounts that differ in significant ways. Whatever one's own specific purpose, one can welcome the existence of apparently competing accounts as revealing a variety of different possibilities within group life.

In this concluding discussion, I continue the conversation begun in the previous chapters, noting, and briefly addressing, some significant issues closely related to what has gone before.

In particular, and in brief: I first consider the relationship of Michael Bratman's and my own accounts of shared (or collective) intention from the point of view of "creature construction." I then return to the topic of collective emotions, distinguishing them from other, consequential emotion-related

Life in Groups: How We Think, Feel, and Act Together. Margaret Gilbert, Oxford University Press. © Margaret Gilbert 2023.
DOI: 10.1093/oso/9780192847157.003.0015

aspects of life in groups, and make a related point about beliefs. Next, I spotlight the idea that conversation—undoubtedly a central component of life in groups—is a context for collective-belief formation, and link this point to classic positions in the philosophy of language. After this I return to a topic of some practical importance that was touched on earlier—collective moral responsibility—and respond to some questions that have been raised about my account of this in other writings.[1] Finally, I briefly explore the relationship of joint commitment thinking to moral thinking, focusing on a related claim from development psychologist Michael Tomasello.

1. Bratman, Gilbert, and Creature Construction

Michael Bratman's classic paper "Shared Intention" starts by alluding to the fact that we often refer to *our* intentions in everyday speech.[2] Shortly afterwards he sets out three roles that he takes such collective intentions to fulfill, and he goes on to suggest that if we can develop an account of a state of affairs involving the intentions of each party that fulfills these roles, we will have arrived at an adequate account of collective intention.[3]

Now, in principle at least, there could be several states of affairs, involving the intentions of each party or not, that are capable of fulfilling these roles. It could be, then, that our everyday notion of collective intention relates to just one of these states of affairs, and that it is not the notion that Bratman's account of collective intention captures.

Setting my usual concern with the everyday notion aside, I want now to look at our two accounts of collective intention in their most recent form from a particular point of view.[4] One might put it like this: if one were creating from scratch creatures that one wanted reliably to fulfill tasks of the type that human beings regularly undertake together, would one do better to endow them with Bratmanian or Gilbertian collective intentions?[5]

---

[1] See chapter 7, this volume ("Collective Remorse," secs. 6–7).   [2] Bratman (1993: 98).
[3] Bratman (1993: 99–100).
[4] "Their most recent form": I have in mind, in particular, Bratman (2014). The full account, with eight clauses, is on p. 84, having been prefaced by a careful discussion of its different elements up until then.
[5] Here I draw on Gilbert (2022), responding to Bratman (2022). Not all acting together would naturally be described as a matter of fulfilling tasks, but much of it is. Think of one of Bratman's central examples: painting the house together; or building a bridge together; or defending the city together. In any case, the question at hand concerns the fulfilling of tasks.

Here I want to emphasize one of the newer elements in Bratman's own creature- construction.[6] The core and original conditions include "We each intend that (e.g.) we go to New York City," and other central conditions also relate to the intentions of each of us—our personal intentions, as I would say—plus common knowledge of these.

The newer element in question concerns what Bratman refers to as the "persistence-interdependence" of these personal intentions. More fully, each creature's personal intention "is set to persist, other things being equal, but only if the other's corresponding intention persists." Moreover, that this is so is "epistemically accessible" to each of the involved creatures.[7]

Now this condition raises some obvious questions. In particular: Are we dealing with personal intentions as these are normally understood, or with something altogether different?

As normally understood, personal intentions can be changed at will by their possessors. In other words, the person with the intention is in a position to change their mind. Bratman clearly does not want to say that each crea- ture's intentions are fixed in place to the extent that their possessor is unable to do away with them without the concurrence of the other party or parties to the collective intention. Indeed, he notes that the creatures involved will not have lost control over their own intentions.[8]

This is in accord with his avowed preference not to introduce radically new elements into his construction of shared intention, such as "we-intentions" in John Searle's sense, and joint commitment in mine.[9] Rather, personal inten- tions of the familiar kind lie at the heart of his construction.

What if the creatures in Bratman's construction were personally to intend not to rescind their first-order intentions as long as the other parties retain theirs? That is certainly possible, but it would not make the collective inten- tion much more stable, insofar as a second-order personal intention not to change a given first-order personal intention can itself be changed at will.

It appears, then, that any one Bratmanian creature who is participating in a collective intention is in a position to rescind its own relevant first-order personal intention at will. Given persistence-interdependence, any one Bratmanian creature is, indeed, in a position to destroy the collective inten- tion altogether. And insofar as any personal intention has a degree of inertia, that is not going to be enough to prevent occasional changes of mind.

---

[6] Bratman uses this phrase, which he takes from Paul Grice, to describe his own agenda in develop- ing an account of shared intention. See, e.g., Bratman (2014: 25).

[7] See, e.g., Bratman (2022).   [8] Bratman (2022).

[9] See Searle (1990); I discuss Searle's "we-intentions" in, e.g., Gilbert (2007).

Bratman may now appeal to the moral sense of the participants in any collective intention.[10] Such a sense may recommend, for instance, that—within certain limits—one avoid disappointing anyone who is or may be relying on one's carrying out a personal intention whose existence is common knowledge between you and that person. Bringing morality into the mix, however, is to take a large step from the original building blocks of Bratman's construction, and to plunge Bratmanian creatures into deep and often contentious waters.

Suppose, then, that we want to construct creatures with stable collective intentions whose stability does not depend on their exercise of a moral sense. It seems that a construction that has a joint commitment of the parties at its core is more to be recommended than one that accords with Bratman's model. Insofar as we humans are the constructions of nature, it would not be surprising to find that we have the capacity to form joint commitments as well as a capacity to form personal intentions.

2. Emotions in Groups versus the Emotions of Groups—and a Related Note on Beliefs

Undoubtedly there are many ways—many important ways—in which emotions, individual and collective, play an important, if not a crucial, role in group life. Social scientists and philosophers have noted the following, among others: *emotional contagion, collective effervescence, feeling-together, feeling-rules*. In the first, roughly, one person's emotion—sadness, say—leads another to be sad also, a process that can be repeated through large numbers of people. In the second, the feelings of each of a group of individuals are intensified by like expressions of feeling from the others. In the third, each of two or more parties in close proximity to one another experiences a particular emotion—enjoyment of a movie they are watching together, say—*as "ours."* In the fourth, there are social rules in a particular group as to how people are supposed to feel in a given situation—one should be sad at a funeral, happy at a birthday party, for instance. People may then feel bound to behave accordingly, even if they do not feel as they are supposed to.[11]

---

[10] He does indeed appeal to it in, e.g., Bratman (2014).
[11] On collective effervescence see Durkheim (1995); on feeling together see, e.g., Zahavi (2015); on feeling-rules see Hochschild (1979).

To acknowledge such phenomena, and their importance, is not to underplay the significance of collective emotions as they have been characterized in this book—nor is it to say that these other phenomena are best characterized as cases of specifically collective emotion.

With respect to feeling-rules, it seems that there can be feeling-rules for individuals, and also feeling-rules for groups. For instance, there may well be a feeling-rule to the effect that a sports team, as such, should be excited after winning a game, or that an army unit that has failed in its mission should be ashamed or regretful. Any such rule evidently presupposes that sports teams as such can be excited, and so on, without telling us what collective emotions involve.

All that said, in the growing philosophical literature on collective emotion the assumption seems to persist that anything appropriately referred to as an emotion, personal or collective, must involve what I have referred to as "feeling-sensations" or, in other words, a certain quality of consciousness in the involved individuals. Alternatively, collective or group emotions are considered to be constituted, at least in part, by individual emotions, whatever precisely the latter are taken to involve.

Thus Michael Brady has carefully developed "a model of group emotion that emphasizes the links or connections between individual emotions."[12] He assumes, indeed, that "group emotion involves or is partly constituted by individual emotions," saying—without explanation—that this "ought to be acceptable by all."

It is hard to be sure why he says this. Why should we assume anything about emotions *in general*, before we have considered both the individual and the collective case?[13]

Brady develops an account of a phenomenon partly constituted by individual emotions which may well occur and have important consequences. It is not clear to me, however, that it rises to the level of an intuitively *collective* emotion, or, as he puts it in relation to his example, that we come *collectively* to grieve purely as a result of a process of "mimicry and synchronization" with respect to the grieving of each.[14]

I have criticized summative accounts of a collective belief along similar lines. More precisely, I have argued not only against a simple "summative" view such that all or most of the group members must believe that such-and-such,

---

[12] Brady (2016: 98).
[13] Cf. chapter 4, this volume, for discussion of the analogous point with respect to belief.
[14] Brady (2016: 99).

but also against that view plus a common knowledge clause, that is: it is common knowledge among the members that all or most of them believe that p.[15] It seems that the same worry arises if the generalized belief that is commonly known became general by reason of the influence of one person's belief on another's, whether through some kind of automatic mimicry and synchronization or some more rational process. It is not clear that even with that added, it is appropriate to say that that we, collectively, believe that p. The same seems to go for emotions understood among similar lines.

In support of this point, note that even on the basis of the facts just supposed, the parties seem not to have accrued the standing to rebuke one another, in the name of what *we* feel, for expressions contrary to the supposedly collective emotion. Yet the potential for rebukes in the name of what we feel seem to be part of the landscape of genuinely collective emotions and, indeed, to be part and parcel of such emotions, as are potential demands of the same type for action appropriate to the emotion in question.

To draw attention to collective emotions in the sense I have articulated here is not to deny that emotions—in a generic sense—can figure in group life in a variety of ways.[16] What you are feeling can indeed influence what I am feeling, and so on. So, too, can what we feel, in the sense articulated here, influence the emotions of the component individuals, and be influenced by them.

Thus, if we are in my sense collectively grieving over some event, in the sense I've articulated, and I am, accordingly, expressing that grief in my conversations with you, I may well start personally to grieve as well, though I did not before. And if all of us are individually grieving, this is likely, through our grief-stricken interactions, to give rise to collective grief.

Just as emotions can figure in group life in a variety of ways, so can beliefs. Collective beliefs as discussed in this book, like collective emotions, are also liable both to influence, and to be influenced by, the beliefs of individuals.

In this connection it is worth saying something about the phenomenon social psychologists refer to as *pluralistic ignorance*. This has been described in different ways. I take it, however, this would count as an instance of that phenomenon: in a particular group, though people generally hold a particular belief, the members think—wrongly—that other group members do not think as they themselves do.

---

[15] Starting with Gilbert (1989: ch. 5).
[16] "In a generic sense." Compare the discussion in chapter 4, this volume, of a generic idea of belief that subsumes the individual and collective cases.

This situation could arise for a number of reasons, and it is describable independently of any reference to collective beliefs as I understand these. That said, one can see how collective beliefs could lead to pluralistic ignorance— and vice versa. Let me briefly focus on the former possibility.

Suppose that a collective belief that, say, vaccinations are harmful has been established at a meeting of a given group, largely as the result of the tub-thumping insistence of Jenny Jones, a particularly vocal member. Once the belief has been established as that of the group, it will dispose group members to express that belief when talking with one another in their capacity as group members. It will then be tempting for a given member to think that his peers personally believe that vaccination is harmful—though he does not believe that, and most of the others do not either. Even Jenny Jones may not believe it, having seized on what she thought was a provocative opinion in the meeting where the collective belief was established, in order to attract attention to herself.

3. The Ubiquity of Collective Belief: The Case of Conversation

I proposed in *On Social Facts* that an important context for collective beliefs on the joint commitment account is everyday conversation. As I put it there, conversations are negotiations—in a broad sense—of collective belief.[17] This proposal needs some elaboration, and in later work I have developed it further in collaboration with Maura Priest.[18]

Taking it on board as just mooted, this proposal can be brought to bear on some seminal contributions to the philosophy of language from David Lewis and Robert Stalnaker. That this is so was suggested to me some time ago by David Lewis in conversation. Indeed, what he wrote independently of any reference to collective belief is very suggestive in this respect.

In the discussions in question, Lewis and Stalnaker were particularly interested in *presuppositions*. The general idea of a presupposition can be introduced by reference to the famous example sentence "The King of France is

---

[17] See Gilbert (1989: 295–8, 476–7). To propose that a conversation is a negotiation of collective belief is not, of course, to attempt a full characterization of conversation. For thoughtful discussion on that score in connection with my account of collective belief, see Schmitt (2018). I take up one issue with this in Gilbert (2018).

[18] See Gilbert and Priest (2013), on which I draw in what follows; also Gilbert and Priest (2022). These amplify the discussion of conversation in Gilbert (1989) and relate the negotiation of collective belief view to a number of other approaches to conversation.

bald." Someone who says this presupposes, but does not state, that there is one and only one King of France.

Here is one of Lewis's key remarks on presupposition in his famous paper "Score-Keeping in a Language Game":

> Say something that requires a missing presupposition, and straightaway that presupposition springs into existence…Or at least that is what happens if your conversational partners tacitly acquiesce—if no one says, "But France has three Kings": or "Whadda ya mean?"[19]

More generally:

> Presupposition evolves according to a rule of accommodation specifying that any presuppositions that are required by what is said straightway come into existence, provided that nobody objects.[20]

In saying that particular presuppositions "straightway come into existence" at a particular time Lewis views them as "abstract entities," as are all of the components of what he refers to as the "conversational score."

This all raises the question of what is going on between the participants in the conversation as the conversational score develops. Taking as an example my saying "The King of France is bald," and your not objecting to that, it is plausible to suggest that once I've said what I said and you've not objected, we then collectively believe that the King of France is bald, and, relatedly, collectively presuppose that there is one and only one King of France.

Here I understand what it is to collectively presuppose some proposition in the way in which I understand what it is to collectively believe one: we are jointly committed to presuppose, as a body, that there is one and only one King of France.

I shall not pursue further here the thesis that conversations are negotiations of collective beliefs. Suffice it to say that if conversations routinely produce collective beliefs, as it is plausible to suppose, the latter will be hard to avoid in any life in groups. They will, then, be forces to be reckoned with in any such life.

---

[19] Lewis (1979: 339).   [20] Lewis (1979: 347).

4. Regarding Collective Praise- and Blameworthiness

As noted in chapter 7, "Collective Remorse," in order for us appropriately to feel remorse over our act, there must indeed be an act that is ours, collectively. That said, for collective remorse, collective guilt feelings, or collective pride to be in place, it seems that more is needed than that we have collectively acted in a way that potentially merits the emotion in question. Rather, we need to be collectively morally responsible for that action.

The approach to our collective psychology exemplified in this book allows us to see how arguably central components of collective moral responsibility—collective praise- or blameworthiness and what lies between—are possible.

Suppose, to fix ideas, that one who performs an action is morally to blame for doing so if and only if the following three conditions are met. First, the action was morally wrong, all else being equal. Second, all else was equal. In particular, one was not coerced into performing the action, which would be at least a mitigating circumstance. Rather, one acted freely. Third, one knew, or was at least in a position to know, that the first two conditions were fulfilled. Here the pronoun "one" is intended to be neutral with respect to the kind of entity involved. In particular, it allows for the possibility that both individual humans, and groups of individual humans, as such, may be morally responsible for their actions.

If something like this is right, then it seems that groups can be morally responsible for their actions, at least given the joint commitment account of collective goals and beliefs, which can comprise moral beliefs, and amount to collective knowledge in the right circumstances.[21]

Note that on the joint commitment account of collective goals, these can be formed as a result of external pressure, including outright coercion. Thus a government, empowered by a basic joint commitment to form goals for a particular political society, may form the collective goal of forcefully resisting a foreign invader intent on enslaving its people.[22] The fact of the invasion and its aim mitigates any blameworthiness of the society that is being invaded for its use of force—which should nonetheless be used in a morally responsible manner.

---

[21] Precisely what those circumstances are is not something on which I have a considered opinion. For an account of what it is for a group belief to be justified that starts from the account of group belief I have developed, see Schmitt (1994).

[22] More fully, the government may in these circumstances institute a joint commitment of the society as a whole to espouse as a body the goal of forcefully resisting the invader.

If collective blame- or praiseworthiness has been established, it is a further question which particular members are personally worthy of praise or blame in relation to the action in question. This is an important consequence of the joint commitment account of collective moral responsibility. The situation of each member of the group needs to be considered on its own merits—or demerits.

Thus I may reasonably be proud of us for some achievement of ours, without thereby being proud of any contribution I have made. I may not have had any relevant role in the matter, and if I had such a role, it might have been no great achievement to carry it out.

The same goes for my personal blameworthiness in relation to our morally blameworthy action. It is important to bear this in mind when facing an individual member of a blameworthy group. Some group members may have fought to the best of their abilities against the performance of the action in question. In that case it would be wrong for anyone to blame them personally for the action.

Before concluding this brief discussion of a topic of some importance in practice, I briefly note and respond to some comments that have been made about the account of collective moral responsibility sketched above.[23]

Marion Smiley has suggested that in order to be morally responsible one must be a unit of some kind. Referring to my work as being unhelpful in this connection, she characterizes me as invoking "shared" commitments.[24] If she has in mind a set of personal commitments of individual human beings—commitments they can personally bring into being and rescind at will—then that is not something that I invoke in discussing collective action and so on: a joint commitment is not a concatenation of personal commitments.

Another concern—from a different direction—has been expressed by Michael McKenna. He prefers not to talk in terms of "irreducible collective agents (or plural subjects)" and doubts the plausibility of understanding "allegedly irreducible" collective agents as potentially morally responsible ones.[25] He doubts this in part because he assumes that the only agents who can be morally responsible are those whose actions exhibit a "rich and stable pattern of responses to reasons," Granting this assumption for the sake of argument, collectives understood as plural subjects constituted by joint commitments can exhibit a rich and stable pattern of responses to reasons, as for instance,

---

[23] This discussion draws on Gilbert and Priest (2020: sec. 2.8).   [24] See Smiley (2010: 182–3).
[25] McKenna (2006: 17).

the relevant people come collectively to adopt a wide range of moral and other principles to inform their collective decision-making.

In some reflections on collective moral responsibility that reference my work, Tracy Isaacs allows that "it makes sense to think of plural subjects as operating on a different [i.e., collective] level of agency."[26] That said, she does not adopt my account of collective moral responsibility, or something like it. She explains that this is because of something she finds troubling: that someone who is a member of a plural subject intent on genocide, for instance, "is obligated to participate unless the others grant him permission to get out."

This claim would indeed be troubling if the obligation in question were understood as a matter of all-things-considered moral requirement, but—as I understand it—it is not. Rather, it is a directed obligation, grounded in a joint commitment, that each party has to each party. Importantly, such obligations are not all-things-considered moral requirements. Indeed, they are not moral requirements at all.

One who accepts the account of collective moral responsibility I have sketched above, then, can certainly agree that if we are collectively intent on genocide, I am *not* morally required, all things considered, to participate. On the contrary, I am presumably morally required to do all that I can to stop this genocide from happening. The same goes for many less terrible collective goals.

Let me briefly mention one further potential concern regarding the joint commitment approach to collective moral responsibility. I have argued that one cannot directly infer anything about the blameworthiness of a given group member from the fact that their group is morally to blame for some action. Does this mean that it will never be right to treat a group adversely in response to its blameworthy action? After all, such treatment is likely adversely to affect potentially innocent group members.

One should of course do what one can to avoid harming individuals who are innocent when responding to their group's blameworthy act. Bearing that in mind, it is worth pointing out that there are ways of responding adversely to a group's action that may not affect their innocent members adversely and may even improve their lives. For instance, were a particular group to be disbanded in response to its blameworthy action, and the relatively few culpable members treated as such, the others may well benefit rather than suffer.

---

[26] Isaacs (2006: 71).

5. The Evolution of Moral Thinking

I have argued that joint commitment is a ground of obligations and rights. These are rights of each party against each party, and correlative obligations of each party to each party. I have emphasized that I do not see these as specifically moral obligations and rights.

There are several reasons for this. For one thing, the argument for their existence seems not to be a specifically moral one. For another, it seems that they can be rights to evil actions, and correlative obligations to perform evil actions, as when one person promises another to perform some evil deed. Though these obligations should not be fulfilled, all things considered, and the right-holders, correspondingly, should not be accorded the object of their right, they retain the standing to demand that object. In other words, they retain the right, and all that it entails.

Alluding to joint commitment in my sense, the distinguished developmental psychologist Michael Tomasello has claimed that the emergence of joint commitment on the human scene was "the decisive moral step that bequeathed to modern human morality all of its most essential and distinctive elements."[27] Given what I have just said, however, and granting that the boundaries of the moral realm are not that clearly marked, I am inclined to doubt that, in and of itself, the emergence of joint commitment involves a moral step at all.[28]

That is not to say that joint commitment thinking cannot easily be seen as an important step towards some central forms of moral thinking. Let me briefly refer here to one of the aspects of moral thinking to which Tomasello alludes: the ideas of fairness in distribution.

Suppose that—long ago—nine of us come back from successfully hunting a stag together. Understand our hunting the stag together as a matter of our severally acting in light of our joint commitment to endorse as a body the goal of catching a stag. Having prepared the stag, we sit down to a long-awaited meal, and you give everyone but me a large piece of stag meat. I may sense that "something is amiss": each of us has worked hard to take the stag, and each of us—I sense—"should" have roughly the same size piece. Here we can say that a "sense of fairness"—or perhaps better, a "sense of unfairness"—has been triggered in me.

In sum, there is something we might call the morality of shared agency, in which concepts such as fairness come into play, along with concerns about

---

[27] Tomasello (2016: 78).   [28] I am in agreement with Stanford (2017) here.

such things as coerced involvement, or unconscionable goals, and positive appraisals of helping and other behavior that is likely to enhance the success of our collective enterprises.

Clearly, the relation of joint commitment thinking and moral thinking, both as to their origins and their connections, both logical and empirical, are of great interest. Joint commitment thinking may indeed predate moral thinking, but should, I think, be distinguished from it—unless our concept of the moral is to become perplexingly broad.[29]

Bibliography

Brady, Michael (2016) "Group Emotion and Group Understanding" in *The Epistemic Life of Groups: Essays in the Epistemology of Collectives,* eds. Michael S. Brady and Miranda Fricker, Oxford University Press: Oxford.

Bratman, Michael (1993) "Shared Intention," *Ethics,* 104.1: 97–113.

Bratman, Michael (2014) *Shared Agency: A Planning Theory of Acting Together,* Oxford University Press: New York.

Bratman, Michael (2022) "A Planning Theory of Acting Together" *Journal of the American Philosophical Association,* 8.3: 391–398.

Durkheim, Émile (1995 [1915]) *The Elementary Forms of the Religious Life,* Free Press: Glencoe.

Gilbert, Margaret (1989) *On Social Facts,* Routledge and Kegan Paul: London (1992) Princeton University Press: Princeton.

Gilbert, Margaret (2007) "Searle on Collective Intentions" (2007) in *Intentional Acts and Social Facts,* ed. Savas Tsohatzidis, Springer: Dordrecht.

Gilbert, Margaret (2018a) "Further Reflections on the Social World" *Protosociology* 35: 257–284.

Gilbert, Margaret (2018b) "Remarks on Joint Commitment and Its Relation to Moral Thinking" *Philosophical Psychology* 31, 755–66; https://doi.org/10.1080/09515089.2018.1486611.

Gilbert, Margaret (2020) "Shared Intentionality, Joint Commitment, and Directed Obligation" *Behavioral and Brain Sciences* 43; https://doi.org/10.1017/S0140525X19002619.

Gilbert, Margaret (2022) "Creature Construction and the Morality of Shared Agency" *Journal of the American Philosophical Association* 8: 412–15.

---

[29] For related discussion see my responses to Tomasello in Gilbert (2018b) and Gilbert (2020). For research suggesting that participation in joint commitments may not mark the divide between our species and some non-human primates see, e.g., Heesen et. al. (2021).

Gilbert, Margaret, and Priest, Maura (2013) "Conversation and Collective Belief" in A. Capone, F. Lo Piparo, and M. Carapezza (eds.) *Perspectives on Pragmatics and Philosophy*, Springer: Dordrecht.

Gilbert, Margaret, and Priest, Maura (2020) "Collective Moral Responsibility and What Follows for Group Members" in Deborah Tollefsen and Saba Bazargan-Forward (eds.) *The Routledge Handbook of Collective Responsibility*, Routledge: New York.

Gilbert, Margaret, and Priest, Maura (2022) "Dialogue and Joint Commitment" (in French translation) in Raphael Kunstler (ed.) *Les Defis du Collectif: ontologie sociale, individualisme methodologique et argumentation.* Hermann : Paris.

Heesen, R., Zuberbühler, K., Bangerter, A., Iglesias, K., Rossano, F., Pajot, A., Guéry, J.-P., and Genty, E. (2021) "Evidence of Joint Commitment in Great Apes' Natural Joint Actions" *Royal Society Open Science* 8; https:/doi.org/10.1098.rsos.211121.

Hochschild, Arlie R. (1979) "Emotion Work, Feeling Rules, and Social Structure" *American Journal of Sociology* 85; https://doi.org/10.1086/227049.

Isaacs, Tracy (2006) "Collective Moral Responsibility and Collective Intention" in P. French and H. Wettstein (eds.) *Shared Intentions and Collective Responsibility, Midwest Studies in Philosophy*, 30.

Leon, Philippe, and Zahavi, Dan (2018) "How We Feel: Collective Emotions without Joint Commitments" *Protosociology* 35: 117–134.

Lewis, David (1979) "Scorekeeping in a Language Game" *Journal of Philosophical Logic* 8: 339–353.

McKenna, Michael (2006) "Collective Responsibility and an Agent Meaning Theory," *Midwest Studies in Philosophy*, 30 (1): 16–34.

Schmitt, Frederick (1994) "The Justification of Group Beliefs" in F. F. Schmitt (ed.) *Socializing Epistemology*, Rowman and Littlefield: Lanham, MD.

Schmitt, Frederick (2018) "Remarks on Conversation and Negotiated Collective Belief" *Protosociology* 35: 74–98.

Searle, John (1990) "Collective Intentions and Actions" in Philip R. Cohen Jerry MorganPhilip R. Cohen Jerry Morgan & Martha Pollack (eds.), *Intentions in Communication*. MIT Press: Cambridge, MA.

Smiley, Marion (2010) "From Moral Agency to Collective Wrongs: Re-Thinking Collective Moral Responsibility" *Journal of Law and Policy* 1: 171–202.

Stalnaker, Robert (1973) "Presuppositions" *Journal of Philosophic Logic* 2: 447–457.

Stanford, P. Kyle (2017) "Bending toward Justice" *Philosophy of Science* 84: 369–376.

Tomasello, Michael (2016) *A Natural History of Human Morality*, Cambridge, MA: Harvard University Press.

Zahavi, Dan (2015) "You, Me, and We—The Sharing of Emotional Experiences" *Journal of Consciousness Studies* 22: 84–101.

Topic Bibliography of the Author's Works Relating to Life in Groups

Books

1. *On Social Facts* (1989) (hardback) Routledge and Kegan Paul: London (in the series International Library of Philosophy); (1992) (paperback) Princeton University Press: Princeton. [OSF].
2. *Living Together: Rationality, Sociality, and Obligation* (1996) Rowman and Littlefield: Lanham, MD. [LT].
3. *Sociality and Responsibility: New Essays in Plural Subject Theory* (2000) Rowman and Littlefield: Lanham, MD. [S&R].
4. *Marcher Ensemble: Essais sur les Fondements des Phenomenes Collectif* (in French) (2003) Presses Universitaires de France: Paris, France. [French translations of some previously published essays by the author with an introductory essay by the author.] [ME].
5. *A Theory of Political Obligation: Membership, Commitment, and the Bonds of Society* (2006) Oxford University Press: Oxford. [TPO].
6. *Joint Commitment: How We Make the Social World* (2013) Oxford University Press: New York. [JC].
7. *Il Noi Collettivo: Impegno Coniunto e Mondo Sociale* (in Italian) (2015) Raffaelo Cortina: Italy [Italian translations of some previously published essays by the author, with introductory essays by the author and the translator.] [INC].
8. *Rights and Demands: A Foundational Inquiry* (2018). Oxford University Press: Oxford. [RD].

Articles and Book Chapters Organized by Topic

Translations of listed articles or book chapters have not been included; individual articles and book chapters that have been reprinted in one of the above listed essay collections—LT, S&R, ME, JC, INC—are noted as such; some articles or book chapters are listed under more than one heading, as appropriate. Each of the essay collections has a substantive introduction written for that volume. These discussions are not listed below.

Our Actions and Intentions

1. "Social Groups: A Simmelian View" (1989) OSF, ch. 4, pp. 146–236.
2. "Walking Together: A Paradigmatic Social Phenomenon" (1990) in *Midwest Studies in Philosophy*, vol. 15, *The Philosophy of the Human Sciences*, eds. P. A. French, T. E. Uehling, Jr., and H. K. Wettstein, University of Notre Dame Press: Notre Dame, pp. 1–14. [LT; ME]

3. "What Is It for Us to Intend?" (1997) in *Contemporary Action Theory*, vol. 2, eds. G. Holmstrom-Hintikka and R. Tuomela, D. Reidel: Dordrecht, pp. 65–85. [S&R]
4. "Joint Action" (2001) in *Elsevier Encyclopedia of the Social and Behavioral Sciences*, eds. N. J. Smelser and P. J. Baltes, vol. 12, pp. 7987–92.
5. "Acting Together" (2002) in *Social Facts and Collective Intentionality*, ed. Georg Meggle, German Library of Sciences, Hansel-Hohenhausen: Frankfurt, pp. 53–72. [JC]
6. "On the Nature and Normativity of Intentions and Decisions: Towards an Understanding of Commitments of the Will" (2005) in *Patterns of Value II*, eds. Wlodek Rabinowicz and Toni Ronnow-Rasmussen, Lund University: Lund, pp. 180–9.
7. "Rationality in Collective Action" (2006) *Philosophy of the Social Sciences*, vol. 36, no. 1, pp. 3–17. [JC]
8. "Acting Together, Joint Commitment, and Obligation" (2006) in *Facets of Sociality*, eds. N. Psarros and K. Shulte-Ostermann, Ontos-Verlag: Frankfurt.
9. "Collective Intentions, Commitment, and Collective Action Problems" (2007) in *Rationality and Commitment*, eds. Fabienne Peter and Hans-Bernard Schmid, Oxford University Press: Oxford, pp. 258–80.
10. "Searle on Collective Intentions" (2007) in *Intentional Acts and Social Facts*, ed. Savas Tsohatzidis, Springer: Dordrecht, pp. 31–48.
11. "Two Approaches to Shared Intention: An Essay in the Philosophy of Social Phenomena" (2008) in a special anniversary issue of *Analyse u. Kritik*, vol. 30, pp. 483–514. [JC]
12. "Shared Intention and Personal Intentions" (2009) *Philosophical Studies* (special issue comprising selected papers from the Pacific APA meetings, Pasadena, 2008), vol. 144, pp. 167–87.
13. "Joint or Collective Intention" (2010) in *Encyclopedia of the Mind*, Sage Publications.
14. "Collective Action" (2010) in *A Companion to the Philosophy of Action*, Wiley-Blackwell: Oxford.
15. "The Nature of Agreements: A Solution to Some Puzzles about Claim-Rights and Joint Intention" (2014) in *Rational and Social Agency*, eds. M. Vargas and G. Yaffe, Oxford University Press: New York, pp. 215–54. [Ch. 1, this volume]
16. "Joint Action," updated version of (4), (2015) in *International Encyclopedia of the Social & Behavioral Sciences*, ed. James D. Wright, 2nd edition, vol. 12, Elsevier: Oxford, pp. 839–43.
17. "Shared Intentionality, Joint Commitment, and Directed Obligation" (2020) invited commentary on Michael Tomasello's target article "The Moral Psychology of Obligation" in *Behavioral and Brain Sciences*, vol. 43. https://doi.org/10.1017/S0140525X19002619.
18. "A Simple Theory of Acting Together" (2022) *Journal of the American Philosophical Association*. https://www.doi.org/10.1017/apa.2021.24.
19. "Creature Construction and the Morality of Shared Agency: Response to Bratman" (2022) *Journal of the American Philosophical Association*. https://www.doi.org/10.1017/apa.2021.25.

Our Beliefs

1. "Modeling Collective Belief" (1987) *Synthese*, vol. 73, pp. 185–204. [LT]
2. "After Durkheim: Concerning Collective Belief" (1989) OSF, ch. 5, pp. 237–314.
3. "Collective Belief" (1992) in *A Companion to Epistemology*, eds. J. Dancy and E. Sosa, Basil Blackwell: Oxford, pp. 70–1.

4. "Remarks on Collective Belief" (1994) in *Socializing Epistemology: The Social Dimensions of Knowledge*, ed. Frederick Schmitt, Rowman and Littlefield: Lanham, MD, pp. 235–53.

5. "Durkheim and Social Facts" (1994) in *Debating Durkheim*, eds. H. Martins and W. Pickering, Routledge: London, pp. 86–109. [ME]

6. "Social Epistemology and Family Therapy" (1995), English original published in Italian translation in *Esperienza e Conoscenza*, ed. G. Piazza, Citta Study: Milan, pp. 247–8.

7. "Credenze Collettive e Mutamento Scientifico" (1998) (English original "Collective Belief and Scientific Change" tr. into Italian by G. Piazza) *Fenomenologia e Società*, vol. 21, no. 1, pp. 32–45. [S&R]

8. "Belief and Acceptance as Features of Groups" (2002) *Protosociology*, vol. 16, pp. 35–69 (online journal: www.protosociology.de). [JC]

9. "Collective Epistemology" (2004) *Episteme*, vol. 1, no. 2, pp. 95–7. [JC]

10. "Croyances Collectives" (2006) in *Le Dictionnaire des Sciences Humaines*, Presses Universitaires de France: Paris, pp. 225–9.

11. "Culture as Collective Construction" and "Joint Commitment and Group Belief" (2010) *Kolner Zeitschrift fur Sociologie*, pp. 384–410. [Chs. 2 and 3, this volume]

12. "Conversation and Collective Belief" (with Maura Priest) (2013) in *Perspectives on Pragmatics and Philosophy*, eds A. Capone, F. Lo Piparo, M. Carapezza, Springer: Dordrecht, pp. 1–34.

13. "Belief, Acceptance, and What Happens in Groups: Some Methodological Considerations" (with Daniel Pilchman) (2014) in *Essays in Collective Epistemology*, ed. Jennifer Lackey, Oxford University Press: Oxford, pp. 190–212. [Ch. 4, this volume]

14. "Collective Belief, Kuhn, and the String Theory Community" (with James Weatherall) (2016) in *The Epistemic Life of Groups*, eds. M. Brady and M. Fricker, Oxford University Press: Oxford, pp. 191–217. [Ch. 5, this volume]

15. "Scientists Are People Too: Comment on Andersen" (2017) *Social Epistemology Review and Reply Collective*, vol. 6, pp. 45–9.

Our Emotions and Related Phenomena

1. "On Feeling Guilt for What One's Group Has Done" (1996) LT, ch. 14, pp. 375–90.

2. "Group Wrongs and Guilt Feelings" (1997) *Journal of Ethics*, vol. 1, no. 1, pp. 65–84.

3. "Collective Remorse" (2001) in *War Crimes and Collective Wrongdoing: A Reader*, ed. A. Jokic, Basil Blackwell: Oxford, pp. 216–35. [S&R] [Ch. 7, this volume]

4. "Collective Guilt and Collective Guilt Feelings" (2002) *Journal of Ethics*, vol. 6, pp. 115–43. [JC]

5. "How We Feel: Understanding Everyday Collective Emotion Ascriptions" (2014) in *Collective Emotions*, eds. Mikko Salmela and Christian van Sheve, Oxford University Press: Oxford, pp. 18–30. [Ch. 8, this volume]

Our Preferences, Values, and Virtues

1. "Collective Preferences, Obligations, and Rational Choice" (2001) *Economics and Philosophy*, vol. 17, pp. 109–19. [Ch. 9, this volume]

2. "Shared Values, Social Unity and Liberty" (2005) *Public Affairs Quarterly*, vol. 19, no. 1, pp. 25–49. [JC; INC]

3. "Corporate Misbehavior and Collective Values" (2005) *Brooklyn Law Review*, vol. 70, no. 4, pp. 1369–80. [Ch. 10, this volume]
4. "Shared Values and Social Unity" (2005) *Experience and Analysis: Proceedings of the Austrian Wittgenstein Society*, pp. 373–6.
5. "Can a Wise Society Be a Free One?" (2006) *Southern Journal of Philosophy*, vol. 44, pp. 1–17. [Ch. 11, this volume]

Our Promises and Agreements

1. "Agreements, Conventions, and Language" (1983) *Synthese*, vol. 54, no. 3, pp. 375–407.
2. "Agreements, Coercion, and Obligation" (1993) *Ethics*, vol. 103, no. 4, pp. 679–706. [LT]
3. "Is an Agreement an Exchange of Promises?" (1993) *The Journal of Philosophy*, vol. 54, no. 12, pp. 627–49. [LT]
4. "Scanlon on Promissory Obligation: The Problem of Promisees' Rights" (2004) *Journal of Philosophy*, vol. 101, pp. 83–109. [JC]
5. "Reconsidering Actual Contract Theory" (2006) TPO, ch. 10, pp. 215–37.
6. "Three Dogmas about Promising" (2011) in *Understanding Promises and Agreements*, ed. H. Sheinman, Oxford University Press: Oxford, pp. 80–108. [JC]
7. "The Nature of Agreements: A Solution to Some Puzzles about Claim-Rights and Joint Intention" (2014) in *Rational and Social Agency*, eds. M. Vargas and G. Yaffe, Oxford University Press: New York. [Ch. 1, this volume]
8. "The Problem Solved" (2018) RD, Part 2, including ch. 6, "Agreements and Promises: Hume's Legacy"; ch. 7, "Problems with Moral Principle Accounts"; ch. 9, "A Theory of Agreements and Promises."

Our Political Obligations, Our Authorities

1. "Group Membership and Political Obligation" (1993) *The Monist*, vol. 6, no. 1, pp. 119–33. [LT]
2. "Reconsidering the 'Actual Contract' Theory of Political Obligation" (1999) *Ethics*, vol. 109, pp. 226–60. [S&R; ME]
3. "The Plural Subject Theory of Political Obligation" (2006), TPO, ch. 11, pp. 238–86.
4. "*A Theory of Political Obligation*: Responses to Horton, Jeske, Narveson and Stoutland" (2013) *Jurisprudence: An International Journal of Legal and Political Thought*, vol. 4, pp. 301–21. [Ch. 12, this volume, is a revised version of this]
5. "Demoralizing Political Obligation" (2014) JC, ch. 17, pp. 389–408.
6. "Commands and Their Practical Import" (2014) JC, ch. 18, pp. 409–26.

Patriotism: Its Nature

1. "Pro Patria: An Essay on Patriotism" (2010) *Journal of Ethics*, vol. 13, special issue ed. I. Primoratz, pp. 319–40. [JC]
2. "On Patriotism" (with Itzel Garcia) (2018) in *The Handbook of Patriotism*, ed. Mitja Sardoc, Springer: Cam. Weblink: https://doi.org/10.1007/978-3-319-30534-9_51-1.

Our Moral Responsibility

1. "The Idea of Collective Guilt" (2000), S&R, ch. 8, pp. 141–53.
2. "Considerations on Collective Guilt" (2001) in *From History to Justice: Essays in Honor of Burleigh Wilkins*, ed. A. Jokic, Peter Lang: New York, pp. 239–49.
3. "Collective Guilt and Collective Guilt Feelings" (2002) *Journal of Ethics*, vol. 6, pp. 115–43. [JC]
4. "Collective Wrongdoing: Moral and Legal Responses" (2002) *Social Theory and Practice*, vol. 28, pp. 167–8.
5. "Who's to Blame? Collective Moral Responsibility and Its Implications for Group Members" (2006) *Midwest Studies in Philosophy*, ed. Peter French, vol. 30, pp. 94–114. [JC; INC]
6. "La Responsabilite Collective et ses Implications" (2008), *Revue Française de Science Politique*, vol. 92, no. 2, pp. 268–85.
7. "Foundations and Consequences of Collective Moral Responsibility" (2011) *Teoria e Critica della Regolazione Sociale*, Quaderno 1. http://www.lex.unict.it/tcrs.
8. "Collective Moral Responsibility and Its Implications for Group Members" (with Maura Priest) (2020) in *The Routledge Handbook of Collective Responsibility*, eds. Deborah Tollefsen and Saba Bazargan-Forward, London and New York: Routledge. pp. 23–37.

Our Conventions, Rules, Norms, Laws

1. "About Conventions" (1974) *Second-Order*, vol. 3, no. 2, pp. 71–89.
2. "Game Theory and Convention" (1981) *Synthese*, vol. 44, no. 1, pp. 41–93. [LT]
3. "Agreements, Conventions, and Language" (1983) *Synthese*, vol. 54, no. 3, pp. 375–407. [LT]
4. "Notes on the Concept of a Social Convention" (1983) *New Literary History*, vol. 14, pp. 225–51. [LT]
5. "Social Convention" (1989) OSF, ch. 6, pp. 315–73.
6. "Rationality, Coordination, and Convention" (1990) *Synthese*, vol. 84, pp. 1–21. [LT; ME]
7. "Norms" (1994) in *Blackwell Dictionary of Social Thought*, eds. W. Outhwaite and T. Bottomore, Blackwell: Oxford, pp. 425–7.
8. "Social Rules: Some Problems for Hart's Account, and an Alternative Proposal" (1999) *Law and Philosophy*, vol. 18, pp. 141–71. [S&R]
9. "Social Rules as Plural Subject Phenomena" (2003) in *On The Nature of Social and Institutional Reality*, eds. J. Kotkavirta and E. Lagerpetz, SoPhi Academic Press.
10. "Political Societies" (2006) TPO, ch. 9, pp. 185–214.
11. "Social Convention Revisited" (2008) *Topoi*, special issue on convention, vol. 27, pp. 5–16. [JC]
12. "Social Rules" (with Maura Priest) (2013) in *Encyclopedia of the Social Sciences*, ed. Byron Kaldis, Sage: Los Angeles, pp. 931–933.
13. "Responses to Some Questions on Social Convention and Related Matters" (2013) in *Convenzioni*, Post n. 4, Mimesis: Milano-Udine.
14. "Demand-Rights, Law, and Other Institutions" (2013) R&D, ch. 13, pp. 293–324.

Joint Commitment

1. "Considerations on Joint Commitment" (Response to critics/comments) (2002) in *Social Facts and Collective Intentionality*, ed. Georg Meggle, German Library of Sciences, Hansel-Hohenhausen: Frankfurt, pp. 73–102. [JC]
2. "The Structure of the Social Atom: Joint Commitment as the Foundation of Human Social Behavior" (2003) in *Social Metaphysics*, ed. F. Schmitt, Roman and Littlefield: Lanham, MD, pp. 39–64.
3. "Acting Together, Joint Commitment, and Obligation" (2006) in *Facets of Sociality*, eds. Nikos Psarros and Katinka Shulte-Ostermann, Ontos Verlag: Frankfurt, pp. 153–162.
4. "Joint Commitment and Obligation" (2006) TPO, ch. 7, secs. 1–2, pp. 125–46.
5. "Mutual Recognition, Common Knowledge and Joint Attention" (2007) in *Hommage à Wlodek*, eds. T. Ronnow-Rasmussen, B. Petersson, J. Josefsson, and D. Egonsson, www.fil.lu.se/hommageawlodek.
6. "Mutual Recognition and Some Related Phenomena" (2011) in *Recognition and Social Ontology*, eds. H. Ikaheimo and A. Laitinen, Brill: Leiden, pp. 270–86. [JC]
7. "Commitment" (2012) in *The International Encyclopedia of Ethics*, ed. Hugh LaFollette, Oxford: Wiley-Blackwell.
8. "Joint Commitment: What It Is and Why It Matters" (2016) *Phenomenology and Mind*, 9, pp. 19–26.
9. "Joint Commitment" (2017) in *Routledge Handbook on Collective Intentionality*, eds. K. Ludwig and Marija Jankovic, Routledge: London, pp. 130–9.

Our Obligations and Rights

1. "Obligation and Joint Commitment" (1999) *Utilitas*, vol. 11, pp. 143–63. [S&R]
2. "Obligation: Preliminary Points" (2006) TPO, ch. 2, pp. 26–42.
3. "Joint Commitment and Obligation" (2006) TPO, ch. 7, sec. 7.4, pp. 147–63.
4. "Rorty on Human Rights" (2010) http://escholarship.org/uc/item/2127z5b4.
5. "Giving Claim-Rights Their Due" (2012) in *Rights: Concepts and Contexts*, eds. Brian Bix and Horacio Spector, Ashgate: Farnham, Surrey, pp. 301–23. [Ch. 13, this volume]
6. "The Nature of Agreements: A Solution to Some Puzzles about Claim-Rights and Joint Intention" (2014) in *Rational and Social Agency*, eds. M. Vargas and G. Yaffe, Oxford University Press: New York, pp. 215–54. [Ch. 1, this volume]
7. "A Fundamental Ground of Demand-Rights" (2018), R&D, ch. 8, pp. 159–87.

Language, Languages, and Conversation

1. "Agreements, Conventions, and Language" (1983) *Synthese*, vol. 54, no. 3, pp. 375–407.
2. "On the Question Whether Language Has a Social Nature: Some Aspects of Winch and Others on Wittgenstein" (1983) *Synthese*, vol. 56, no. 3, pp. 301–18. [LT]
3. "Action, Meaning, and the Social" (1989) OSF, ch. 3, pp. 58–145.
4. "Group Languages" (1989) OSF, ch. 3.6, pp. 132–45.
5. "Another Context: Conversations" (1989) OSF, ch. 7.3 pp. 294–8.

6. "Group Languages and 'Criteria'" (1996) LT, ch. 10, pp. 249–62.
7. "Conversation and Collective Belief" (with Maura Priest) (2013) in *Perspectives on Pragmatics and Philosophy*, eds. A. Capone, F. Lo Piparo, and M. Carapezza, Springer: Dordrecht, pp. 1–34.
8. "Dialogue and Joint Commitment" (with Maura Priest), (2022) in French translation in *Les Défis de Collectif*, eds. Raphael Kunstler et al.

Social Groups, Social Unity, Sociality

1. "Everyday Concepts and Social Reality" (1989) OSF, ch. 1, pp. 1–21.
2. "'Social Action' and the Subject Matter of the Social Sciences" (1989) OSF, ch. 2, pp. 22–57.
3. "Social Groups: A Simmelian View" (1989) OSF, ch. 4, pp. 146–236.
4. "On Social Facts" (1989) OSF, ch. 7, pp. 408–45.
5. "Folk Psychology Takes Sociality Seriously" (1989) *Behavioral and Brain Sciences*, vol. 12, pp. 707–8.
6. "Wittgenstein and the Philosophy of Sociology" (1990) in *Ludwig Wittgenstein: A Symposium on the Centennial of His Birth*, eds. S. Teghrarian, A. Serafini, and E. M. Cook, Longwood Academic: Wakefield, NH, pp. 19–29.
7. "Walking Together: A Paradigmatic Social Phenomenon" (1990) in *Midwest Studies in Philosophy*, vol. 15, *The Philosophy of the Human Sciences*, eds. P. A. French, T. E. Uehling, Jr., and H. K. Wettstein, University of Notre Dame Press: Notre Dame, pp. 1–14.
8. "Fusion: Sketch of a Contractual Model" (1990) in *Perspectives on the Family*, eds. R. C. L. Moffat, J. Grcic, and M. Bayles, Edwin Mellen Press: Lewiston, pp. 65–78. [LT; JC; INC]
9. "Me, You, and Us: Distinguishing Egoism, Altruism, and Groupism" (1994) *Behavioral and Brain Sciences*, vol. 17.
10. "Sociality as a Philosophically Significant Category" (1994) *Journal of Social Philosophy*, vol. 25, no. 3, pp. 5–25.
11. "Concerning Sociality: The Plural Subject as Paradigm" (1997) in *The Mark of the Social*, ed. J. Greenwood, Rowman and Littlefield: Lanham, MD.
12. "In Search of Sociality: Recent Developments in the Philosophy of Social Phenomena" (1998) *Philosophical Explorations*, vol. 1, no. 1, pp. 233–41. [S&R]
13. "Sociality, Unity, Objectivity" (2000) *Proceedings of the 1998 World Congress of Philosophy: Invited Papers*, pp. 153–60.
14. "Philosophy and the Social Sciences" (2002) in *In the Scope of Logic, Methodology and Philosophy of Science*, eds. P. Gardenfors, J. Wolenski, and K. Kijania-Placek, Kluwer, pp. 439–49. [ME]
15. "A Theoretical Framework for the Understanding of Teams" (2004) in *Teamwork Multidisciplinary Perspectives*, ed. N. Gold, Palgrave-MacMillan: London, pp. 22–32.
16. "Social Groups: Starting Small" (2006) TPO, ch. 6, pp. 93–124.
17. "Societies as Plural Subjects" (2006) TPO, ch. 8, pp. 165–81.
18. "A Real Unity of Them All?" (2009) *The Monist*, special issue on Europe, vol. 92, no. 2, pp. 268–85. [JC; INC]
19. "Further Reflections on the Social World" (2018) *Protosociology*, vol. 35, pp. 243–69.

Rational Individuals Interacting One-On-One

1. "Game Theory and Convention" (1981) *Synthese*, vol. 44, no. 1, pp. 41–93. [LT]
2. "Coordination Problems and the Evolution of Behavior" (1984) *Behavioral & Brain Sciences*, vol. 7, no. 1, pp. 106–7.
3. "Rationality and Salience" (1989) *Philosophical Studies*, vol. 55, pp. 223–39. [LT]
4. "Rationality, Coordination, and Convention" (1990) *Synthese*, vol. 84, pp. 1–21. [LT; ME]

Responses to Comments include:

1. "More on Social Facts: Reply to Greenwood" (1991) *Social Epistemology*, vol. 5, pp 233–44. [LT]
2. "Aspects of Joint Commitment" (2002) in *Social Facts and Collective Intentionality*, ed. Georg Meggle, German Library of Sciences, Hansel-Hohenhausen: Frankfurt, pp. 73–102. [JC]
3. "Response to Objections" (2006) ch. 11. Sec. 3, TPO, pp. 266–74.
4. "Joint Commitment and Group Belief" (2010) in *Kolner Zeitschrift for Sociologie*, pp. 384–410 [Ch. 3: this volume].
5. "Responses to Some Questions on Social Convention and Related Matters" (2013) in *Convenzioni*, Post n. 4, Mimesis: Milano-Udine.
6. "*A Theory of Political Obligation*: Responses to Horton, Jeske, Narveson and Stoutland" (2013) in *Jurisprudence: An International Journal of Legal and Political Thought*, vol. pp. [Ch. 12, this volume, is a revised version of this.]
7. "Further Reflections on the Social World" (2018), *Protosociology*, vol. 35. pp. 243–69.
8. Precis of *Rights and Demands* and Responses to Comments from Arneson, Darwall, Helmreich, and Watson (forthcoming) *Philosophy and Phenomenological Research*.

Subject Index

Notes: Technical terms of the author are printed in boldface type

Several topics are treated relatively extensively in more than one chapter; this index lists at least one such treatment of each of these topics.

For the benefit of digital users, indexed terms listed as spanning two pages (e.g., 52–53) may, on occasion, appear on only one of those pages.

Name Index

For the benefit of digital users, indexed terms listed as spanning two pages (e.g., 52–53) may, on occasion, appear on only one of those pages.

Name index compiled by Tiffany Zhu